11 —

MW01039955

THE NEW URBAN PARK

DEVELOPMENT OF WESTERN RESOURCES

The Development of Western Resources is an interdisciplinary series focusing on the use and misuse of resources in the American West. Written for a broad readership of humanists, social scientists, and resource specialists, the books in this series emphasize both historical and contemporary perspectives as they explore the interplay between resource exploitation and economic, social, and political experiences.

John G. Clark, University of Kansas, Founding Editor
Hal K. Rothman, University of Nevada, Las Vegas, Series Editor

THE NEW URBAN PARK

Golden Gate National Recreation Area and Civic Environmentalism

Hal K. Rothman

July 31, 2004
To Jan Blum
with warm regards

University Press of Kansas

© 2004 by the University Press of Kansas

Published by the University Press of Kansas (Lawrence, Kansas 66049), which was organized by the Kansas Board of Regents and is operated and funded by Emporia State University, Fort Hays State University, Kansas State University, Pittsburg State University, the University of Kansas, and Wichita State University

Library of Congress Cataloging-in-Publication Data

Rothman, Hal, 1958–
    The new urban park : Golden Gate National Recreation Area and civic environmentalism / Hal K. Rothman.
        p. cm. — (Development of western resources)
Includes bibliographical references and index.
        ISBN 0-7006-1286-6 (alk. paper)
    1. Golden Gate National Recreation Area (Calif.)—History. 2. Urban ecology—California—San Francisco—History. 3. Environmentalism—California—San Francisco—History. 4. Urban parks—United States—Case studies. 5. Urban ecology—United States—Case studies. I. Title. II. Series.
    F868.S156R68 2003
    333.78′3′0979461—dc21   2003013216

British Library Cataloguing in Publication Data is available.

Printed in the United States of America

10 9 8 7 6 5 4 3 2 1

The paper used in this publication meets the minimum requirements of the American National Standard for Permanence of Paper for Printed Library Materials Z39.48-1984.

Contents

Acknowledgments

This administrative history could not have been written without the help of Golden Gate National Recreation Area Superintendent Brian O'Neill and his staff. Stephen Haller took the lead role in handling the details, and his efforts made this one of the best-managed national park projects Rothman and Associates has ever undertaken. Special thanks also go to Diane Nicholson, Ric Borjes, and Paul Scolari, who smoothed the way at every opportunity. Susan Ewing-Haley proved invaluable as a guide through the park archives and played a key role in ensuring accurate citations throughout the book. John Martini provided considerable insight in many key areas of this study. Greg Moore of GGNPA also provided important observations and perceptions. Rich Weideman gave a fine tour of Alcatraz, and a number of staff members added important dimensions to the project with their interviews and e-mails. Dan Holder played his usual critical role in the project's development. He supervised the research, handled the massive collection of documents, copyedited and offered suggestions throughout, and made sure of the countless details that compromise any such endeavor. Without his efforts, it's safe to say, the project would be much different. Brian Frehner developed into a key member of the research team. Bill Issel of San Francisco State and Terry Young of the Huntington Library both read the manuscript, providing the benefit of their vast knowledge of San Francisco and its parks.

Golden Gate National Recreational Area is young enough to benefit from the insights of its founders, of the people who made the park happen and who influenced it as it developed. Their presence and their contribution to this book have provided a measure of depth that belies documents alone. The people who have offered their memories and observations for this revised version include Amy Meyer, Edgar Wayburn, Doug Nadeau, Rich Bartke, and Bill Whalen.

Writing history is a complicated and contentious process, made even more so when the participants in the events in question are still active. Historians cannot rely on memory alone, for as any attorney will tell, it is the most fallible and malleable form of historical data. "The palest of ink," the medieval scribes averred, "is better than the sharpest of memory," and with good reason. In the historian's creed, documents from the historical moment supersede any after-the-fact account, and responsible historians must try to reconcile the differences that inevitably emerge. Nor is a history an encyclopedic account of every event that occurred in a time and place. Instead it is an effort to represent the past through the use of selective examples that illustrate dominant trends. The history of Golden Gate National Recreation Area is filled with stories that are important in and of themselves, but tell little about the park's overall evolution. Sadly, many of these have had to be omitted in this volume.

In the end, the historian is asked to make decisions about historical events and their meaning. Especially in the study of the recent past, this is a task that is sure to cause controversy, to enrage proponents of one or another point of view. Yet historians must hold a steady course. Achieving a balance between personal points of view and documents from the time, judiciously choosing examples that explain larger themes, setting them in the context of professional scholarship that addresses the field, the time, and the place, is the historian's goal in any study. It is my hope that I have achieved such a balance here.

Introduction

Golden Gate National Recreational Area represented a new model for the National Park Service when it was established in 1972. For most of its history, the Park Service had been concerned with spectacular nature, a bias that still permeates the agency as the twenty-first century begins. In the 1960s, a transformation of American society led the agency to develop the broader representations of national heritage already contained within its purview and add breadth and depth to them. At the same time, a neopopulist idea, "parks for the people, where the people are," a legacy of Lyndon Johnson's social policy that came to fruition during Richard M. Nixon's administration, forced federal agencies and particularly the Park Service to find ways to serve urban constituencies. With its peer, Gateway National Recreation Area in New York, Golden Gate National Recreation Area became part of the vanguard of a reenvisioning of the ideal of national parks in American society.

Yet as the 1970s began, the Park Service had little experience with urban parks. Since its founding in 1916, the agency had been primarily concerned with large scenic natural areas, initially adding American history to its purview during the New Deal. The agency had possessed archaeological sites since its inception, but they had been and remained ancillary to the primary development of the park system. Recreation was even further from the agency's idea of its responsibilities, somewhere far below the hefty obligation to protect the places that defined the American nation. By the 1960s, the agency finally embraced recreation as other challengers in the federal bureaucracy claimed the same turf, but the Park Service limped toward a functional grasp of such a different responsibility.

The changes further accentuated the agency's need to respond more broadly to public demands for recreational space, but only after the founding of Gateway and Golden Gate did the Park Service find itself with competing missions in urban space. The combination of recreation, history, wilderness, and nature that defined Golden Gate National Recreation Area became the archetype of a new Park Service, one that finally moved beyond the neoelitist conceptualization that marked its birth and attempted to reach the broadest range of the rapidly changing American public.

Urban parks such as Golden Gate National Recreation Area inherently reflected the most basic tension in the agency mission, the dichotomy between preservation for the future and available public use in the present. The

agency had always been torn between these two precepts of its organic legislation, and the pressure of urban use exacerbated an already difficult situation. In San Francisco and the surrounding area, the park that was created
had already been defined as specific spaces for various purposes. The public
knew these spaces, sometimes called them by their own names, and had a
clearly articulated vision of what they meant. Often Golden Gate National
Recreation Area's components were better known as local features rather
than as part of a national park area, and building an identity for the new
national park area became a struggle. Even more, the uses of various parts
of the park by the public preceded and sometimes trumped park goals, leading to a complicated management process that spoke volumes about the
changing role of government and institutions in American society.

Much of the core of this tension stemmed from the fundamentally political nature of national parks and parklands in general. Despite the tendency
of scholars to regard the history of the parks as based in the preservation of
resources, a closer look reveals that fundamentally political nature of park
policy and management from the inception of the agency. In the Bay Area,
politics dictated to the new park even before its establishment. The park resulted from the actions of civic-minded interest groups that allied with a
powerful congressional representative, and ever after politics—local, county,
state, and national, inside and between counties and municipalities—became
the driving force in the history of the park. Unlike Yellowstone and the other
crown jewels of the park system, where the Park Service was the dominant
influence on the entire surrounding region, at Golden Gate National Recreation Area and its peers, the Park Service held only one of many seats at a
regional political and economic table. The limits on the agency's ability to
implement its policies were varied and vast.

Even the constituencies shifted in the Bay Area. The Park Service found
itself not only with its usual supporters, outdoors people such as Sierra Club
members and other conservation advocates, but also with a range of local
neighborhood, ethnic, and even labor interests with a vested interest in the
park and a vision of what it should provide. Some of these users claimed
their right by prior use, others coveted structures or programs that went on
within the park, and still more sought to use the park to protect their prerogative, a time-honored practice in the United States. The difference between conventional conservationists and recreational users led to strife, as
did that between neighbors who wanted a pristine environment to insulate
them from growth and those who wanted to use the park to decompress
from the tight urban situation in the Bay Area. Golden Gate National Recreation Area was asked to be all things to all people all of the time; each of its
myriad constituencies simultaneously wanted it to be theirs alone.

This sparked a continuous set of antagonisms, sometimes directed at
the Park Service and other times during which the Park Service was asked

to referee, that became much of the basis of environmental politics in the Bay Area. The nature of the tension pitted urban and rural groups and individuals against one another, highly educated white-collar people against working class communities and individuals, newcomers against old-timers, and countless other combinations. All of them had a claim on some dimension of the park; all of them wanted precedence for their way of using its resources.

In short, Golden Gate National Recreation Area became an archetype of modern society as well as a prominent example of the problems of constituency management in the age of entitlement. Its issues, largely dissimilar from those of the older national parks but grandly foreshadowing the future of the park system in a changing nation, suggested a transformation in the principles of federal land management agencies. No longer could they dictate terms; instead they had to negotiate, in no small part in the hope of maintaining complicated alliances that helped protect the park and its budget at the national level. Superintendents could be forgiven for thinking that they had stumbled across insoluble dilemmas. Balancing urban structures and green space, recreational day use and wilderness, and hiking and hang gliding in the context of an energized city was a task that required more than intelligence and discretion. Golden Gate National Recreation Area foreshadowed a world where no entity could take its support for granted. As the Park Service learned to work for its constituencies there, it created a blueprint that has served it well as the agency has pursued partnerships in the parks. Long before the twenty-first century, Golden Gate was a twenty-first-century park. As such, it provides a model for the park system in the new century.

THE NEW URBAN PARK

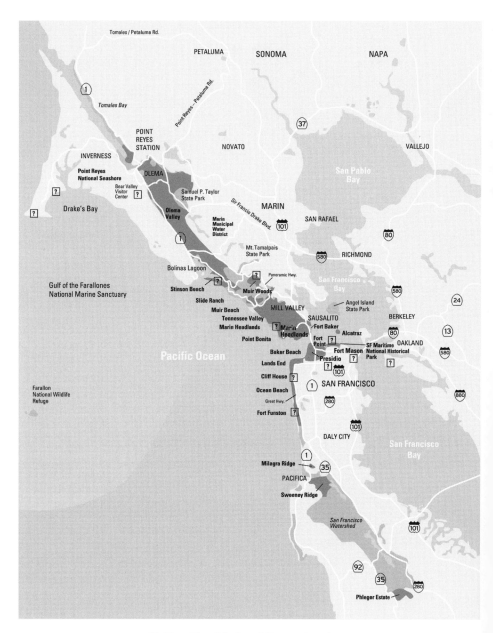

Golden Gate National Recreation Area

CHAPTER ONE

National Parks and the Bay Area

If there is one genuine contribution that the United States has made to the application of the principles of democracy, the most likely candidate is the national park. Prior to the Age of Enlightenment—the eighteenth-century intellectual and ultimately social revolution that insisted individuals possessed natural rights and added the concept of a relationship between the governors and the governed to human affairs—the idea of a park owned and used by the people was entirely unknown. In most cultures, especially monarchies and other forms of hereditary government, parks were the provinces of the nobility and wealthy, kept and maintained for their use alone. Common people were forbidden to use designated lands, sometimes on the penalty of death. Many stood outside the boundaries of such areas and looked in with envy, conscious of the wealth of natural resources and aesthetic pleasures within and equally aware of the huge price to be paid for violating the liege's prerogative. Such parks, like the forests set aside for royal hunts, served as manifestations of power, markers of different standing in a society riven by social distinctions. They were also the flash points of class-based tension. The story of Robert of Locksley, a member of the twelfth-century English gentry who as Robin Hood took to the woods after defending a man who stole a deer from restricted land to feed his starving family, clearly illustrated the tension inherent in the traditional organization of private parklands.[1]

U.S. history followed a different vector, for the acquisitive nation of the nineteenth century encompassed more land than its people could then inhabit. The great beauty and uniqueness of much of this land inspired a culture that saw itself as a light to nations, one that believed it was in the process of perfecting human endeavor in a way earlier societies had not. Such lands answered the dilemma of the nineteenth century. They demonstrated a distinctiveness in nature that Americans saw in their society; they served as a counterpoint to European claims that the New World was inferior in every way. Yet nineteenth-century America was a commercial society devoted to economic wealth by the measures of industry. Parkland could not impinge on economic effort, on the process of observing, demarcating, and then harvesting the bounty of the land. The parks' contribution to the purpose of nation-building must be more valuable as symbol than as reality; awe-inspiring scenery had to outweigh ranch and agricultural potential at the time momentum for a park gathered. The first parks, including Yellowstone, Yosemite, Sequoia, General Grant—now part of Kings Canyon, Crater Lake, and their peers, all shared a combination of beauty and inaccessibility for commercial economic purposes that made them valuable manifestations of American cultural needs instead of sources from which to wring wealth.[2]

The crucial feature of these parks in the nation's ideology was the principle of their openness to all Americans. In the eyes of supporters, national parks were testimony to the patrimony and heritage of a country that intended to reinvent the relationships between government and its people. During the late nineteenth century and the first decade of the twentieth, those people who professed goals of community instead of individualism saw in the national parks not only an affirmation of their nation but also a clear and distinct way to articulate one of the prime assumptions of the time: that a society's institutions should serve the economic, social, spiritual, and cultural needs of its people. This principle, deeply ingrained in the concept of national parks—if not always in the motives behind their creation—became an underlying premise in the evolution of American conservation.[3]

This seemingly contradictory impulse revealed much of the goals and pretensions of the United States as the twentieth century began. Economically and politically powerful families wanted the feeling of European aristocracy, the sense of having large areas devoted to aesthetic and ultimately recreational purposes, while supporting the democracy that Americans were certain made their nation special. The process of creating a nation that sprawled from the Atlantic to the Pacific challenged many of the ideas of democracy, but in these huge natural parks, Americans could see the fruition of their nineteenth-century idea, a transcontinental nation that practiced democratic ideals. As the twentieth century dawned, no more powerful proof of their commitment to democracy existed than the patrimony of national parks.

Yet an enormous gap existed between the rhetoric of the time and the actuality of the national parks that were created. The language of democracy trumpeted openness, but the parks Americans created catered to only one segment of society, the people with the time and resources to travel and the education to regard nature as part of their cultural heritage. The Americans who traveled to parks were the winners in the transition to industrial society. The ones who might most benefit from such public patrimony usually lacked the resources, inclination, and even the awareness that such parks existed. As democratic institutions, early national parks functioned more as symbols than as participatory reality.

The San Francisco Bay Area served as one of the key points of genesis and promotion of the idea of national parks. The queen city of the West at the turn of the twentieth century, San Francisco enjoyed a beautiful setting that could not help but inspire an appreciation of scenery. People's beliefs in the beauty and value of the natural environment and the wealth that the community held provided other obvious precursors of support for national parks. The institutions spawned there played essential roles in shaping the conservation movement around 1900. California's mountains, especially the rugged Sierra Nevada, fostered a sense of longing among wealthy urbanites who faced cultural transformation from which they benefited economically, but who felt spiritually and sometimes even morally impoverished. Residents responded by making the wild outdoors the visible symbol of their longing for a simpler, less urban past. In essence, they sought to have the benefits of industrialization in their lives and to use a small part of the wealth they created to maintain a pristine natural world, away from the smoke and thunder of a modern city.[4]

With the enigmatic Scot John Muir, the emblematic "John of the Mountains" as a living symbol, this local conservation movement gained national momentum. Muir's wilderness philosophy led to the creation of the Sierra Club, which counted many Bay Area notables among its founders and early leaders. The movement also was connected to national figures. The University of California at Berkeley produced the first two leaders of the National Park Service, Stephen T. Mather and Horace M. Albright, as well as President Woodrow Wilson's secretary of the interior, Franklin K. Lane, who brought Mather to Washington, D.C., to run the parks.[5]

San Francisco and its environs became a hotbed of conservation sentiment at the start of the twentieth century. Displaying both their democratic instincts and their political power, community leaders advocated huge natural parks, not for themselves they believed, but for the nation. Strong and widespread support for national parks, especially among the most influential segments of the community, characterized the region. At the beginning of the twentieth century, the Bay Area legitimately claimed the title of the urban area most thoroughly devoted to national parks.

The national parks that Bay Area residents so touted were large natural areas, far from urban centers such as San Francisco and Oakland. In the formulation of the time, places that merited protection from development were "sacred" while those that could be developed for commercial uses were loosely labeled "profane." Influential conservation leaders, deeply involved in economic development, understood and supported this distinction, for it allowed them to achieve an important end for the privileged class of the turn of the century—the creation of permanent places that protected them from the chaos of modernity on which their wealth depended. These leaders did not see a contradiction in developing one kind of land and protecting another. In this belief they were part of their moment, best expressed in the divided mandate the National Park Service received at its founding, to "maintain in absolutely unimpaired form and to set aside for use."[6] Division of space into sacred and profane seemingly created parallel universes of pristine nature and industrial development. The seventy-five years that followed the creation of the Park Service proved these seminal ideas hopelessly contradictory, but as the century began they were generally regarded as entirely compatible.

Against this backdrop of rapid growth and social change, the enthusiasm for a national park in the Bay Area gathered powerful momentum. The rise of progressivism in California played a significant role. During the late nineteenth century, Muir and the Sierra Club had been active advocates of national parks, especially Yosemite Valley, then a state park about 140 miles east of San Francisco. Yosemite's combination of values resonated as the goals of reform swept California along with the rest of the country. At the turn of the century, national parks spoke to important needs and insecurities in American society, and for San Francisco, flush with a sense of its own importance, adding such a prize was a meaningful and viable objective. The transfer of Yosemite from state park to national park status and the creation of General Grant, Sequoia, and other national parks opened up opportunities for more national parks. Success seemed to create the prospect of greater successes.[7]

Despite all the forces that indicated the viability of a Bay Area national park, a major ingredient of the park proclamation process was completely absent in the San Francisco region: there was no public domain land in the immediate vicinity. At the turn of the century, public land remained the primary building block of national parks, and it offered an enormous advantage. Congress was unlikely to appropriate money to purchase parkland, and public lands could be set aside by presidential or congressional authorization with nary a thought to cost. No one needed to allocate money to purchase land, and at the time, while the U.S. Army administered the national parks before the National Park Service was established in 1916, funds for personnel or other costs did not need to be part of the equation. In places where a ready store of public land did not exist, the federal government could depend only on gifts of land from which to fashion national parks. The power of eminent domain—condemning private property for public use—was a risky strategy. In most circumstances, such gifts were rare and occurred only under unusual circumstances.[8]

The great San Francisco earthquake of April 1906 became the catalyst for a gift of land that led to the Bay Area's first national park area. The earthquake was a deadly calamity; San Francisco had been built piecemeal, its infrastructure a combination of public and private entities all building to their own specifications. When the quake came, buildings toppled, the rudimentary water system failed, and fires engulfed the town. Days later the fires burnt out, leaving the wreckage of a city strewn across the landscape. The near-total collapse of the infrastructure during the quake gave ammunition to a Progressive Era obsession. Progressives insisted that public entities—city, county, state, and federal government—should provide cities with water, power, and other necessities of modern life. Public control would assure the equity, dependability, and fairness that business could not always be relied upon to provide. A dependable water supply remained a crucial issue in San Francisco. Despite the bay and an annual precipitation rate that exceeded twenty inches, questions concerning both the source of water and making it accessible to the public vexed private providers. In the aftermath of the quake, the problem worsened. Water was in short supply, and a number of companies scurried to fill the void with water sources, new reservoirs in particular, to supply the city.[9] It was a profit-making opportunity that certainly galled good government advocates.

James Newlands, president of the North Coast Water Company, saw the city's need as an opportunity for personal profit. Assessing potential reservoir sites, Newlands, nephew of Francis Newlands, the Nevada congressman who authored the Reclamation Act of 1902, came across a grove of redwoods in Marin County, owned by William Kent, a wealthy Bay Area native who returned home after a career of municipal reform in Chicago to settle on the beautiful forty-seven-acre tract. Kent hailed from a family with a long tradition of reform and shared with many of his Progressive peers a distaste for monopolies. Recognizing San Francisco's desperate situation and the potential of the grove as a reservoir, Newlands approached Kent to purchase the land for a reservoir. Kent declined; he wanted the property for its beauty, often calling it the last intact stand of redwoods in the Bay Area, and emphatically stated that he did not want to see it become a reservoir.[10]

When he denied Newlands's request, Kent bucked the spirit of the Bay Area in the earthquake's aftermath. The community needed a new infrastructure, and water was crucial to its rebirth. Well connected through his uncle and his business, Newlands recognized that local and state governments would support his objectives. He filed a condemnation suit in state court, arguing that the public good of the reservoir exceeded Kent's right to keep the property. A dubious argument in American statutes, Newlands's contention received a sympathetic hearing in the months following the earthquake. Progressivism policy making was predisposed to its conception of the public good and San Franciscans' circumstances were extreme. In this situation, it was easy for a local court to construe Newlands's request as a form of public service. The politically savvy Kent recognized the implicit danger in Newlands's endeavor, with California state courts likely to rule favorably on the lawsuit. San Francisco stood to benefit greatly from the private reservoir, while at the same time Newlands made a fortune through his water company. Recognizing his vulnerability, Kent devised a means to thwart the lawsuit. He sought to preserve the redwoods, not necessarily to keep the property, and he knew of a new law that allowed him to achieve his goal. His attorney sent a letter to the Department of the Interior, offering the land as a gift if the government would designate it a national monument.[11]

The Antiquities Act of 1906, the law that allowed the establishment of national monuments, was a recent but potent addition to the arsenal of conservation. Signed into law by President Theodore Roosevelt in 1906, the act was vague. It permitted the president to proclaim as national monuments any part of the public domain with only a signature of the executive pen. Although the framers of the bill claimed that its primary use would be the reservation of small areas of prehistoric significance, it was an important part of a trend that granted the chief executive considerable control over public lands. In the hands of a president such as Roosevelt, the power to establish national monuments was a valuable asset for conservation goals.[12]

Roosevelt's reliance on the Antiquities Act increased during 1907 when Congress stripped him of the power, established under the Forest Reserve Act of 1891, to proclaim national forests in fourteen western states. Finding one avenue to achieve his conservation agenda blocked, he utilized another. The first group of national monuments proclaimed in 1906—which included Devil's Tower in Wyoming, Arizona's Petrified Forest, and El Morro in New Mexico—fit the expectations of the act's framers, but Roosevelt planned a much larger coup. The Grand Canyon faced threats of development, and Roosevelt was prepared to create a national monument of more than 800,000 acres in Arizona to protect this powerful symbol of American intellectual and cultural transformation.[13]

Just before this defining moment in conservation and national park history, Kent circumvented the condemnation suit in California. On December 26, 1907, he mailed the deed to 295 acres of his land, including the 47-acre tract targeted by the lawsuit, to Secretary of the Interior James R. Garfield, son of the former president, requesting that the government accept the gift for a national monument named in honor of John Muir. Kent had not yet been served in the suit, so his action could not be construed as avoiding state jurisdiction. He urged quick federal action on his gift. Twelve days later, just two days before he proclaimed Grand Canyon National Monument, Roosevelt signed a proclamation establishing Muir Woods National Monument. Newlands's situation was inexorably altered. To obtain Kent's land for a reservoir, he now had to sue the U.S. government in federal court, a far more daunting prospect than action against one citizen. Newlands persisted until Kent agreed to sell him another tract. The North Coast Water Company dropped its lawsuit and built its reservoir elsewhere.[14]

The establishment of Muir Woods National Monument illustrated the difficulty of maintaining the sacred-profane distinction that marked earlier conservation efforts. Kent's sacred space was Newlands's utilitarian reservoir, and ultimately the resolution relied on political relationships and position, not any objective assessment of the site's merit. In short, power played an enormous role in shaping the fate of Kent's forty-seven acres of red-woods, and the issue at Muir Woods foreshadowed the tendentious battle over Hetch-Hetchy Dam in Yosemite National Park. The argument between Kent and Newlands was the first sign of a deeper rift among conservation-ists. Former allies found that although they agreed in principle, their objec-tives in specific cases differed. Simply put, they placed higher value on different sides of the same question, leading to contentiousness and acri-mony among partners that threatened to fracture alliances and negate the gains of a decade of legislation.

The battle over the Hetch-Hetchy Dam shattered the illusion that only one approach to conservation existed. A valley within Yosemite National Park, Hetch-Hetchy was prime territory for the major reservoir that San Francisco needed. A seven-year battle over the dam that finally ended with its authorization in 1916 pitted longtime friends such as Muir and Kent against one another and bitterly divided the conservation movement. A few years after the gift of the woods in Muir's name, Kent said of his friend's stance against the dam that Muir "has no social sense, with him, it is God and the rock where God put it and that is the end of the story." Muir saw the damming of Hetch-Hetchy as the destruction of a natural temple. Kent and others like him recognized the damage but placed greater weight on the need for a dependable and publicly owned water supply for a major metropolitan area. When the U.S. Senate approved the dam, it fractured the loosely connected advocates of preservation and conservation. Conserva-tion gained a triumph at the expense not of rapacious users of resources, but of its preservationist allies. By 1914, the dam was in place, inundating the valley after highlighting the inherent contradictions in conservation.[15]

Hetch-Hetchy so complicated relationships in the conservation move-ment that further efforts to create national park areas in the Bay Area were stymied for more than a decade. Instead of a coalition of like-minded indi-viduals close to the levers of power, Hetch-Hetchy left a contentious and frac-tured group that did not trust one another and could hardly ally to achieve conservation goals. Despite powerful leadership and strong fealty to Muir's goals, especially after he died on Christmas Eve 1914, in the aftermath of the Hetch-Hetchy crisis the focus of the Sierra Club shifted away from San Fran-cisco to an effort to include remote redwoods in the national park system. The dire situation of redwoods in northern California made their protection essential. Club members could agree on the need to preserve the magnifi-cent trees; they could not yet civilly discuss the needs of the Bay Area, and so the region remained without a signature national park.[16]

By the 1920s, the move to create a larger and more significant national park near San Francisco regained some momentum. William Kent, by this time a fixture in California progressive politics, played a catalytic role. With his powerful affection for Marin County he became the leading advocate of preserving Mount Tamalpais, just above Muir Woods National Monument. Kent displayed the sometimes contradictory sentiments of conservation. At the same time that he supported preservation, he was the major force behind the creation of a railroad spur to Bolinas. The new line complemented the Mill Valley and Mount Tamalpais Scenic Railway, first built in 1896 and long known as the "crookedest railroad in the world" for its 281 curves on the way to the peak. In 1903, four years before he gave Muir Woods to the federal government, Kent founded the Tamalpais National Park Association. "Need and opportunity are linked together here," Kent told Gifford Pinchot, the leading utilitarian forester in the nation, San Francisco mayor James D. Phelan, and other supporters at the group's inaugural meeting. Kent himself bought much of the land on the mountain, and the Marin Municipal Water District, established in 1912, purchased the Lagunitas Creek drainage near Mount Tamalpais. When an effort to establish a national park failed, Kent donated the land to the state of California, and in 1928 Mount Tamalpais State Park came into being. At about the same time, one of the best local park organizations in the country, the East Bay Regional Park District, created a greenbelt in the East Bay Hills.[17] Local and state level momentum remained strong.

The combination of the Great Depression and World War II muted national park efforts in the Bay Area until 1945. The depression was as devastating to San Francisco as it was elsewhere in the nation. The unemployment rate topped 30 percent in the Bay Area, and Oakland, which had become an industrial city and fancied itself the "Detroit of the West" in the 1920s, experienced the fate of other industrial towns. Factories closed and workers were laid off. The remedy, public works projects, was as welcome in the Bay Area as elsewhere. The most prominent of these undertakings, the Golden Gate Bridge, became not only a symbol of the Bay Area, an important infrastructural link that also seemed to visually complete the bay, but a national symbol as well. After its construction, many who saw the bridge remarked that they could no longer imagine the space between San Francisco and Marin County without its rust-colored, elegant lines. American soldiers and sailors fighting across the Pacific linked it to their return home, predicting with muted enthusiasm "The Golden Gate in '48." The bridge was a powerful symbol. During the 1940s, physician and Sierra Club president Edgar Wayburn and noted photographer and club board member Ansel Adams proposed that the lands around the Golden Gate be designated a national monument.

World War II transformed the western states, and California was the greatest beneficiary. Not only did the state's population increase by 1.5 million between 1940 and 1944, the federal government spent $35 billion, almost 10 percent of its total expenditure between 1940 and 1946, in California.

The Bay Area experienced a comprehensive transformation, gaining half a million people during the war years alone. San Francisco and Oakland ports became staging grounds for the war effort. Military installations, already prominent, grew in number and size. Combat in the Pacific theater transformed half-century-old patterns in the region. San Francisco became economically more significant than it had been prior to 1941, when maritime operations, printing, construction, and light manufacturing dominated the local industrial scene and downtown was only a nascent financial and service center. Although multiethnic, the city's population was 95 percent white when the war began. With the major exception of Asians, Oakland and the East Bay, long home to industry, were equally monochromatic. Before Pearl Harbor, nowhere in the East Bay did African Americans make up more than 4 percent of the population. During the war, the Bay Area's population increased almost 40 percent, and diversity became typical. San Francisco's population increased by more than 30 percent, filling urban neighborhoods with newcomers, including as many as 40,000 African Americans. The long process of suburban migration began with the construction of trains, bridges (of which the Golden Gate was the first to open), and ferries to Marin and Contra Costa counties north of San Francisco. Easy commuting to the city became possible, and many embarked on this course. They followed an age-old pattern of prosperous Americans; they moved farther from the sometimes smelly and noisy sources of their wealth into often stunning hinterlands that faced ongoing development. The East Bay grew so fast that by the end of the war it exceeded San Francisco and the peninsular counties in population. By the time Japan surrendered in 1945, the Bay Area was a more crowded, more diverse, and more industrial region than it had been before the bombing of Pearl Harbor.[18]

Not even the experience of the war prepared California for its remarkable postwar growth. The Golden State came into its own in the aftermath of World War II, increasing in economic opportunities and population with unequaled speed. In 1962, it surpassed New York as the most populous state in the Union. Federal dollars provided the basis for much of the growth. Not only did government contracts underpin the development of numerous industries, but federal dollars also supported the growth of an enormous and sophisticated transportation network. Construction and other light industries provided homes for the swarm of new residents, adding another dimension to the economy. Within a decade of Japan's surrender, California had become one of the most powerful economic engines in the nation and indeed the world. The physical plant constructed during the war fused with cold war government contracts in its aftermath to turn the American Dream into the California Dream. In the two decades following World War II, no state was more central to the vision of what the United States could become.

California also illustrated the problems of the nation's future. Not only did smog dominate the state's skies as the freeways filled with traffic so quickly each day that many became parking lots, but the people of California lacked recreational space. In San Francisco and the Bay Area—one a small peninsula and the other limited in growth by the mountains—the need was exacerbated. A crowded city in a beautiful region, with strong blue-collar unions and powerful ethnic constituencies, demanded recreational space of the sort that the wealthy who fled the urban area possessed. In the prosperous postwar era, when anything seemed possible, the demand for public recreational space became one of many essential goals for the society of the future, the image California held of itself and its place in the nation.

The late 1950s and early 1960s provided Americans with a unique opportunity to expand their national park system. In 1956, Mission 66, a ten-year program to upgrade facilities and expand the system before the fiftieth anniversary of the 1916 founding of the National Park Service, received unqualified congressional support. Development of existing parks and the addition of new ones became goals not only for the agency, but for Congress and the public as well. In this context, the San Francisco Bay Area again came to the attention of Park Service officials. The federal government had been lax about preserving seashores and lakeshores. The first such efforts began during the 1930s, more than a half century after the establishment of Yellowstone National Park. By the late 1950s, only one area, Cape Hatteras in North Carolina, had been established. The growth of American cities between the 1930s and the 1950s put tremendous pressure on shorelines and lakeshores, which seemed likely to become privately owned and off-limits to much of the American public.

After the publication of "Our Vanishing Shoreline," a 1955 Park Service survey sponsored by the Mellon family, impetus for the establishment of national seashores and lakeshores gained momentum. When Congress established the Outdoor Recreation Resources Review Commission (ORRRC) in 1958, the Park Service embarked upon a comprehensive program to evaluate shoreline resources and produced three additional surveys, "A Report on the Seashore Recreation Survey of the Atlantic and Gulf Coasts," "Our Fourth Shore: Great Lakes Shoreline Recreation Area Survey," and "Pacific Coast Recreation Area Survey." The interest spurred others to action, and in 1959, U.S. Senator Richard Neuberger of Oregon, a longtime conservation advocate, proposed the authorization of ten national shoreline recreation areas, a new and confusing designation to add to the plethora of names that already existed for national park areas.[19]

The San Francisco Bay Area enjoyed a powerful claim on the commitment of federal resources to preserve open space. Point Reyes, to the north of the Golden Gate Bridge in Marin County, was a beautiful stretch of coast mainly leased to dairy farmers since the nineteenth century. The area remained remote, for to reach it a traveler had to cross the undeveloped lands of West Marin, bordered by the scenic army posts of Forts Baker, Barry, and Cronkhite and, after the turn of the twentieth century, Muir Woods National Monument and Mount Tamalpais and Samuel P. Taylor State Parks. To the people of Point Reyes, this isolation mattered little. They produced butter for the outside world, often the sum of their connection to modernity, and lived in a seemingly fixed moment in the past.[20]

As national interest in shorelines and lakeshores grew, Point Reyes's remote location and the poor financial fortune of landowners made it a likely candidate for inclusion in the park system. The National Park Service (NPS) revived its interest during the 1930s, when the Great Depression and New Deal combined to send NPS representatives to nearly every scenic spot in the nation, but only in the 1950s, with the Pacific Coast Recreation Area Survey, did efforts to preserve the area begin. By that time, freeways and suburban sprawl had spread into Marin County, piercing the quiet in which the Point Reyes area so long had slumbered. A rapid response was so essential that George L. Collins, chief of the agency's planning team and a long-time Park Service professional closely connected to power in the agency, paid for publication of the Pacific Coast shoreline survey out of his own pocket. Sierra Club activity furthered the cause. In 1958, the *Sierra Club Bulletin* devoted an entire issue to the establishment of a protected area at Point Reyes.[21]

Outdoor recreation became an important social issue in a prosperous but increasingly confined society, and Stewart Udall's Department of the Interior assumed responsibility for providing the public with recreational options. Americans wanted to have it all, and for the first time, they expected not only leisure time but facilities in which to enjoy recreation. The National Park Service seemed to be the logical agency to manage recreation, but Udall held an older view of the value of the park system. His preservationist tenets, expressed clearly in his 1963 best-seller, *The Quiet Crisis*, illustrated his leanings, a point of view that led him to regard national parks as places of reverence rather than recreation. Udall's vision of the national parks curtailed NPS prerogative.[22] At the moment when the National Park Service was best prepared and most inclined to manage recreation, Udall supported the establishment of the Bureau of Outdoor Recreation (BOR) in the Department of the Interior. He shifted recreation management to the new agency.

Public recreation had been a long-standing sore point with the Park Service. Recreation offered a ready-made constituency for the NPS, but to purists in the agency, recreational areas diluted the stock—in the timeworn phrase—of the national parks. The NPS had been intermittently involved in recreation management since before the New Deal, but its efforts ran into Congress's sense that the national parks meant something other than recreation. The Park Service also encountered resistance from other federal agencies that claimed the turf. NPS battles with the Forest Service over recreation were legendary, but only with the creation of BOR did resistance come from within the Department of the Interior. Faced with a much larger agency in its own department that claimed its mission, BOR immediately sought distance from the better positioned NPS, exasperating Director Conrad L. Wirth and other politically supple leaders of the Park Service. A Forest Service bureaucrat was chosen as BOR's first administrator, and BOR used its resources to support recreation in nearly every federal agency—except the Park Service. This typical contest of mission and constituency compelled aggressive NPS action.[23]

At Point Reyes, the Bureau of Outdoor Recreation presented little threat to the Park Service. The seashore and lakeshores surveys focused on Point Reyes, and while the area did not offer the kind of easily accessible recreation that BOR supported, it did offer recreational potential and in the Bay Area, powerful psychic cachet. Although timber and development interests opposed a reserved area at Point Reyes, the Kennedy administration's support for the goals of outdoor recreation—clearly expressed in the outdoor recreation commission's final report—and the election of Clem Miller as the congressional representative from Point Reyes and the northern coast substantially increased the chances of inclusion in the park system. Miller strongly advocated the creation of a national reserve at Point Reyes and made this one of his primary goals in Congress. He also lobbied for inclusion of Marin County's excess military land in a park area. One of California's U.S. senators, Clair Engel, also supported the park. Sierra Club leaders were instrumental in founding the Point Reyes Foundation, reflecting the powerful interest among Bay Area residents in preserving the wild coast. Another group, Conservation Associates, which included NPS veteran George Collins among its founders, acted as an intermediary between industry and conservationists. Even when Pacific Gas and Electric announced plans to build a nuclear power plant at Bodega Bay, north of the proposed seashore, interest in Point Reyes did not diminish. After the 1962 ORRRC report categorized the need for urban recreational lands as urgent and after much lobbying, Congress passed the Point Reyes National Seashore bill in August 1962, and President John F. Kennedy signed it into law on September 13.[24]

Authorization was only the first step in the process of preserving wildland. Point Reyes was a second-generation national park, created not from the public domain, but by purchasing lands from private owners, exchanging tracts with businesses, and relying on the cooperation of state governments. The proclamation signed by Kennedy was merely a promise to create a park. The real work took negotiations and counteroffers, highlighting how much more difficult establishing new national park areas had become. Although the money set aside for land acquisition in California was insufficient and nearly a decade passed before the Park Service acquired enough ground to establish the park, Point Reyes National Seashore was a major achievement. The Bay Area had its second national park area, this one potentially larger by far and with a cultural meaning that transcended the sacred-profane distinction embodied in Muir Woods National Monument. It also set a new pattern that could be repeated elsewhere in the populous metropolitan area. Point Reyes became the cornerstone of a drive to establish a major national park area in northern California.

In response to the changing look of the Bay Area, residents expressed the combination of nostalgia for the past and fear of change that underpinned much of the preservation movement in the United States. As did many American cities in the late 1950s and the early 1960s, San Francisco and its surrounding communities embraced urban renewal. Conceptually a solid idea, urban renewal promised renovation of the downtown areas that became blighted as post–World War II suburban growth drew economic and social activity away from urban cores. Simultaneously it often became a way for powerful civic interests to use federal might and money to acquire land, demolish low-income and minority neighborhoods under the loose rubric of "progress," and gentrify attractive urban areas. When it worked well, urban renewal temporarily resuscitated declining cities. When it became a manifestation of poorly distributed wealth and power, it could be a very divisive program.[25]

San Francisco revealed both dimensions of urban renewal's impact. Much of the city's population and especially East Bay and Marin County commuters experienced great benefits from urban renewal. A small downtown office district had long hampered the city's ability to compete as a regional, national, and international service center. To foster growth required more space, and in densely populated San Francisco, there was little room for easy expansion. North of downtown lay intact, vibrant neighborhoods such as Chinatown and North Beach; to the west were hilly topography and the prime retail and high-end hotel district, and beyond that the expensive neighborhoods of Pacific Heights as well as the Presidio and the military apparatus it contained. The bay stood east of downtown. The only direction available for growth was south, across one of the city's symbolic barriers, the 120-foot-wide Market Street that separated affluent San Francisco from the economically disadvantaged South of Market area.[26] Development below Market Street meant greater prosperity for white-collar Bay Area residents, more and more of whom headed across bridges each day on their way to work.

From a developer's perspective, rewards for projects south of Market Street were considerable. Hundreds of acres, relatively cheap in cost and mostly populated by people who in the 1950s lacked access to the mechanisms of power, awaited innovative utilization. Urban renewal provided the vehicle fueled by federal dollars, and the city's most powerful entities lined up in support of development. Some of San Francisco's prominent planning organizations, including the Blyth-Zellerbach Committee, an off-shoot of the Bay Area Council (BAC), one of the oldest planning entities in the region, the San Francisco Planning and Urban Renewal Association (SPUR), and the San Francisco Redevelopment Agency (SFRA), strongly advocated development. Their influence created a parallel power base in favor of development that offset the long-standing influence of San Francisco's neighborhood organizations, working-class clubs, and unions. A coalition of developers that took shape sought to transform the city and make it into a financial center and tourist destination. The boldest among them envisioned retaking the title of the primary city in the West from the upstart to the south, Los Angeles. In this heady environment, many Bay Area residents bought into the dream of becoming the Manhattan of the West.[27]

After 1945, large-scale development goals in the United States typically encountered two related but very different kinds of issues that furthered preservation goals. In this era, American cities competed to establish a unique character based on their history, cultural attributes, and general ambience. Since the days of the gold-seeking forty-niner and accentuated by the novels and stories of Jack London, San Francisco had been known as a city with unique charm. As the 1960s began, it had yet to clearly portray its rich and complicated history, an absolutely necessary ingredient if the city was to stake a claim to the kind of high culture preeminence it sought. Urban renewal seemed the ticket to faux culture and history, precisely the kind of presentation of the past that helped cities but often hurt residents without the means or desire to participate in change. Redevelopment always prompted a twinge of discomfort, similar to the sentiments of William Kent earlier in the century. A sense of loss accompanied change, for the powerful as well as the disenfranchised. Growth meant the destruction of familiar landmarks, assuring that symbols of communities and their patterns of living would be different. Even beneficiaries felt the sense of loss.[28]

These twinned but contradictory sentiments contributed to a growing preoccupation with cultural preservation in the Bay Area. A strong and long-term military presence was also a crucial factor; the region contained numerous military reservations, forts, and gun batteries, a few operational and others relics of earlier eras. Since 1850 the lands included in these reservations created de facto open space that permitted some public use. Military personnel, and increasingly service retirees, made their homes in the region. Proud of their heritage and seeking validation of their contribution to American society, military retirees took special interest in the symbols and structures of their effort. Fort Point, under the Golden Gate Bridge, became the focus of their efforts.

Built on the location of a tiny Spanish gun battery, called Castillo de San Joaquin, Fort Point was one of the first major U.S. Army installations in the Bay Area. Constructed during the 1850s, the fort became the front line of American defense on the Pacific Ocean. The Civil War never reached the fort, but it remained a barracks for the better part of the next fifty years. It was gradually incorporated into the Presidio, the Bay Area's primary army installation. In 1926, the barracks closed and the fort was abandoned. During construction of the Golden Gate Bridge in the 1930s, serious discussions about Fort Point's demolition began. Only the intervention of Joseph Strauss, the powerful and authoritarian chief engineer of the Golden Gate Bridge project, prevented its destruction. Strauss initially thought that the site offered the best location for the caisson that would anchor the San Francisco end of the bridge, but a tour of the fort persuaded him that it was worth preserving. He redesigned the bridge and moved the caisson several hundred feet. During World War II, when the threat of Japanese invasion of the West Coast seemed real, soldiers again were stationed at Fort Point. After the end of the war, the fort was again abandoned and stood vacant in the shadow of the Golden Gate Bridge.[29]

Long regarded as an outstanding example of masonry fort construction, Fort Point had been the subject of preservation interest since the 1920s. In 1926, the American Institute of Architects expressed concern about the fort's deterioration to Secretary of War Dwight Davis. After World War II, when the fort was finally and permanently shuttered, preservation advocates and military retirees combined to spur a preservation drive. In March 1947, to commemorate 100 years of American military presence at the site, the army hosted an open house at the fort. General Mark Clark, the venerated leader of World War II who commanded the Sixth Army, then headquartered at the Presidio, proposed that the fort be declared surplus and released to an agency with the expertise to manage it. Clark's optimistic hope failed to materialize. The War Department decided not to release the fort to the War Assets Administration, the agency responsible for disposing of surplus properties.[30]

During the subsequent decade, Fort Point languished. Military property, it remained off-limits to the public except for annual Armed Forces Day celebrations. Infrequent tours took place, usually at the request of a visiting dignitary or a professional with some interest in the fort's past. A few grassroots movements that sought to preserve the fort made noise in the community, but little if any preservation work was accomplished. Fort Point simply stood decaying, and the estimates of the cost to restore it increased with each passing year.

By the late 1950s, when California surpassed New York as the state that received the largest percentage of defense contracts and the San Francisco Bay Area contained no fewer than forty separate military installations, many people with close ties to the military reached the stage of life where preservation was a worthwhile investment of their time and energy. In 1959, a group of these people—military retirees and civilian engineers impressed with the structure—formed the Fort Point Museum Association. They raised funds for preservation and lobbied for the establishment of a national historic site at the fort. A decade-long grassroots movement to save the fort from decay took shape. With the Sixth Army's moral and financial support, the association cleaned up the fort grounds, built safety barricades, sponsored special events, hosted school groups and civic organizations, and entertained growing numbers of weekend visitors.[31] The public began to perceive Fort Point as more than an abandoned military installation.

This interest became a place to begin, a jumping-off point from which a variety of individuals and concerns could start to look at a larger conception of public preservation for the Bay Area. Fort Point was an important historic relic, a piece of the area's past that made the transition from use to symbol ahead of many similar places. Yet as the Bay Area was transformed both economically and culturally, the expectations of its people grew in scope. A small fort under the Golden Gate Bridge did not represent the region's conception of its merits. Creating a national park area that reflected the self-image and grandeur of the region required a much greater vision.

CHAPTER TWO

A National Park for the Golden Gate

The Bay Area treasured its idiosyncratic self-image. Cultivated out of a long history of opposing the norms of American society, San Francisco's image illustrated that the Bay Area valued itself in a way different from the rest of the nation. Neighborhoods served as organizational centers and provided a sense of identity and purpose. Ethnic and class-based communities, concerned with preserving their neighborhoods' character, regarded progress with great—and largely negative—gravity. In 1959, to the shock and dismay of the California Department of Highways, the San Francisco Board of Supervisors voted down seven of ten planned freeways through San Francisco, including one through Golden Gate Park and another on the waterfront. George Moscone and Willie Brown, who both went on to prominence, led the Freeway Revolt, which in turn energized the Sierra Club and Edgar Wayburn to pioneer the development of a powerful slow growth movement well ahead of the rest of the nation. In 1950s San Francisco, an early version of the quality of life issues that later vexed American society played a significant role in slowing urban development. That attitude continued into the 1960s, when the Bay Area became ground zero for the American cultural revolution and ordinary San Franciscans battled freeways they regarded as a portent of doom.[1]

Across the bay in Berkeley, a movement that reshaped the definition of individual rights in American society erupted over the issue of political organizing on the University of California–Berkeley campus. Borrowing the techniques and strategies of the civil rights movement in the South, the free speech movement (FSM) reinvented the prerogatives of the individual in American society and set off the student revolts of the 1960s. From FSM came the antiwar movement, which focused on bringing the American involvement in Vietnam to a halt. In one of the countless demonstrations that dotted the late 1960s, Berkeley students marched on the Oakland induction center with the goal of closing it down. They succeeded for a day, a prelude to the October 1969 antiwar moratorium and the march on the White House by 40,000 people the following month, the high points of antiwar activity in the United States.[2]

At about the same time, a loosely constructed and conceived movement, detached from the political struggles of the day and utopian in character, also found a home in the Bay Area. Descended at least in part from the Beats of 1950s North Beach, the hippies of San Francisco's Haight-

Ashbury neighborhood created a new consciousness. They did not see the point of battling what they called the "straights." They aimed for a new reality, assisted by psychedelic drugs, that would run parallel to the temporal world. Labeled the counterculture, this loose grouping offered another of the countless variations on the mainstream that came to characterize the decade. If cultural innovation of any sort was to occur in 1960s America, the Bay Area was likely to be its focus.

In a unique way, the cultural revolution in the Bay Area and the idea of service-sector growth through urban renewal melded together to create in San Francisco an idyllic place that stood out for its culture as well as its beauty. One result was increasingly stringent opposition to growth and the spread of suburbia. After 1945, suburban growth in the United States gobbled up huge tracts of land, devouring the open space that generations of Americans long took for granted. Between 1945 and the early 1970s, American suburbs grew so fast that their population eclipsed the cities they surrounded.[3] Freeways extended far into the hinterlands around every city of significance. Developers eagerly built new homes, shopping centers, and other amenities of postwar life, aided by massive federal funding for roads and highways. Many more people could enjoy the fruits of prosperity, but these came at a cost—the loss of the freedom to roam in undeveloped space. As the suburbs grew, efforts to retain that space became a prominent goal of the families that moved to these new communities. The last to come were often the first to complain about the impact of which they were an intrinsic part.

In the battles of the 1960s in the Bay Area, local residents cloaked themselves in the quality-of-life environmentalism that rose to the fore as Americans came to believe that they could have it all without risk. These attitudes differed greatly from turn-of-the-century conservation; quality-of-life environmentalists became extremely skilled at a strategy that would come to be known as NIMBY, "not in my backyard." They regarded themselves as entitled to freedom from the consequences of the progress that gave them leisure, offering an environmentalism that depended on the affluence of their society for its claims to moral right. As long as American society remained prosperous, such arguments held great sway. In the mid-1960s, the combination of affluence and idealism gave such attitudes a currency they have yet to regain.[4]

The vibrant cultural community in the Bay Area took advantage of the growing interest in the publicly preserved past to seek another kind of federal perquisite. The struggle over development illustrated the era's tensions and hastened the establishment of a national park area near San Francisco Bay. Powerful efforts to create state and local open space helped seed a climate that valued public parklands, and even in the heyday of California, national parks were a coveted prize. National park areas had long been regarded as marvelous additions in most areas of the country, but until the New Deal, NPS area designations other than "national park" were neither economic prizes nor powerful cultural symbols. They lacked the cachet that accompanied federal development money and the revenue generated by visitation of the crown jewels of the system. Most were second-class sites, areas passed over unless the agency received extraordinary levels of funding. After World War II, new national park areas proliferated as the nation self-consciously broadened the themes included in this primary form of official commemoration. A new park area might well be the ticket to construction contracts and other kinds of development. With the beginning of Mission 66, national park areas became economic engines as well as markers of historical, cultural, and scenic significance. Residents of the Bay Area recognized the emerging twofold advantages of inclusion in the park system.[5]

In the San Francisco region, the combination of interest in cultural and economic development translated into three designations, two as individual park areas and the third as a national landmark. A clear tie between the military experience and cultural preservation began when the Presidio was designated a National Historic Landmark in 1962. Official preservation took nonmilitary forms as well. In 1964, the John Muir National Historic Site was established in Martinez, northeast of Oakland, to commemorate the life of the great preservationist, who moved to the town after his marriage and operated his wife's family's large fruit ranch. In addition, the Eugene O'Neill National Historic Site in Danville, east of Oakland, was authorized in 1976 and established in 1982 to celebrate the achievements of the famous American playwright. The new parks represented an important additional source of federal largesse as the military considered downsizing its presence in the Bay Area.

By the early 1960s, the Bay Area faced significant economic challenges closely related to the changing nature of the military presence. The San Francisco region competed with other western cities for federal dollars, but like many similar areas, northern California was limited by its military facilities. It had been the western capital of shipbuilding, an advantage as long as sea power was a crucial military activity. The rise of aerospace limited the Bay Area's fortunes. Especially during the early 1960s, the momentum shifted away from the Bay Area to southern California, long a chief rival. The Bay Area had research laboratories, Lawrence Livermore and NASA–Ames Research Laboratory in particular, but the bulk of its military support apparatus was blue-collar and industrial, especially the docks and warehouses that supported America's overseas expeditions. In an increasingly highly technological industry, the Bay Area lagged behind greater Los Angeles, with its Jet Propulsion Laboratory in Pasadena and massive aerospace industrial presence.[6]

One manifestation of the shift in federal emphasis from blue- to white-collar endeavors was the divestiture of excess federal land, a process that occurred throughout the country. As early as the 1850s, the military held enormous reservations of land in the Bay Area, and in the twentieth century, its reach expanded. The military quickly acquired land for installations before, during, and after World War II, and by the end of the 1950s, other federal agencies, states, cities, and communities clamored for title. Often, military officials were willing to give up the properties. The cost of maintaining land was high, and few Pentagon officials wanted to rankle always delicate regional relationships by holding on to land that they did not really need. Across the nation, military and defense-industry land became parks, forests, public projects, or private developments.[7]

In the Bay Area, federal divestiture began in 1960 and grew in scope and scale. The Park Service was slow on the uptake. Although noted conservationist Edgar Wayburn worked to transfer these lands to the park system, the Park Service was uninterested. In 1961, the military turned over to California the undeveloped areas of Fort Baker, across the Golden Gate from the Presidio, to be used as Marin Headlands State Park. After a concerted effort by the state, Angel Island State Park followed a few years later.[8] In 1962, the Department of Defense declared Fort Mason surplus property after transferring the remaining military functions to the Oakland army base. The opportunity excited local interest in a number of ways. In August 1964, the San Francisco Board of Supervisors passed Resolution no. 472-64. It requested the establishment of Fort Mason as a national historic site and, if that could not be achieved, asked the General Services Administration (GSA) to give Fort Mason to San Francisco as a park and recreation area. The process was typical; excess federal land had enormous potential for cities if they were adapted to new purposes.

The real contest during the divestiture process was the battle for the famous federal penitentiary on Alcatraz Island. After the Mexican-American War in 1848 and the United States's annexation of California, Alcatraz Island served as a lighthouse, a well-armed fort, a military prison, and finally after 1934, as the federal system's most vaunted penitentiary. The hardest of the hard cases found their way to "Uncle Sam's Devil's Island," as one reporter labeled the facility. With the appearance of Al "Scarface" Capone, "Machine Gun" Kelly, and other notorious criminals, Alcatraz became a national symbol, full of the mystery and fear that mainstream society attributes to its deviants.[9]

Penitentiaries enjoy an unusual, almost prurient popularity with the American public, and Alcatraz Island, known as The Rock, possessed a particularly terrifying reputation. Everything about it seemed brutal, even its location. The cool San Francisco Bay climate crumbled the masonry structures, and salt water corroded the plumbing. By the early 1960s, Alcatraz required at least $5 million for maintenance and repairs. The enormous cost of shipping everything to The Rock, even fresh water, drove expenses skyward. The penitentiary became untenable, a relic of an era that envisioned imprisonment as punishment rather than a means of rehabilitation. In June 1962, U.S. Attorney General Robert Kennedy announced that Alcatraz would be phased out of the penitentiary system. On March 21, 1963, the prison closed, and the last inmates were transferred off the island to the maximum security facility at Marion, Illinois. The last prisoner, Frank Weatherman, told reporters, "It's mighty good to get up and leave. This rock ain't no good for nobody." An era came to an end. Alcatraz was no longer a prison; unneeded by the federal government, its future remained unclear.[10]

To many, the island seemed the ultimate prize, and no shortage of claimants followed the April 1963 General Services Administration announcement that Alcatraz Island was excess property. It was not an ordinary piece of property. Alcatraz enjoyed a powerful cultural cachet in many different circles, and long and arduous debates about its use ensued. The interest stretched from Washington, D.C., across the country. In 1964, five Lakota people seized Alcatraz Island and held it for four hours. Under their interpretation of the 1868 Fort Laramie Treaty, all abandoned federal land once held by the Lakota reverted to them. Before the heady days of the free speech movement, such an action seemed eccentric, and Assistant Attorney General Ramsey Clark dismissed any legal standing for the action.[11] In March of that year, the President's Commission on the Disposition of Alcatraz Island was empaneled. Two months later, the commission recommended that the island be used to commemorate the founding of the United Nations in San Francisco, but no action followed. The proposal seemed impractical, and in subsequent years no one came up with a viable alternative. The cost of repairs on the island was daunting, the logistical problems of moving people and supplies were enormous, and for many agencies, strapped with growing costs and finite resources, the island remained appealing but looked more and more as if it were a management nightmare. By 1968, most public entities gave up on the island. Nearly every federal and California state agency indicated to the General Services Administration that Alcatraz Island was not in its plans.[12]

Alcatraz was too important a symbol to simply let slide away, however, and Bay Area governments searched for a way to use the island. The City of San Francisco became interested in acquiring the island in 1968 and asked for development proposals. Almost 500 different proposals were submitted. Texas billionaire tycoon H. Lamar Hunt proposed high-end condominiums, restaurants, and other urban uses for the island, intending them to be a space-age counterpart to New York City attractions. In September 1969, the San Francisco Board of Supervisors approved the plan. The uproar was instantaneous. People all over the country wrote Secretary Hickel and other federal officials asking for intervention. After receiving 8,000 protest coupons, clipped from local newspapers, the board of supervisors agreed to revisit its decision.[13]

The increasingly vocal pan-Indian Native American population also had plans for the island, including a cultural center with a spiritual shrine, a museum, and a vocational training program facility. After the San Francisco Indian Center on Valencia Street burned down on October 9, 1969, the quest for the island took on new urgency.[14] Alcatraz Island came to symbolize the injustice American Indians experienced, and urban Indians moved to solidify their claim to the island. In the more dramatic style that derived both from the civil rights movement and the American cultural revolution, Indian people seized Alcatraz Island twice in November 1969.[15]

The Bureau of Outdoor Recreation revived its interest as well, commissioning studies of Alcatraz and nearby Angel Island. The most important of these, "Golden Gate: A Matchless Opportunity," built on more than twenty years of ideas for a park in the region.[16] The study played a catalytic role in initiating the park proclamation process. "The bureaucratic spark," Doug Nadeau recalled, that helped generate support for the park was "a crash project" prepared by a small government planning team December 4–9, 1969, entitled "A New Look at Alcatraz." Based upon this document, Secretary of the Interior Walter J. Hickel made the decision to authorize the preparation of a conceptual plan for the Golden Gate National Recreation Area.

Although local support alone eventually might have succeeded in securing legislation to establish the park, Congress typically relied on the Park Service to recommend new park areas. At the time "A New Look at Alcatraz" was in preparation, no one else proposed a national park at the Golden Gate. Nor was the study team aware that Ansel Adams and Edgar Wayburn had earlier made such a proposal. To prepare the conceptual plan for the park, which became the basis of NPS support of authorizing legislation, the Park Service assembled a planning team that included representatives from outside agencies, a novel concept. This small gesture foretold the park's signature pioneering in public involvement. Even more, the plan "literally introduced Amy Meyer to the concept" of a park, Nadeau recalled. "She of course picked up the ball and ran with it much further than any of us had dreamed."[17]

In 1969, Amy Meyer, an activist, artist, homemaker, and resident of the Richmond District, attended a meeting about excess military land and learned that the General Services Administration planned to build a football field–sized National Archives branch office overlooking San Francisco Bay near her home at Fort Miley. In the age of urban renewal and strong central government, the concept seemed feasible. Even in the late 1960s, governments acted with a sense of destiny and sometimes without considering the implications for communities, and such unsightly structures had become a hallmark of American public architecture. San Francisco was different, more tied to its cultural past and more cognizant of the significance of neighborhoods and micro-communities. Where cities all over the country simply accepted construction that destroyed historic downtowns, San Francisco erupted in indignation.

For Meyer, the idea that the government could simply put a building three blocks from her home spurred her to action. Her husband was working long hours as a psychiatrist and she was raising two small children. "I stumbled into this and said, 'gee this is interesting, what a nice little project I could work on,'" she laughed during an interview in 2002. "The next thing I knew I had this sort of tiger on my hands." She was fortunate to step into a situation in which federal planning teams had already laid the groundwork. The 1969 GSA plan and the BOR/NPS study created a context in which Meyer could act and federal agencies with prepared plans could help.[18] It set her forward on a more than thirty-year career as a conservation activist.

Opposition created a coalition of disparate interests. John Jacobs, who headed the San Francisco Planning and Urban Renewal Association (SPUR), thought the proposal obnoxious, an affront to neighborhoods. Others held similar opinions. A tenacious individual, Meyer regarded the proposal as a threat to her and her neighbors' way of life, an assault on the entire Richmond District. "What I know how to do is organize people," she later ventured in a discussion of her role. She connected more than seventy neighborhood organizations and encouraged the Sierra Club to complain about the transformation of open space into a government complex. Meyer's energy was palpable, and the Sierra Club appointed her leader of the chapter conservation committee, the entity with responsibility for protecting the local environment.[19] Supported by the club's influence and her unbounded energy, she headed the challenge to the Fort Miley development.

For national park area proponents, the GSA proposal was a fortuitous circumstance that galvanized a number of disparate currents in the Bay Area. San Francisco's history of strong neighborhood activism created powerful grassroots constituencies that were influential in local politics. The Outer Richmond Neighborhood Association, of which Meyer was a member, and other similar groups held clear and firm points of view about issues that affected them. They shaped dialogue about urban growth. Many of these associations had their roots in the nineteenth century and took on ethnic character as the Bay Area developed early in the twentieth century. They became reconstituted as geographic alliances in the post–World War II era. The antifreeway battles of the 1950s and 1960s shaped these new grassroots alliances, and power drifted from working-class neighborhoods to more affluent ones. Pacific Heights, one of the more posh neighborhoods, emerged as a leading force in the city. Its residents and those of another similarly affluent district, St. Francis Woods, comprised nine of the eleven members of the board of supervisors, elected from the city at large, as late as the early 1970s.

Antagonizing such groups was a dangerous strategy even for powerful financial and development interests; the groups possessed wealth, power and access, a strong sense of local and regional identity, and a history of protecting their interests.[20]

Across the Golden Gate Bridge, similar community activism enjoyed an equally long history. Edgar Wayburn, former president of the Sierra Club, was already a longtime leader in regional conservation, a visionary who understood the complicated nature of urban conservation long before such thinking became fashionable. Wayburn recognized the importance of open space close to people even as the postwar Sierra Club focused on faraway wilderness. "Wilderness begins in your own backyard," he often retorted to claims of the debased nature of urban areas. "People have to have places that they go to nearby." Wayburn anticipated the trends of the 1960s more than a decade ahead of the rest of the conservation community. His interest in Marin County was spurred by the reality that in 1947, less than 1,400 acres were in reserves. In the late 1940s, Wayburn began to talk of enlarging Mt. Tamalpais State Park, a project that added more than 5,000 acres to the state park between 1948 and 1972. He envisioned even more, as early as the 1940s conceiving of an open-space link between Tomales Point near Point Reyes and Fort Funston in San Francisco.[21]

Turning even 100,000 acres of Marin County into parkland juxtaposed different visions of the region. Wayburn and his friends brought postwar vision to the area, while communities such as Bolinas and the ranchers of the Olema Valley were equally adamant about being left alone. Such communities opposed a park, but they feared suburban development even more. The Indian occupation of Alcatraz, the changing social climate, and the prospect of the Marincello development also demanded the attention of Marin County activists. Marincello had been the brainchild of Thomas Frouge, a self-made millionaire who teamed up with Gulf Oil to build the 18,000-person community. After nearly eight years of political opposition and litigation, Marincello was sold to the Nature Conservancy on December 22, 1972. One of the project's first steps had been gates erected at the entrance to the Marincello development. After the project's demise, the gates stood decaying until 1978, when they were taken down by the Park Service. The symbolism was powerful, if by 1978 a little bit frayed. The primary vestige of private development in the headlands came down at the hands of an agency responsible to the entire public.[22]

The obvious threat of development lent a sense of urgency to preservation and ripened the region for the grassroots organizing at which the Sierra Club excelled. Pressure for the development of the underutilized Marin Headlands military installations—Fort Baker, Fort Barry, and Fort Cronkhite—galvanized Marin County resistance. Under the circumstances, local residents regarded a park as a better option than miles of subdivisions populated by commuters. Wayburn found a conservation community in Marin and with Katherine Frankforter shaped an organization that sought the inclusion of Marin Headlands in a national park area. Soon called Headlands Inc., the group sought to keep excess military lands from being subdivided, using zoning, precisely the kind of mechanism that many rural people feared, as a primary technique. By preventing excess military and agricultural land from being subdivided, the organization could slow subdivision development and preserve the qualities that would contribute to a park area. The ranching industry in Marin County, perched on the edge of major metropolitan area, recognized the advantage of these new urban allies. Instead of fighting zoning and other mechanisms, they saw in regulations a strategy that helped preserve their way of life. A diverse constituency formed that supported the idea of restricted use of much of west Marin County.[23]

The diverse grassroots energy generated around the Bay Area coalesced in an organization called People for a Golden Gate National Recreation Area. It took the awful acronym PFGGNRA for its own. When Wayburn thought up the name, he remarked that "it sounds like a social disease." But despite the unwieldy handle, the organization developed wide influence. Amy Meyer became its heart and soul; as architect and founder, Wayburn applied the knowledge he had acquired in almost thirty years of conservation activism to become its conscience and voice of reason. Environmental organizations, such as the Sierra Club Bay Chapter, and development groups such as SPUR recognized that PFGGNRA was more than the typical neighborhood organization. Recognizing their commonality of purpose, more than sixty-five Bay Area groups joined PFGGNRA, making it one of the region's most broad-based citizens' movements. "All the people I work with care passionately about this place," Amy Meyer asserted in 2002. "We love it. We think it is the most special place on the face of the earth. . . . I would say that the thing that everybody has in common is this enormous love of the earth and the things that are on it, and particularly in this—perhaps particularly most of all—in this place." That broad base of support, its ties to power and influence, and a reservoir of public credibility put PFGGNRA in the lead in the drive for a national park unit in the San Francisco Bay Area.

The energetic and powerful U.S. Representative Philip "Phil" Burton of the Fifth District in California soon lent his considerable charm, muscle, and political acumen to the park project. Burton, born in Ohio in 1926, moved with his family to San Francisco just before World War II. A classic liberal closely tied to organized labor, he developed into a machine politician who built alliances with charisma. When that did not work, he backed reluctant allies into corners from which they could not extricate themselves without his power. A physically large man who chain-smoked and favored vodka, Burton was hardly an outdoorsman. He once said that "a wilderness experience for me [is] to see a tree in a goddamn pot." Possessed of an extra-ordinary instinct to favor the underdog and committed to an older style of politics that demanded bringing home the bacon, Burton was in the middle of a meteoric and sometimes contentious rise to power in Congress. Although he did not represent the part of the Bay Area in which much of the proposed park was located, he intuitively understood its importance and took it on as his cause. When Wayburn brought him a truncated pro-posal and said he offered it because what he wanted was not politically fea-sible, Burton bellowed, "You tell me what you want, not what's politically feasible, and I'll get it through Congress!"[24]

Burton's motivations were as complex as the man himself. A champion of liberal causes, he was an early adherent to the ideas of quality-of-life envi-ronmentalism that came to fruition during the late 1960s. He believed that government should help people to help themselves and initially did not grasp the role of parks in that formula. He once told San Francisco writer Margot Patterson Doss that parks "were a rich man's game and I'm a labor candidate," but when she pointed out that the rich had private homes at Lake Tahoe and that "the working stiff" needed public parks, Burton was persuaded. "By God, you're right!" he shouted. "You'll get your parks." In 1964, he lauded the passage of the Wilderness Act as a triumph of Ameri-can vision. Ever after, Burton regarded parks as a symbol of the good life and remained committed to the principle that everyone in a democratic and affluent society should have access to public largesse. In this respect, "parks for the people, where the people are," even with its association with the Nixon administration, was natural for him. It brought the benefits of an affluent society to people who otherwise might not receive them.[25]

On June 16, 1971, Burton introduced a new proposal for a national re-creation area in the Golden Gate area. U.S. Representative William Maillard, a Republican from the Bay Area, had proposed a smaller park bill at Way-burn's earlier request. Burton was livid about the limits of the proposal. Not only did the Republican proposal circumvent him and supersede his plans, it was minuscule in comparison to his own ideas. Burton's initial Golden Gate National Recreation Area proposal reflected the verve and style of the congressman and larger goals of his conservationist friends. Wayburn envi-sioned the proposal as the culmination of his twenty-five-year effort to pre-serve Point Reyes and San Francisco. A proposal of this scope upset the existing balance of power in Bay Area land use. Political interests of all kinds squawked loudly at the proposal, the Park Service thought it far too large, and even Wayburn, its architect and greatest proponent, labeled the plan "outrageous."[26] In one dramatic maneuver, the park proposal recast the future of Marin County, moving away from commercial resource use and toward the combination of open space and bedroom community status that became common in outlying areas after World War II.

Conceived by Wayburn and Meyer, Burton's bill was audacious. In Marin, it included Forts Baker, Barry, and Cronkhite, the Olema Valley, Marin Headlands State Park, Angel Island State Park, and the former Marincello housing project. In San Francisco, Burton proposed encompassing Fort Funston, Fort Miley, Fort Mason, and Fort Point, 700 acres of the Presidio, Baker, Phelan, and Ocean Beaches, and most of the city's Lincoln Park. Together with his conservationist friends, Burton soothed local fears about the loss of the military presence and its vast economic impact at the Presidio by concentrating on Marin County. He also got the Department of the Interior veto power over any new development in the Presidio, a remarkable reversal of the power relationships in government that played to one of the military's fears.

The Presidio had been in military hands for more than a century, and as San Francisco grew, it became the last large piece of underdeveloped land in the city. Spectacularly scenic, with acres of mature trees and pristine lawns, the Presidio had become a prize for which many would fight if the federal government ever gave it up. Burton wanted to prevent private development of the tract and, with the inclusion of the post in the proposed park, offered the military a way to preserve its domain without private development pressure. If the military would concede the Presidio after it no longer needed the post for military purposes, private developers would be thwarted. The disposition of the Presidio complete, developers would have to look elsewhere for land for new projects. The Department of Defense enjoyed far greater power than did the Department of the Interior, and Interior's veto was an exceptional maneuver. All in all, the proposal was unique in the annals of American park proclamation, representing the largest expenditure of federal money to purchase parkland in U.S. history. The cost of the 34,000-acre park project was estimated at $118 million, with $60 million for land acquisition alone. Success in the project would have created more than 100,000 acres of open space in San Francisco and Marin County, 64,000 in the Point Reyes National Seashore, 17,000 in the Marin Municipal Water District holdings, and 34,000 in the proposed national recreation area.[27]

The proposal also revealed Burton's political sympathies and his penchant for outraging the conventions of politics. Where Maillard's bill proposed including Alcatraz in the park, Burton's proposal left the island out. The Alcatraz occupation compelled some sort of government response, mostly in an effort to deflect any enhancement of the widely held sense that Indians had been unjustly treated. What began as a brief adventure became a twenty-month ordeal that captured national attention. An oppressed minority group sought redress of grievances and offered a program of self-improvement called "Thunderbird University." Within a few months, when it was clear that the Indians were not going away anytime soon, President

Richard M. Nixon growled at his secretary of the interior, Walter (Wally) J. Hickel of Alaska, "Get those goddamn Indians off Alcatraz."[28] Burton's proposal, introduced just five days after federal marshals evicted the last Indians from Alcatraz, suggested that the federal government sell the island to the Indian people for their asking price: the same $24 in beads, trinkets, and cloth that Peter Minuit reportedly traded for Manhattan Island in 1692.[29]

Pure political theater, Burton's gesture played well in the Bay Area. It seemed to occupy the moral high ground, an important concept in a frayed society. It acknowledged and sought to rectify old wrongs and provided for the empowerment of a minority group. While the actual transfer was unlikely in any circumstance, the statement offered a powerful pronouncement of Burton's political posture.

His Golden Gate National Recreation Area bill revealed the extent of his political power and his adept maneuvering. In the initial proposal, Burton included the Presidio golf course, one of the most beautiful in the world and a prime perquisite of Bay Area military officers. When the army screamed in outrage, as Burton knew it would, he removed the golf course from the proposal and substituted Crissy Field, the former Army Air Corps base adjacent to the bay. Crissy Field had been Burton's objective for the park; it was better suited for recreational use than the golf course, and he manipulated the circumstances to attain his goal. U.S. senator from California Alan Cranston, a Democrat, supported Burton. By the middle of 1972, when Burton's bill emerged from committee, Alcatraz Island had been added to the proposed park, and the broad outlines of the project were secure.[30]

The bipartisan nature of 1970s conservation assisted in bringing the project to fruition. In the early 1970s, northeastern Republicans were often among the most avid supporters of conservation. Secretary of the Interior C. B. Rogers Morton, Hickel's successor and a former governor of Maryland, championed the park. He flew over the area twice and advocated the larger version of the park. From northeastern Republican tradition that spawned so many leading political conservationists, he became a strong proponent of the park. In front of the U.S. Senate, Morton argued for Wayburn's view of a larger park over the more conservative Park Service version.[31]

A range of local obstacles stood in the way of the project, and most of them involved the Presidio. Because of the unprecedented transfer of city, county, and state land to the new park, a range of governing bodies had to approve the bill's outlines. Some entities stood to gain, others to lose. One, the U.S. Army, stood to lose more than it could accept. The military sought to reduce the 34,000 acres in the proposal to 24,000, which meant deleting the Presidio from the park. Although the San Francisco Board of Supervisors voted to include the Presidio in the proposed park, Mayor Joseph Alioto sided with the military. He wanted the Presidio to remain under army control and vetoed a board of supervisors' resolution to include it.

Amy Meyer later remembered that Alioto was "very afraid we would do-in the Presidio," with all the jobs and revenue it brought into the Bay Area. Alioto's decision went against public sentiment and even the wishes of some of his powerful political allies. Even John Jacobs of SPUR, one of the most powerful pro-growth organizations in the Bay Area, favored the inclusion of the Presidio in the park; "The wolves are tending the flock," he told the supervisors.[32]

The board of supervisors played an important role in creating the context in which the Golden Gate National Recreation Area bill could be passed. At a U.S. House of Representatives Subcommittee on National Parks and Recreation hearing on the question of Golden Gate National Recreation Area, Supervisor Robert E. Gonzales spoke in favor of the park, which under the bill he favored would be called the Juan Manuel de Ayala National Recreation Area. He supported inclusion of nonmilitary areas within the Presidio and the controversial clause that the military be required to secure permission from the Department of the Interior for any construction project. Gonzales also wanted a provision that required the military to demolish square footage equal to any new construction in the authorizing legislation. Supervisor Robert H. Mendelsohn echoed the sentiments in an articulate speech.[33] Clearly, the park had local support in a community with a strong history of political activism in a state with great and growing political cachet.

Hurdles to creation of the park remained. In the U.S. Senate, Alan Bible of Nevada, chairman of the Subcommittee on Parks and Recreation, delayed hearings and eliminated much of the Presidio acreage and Cliff House from the bill. The frustrated Amy Meyer called her counterparts in New York who advocated the establishment of Gateway National Recreation Area, regarded as a fait accompli. Rogers Morton suggested that a visit by President Nixon, then in the middle of a reelection campaign, would help the cause. John Jacobs of SPUR, a prominent Bay Area Republican, arranged a boat tour of the Bay Area. Nixon brought along powerful park advocate Laurence Rockefeller and met with Meyer, Wayburn, and others from PFGGNRA. On the former mine depot wharf at the Presidio, Nixon endorsed the proposal.[34]

Nixon's promise gave Burton considerable room to maneuver. Realizing that Nixon was committed and could not back out in an election year, the congressman immediately had his aides add land in Marin County that Meyer and Wayburn suggested but that had not been included in the measure. "Put it in," Burton told Bill Thomas, his longtime aide who had just returned to the *San Francisco Chronicle* but continued to work closely with Burton, since Nixon "can't oppose it now." Burton maneuvered a compromise bill that satisfied the army and mirrored the Senate bill. Bible scheduled hearings two days later, and after the September 22, 1972, hearing, Golden Gate National Recreation Area seemed a certainty.

One enormous obstacle remained. Burton and Armed Forces Committee Chairman Edward Hebert, also a Democrat, developed an adversarial relationship. After Burton and the Louisianian disagreed on the House floor, Hebert was livid. He decided to use his committee to block the bill and pressured Speaker of the House Carl Albert to keep it from a floor vote. The dispute started when the Armed Forces Committee overlooked Burton's initial bill. After the committee did not act, Burton did not point out their lapse. After all, the bill divested the military of considerable land and, as a result of Burton's persuasive maneuvering with military officials, now included the entire Presidio, which would be transferred at the time the military declared the land excess to its needs. Hebert started a last-minute effort to derail the bill, sending a letter denouncing Burton and the bill and bringing military leaders to Congress to lobby against it. The *San Francisco Chronicle* entered the fray, calling the military's position "unconscionable." At the behest of park advocates in the Bay Area, Representative William Mailliard, who enjoyed a better relationship with Hebert despite their different party affiliations, beseeched the chair. Hebert agreed to let the bill go.

As always, Burton counted his votes in the House and knew he could pass the bill. He met with Albert, who assured him the vote would take place.[35] When the bill came before the House on October 11, 1972, Burton's count was accurate, and the junior congressman gained a major victory. The following day, the Senate passed the bill. On October 27, 1972, during the last week of his reelection campaign, Richard M. Nixon signed the Golden Gate National Recreation Area bill along with legislation to establish the Gateway National Recreation Area in New York. These election-year gifts to the states with the first- and third-largest number of delegates to the Electoral College may have smacked of politics, but they created an important social objective during the 1970s. These were national parks that were truly within the reach of ordinary people.

Burton's motives were simultaneously altruistic and pragmatic. A savvy politician, he recognized the constituency-building power of federal parks. National parks served as a medium through which he could build local support and stymie opposition. His efforts superseded those of the Park Service, which desperately wanted a major park in the Bay Area but found its resources directed elsewhere in the early 1970s. Burton carried the agency in his powerful wake, using his political base in the Bay Area and in Washington to further the creation of the park. Even his opponents could hardly resist a park area; few argued against the idea of public recreational space in the heady idealism and affluence of the 1960s and early 1970s. The battle for Golden Gate National Recreation Area became the stepping-stone to power for Burton as well as a catalyst for his later efforts that transformed the national park system.

Golden Gate National Recreation Area and Growth: Land Acquisition in the Bay Area

One of the most aggressive and adept congressional representatives of his era, Phil Burton recognized that he had struck political gold with Golden Gate National Recreation Area. As a political device, the Bay Area park had no parallel for the intrepid congressman. It met the needs of a variety of constituencies, forged political alliances with people predisposed to disagree with Burton, focused on urban areas in a time when that emphasis was mandatory for federal programs, held an important place within his liberal worldview, and muted most potential political adversaries. Golden Gate National Recreation Area, Burton quickly recognized, was more than a regional asset; it gave him new leverage in Congress as well. The park became a symbol of his foresight and leadership; it illustrated his deft maneuvering and ability to build coalitions. Golden Gate National Recreation Area's establishment signified more than a triumph of environmental sentiment and egalitarian democracy. It also initiated a repeatable political strategy not only in northern California but elsewhere in the nation as well. Beginning with Golden Gate National Recreation Area, Burton set in motion a series of park proclamations that continued throughout the subsequent decade and gave the ebullient congressman almost unequaled power in the U.S. House of Representatives.

He was assisted on all fronts in the Bay Area by a remarkable network of activists, headed by Amy Meyer and Edgar Wayburn. By 1972, the two founders of People for a Golden Gate National Recreation Area (PFGGNRA) gathered around themselves a loosely knit confederation of individuals and groups that together wielded enormous influence in the Bay Area. With significant numbers of people and access to the funds necessary to reach a larger public, this group became a force in regional environmental politics and policy making. They and their friends were affiliated loosely, allowing a dexterity that let their organization function in a variety of contexts. Although PFGGNRA was generally adroit at political maneuvering, its actions sometimes alienated local and regional politicians and on occasion failed to connect with on-the-ground activists who might be good supporters. In a few cases, PFGGNRA came to be regarded as arrogant and uninterested in the local consequences of regionwide actions, but generally, the coalition of activists was extremely effective in lobbying for the acquisition of new parklands.

At its 1972 establishment, Golden Gate National Recreation Area was a pastiche, an unwieldy mix of civilian and army lands defined as much by the military's willingness to release their properties as any other circumstance. The park boundaries had been hastily drawn, and a range of other constraints impaired the establishment process. Much of the incredibly valuable land adjacent to the park was not included within the initial boundaries. State and local recalcitrance, opposition, or even slow response to planned development left some tracts beyond reach. Other lands belonged to private owners, some of whom feared federal intrusion. Even when some sellers were willing to deal, federal funds for acquisition could not always be easily secured, and the transfer of land from other public jurisdictions could be a complex process. When Amy Meyer, Edgar Wayburn, and Phil Burton looked at the park they created, they could celebrate. However, all three recognized that they had begun, but not finished, the process of securing recreational and wildlands for the Bay Area.

Thus, even before the ink was dry on the Golden Gate National Recreation Area enabling act, the indefatigable Amy Meyer and Edgar Wayburn already planned additions to the park. The extent of the original Golden Gate National Recreation Area—more than 34,000 acres—was a remarkable accomplishment, but to this duo only a starting point for the drive for the nation's most impressive urban national park area. Meyer and Wayburn conceived of the park as a testimony to the power of grassroots activism and sophisticated political maneuvering. Their optimism was well-founded. Their initial success came at the propitious moment when urban parks received congressional attention, and they had the full backing of one of the rising Democratic politicians on Capitol Hill. The public reliance on government to solve social ills that defined the 1960s began to abate early in the 1970s, but many people, especially in the Bay Area, retained faith in the government's ability to balance interests in a democratic and chaotic society. The old Progressive faith in fair government as the solution to all kinds of social disputes retained many adherents, especially in California, and the idea of urban green space under federal management held great promise.

Divided by the entrance to San Francisco Bay, the original Golden Gate National Recreation Area was essentially two very different kinds of parks under one management rubric. Urban recreational space was one dimension. Located primarily in San Francisco, features such as Fort Mason, Fort Funston, Fort Miley, and Crissy Field were historic landscapes that became surrounded by homes, businesses, roads, and other urban structures as the city grew during the twentieth century. They served a variety of functions in the crowded city. Americans loved military architecture; they had come to expect and admire forts and the other relics of American history, and the emphasis on history in the park system made possible by the addition of historic battlefields and other areas during the New Deal contributed to the feeling that historic forts were an important part of national memory.

Forts and other facilities also offered a respite from pressing urbanity as well as opportunities for civic uses—education, community activity, and other similar concepts—that were not historically functions of national park areas. As San Francisco pinned more of its economic hopes on tourism, the park grew in importance. Alcatraz especially enjoyed great cachet with the public and possessed enormous potential as a destination for out-of-town visitors. To the north of Golden Gate Bridge, the rest of the park offered more traditional national park features. Semiwild lands, mostly located in Marin County, provided vistas and recreational potential. From the headlands to Point Reyes, a connected greenbelt that skirted urbanity offered more traditional national park experiences. The beauty of the rugged coast, old military forts, and stunning natural vistas offered the kinds of features that Americans expected from their national parks throughout the first seventy years of the twentieth century.

But the park was disjointed, its flow broken by inholdings and boundaries that made important features difficult to reach. Because most of the pieces of Golden Gate National Recreation Area had distinct identities before the park was established, the new national recreation area faced an enormous problem: the public regarded it as a series of unconnected segments instead of as a unified national park. A certain amount of that perception was cultural; people saw with the same eyes they had always had, and new signs announcing the national park did little to change public perception.

PFGGNRA worked hard, however, to weave the loose components into the conceptualization of an expanded national park. When they first conceived of the park, Meyer and Wayburn had little power or influence; most of what clout they possessed came from Wayburn's Sierra Club experience and Meyer's gritty determination. By the time they sought expansion of the park boundaries in early 1973, they and PFGGNRA were major players in Bay Area environmentalism. Questions of land use and quality-of-life environmentalism, both central to the formation of Golden Gate National Recreation Area, had already become important national themes. The "Environmental Crisis," as Americans knew the issue, reflected the national ideal of living in a plentiful world without being bothered by the consequences of creating that abundance. Nowhere was that idea more a part of local and regional self-image than in the Bay Area. As a result, PFGGNRA's founders became well-known—loved and feared—civic leaders and activists whose actions and plans caught the attention of most and the ire of some.

For the National Park Service, the emergence of PFGGNRA was both a tremendous advantage and a potentially divisive issue. Since its founding in 1916, the Park Service catered to the American mainstream, first with an elite, class-based orientation and later with an approach that facilitated automobiles and the broad group of visitors they carried. The Park Service hewed closely to its core mission for most of its first half-century. As late as 1964, only six directors had led the agency, and four of them had been with the Park Service since its founding. Leaders came up through the ranks, learned the Park Service way, and implemented it when they reached the top. From Stephen T. Mather through Conrad L. Wirth, this mission meant serving visitors. In this sense, the NPS understood its core constituency—by the 1950s, people with two weeks of vacation each year who chose to see the national parks, usually with their often reluctant children in tow.[1]

During the 1960s, government in the United States sought to serve a broader public than ever before. Urban and minority communities demanded all the services that more affluent groups received, which included access to national park areas. As a result of the riots that plagued American cities after 1965, placating urban America became a significant goal of government policy. Urban national parks became the primary response, placing the Park Service in a new arena in which it had little experience. Saying that "we have got to bring the natural world back to the people, rather than have them live in an environment where everything is paved over with concrete and loaded with frustration and violence," Secretary of the Interior Walter J. Hickel coined the idea of "parks for the people, where the people are" and offered a comprehensive proposal that included national recreation areas at Gateway around the New York/New Jersey shore, in Ohio's Cuyahoga Valley, in the Santa Monica Mountains near Los Angeles, and on lands surrounding the Golden Gate. These were the first full-scale proposals to fulfill Stewart Udall's axiom to bring "the battle lines of conservation into the cities."[2]

Despite this transformation, by the 1970s, the Park Service could no longer count on a supportive public, docilely loyal to the agency's agenda. Especially in the battles over designated wilderness, the Park Service found that it enjoyed a vocal constituency that would support parks—but not necessarily the agency's programs for them. As a result, public constituencies exerted growing influence over agency policy, a change most visible at the local level.[3] PFGGNRA possessed a proprietary feeling about Golden Gate National Recreation Area; for the Park Service, the group's perspective and the power it accrued could be a double-edged sword. The Park Service and PFGGNRA were united in their perception of threats to the park. Suburban development in Marin County posed the largest single obstacle to park expansion, and PFGGNRA applied its hard-won influence to growth questions there. Every subdivision, every road, every new commuter meant additional pressure on finite space, and every decision to develop curtailed the options of park managers and their advocacy groups.

Faced with the threat of developments that impaired their paradise, Marin County residents embraced the kind of quality-of-life environmentalism that marked the 1970s. Zoning and planning were key dimensions of this strategy.[4] Implementation meant forging relationships with government, sometimes difficult for longtime rural residents accustomed to operating on their own in a world without restrictions. Local communities sought new strategies, and the neonatives—the recent arrivals in Marin County who wanted to preserve its way of life—became the best allies of longtime local residents. These newcomers shared a similar perspective and seemed to dairy farmers and ranchers to share their appreciation for Marin County as it was. They quickly recognized that the park provided an important barrier to unwanted and hasty change, and after the establishment of Golden Gate National Recreation Area, adding additional lands to the park seemed the most viable strategy for protecting local interests.

After dodging the Marincello development, Marin County leaders recognized that the national park was an asset. County strategists embraced organized countywide planning as protection from the worst excesses of suburban growth. Other communities, such as Sausalito in the shadow of the Golden Gate Bridge, also recognized the commonality of their and the park's interests and added their support. After the establishment of Golden Gate National Recreation Area, PFGGNRA issued a white paper calling for minor boundary adjustments. As in any large transfer of land, a number of pieces were inaccurately described, leaving some acreage designated for inclusion outside of the park and other privately owned land within its boundaries. The Marin County Parks and Recreation Department worked closely with PFGGNRA to alleviate this problem, establishing a relationship that developed into a formidable alliance.

In 1972 and 1973, the Marin County Planning Commission held hearings on the Marin County Plan (MCP), its countywide management framework. With its recent and widely acknowledged success, PFGGNRA participated in the debate and found much to like about the plan's emphasis on open space, quality of life, needs of visitors, and mass transit. The alliance opened other opportunities. The Marin County Board of Supervisors recognized that the park's establishment gave PFGGNRA, the Park Service, and the county similar obligations and needs. MCP also recognized the park's value both as an economic device and as a strategy for controlling growth and its consequences. Aware of the value of local allies and the significance of planning for Marin County, PFGGNRA warmly endorsed MCP.[5]

The alliance proved valuable when the Nixon administration declined to include funds to purchase 16,500 acres in west Marin County in the 1974 budget, breaking a promise made during the election campaign and effectively halting the prospect of additional lands for Golden Gate National Recreation Area. Although the Nixon administration presented it as a cost-cutting measure in a time of inflation, some regarded it as retribution by Armed Forces Committee Chairman Edward Hebert for Burton's 1972 end run that created the park. Faced with this setback, PFGGNRA, Burton, and the park constituency mounted a forceful attack on the decision. Mailliard, the Republican congressman, made a personal appeal to Nixon, Burton mustered his influence, and the Park Service looked for alternatives. The Department of the Interior found itself with $5.8 million for national park acquisition that had not been allocated, and Mailliard proposed its transfer to Golden Gate National Recreation Area for land purchases in Marin County. Although the sum was not sufficient to accomplish everything that had been planned, it was significantly better than nothing.[6]

Marin County public officials also actively supported park expansion. On May 9, 1973, County Supervisor Peter Arrigoni addressed the Department of the Interior Subcommittee of the U.S. Senate Appropriations Committee, requesting $25 million to purchase land in West Marin for Golden Gate National Recreation Area. Upon his return from Washington, D.C., Arrigoni announced that he believed a portion of his request for acquisition funds would be included in the final budget.[7] An alliance between local government and the Park Service and its supporters indicated the significance of Golden Gate National Recreation Area and its local importance as a barrier to unchecked growth.

Despite the support of Arrigoni and the board of supervisors, the growth of Golden Gate National Recreation Area in Marin County faced obstacles from state government. The establishing legislation allowed for the transfer of state parklands surrounded by the park. These included Mount Tamalpais, Angel Island, Stinson Beach, Muir Beach, Marin Headlands, and three state beaches in San Francisco, Phelan, Baker, and Thornton. In 1973, when the Park Service pursued transfer of title, William Penn Mott Jr., director of California Parks and Recreation who more than a decade later became director of the National Park Service, mounted a campaign to thwart the Park Service. Some people regarded his objections as a turf battle, a contest of mission and constituency, but Mott expressed genuine reservations about the value of national park area designation for state parks, reimbursement for money spent to acquire lands, and the ability of the National Park Service to secure funds for management of the state areas. The California State Park System, he averred, "can do the job, and we can do it at less cost and better than it can be done by the Federal Government."[8]

On February 21, 1973, William J. Whalen, the first superintendent of Golden Gate National Recreation Area, NPS Western Regional Director Howard Chapman, Special Assistant to the GGNRA Superintendent Douglas B. Cornell Jr., and Jack Davis, superintendent of Redwood National Park, met with Mott seeking to resolve the widening gulf between federal and state park managers. In a tense exchange, Mott held firm; he simply could not foresee the transfer of state parklands to federal jurisdiction. The meeting reached an impasse, and Mott prepared to leave. As he stood, he asked for a clear definition of NPS objectives. When Chapman outlined those priorities as donation of the state parklands, a management agreement that allowed NPS to manage the state parks in question and a transfer agreement at a less-than-fee cost, and a detailed management and planning agreement that would involve joint construction, development, planning, and expenditures, the impasse broke. Both sides had been so adamant about their position that they failed to see the commonality of purpose. Although he could not countenance a transfer of land to expand Redwood National Park, Mott found the NPS proposal more reasonable once it had been clarified and agreed to explore options at Golden Gate National Recreation Area with other state officials. At the end of the meeting, the Park Service remained hopeful about an arrangement of some kind.[9]

At the same time, NPS officials negotiated with other property holders to resolve boundary and transfer concerns. The boundary issues presented a legislative nightmare. Several locations—Haslett Warehouse in San Francisco, a 214-acre parcel of Wolfback Ridge adjacent to Sausalito, 145 acres in the Tennessee Valley, and about 4 acres near Muir Beach—had been omitted from the final legislation in the haste to finish the bill. Almost 50 acres of home sites near Stinson Beach had been included within park boundaries as a result of an incorrect description. To save time, money, and effort, NPS officials sought to rectify these issues administratively rather than through legislation. Park officials brought congressional staff members to Golden Gate National Recreation Area to make their case for administrative transfer. PFGGNRA supported the agency, with Wayburn and Meyer making the case to Nathaniel P. Reed, assistant secretary of the interior for national parks. Reed recognized the value in proceeding at the administrative level but found that congressional subcommittees thought that legislative action was necessary in a number of transfers,[10] which required following a process similar to the one used to found the park. Meyer and Wayburn went back to work, this time with the support of the emerging park apparatus and the well-established Regional Office in the Bay Area and well aware that the full power of the energetic, combative, and determined Phil Burton still stood behind them.

The process of building a constituency for boundary revisions required not only action by PFGGNRA but Park Service efforts as well. Local alliances helped the Park Service in this process. Although many private landowners felt betrayed when they found that the Nixon administration refused to fund the purchases authorized in the establishing legislation and the Department of the Interior only peripherally contested the White House decision, the support of public institutions in Marin County for the deletion helped mute most tension. Acquiring land in Marin County seemed possible as summer 1973 began.[11]

In the summer, Whalen could see evident progress in the acquisition of a number of key parcels. Military transfers proceeded most rapidly. Fort Mason and most of the San Francisco properties were already under NPS management. The Marin forts—Baker, Barry, and Cronkhite—also came to the Park Service in 1973. Each of these had been divided under the statute, with the eastern portion of Fort Baker remaining under the administration of the Department of Defense. Parts of Forts Barry and Cronkhite reverted to the State of California. The General Services Administration turned Alcatraz over to the Park Service in April 1973.

Private acquisitions required funding and an elaborate array of hearings and public discussion that conveyed local and regional sanction. The process took longer, faced greater and often unexpected obstacles, and required capital that the Park Service did not always have.[12] In August 1973, Secretary of the Interior C. B. Rogers Morton and the Park Service announced the purchases of the first private lands included in the establishing legislation. The Wilkens Ranch in Bolinas Lagoon, a 1,332-acre tract that the Trust for Public Land (TPL) had previously purchased, was transferred to the Park Service for $1.15 million. A 103-acre tract in Tamalpais Valley cost $635,000. The Park Service also obtained a two-year option to purchase the Marincello property from the Nature Conservancy as well as options on Slide Ranch, along the ocean near Bolinas. In addition, the organization agreed to donate the 500-acre Green Gulch Ranch to the park. Negotiations were also under way to purchase additional tracts of private land included in the establishing act.[13]

Private conservation groups such as the Nature Conservancy and the Trust for Public Land provided the impetus necessary to complete land transactions. Able to act independently of governmental agency constraints, the groups secured options on the properties in advance of park creation or in some instances, with the cooperation of the Park Service, in anticipation of legislation that would fund land acquisition and add it to the park. With their resources, they were able to serve as stewards until a federal arrangement, such as an authorizing bill or an acquisition appropriation, could be passed. In this approach, the private groups mirrored a familiar process of national park proclamation. The Antiquities Act of 1906, which allowed the president to proclaim national monuments from public land, served a similar function. After 1945, Congress refused to recognize such executive decision making by withholding funds for national monuments created without congressional approval. Conservation groups filled that gap by acquiring land that was threatened, and their resources also made it possible to include private land in the system. Private conservation groups engaged in land transfers and exchanges and, in some cases, purchased property that the Park Service or park advocates coveted. Their presence in the Bay Area created a level of flexibility for the Park Service that alleviated many of the constraints on agency activities.[14]

Boundary adjustments continued to play a primary role in acquisition strategy at Golden Gate National Recreation Area. A draft revision bill was introduced late in October 1973 and by November 12, 1973, it reached the desk of Carl Albert, Speaker of the House of Representatives. The bill substituted a revised boundary map for the one used in the authorizing legislation, adding 373.68 acres to the park while deleting 50.68 acres. The additional cost exceeded $1.245 million; acquiring all the lands described in the initial legislation had been projected to cost about $1.88 million. Sale of the lands excised was estimated to bring $635,000, which could be used to reduce the cost. Agency officials anticipated that the smaller cash outlay would diminish any opposition to the process.[15]

They misjudged both the political and the local response to the program, for acquisition ran up against one of the antecedents of the property rights movement. Within days of the introduction of the proposed bill, F. W. and June Warren, owners of one of the Wolfback Ridge parcels, expressed their dismay at what they regarded as a grab for their property. In an October 30, 1973, joint meeting of the Sausalito City Council and Planning Commission, the Warrens first saw the plans put forward by Burton that included their holdings. They regarded their property as a buffer zone between public and private land, and inclusion of their land in the park was, in their estimation, akin to "amputating a vital functional part of this community and dangerously isolating a vulnerable finger of residences to public access from all sides. This community has been conceived as an integral whole since its inception in 1945"; they finished with a flourish: "And we strongly protest its dismemberment." Representative Mailliard was noticeably sympathetic to the Warrens and included their perspective when he discussed the bill in committee. The San Francisco Republican recognized the importance of local opposition and likely sought to undermine Burton. The two were cordial, but they represented different parties, and Burton had stolen Mailliard's idea when he pursued Golden Gate National Recreation Area. Turnabout was surely fair play.[16]

The opposition of area residents such as the Warrens was rooted in Marin County, but the rest of the resistance to the park addition could be construed as intraparty posturing in Washington, D.C. Democrats controlled Capitol Hill and Burton was powerful within the party. He had antagonized Representative Hebert over the Presidio situation, and his relations with the "Water Buffalos"—the cadre of western Democratic congressmen and senators that included Senator Alan Bible of Nevada, Senator Clinton P. Anderson of New Mexico, and Representative Wayne Aspinall of Colorado, who used large-scale federally funded irrigation and water storage projects as a way to bring home the bacon and to build political alliances—were often tenuous, but Burton could always count votes. He excelled in keeping much of Congress in his debt and benefited from

Democratic control of the California legislature, which redistricted Mailliard out of any chance of retaining his seat in an election. Mailliard resigned from the House and accepted appointment as ambassador to the Organization of American States. Appointed to Mailliard's seat, Phil Burton's younger brother, John Burton, used the few months before the general election to secure his House position, and he triumphed in November 1974. With another Burton representing Mailliard's district, which combined parts of San Francisco and Marin County, Phil Burton could count on stronger support from Marin County in Congress.[17]

In December 1974, after a compromise about land acquisition had been worked out, both houses of Congress passed the boundary revision bill. When President Gerald Ford signed the bill on December 26, 1974, the inaccuracies in the original park boundaries were clarified. The authorization to acquire Oakwood Valley, Wolfback Ridge, Stinson Beach, Muir Beach, and Haslett Warehouse was complete. The conservation land trusts had prepared the way with options and prior purchases, and the transactions went smoothly.[18]

The success of national park expansion only enhanced the threat to state parks. Despite William Penn Mott Jr.'s willingness to negotiate, his successors mounted effective resistance against Golden Gate National Recreation Area. After Ford signed the land acquisition bill, California State Parks and Recreation directors Leonard Grimes Jr. and Herbert Rhodes commissioned a 1975 study to assess the viability of the transfers. The study rejected federal control, instead offering a plan for a "Golden Gateway State Urban Park." The authors pointed to the almost twenty years of state stewardship at Angel Island and San Francisco Maritime State Historic Park as well as the need for recreation for the growing urban population of the Bay Area. They candidly observed a number of significant problems for the state parks: insufficient funding, a growing backlog of deferred maintenance, and an overall lack of planning for Haslett Warehouse and other state-owned areas. In the end, the study followed Mott's reasoning: turning the parks over to the federal government amounted to an abdication of the state's mandate.[19]

The Marin County state park controversy continued for most of 1975. The California Department of Parks and Recreation fought any transfers, enlisting its individual and organizational supporters. The Contra Costa Hills Club, Marin Conservation League, Tamalpais Conservation Club, Sempervirens Fund and others who opposed the transfer were particularly potent opponents. They were conservation advocacy groups and had supported the concept of a Golden Gate National Recreation Area. Often their letters expressed admiration for the process that created the national park and support for the expansion to the south, but strong opposition to turning the Marin County state parks over to the federal government. Influential elites, these Marin County conservation groups used both their experience and their standing. With such support, the California Parks and Recreation

Commission executed a political maneuver that led to the demise of the proposed transfer of state parkland. As the California legislature moved to authorize a transfer of nine Bay Area state parks at the behest of state senator George Moscone and Ninth District assemblyman Michael Wornum, two Democrats who were the most prominent legislative advocates of including state parks in Golden Gate National Recreation Area, the parks commission unanimously voted against a transfer without payment to California for the value of the lands. The Park Service lacked the funds to compensate the state. Without the commission's support, the transfer was dead, a victim of state politics. Even though the legislature passed the bill, Governor Edmund P. "Jerry" Brown Jr. vetoed it.[20]

The following year, a new effort that smoothed over the differences in the state and federal perspectives took shape. A compromise between the governor and Bay Area legislators such as Michael Wornum and John Foran led to approval of the transfer of Stinson Beach, Muir Beach, and Marin Headlands state parks. Mount Tamalpais was to remain in the state park system, and the legislation gave the governor the discretion to shift Angel Island, Haslett Warehouse, and San Francisco Maritime State Historical Park to federal jurisdiction. Although the state did not keep everything, it kept its most important Bay Area state park, Mount Tamalpais, and shed the enormous financial responsibility for the upkeep of historic ships. "I feel better now," observed California State Parks Director Herbert Rhodes, who vociferously objected to any transfer in 1975.[21]

Initial efforts at expansion south of Golden Gate National Recreation Area also met considerable local resistance. In 1973, Congressman Leo Ryan expressed dismay that San Mateo County had been excluded from the initial Golden Gate National Recreation Area proclamation. His district had been left out of a plum that brought it status and offered employment possibilities. Ryan believed that within a few years, persuasive leadership might sway local opposition to favor an addition. In May 1975, PFGGNRA and the National Park Service made public a proposal for a huge addition to Golden Gate National Recreation Area. The proposed land acquisition stretched from the park's existing southern boundary near Pacifica down the coast past Half Moon Bay and the San Mateo County line, extending nearly all the way to Santa Cruz. The more than 170,000 acres proposed would give Golden Gate National Recreation Area, or "Golden Gate National Seashore," as some proponents labeled the project, control of almost 150 miles of coast. Although the proposed additions looped around the existing villages and Whalen regarded the cost as "in the $100 million class," making its completion unlikely at best, the announcement sparked local resistance up and down the coast.[22]

The proposal fueled an already tense situation. The efforts at planning that produced results in San Francisco and Marin County stalled in Pacifica to the south. In San Francisco proper, the need for planning was obvious to all. Without it no recreational space would exist. Neighborhoods joined together with labor and ethnic groups there to support preserving open areas. In Marin County, the white-collar invasion that followed 1945 led to prerogative protection—what a later generation would call NIMBY—as well as support for parklands as protection from inundation. But in traditionally blue-collar Pacifica, concerns about open space and parks only inspired suspicion, even as the area dealt with the threat that the Bay Area loved to hate, freeway development.

The Association of Bay Area Governments (ABAG) and the Metropolitan Transportation Commission policy committee recommended that open areas on the coast be reserved from development and road construction. Within a week, the Golden Gate National Recreation Area expansion proposal was announced. Coastal San Mateo County felt that it was being cut out of an opportunity for growth and prosperity in order to meet the demands of its more affluent neighbors to the north and its prosperous residents along the Highway 101/280 corridor. This was a typical refrain, a response by those who had not enjoyed the full benefit of postwar prosperity against those who had already made their money and now appeared to be trying to stop others from doing the same. Environmentalism, which included national park expansion, became the leverage point of a great deal of that tension. The Bay Area organizations that protected community ways of life had much power; the juxtaposition of their objectives and those of San Mateo County was a prelude to great tensions.[23]

Some of the strain could be directly attributed to the earlier successes of PFGGNRA and its leadership's occasionally heavy-handed and self-assured style. By all accounts, Ed Wayburn and Amy Meyer were opposites. Wayburn was a formal and cordial southerner, while Meyer was New York City born and bred and had the tenacity often associated with its natives. They made a devastating team, but the way that they sometimes operated could alienate even their friends. Perhaps reading too much into their initial success, PFGGNRA pushed forward, only to encounter some close allies who thought the proposal did not satisfy local needs or duplicated state or county efforts. Betty Hughes, secretary of the Citizens' Advisory Committee for the Forest of Nisene Marks State Park, critiqued the expansion to Wayburn. In such situations, "we, the public, wind up with a few scraps of land and forest instead of a truly significant saving of *new* lands in national protection," she wrote. Instead of adding existing parks to Golden Gate National Recreation Area, PFGGNRA should try to acquire lands without park status. "How presumptuous of your committee," Hughes exclaimed.[24]

Before the proposal to expand to the south of San Francisco debuted, PFGGNRA had not engaged in enough legwork along the coast. The lack of involvement with San Mateo County activists during planning meant that local residents sometimes bristled about do-gooding outsiders. Although Wayburn's charm could contain much of that damage, resentment fueled local opponents. One group put out a widely circulated flier that voiced every rural landholder's nightmare: "Warning: Your Land and Home Are in Danger of Being Confiscated for Use as a National Park." More than a decade and a half before the "takings" revolution—the articulation of the principle that even with the power of eminent domain, the government had no legal standing to take property and compensate for it in the name of the public good—these very sentiments were located firmly at the core of a key anti-park coalition.[25]

Although PFGGNRA typically responded to such challenges by marshaling a long line of public supporters with diverse and persuasive rationales, the extension southward developed into a question of relative political influence. Congressman Paul McCloskey, who represented western San Mateo County, came to his district to sell the project. He faced 200 angry constituents at one meeting in San Gregorio. A special hearing of the La Honda–Pescadero School Board erupted when 400 people jeered the pro-park presentation and hooted presenters off the stage, inspiring an impromptu rally that led to the founding of "People Against a Golden Gate National Recreation Area." Where Wayburn and Meyer saw public protection of lifestyles in the bill, residents saw the dismantling of their communities and the culture that underpinned them. Resistance was fierce; opponents felt their homes, livings, and even their identity threatened by the proposal.[26]

Ryan's introduction of a bill to study the park expansion proposal did little to quell local opposition. The bill proposed a study of the feasibility of enlargement, something opponents should have favored. Ryan announced that his measure enjoyed the endorsement of PFGGNRA, the Sierra Club, and the National Park Service. The coastal communities raised an uproar. La Honda–Pescadero, which feared the disappearance of its taxable land base, resisted most vociferously. Three separate organizations formed there to fight the endorsement. Ryan had clearly misjudged public opinion. When he addressed a meeting of the San Mateo county supervisors, he was interrupted by hostile ranchers and jeered throughout the meeting. His pronouncement that he would only support the inclusion of lands that the study recommended did little to pacify the hostile crowd. "My family has been six generations on the same land," said Homer McCurry, a rancher whose property abutted the Santa Cruz County line announced at the meeting. "We will be there when the government comes and we will not be moved by anything."[27]

Pronounced local opposition doomed any southern expansion in the mid-1970s, a harbinger of the kind of resistance park growth soon faced in other areas. "We wonder just how much parkland we can afford," an editorial in the *Santa Cruz Sentinel* asked, linking cost to quality of life, a relationship already on the cusp of gaining widespread following in American society. "It is not difficult to understand," a *San Mateo Times* editorial explained, "the critical and even hostile reception" to the proposal. When rural populations felt threatened by government and as long as the state could fund the range of services Californians had come to expect of their government, efforts to expand the park looked to local residents all too much like a raid on the country by the city.[28]

In the city of San Francisco, a different constellation of circumstances made additional parkland more compelling to local interests. By 1975, San Francisco had completed the initial stage of full-scale downtown redevelopment. Work on the area south of Market Street was under way, but the project, the Yerba Buena Center, was in deep financial trouble as a result of a host of antidevelopment lawsuits. Barred by law from seeking a third term as mayor, Joseph Alioto gave way to George Moscone, a new-style ethnic politician who previously served in the state senate and conceived of his constituency in a broad fashion. Moscone led the way to more inclusive local politics, valuing neighborhood power over development dollars and railing against the Manhattanization of San Francisco. In essence, he was a kind of urban populist, tied to the grass roots with faith in government as a remedy for social ills. He embraced the principle that all groups were minorities, an idea that made mutual tolerance and cooperation the only workable strategy. Moscone decentralized power and distributed it back to the grass roots, especially to the neighborhoods. His election proved an advantage for PFGGNRA and the coalitions that favored expansion of parklands in San Francisco.[29]

By September 1976, one of the primary goals of initial expansion and boundary revision efforts approached completion. California governor Jerry Brown signed a bill approving the transfer of the state holdings around Hyde Street Pier to Golden Gate National Recreation Area as the summer ended. The city kept ownership of the pier and leased it to the Park Service. Whalen announced that the Park Service intended to assume administration before the year ended. The transfer included Hyde Street Pier and its collection of historic ships and Haslett Warehouse. The city ceded Aquatic Park and its bathhouse. "For the first time, all of the public holdings between Fort Mason and Fisherman's Wharf," Whalen effused, "will be brought together for a major recreational and historical complex." Haslett Warehouse still contained more than 100 tenants, and the San Francisco Maritime Museum Association, which owned the *Balclutha*, the *Eppleton Hall*, and an extensive museum collection, still needed to make a formal donation of its holdings to the government. Observers expected the financially strapped organization to rush to formalize the transfer, but almost two years passed before the association signed the papers. The San Francisco Maritime State Historic Park was transferred to Golden Gate National Recreation Area on September 16, 1977.[30]

The 1978 addition of parcel four of Playland, an old amusement park, typified the kind of adaptive use of out-of-date urban space at which Golden Gate National Recreation Area excelled. Begun in the 1920s as a local amusement park, Playland at the Beach became a landmark, a recreational place with memories for generations of Bay Area residents. By the 1960s, like many similar attractions, it fell on hard times and closed in 1972. The amusement park was located on prime beachfront property, and with its demise, developers eagerly eyed its economic potential. In April 1972, the Seal Rock Development Company announced plans for 900 units of condominiums and high-rises. In June 1972, the planning commission gave approval for 724 units and 230,000 square feet of commercial space. In December, the approval was trimmed to a smaller project. The planning commission was only the first hurdle for the developers in the maze of regulations. As a result of Playland's beachfront location, the state's Coastal Commission also had to rule on the project. In June 1973, it approved an even more limited scale. By 1977, trimmed in size and scope and subjected to five years of repeated analysis, the development stalled.[31]

Much of the public rejoiced as the developers ran out of money. Many viewed the conversion of recreational space into private commercial and residential space with trepidation. Even though Playland had never been free, commercial development of the site was hugely unpopular with the public. The creation of Golden Gate National Recreation Area made the public keenly aware of both the advantages of urban recreational space and the acute shortage of such areas. Playland seemed to achieve its highest use as public recreational space, and the public emphasized its support of that idea with petition after petition in favor of its inclusion in Golden Gate National Recreation Area. Burton's support was enlisted, and Playland became part of the expansion efforts. Burton guided the acquisition to fruition, and part of the old amusement park joined the new national recreation area. Condos eventually were built on the rest.

Despite such successes, the expansion of Golden Gate National Recreation Area in San Francisco became a political issue, full of the jockeying associated with local, state, and federal relationships. Mid-1970s inflation began to drain the resources of even communities as large as San Francisco. Especially in California, with its very high public expectations of government services, costs spiraled out of control. Local leaders pointed to tax-exempt federal lands as a remedy for financial woes. If those lands could be taxed or returned to taxable status, many of the problems of local communities could be solved. Dianne Feinstein, president of the San Francisco Board of Supervisors, followed this line of reasoning. She argued against further federal expansion in the city because it compromised property tax revenues. By 1978, 51 percent of the land in San Francisco was tax-exempt; the federal government owned 35 percent of all government-held land in the city. In Feinstein's view, running an American city in the late 1970s without the revenue from half of the property tax base was at best ludicrous. In San Francisco, city officials felt increasingly threatened by the growth of Golden Gate National Recreation Area.

In Marin County in 1976 and 1977, similar circumstances produced very different results. Even before Marincello, Marin County had become the scene of what a later generation labeled "gentrification." When rural Marin County—the old dairy ranches and other agricultural and ranching operations—survived, they did so in two netherworlds controlled by outside forces. In one, the federal government, increasingly in the guise of the Park Service, served as an important barrier to wholesale change. Golden Gate National Recreation Area's presence increased land values, but it filled up enough space that the kind of wholesale development exemplified by Marincello was only occasionally possible. In most instances, the rising cost of land drove housing prices skyward and made it economically unfeasible for developers to convert tracts of land into subdivisions. Neonatives, typically wealthy residents of the Bay Area who bought land in Marin County for a retreat, second home, or sometimes to commute, changed by their presence the very paradise they sought.[32] The interests of these neonatives often coincided with those of longtime rural residents, and the neonatives' wealth, power, and social and political sophistication helped serve as a drag against wholesale and unchecked change.

John Jacobs of the San Francisco Planning and Urban Renewal Association (SPUR) provided one illustration of the powerful and complicated role of neonatives. Jacobs's park credentials were impeccable. He resisted the federal government's attempt to place the National Archives branch at Fort Miley, and the facility was eventually located at San Bruno. His Republican Party ties helped bring about the establishment of Golden Gate National Recreation Area, and he offered tacit support as Amy Meyer and her friends never stopped trying to expand the park. By late 1975, they sought to fill a gap in the heart of Marin County between Samuel P. Taylor State Park, Point Reyes Station, White House Pool, and Olema by adding the Cheda Ranch area, Lagunitas Creek Loop, and Olema Valley Meadow. The extension provided better continuity of parkland on the Marin County coast and had been a goal beyond the reach of PFGGNRA in 1972. Jacobs and his wife were partners in the Mesa Ranch just north of Bolinas, in the area that PFGGNRA coveted for the park. With what Jacobs called "the full realization that success . . . might doom our chances for a vacation home on Bolinas Mesa," he and his associates, led by managing partner Anton G. Holter, agreed that the ranch belonged in Golden Gate National Recreation Area.[33]

The 210-acre Bolinas ranch and the nearby 1,100-acre RCA property became one of the foci of local backlash. Local opponents claimed that inclusion in the park of these tracts would damage the agricultural base of rural Marin County, but Holter rejected that claim, stating, "Frankly, I don't think these people are farmers. Writers, lawyers, teachers, architects, and gardeners, yes." The opposition came from neonatives who preceded Holter and Jacobs into the area, similar amenity migrants drawn to the area for the same reasons as the Mesa Ranch owners but with a different sense of individual prerogative and social objectives. Although Jacobs railed that his opponents sought 50- to 100-acre ranchettes on adjacent lands, profiting from the presence of the park and the lack of development to offer tracts that only the wealthy could afford, it was just as likely that they simply wanted to pull up the figurative ladder to the exclusive tree house of Marin County after they entered. In this sense, Jacobs and Holter could see public purpose more clearly than neighboring landowners.[34] The struggle over Jacobs's land and the RCA property revealed how class, wealth, and perspective could alter the relationships between natives, neonatives, and newcomers. Questions of land use contained the potential to crack apart existing alliances.

Despite the stance of Jacobs and Holter, H.R. 10398, the bill they supported, failed to reach the floor of the U.S. House. John Burton introduced it in December 1975, and held hearings in Marin County early in 1976. Opponents spoke loudly and vociferously against the bill, while its advocates offered only muted support. "You're taking all the property where it is feasible to build a motel," complained Don DeWolfe of Point Reyes Station. Another opponent called the purchase a rip-off of taxpayers. Before the meeting, Amy Meyer authored a justification for the bill that she circulated to Marin County officials through Jerry Friedman, one of the planning commissioners. She made a "heroic effort at defense," a report observed, "but was clearly outgunned." Even Friedman and other supporters sounded lukewarm in the face of angry voters.[35] After recognizing that he incorrectly assessed the powerfully negative local sentiment, John Burton withdrew his bill.[36]

This political ambivalence characterized questions of land acquisition in Marin County. Powerful advocates sought inclusion of much of West Marin in the park, but many of those supporters were from the San Francisco side of the bay. In retrospect, H.R. 10398 came forward without enough input from local constituencies. In one account after the demise, Alice Yarish of the *Pacific Sun* suggested that none of the landowners were included in the discussions leading up to the bill. While the statement was arguably hyperbole, it also clearly articulated the resentment of local landowners. By the mid-1970s, fears of government action were widespread, and rural communities felt especially threatened. When they heard the park expansion proposal at the meeting, many residents were upset; a few were enraged.[37] Many resisted, some for personal reasons, some for economic ones, but the opposition made the going too rough for John Burton. In his first term as congressman, he wisely followed the loudest group of constituents. His older brother might have played the situation differently, but John Burton was not yet as adept a political power broker as Phil Burton.

The defeat barely deterred PFGGNRA, and Amy Meyer made Marin County one of her primary objectives. Within one year, Meyer and Bob Young circulated a new set of justifications for acquiring the same properties. Meyer was indefatigable; she repackaged the initial proposal with a new rationale and even added recommendations for additional, more expensive land. Meyer divided the land in question into two basic categories. The first encompassed the roughly 4,000 acres of the year before; the second contained about 2,000 acres that were more controversial. Her proposal included privately owned ranches, some private residences and businesses, part of the town of Olema, and several other parcels. The threat of development underpinned her desire for acquisition. Holter, Meyer claimed, planned a 200-unit hotel on the Mesa Ranch because of his unsuccessful efforts to sell the land to the park system. The Cheda Ranch, owned by a real estate company, faced imminent development. The entire package, Meyer thought, could be acquired for between $13 million and $15 million.[38]

Throughout 1977, the debate raged across Marin County. A new series of public hearings took place in which the acquisition was debated. By the fall, a loose consensus appeared to be coalescing. On September 13, 1977, the *Pacific Sun* reported that a proposed 15,000-acre expansion of Golden Gate National Recreation Area drew "hardly a murmur" at the Marin County Board of Supervisors. As the consensus emerged, the lands of the few individual landowners who did not want to sell were excluded. The focus shifted away from questions of acquisition to remedies for problems, such as loss of tax revenue, that federal ownership might create. By October, John Burton had sufficient local support to proceed.[39]

The coalition John Burton assembled in Marin County to encourage the expansion of GGNRA came together as Phil Burton embarked on a campaign aimed at redefining reform politics in the U.S. House. Always a master political strategist, Burton grasped the levers of political coalition-building more completely. Following his always savvy political instincts, he functioned as a different kind of power broker. His efforts recycled an existing political form—the local demands for "pork" catered to by the old Water Buffaloes—and put it in a new setting. Burton became the person who put together unstoppable public works coalitions, and national park areas became the linchpin of that strategy.[40]

The national political climate changed dramatically in the late 1970s, and Phil Burton was an unlikely person to intuit, understand, and capitalize on the changes. The "Great Aberration," the period of time between 1945 and 1974 when more Americans did better economically than ever before and that created deceptive views of the American norm, came to an end in the OPEC (Organization of Petroleum Exporting Countries) oil crisis and the resulting explosion of global inflation. California, which had been regarded as the American Dream, felt the hit as hard as anywhere. Postwar prosperity in California brought with it a state-run vision of a Great Society that paralleled Lyndon B. Johnson's hopes for the nation. The state became a seemingly independent entity that made its own rules and paid its own way. State taxes were high, but the quality of life made it all worthwhile. Although critics often bashed the state as a socialistic entity, Californians generally adored their paradise. But its future depended on a large influx of ongoing revenues, and after 1975, as the world economy shifted and California experienced a decline in financial resources, the miracle started to fray at the edges.

The catalyst that upset the State of California's relationship with its citizens came from Howard Jarvis, a retired lobbyist for apartment building owners, and his successful efforts to cap property taxes. Between 1973 and 1978, California real estate values soared. For many, this gain provided a benefit of epic proportions, but these unearned increments seemed equally unreal and unstable. With an attendant rise in property tax payments, the increments hurt some sectors of homeowners, especially retirees and those on a fixed income. The California legislature could not agree on property tax relief legislation at a time when the cost of homes—and their tax bills— soared. In 1976, Governor Jerry Brown held onto billions in tax surpluses instead of returning them to a groaning public. Public grumbling mounted, and calls to divest the state of its power grew louder. In this climate, Jarvis and his compatriot Paul Gann seized on a formula to return billions of dollars to taxpayers. They sponsored a ballot initiative to roll back property taxes. Called Proposition 13, the initiative quite simply threatened the California way of life that was intrinsically tied to postwar prosperity. When Proposition 13 passed in June 1978, it represented a watershed moment in California history. State government was crippled, state revenues decreased dramatically, and programs that many valued soon came to a halt. Surpluses were no more, but Californians expected no less from their government.[41] Instead of residing in a state where people paid for the vast array of services they received, Californians became the progenitors of the national "Me, Me, Me, Now, Now, Now" culture of the end of the twentieth century.

The California state park system experienced notable difficulties as a result of Proposition 13. Californians thought of their state parks as equals of the national park system in scenery and beauty, and anyone standing atop Mount Tamalpais would be hard-pressed to disagree. William Penn

Mott's strong stance against the transfer of state lands to the Golden Gate National Recreation Area stemmed from that very sense of California exceptionalism. In the post–Proposition 13 climate, and especially after the Jarvis-Gann bill, also known as Jarvis II, which planned to cut California state income tax by 50 percent, his point of view became untenable. Without tax revenues, the state park department simply could not maintain its properties. The California Department of Parks and Recreation transferred three parks to the federal government, granting $1 billion of value in a lease that required only $1 each year. The decision revealed a dramatic shift in the role of the state. After Howard Jarvis's bill, without resources, the state quietly shelved any such plans and became amenable to the Park Service's management of state parkland.[42]

The city of San Francisco and other urban entities faced the same constraints as the state. Mayor Dianne Feinstein faced a crisis at the city's Golden Gate Park that stemmed directly from the loss of revenue as a result of property tax caps. At the same time, federal dollars for the development of McLaren Park showed that the federal government still supported endeavors that Californians demanded. The lesson was not lost on either Feinstein or any other local or state politician in California. Jarvis-Gann, the plan that cut California's income tax in half, took away the state resources that provided precisely the public services that the public most appreciated. Fiercely strapped, local and state entities looked to agencies in Washington, D.C., for more help than they had since the New Deal.

Jarvis-Gann created an opening for Phil Burton that the congressmen used to his advantage. If California, one of the wealthiest states in the Union, would not support its parks, Burton could arrange for the federal government to step in and take them over. This approach had two enormous political advantages: it brought home millions of dollars in federal largesse for which Burton alone was responsible, and it protected the recreational prerogatives of people who believed in their entitlement to the good life. Ousted as House majority whip by his loss in the Speaker's race and cut out of the power structure by Representatives Tip O'Neill, Dan Rostenkowski, and Jim Wright, Burton needed another strategy to maintain power in the House. Recognizing that countering the impact of Jarvis-Gann by transfer of responsibility gave him a template that could be applied in other places, Burton began to assemble the most complex piece of legislation in national park history.

Formally titled the National Parks and Recreation Act of 1978, but colloquially known as the Omnibus Bill of 1978, Burton's legislative masterpiece created the park system's greatest single expansion. Passed in time to let representatives receive its largesse before the 1978 elections, the act benefited more than 100 congressmen and -women in forty-four states. The bill included more than 100 projects, expanded thirty-four individual park areas, added nine historic areas and three parks, tripled the size of the national wilderness system, created five national trails and eight wild and scenic rivers, and authorized the study of seventeen other river segments for possible inclusion in the national park system. Although Burton's detractors called the legislation a naked power play designed to put the congressman back into the House Democratic power structure, the bill did much more.[43] It shaped Burton's legacy, one that forged recreational and reflective space for an increasingly crowded nation.

At Golden Gate National Recreation Area, Phil Burton's personal favorite project, the National Parks and Recreation Act of 1978 formalized the acquisitions that had been under discussion in Marin County for the better part of the decade and provided funds to close the purchase of previously authorized lands. The bill targeted for purchase 3,741 acres involving fifty-six property owners, with an expected cost of $15 million.[44]

Passage of the National Parks and Recreation Act of 1978 allowed one more close look at the acquisition plans of the federal government in Marin County. At John Burton's request, the Marin County Board of Supervisors held three public hearings, September 13, September 20, and November 29, 1977, and collected letters and position papers from as many as 300 individuals. The people of Bolinas participated in an advisory poll on November 8, 1977; board of supervisors chairman Gary Giacomini held a public hearing in Bolinas on November 14, 1977; and the board solicited comments and recommendations from a range of city, county, and state government agencies. Although generally willing to support the acquisitions, the board of supervisors sought a number of guarantees. It accepted the priorities established by the Marin Conservation League, which placed completing park boundaries first, followed by protection of natural resources, recreational needs, and land-use values with an emphasis on preserving agricultural land, and strongly cautioned against transformation of the acquired lands. County representatives believed that leases for continued agricultural use to former landowners would mitigate any negative changes that resulted from the transfer. They also insisted that the county and its townships be fairly compensated for lost tax revenue.

In the end, the board agreed that the transfer of Muir Beach, Stinson Beach, the lands between Samuel P. Taylor State Park and Olema, and the Haggerty Gulch should proceed as proposed, but questions about Bolinas and the Lagunitas Loop loomed large. The board sought the inclusion of Bolinas in Point Reyes National Seashore rather than Golden Gate National Recreation Area, believing that the national seashore's management was more in keeping with the nature of life in the area. The input on Lagunitas Loop was split. Local environmentalists and the county planning department opposed inclusion; the county parks and recreation department and PFGGNRA and other broader-based groups supported inclusion. The board recommended compromise. The Giacomini Ranch, a thriving agricultural operation run by a cousin of board chairman Gary Giacomini, remained beyond Park Service reach.[45]

Conservation groups again proved helpful in issues of land acquisition. The Trust for Public Land and the Nature Conservancy both had important stakes in the region. Acquisition of the Nature Conservancy tracts, Marincello and Slide Ranch, required negotiation with that organization. The more expensive of the two, Marincello, seemed most likely to be purchased in pieces. The Park Service agreed to acquire Slide Ranch at the Nature Conservancy's cost with reasonable overhead in exchange for Conservancy donation of the Wheelwright property in the Tennessee Valley and the purchase cost of Marincello. At the cost of $3,860 per acre, the amount specified in the Nature Conservancy's purchase agreement with Gulf Oil for Marincello, the Park Service could only muster funds to pay for 87 of the 2,138 available acres.[46]

By 1980, the first phase of land acquisition at Golden Gate National Recreation Area was drawing to a close. During the park's first eight years, the Park Service acquired nearly all of the roughly 17,000 acres of private land included in the original proclamation, as well as 2,801 of the approximately 4,577 acres held by other federal agencies that had been authorized but not included in the original establishment. In addition, the army issued the Park Service an irrevocable permit for recreation use and development of shoreline Presidio lands, a decision that amounted to a de facto transfer of 150 acres of waterfront acreage. The initial park statute required that any lands acquired from California be the result of a donation. After a 1978 referendum, the City of San Francisco donated 600 acres, including parts of Playland and city beaches, to the park. The state legislature transferred another 4,710 acres mainly in Marin County. With most of the initial boundary questions resolved and the bulk of the acquisitions of the 1978 Omnibus Bill accomplished, the time had come for a reassessment of park objectives.[47]

As with nearly every other dimension of the first decade of Golden Gate National Recreation Area, Phil Burton played an instrumental role in furthering the development of the park. The strategy he developed in 1978 became his signature, a path to exercise power and build consensus while shut out of the House Democratic power structure. It culminated with the National Parks and Recreation Act of 1980, which Arizona congressman Morris "Mo" Udall called "one of the supreme acts of chutzpah" that he had ever seen in the House of Representatives. Burton presented H.R. 3 as a two-line bill to add a small amount of land to Golden Gate National Recreation Area. He then asked the House for unanimous consent to technical and conforming amendments, typically very short, but in this case seventy-five pages that were the meat of the bill. The legislation Burton authored spent $70 million and included Channel Islands National Park, the Martin

Luther King Jr. National Historic Site and Preservation District in Atlanta, Chaco Culture National Historical Park in New Mexico, the Women's Rights National Historical Park in Seneca Falls, New York, $10 million for Olympic National Park in Washington state, and $5 million for acquisition of 2,400 acres at Point Reyes National Seashore as well as $15.5 million for as many as 5,400 acres in San Mateo County for Golden Gate National Recreation Area.[48] When the bill passed in February 1980, Burton's influence on national park proclamation reached its pinnacle as an era came to an end.

In the history of the role of government in American society, 1980 became a pivotal year, the moment of a clear and evident shift in the conception of federal obligations. Burton's strategy of delivering the bacon to districts across the country had, in one form or another, dominated political negotiation since the New Deal of the 1930s. The combination of rising interest rates, the decline of the industrial and manufacturing economy, and the election of Ronald Reagan on a conservative, antigovernment platform in November 1980 spelled the end of Democratic pork-barrel politics. Detractors often referred to Burton's activities as "park-barreling" in an effort to equate them with the pork-barreling for which Congress was famous, but his ability to accomplish his goals depended on a compliant power structure. Even those who detested him and those who railed about excess and unnecessary government spending were charmed by the inclusion of parks for their districts.[49] Before 1980, no one—at least no one who wanted to retain a seat in Congress—opposed a project that delivered federal dollars to his or her home district. The Reagan administration purposely halted Burton's style of bringing home projects for home districts, and the changing economic situation made his strategy obsolete.

Burton managed to retain both his vision and maneuvering skills in the changing climate. When asked if Golden Gate National Recreation Area was now complete after the passage of the National Parks and Recreation Act of 1980, he responded with characteristic aplomb: "Please, I'm headed South." Golden Gate National Recreation Area remained his pet project, his prize, and increasingly his legacy. Even in the dire early years of the Reagan administration, when Secretary of the Interior James Watt froze parkland acquisition during the painful recession of 1981 and 1982, Burton pushed for growth and continued the supple power-brokering that brought more land to his park. The acts authorizing transfer became law before Reagan was elected. Finding the money to run the new lands after Reagan took office proved a challenge. "How can I accept land in San Mateo when I can't care for what I have?" Whalen asked reporters in the clearest articulation of the problem.[50]

In the 1980s, Golden Gate National Recreation Area finally succeeded in growing to the south, eventually including Sweeney Ridge and other lands in San Mateo County. Democrats in Congress recognized that they faced a new era. A spate of lame duck legislation was hustled through Congress for the president's signature, including the Alaska National Interest Lands Conservation Act (ANILCA) on December 2, 1980. Among the pieces of legislation that came through during the brief window was S. 2363, which had been authorized under the National Park Act of 1980 and provided for the expansion of Golden Gate National Recreation Area into San Mateo County. A reticent Doug Nadeau, chief of the Division of Resource Management and Planning, initiated meetings with the communities and local residents affected by the new legislation. A Park Service veteran who served at the park from its founding, Nadeau observed the PFGGNRA fiasco in San Mateo in the mid-1970s and recognized the need to learn from earlier mistakes. In a different climate, when communities such as Pacifica actively sought to shed the cost of park and even public property management, Nadeau faced a much easier task than could have been anticipated even three years earlier.[51]

Long-standing relationships with conservation organizations served the NPS well in the move to implement the National Park Act of 1980 and include parts of San Mateo County in Golden Gate National Recreation Area. The Trust for Public Land (TPL) held an option on Sweeney Ridge, but efforts to transfer it to the park system slowed when the Reagan administration froze park acquisitions. In 1981, the park system did not add a new park area for the first year since 1945. In 1982, with Assistant Secretary of the Interior Ray Arnett insisting that every land purchase be reviewed in his office and with Ric Davidge, formerly managing director of the National Inholders Association, a group of people who owned land within national park area boundaries, overseeing land acquisition for the park system, the Department of the Interior spent only half the money Congress allocated for land acquisition. High-level administrators served as a block against park expansion and TPL and NPS officials met repeatedly to find ways around the predicament. TPL was in the business of acquiring land for public purposes, and mere administrative fiat would not change the organization's long-term objectives. The General Services Administration agreed to exchange excess or surplus property until new funding could be secured. At long last, in September 1986, the San Mateo County Board of Supervisors gave final approval to the transfer of 287 acres of open space to Golden Gate National Recreation Area.[52]

As GGNRA became a fixture in the Bay Area and agriculture continued to decline in Marin County, a continuous stream of small properties, typically ranches, were purchased and included in the park. After James Watt's 1983 departure from the Department of the Interior, the Reagan administration eased its strictures against land acquisition. The prospect of the 1984 election turned many Republican congressional representatives back into pork- and park-barrelers, and a plethora of new areas again joined the park system. At Golden Gate National Recreation Area in 1983, the 1,065-acre McIsaac Ranch in Marin County was purchased for nearly $2 million. The McIsaac family received a twenty-five-year leaseback that allowed them to continue to operate their cattle ranch. The agreement came to typify the kinds of concessions NPS officials had to make to complete Golden Gate National Recreation Area.

Between the end of 1983 and 1986, 1,636.37 acres were purchased for the park. Priorities in Marin County included the Jensen Oyster Company land near Tomales Bay, the nearby Martinelli Ranch that had been sold to a developer but whose plans faced public opposition, and the Gallagher, McFadden, and Genazzi ranches in Lagunitas Loop. Elsewhere, small areas in Sutro Heights and a twelve-acre parcel at Sweeney Ridge owned by the California Department of Transportation, all which had been authorized under the 1980 park act, rounded out park objectives. GGNRA retained almost $2.7 million in previously allocated acquisition money, enough for the top six properties on the list. The formidable duo of California senators, Alan Cranston and Pete Wilson, supported a $3.1 million appropriation to buy the rest.[53]

The process of rounding out Golden Gate National Recreation Area continued and remained a constant feature of park management. Outside organizations made several recommendations. In 1988, the National Parks and Conservation Association identified desirable additions. The purchase of the Genazzi Ranch in 1988 brought the park closer to completing its acquisitions in the Lagunitas Loop. The transfer of Cattle Hill, a 261-acre tract that abutted Sweeney Ridge in Pacifica was completed in 1992, another in the seemingly endless parade of additions that consolidated park boundaries. After a long and complicated battle that took almost fifteen years, the Giacomini Ranch was finally part of the park. The inclusion of Phleger Estates near Woodside in the southern portion of Golden Gate National Recreation Area in 1994 seemed to close out a generation-long process.[54]

Only one acquisition issue remained, but it was the largest and most significant of them all. More than any other piece of property, the transfer of the Presidio from the military to Golden Gate National Recreation Area signified the park's completion. Phil Burton again served as the catalyst. The dynamic congressman lived hard, drinking and smoking with furious intensity. He collapsed and died of a sudden heart attack in the early morning hours of April 9, 1983. His death ended an era but did not diminish his legacy, of which the primary piece became the transfer of the Presidio in 1994. Without Burton's foresight, the Presidio, one of the most spectacular pieces of property in the United States, would have escaped inclusion in the park system. In the 1970s, long before anyone anticipated the end of the cold war and the end of a military-based economy, Burton took a bold step that envisioned this prime piece of property as a way of filling out the park, making it genuine urban open space that served the community. Simultaneously, his 1978 National Parks and Recreation Act secured an ongoing federal presence in the event of the army's retrenchment. Phil Burton assured that the Presidio would remain public space instead of becoming high-end beachfront property. This was an enormous gift to the park and city that he loved.

Although the real legwork for land acquisition at Golden Gate National Recreation Area came from organizations such as PFGGNRA, Phil Burton remained the visionary whose support translated grassroots action into law. In retrospect, he seems clairvoyant. In 1972, during the Vietnam War, the prospect of the army ever leaving the Presidio was remote at best. Military expenditures constituted an ever-growing segment of the economies of the Golden State and the Bay Area, and the prospect of a military departure should have sent a cold shudder down the spine of anyone who represented California at the state or national level. Yet, Phil Burton looked ahead in ways his contemporaries did not, a vision that the National Parks and Recreation Act of 1978, which included the remarkable caveat that the military could not undertake construction or any similar activity in the Presidio without NPS permission, confirmed.

Before the industrial economy lost ground to postindustrial service pursuits, before the cold war came to an end and took military-driven prosperity from California and the Sunbelt states, Burton anticipated the long-term value of urban recreational space. He recognized the coming of a time when such resources were more valuable as scenery and recreation than they could ever again be as part of the military-industrial complex. This early cognizance of the meaning and impact of the transformation to a service economy made Burton prescient, a true visionary, the individual most entitled to the credit for the final outline of Golden Gate National Recreation Area.

CHAPTER FOUR

How to Build an Urban Park

Planning at Golden Gate National Recreation Area followed a distinct process. The Park Service assessed its existing policies, adapting standards to the realities of the Bay Area and its many energized constituencies. The Park Service also responded to public activities for which it had no existing policy or practice. It learned to cooperate, engaging in joint endeavors with its advisory commission and devising other tactics and programs that helped the agency take the pulse of the public and incorporate its views into policy and practice. Despite utilizing this essentially reactive pattern, the Park Service was able to invent a set of practices that adhered to agency standards and reflected the circumstances of urban national park areas with complicated constituencies.

Superintendent William Whalen liked to say that planning began the first day he visited Golden Gate National Recreation Area. Although Whalen certainly began crafting a vision that December day in 1972, comprehensive planning required a great deal more time to take shape. Initially, the Park Service was on the defensive in the Bay Area. Other than Muir Woods National Monument and Point Reyes National Seashore, its prior presence in the region had been limited to the Western Regional Office, established in 1935, but without a major national park in the vicinity, the Park Service was overshadowed by other federal agencies, most prominently the military. The establishment of the John Muir National Historic Site in 1964 and the Eugene O'Neill National Historic Site in 1976 altered that trend, but as long as the Regional Office was its primary presence, the agency had little need for knowledge of local politics, alliances, and its constituencies.

After the establishment of the new park, the Park Service faced a plethora of users who felt a proprietary interest in GGNRA and found itself at a severe disadvantage. Before the area was added to the national park system, these users engaged in activities that they felt were justified and protected by law. To make the area into a national park sometimes required that the Park Service change such patterns, almost always inspiring outrage. When that happened, these citizens of a fractious but open metropolitan area, where it was easier to get a hearing for any point of view than in many other communities, argued their case loudly and vociferously. They marshaled whatever influence they could and took on the agency and its representatives.

For the better part of the 1970s, the Park Service's posture at Golden Gate National Recreation Area reflected such challenges. People brought their issues to the park, and staff responded on a case-by-case basis. Although this approach did not always meet the post–National Environmental Policy Act of 1969 standards for federal decision-making, it was a necessary phase in developing park planning, allowing planners to build toward larger integrated goals with a set of checks and balances that simultaneously explained to the public that the agency had a different mission than previous managers and that it needed to eliminate some uses while keeping its options open.

Golden Gate National Recreation Area's establishing legislation contained another unusual mandate. Historically, most national parks operated independently of local authority; the most significant, Yellowstone and its ilk, dictated terms to local government, for they were often the engine that drove the regional economy. In rural places by midcentury, a national park was a ticket to an economic future; in urban areas, it had none of that primacy. As a result, the agency had to share power. At Golden Gate, that sharing began with an advisory commission. Such committees had become common in the national park system as it expanded, but most were appointed by the secretary of the interior. In the confrontational climate of the 1960s and early 1970s, opponents caustically referred to such organizations as "captives."

At Phil Burton's behest, the park was required to establish a Citizens' Advisory Commission (CAC). The clause did not mandate specific actions, giving no real form to the concept of citizen participation. As the Golden Gate National Recreation Area bill made its way through the House and Senate, the question of the commission's composition became an issue. Local activists wanted more control over the appointment process. The Park Service and Secretary of the Interior Rogers C. B. Morton remained uncomfortable with the idea of an advisory group. After the establishment of the park, Whalen was left to sort out the recalcitrance of the government and the enthusiasm of the activists. Following a different management model than the traditional Park Service, he regarded citizen involvement as a tremendous advantage for the park. From its inception, the advisory commission played an important role. Whalen intended to "nurture and refine" the commission, allowing it to serve as liaison between the park, its planners, and Bay Area communities.[1]

The Citizens' Advisory Commission slowly took shape. Although Edgar Wayburn and other activists were contacted about nominating people to the commission, during the first year of the park's existence, no one was appointed to any of its fifteen seats. Many who helped found the park were bemused, befuddled, mistrustful, or angry. They thought that government officials purposely stalled the advent of the commission. On October 27, 1973, the first anniversary of the founding of Golden Gate National Recreation

Area, conservationists in Marin County and San Francisco voiced their complaints about the slow process. National Park Service director Ronald Walker promised "imminent" appointments, but the locals expressed incredulity and loud disbelief. "I was told that in November of last year," Robert F. Raab, president of the Marin Conservation League, vehemently retorted. "I just can't figure out why it would take a year to appoint fifteen people. There is a veritable plethora of qualified people in Marin and San Francisco and the Bay Area." Amy Meyer, the driving force behind the park, described herself as "furious" at the inaction. The very people Whalen hoped to include were livid. They felt excluded from the park they had helped create.[2]

Trying to turn animosity into action, Whalen began to build bridges to the people who would become the CAC. For leadership and to reflect the importance of military lands, Whalen turned to the military. He enlisted Frank Boerger, a retired army colonel and engineer, to head the group. "We were in absolutely unknown territory," Boerger remembered of the early days of the commission in 1974. "No one, including the park, knew what an advisory commission was supposed to do." The group reflected the breadth of the Bay Area. The secretary of the interior appointed five members, including Boerger, while PFGGNRA chose five more. Three of PFGGNRA's five had to be members of minority groups. San Francisco and Marin County each appointed two representatives, and the East Bay Regional Parks selected the final representative.[3] The remarkable caveat in the legislation that granted a private organization control of one-third of the board appointments revealed much about power and, to a lesser degree, patronage at Golden Gate National Recreation Area. In a way they had never been at any other park, the activists, from the park's inception, became part of its power structure.

This was another aspect of Burton's legacy. Commissioner Richard Bartke remembered that Burton attended the commission's second meeting in 1974, "and gave us our goal 'to give advice to the Secretary of the Interior, and to be the eyes and ears of Congress.'" Despite this charge, Park Service officials were still not sure what to make of the new commission. Officials may have feared politicized local involvement and special interest pressure, and a glance at politics in the Bay Area could easily confirm such fears. Furthermore, the Park Service itself had come through an era of turmoil. First its always dependable friends, such as the National Parks Association, which became the National Parks and Conservation Association in 1970, had become critical of the agency and its policies and goals. The appointment of Ronald Walker, an advance man in Richard M. Nixon's reelection campaign with no previous park experience, to lead the Park Service after George B. Hartzog Jr. was forced out at the insistence of presidential friend Charles "Bebe" Rebozo politicized the directorship. The long tradition of rising through the ranks and earning the directorship came to an end, leaving a momentarily timid agency short of leadership and in disarray. In this climate, the agency was unlikely to encourage local groups to claim a larger part of decision-making power.[4]

For activists, this was a daunting and problematic situation. If the agency did not trust its supporters, then the commission could be little more than window dressing. Whalen's integrity saved the situation. The superintendent was skilled at managing constituencies and practiced at the fine art of negotiation. He did not want "a rubber stamp," instead seeing the advisory commission as an important liaison between the park and its many and vocal constituencies. The CAC embraced Whalen's vision and quickly established a consensus about the group's mission. "Our task was to inspire the public to want to come," Boerger recalled.[5]

Once the appointments came through and Boerger took the lead, the advisory commission moved quickly. The CAC established its own direction and throughout the 1970s played a significant role in forming park policy. Among its important innovations was the creation of the Fort Mason Foundation, an umbrella organization that administered many of the historic properties at Fort Mason for community purposes. The CAC also played a significant part in the development of park planning. Boerger retained independence for the commission, which often found itself critical of Park Service policy at Golden Gate National Recreation Area. "We respect regulations," Boerger allowed, "but we don't always agree with them. When we don't, we say so." This ability to be critical has yielded important benefits. In every case that the CAC made recommendations different from those of the Park Service, the park accepted the commission's suggestions. The result was a close partnership, replete with mutual respect.[6]

The partnership worked well throughout the 1970s. With Golden Gate National Recreation Area's first General Management Plan (GMP), which debuted in draft form in 1979, looming in front of the agency, the CAC took on the responsibility for providing community input. Especially in the highly charged Bay Area, a direct forum for community participation and a filter for the points of view of many constituencies was essential in negotiating the pitfalls of local politics. Even after he left San Francisco for the director's chair in Washington, D.C., Whalen recognized and appreciated the significance of the commission. "We need a citizens' commission to run interference for the bureaucracy," he told Frank Boerger in 1979, "and also to be a listening post and advisor." The CAC at Golden Gate National Recreation Area, Whalen had come to believe, could serve as model for park-public cooperation at a number of the new parks he now oversaw.[7]

Even as the CAC developed its point of view, Whalen faced a mighty task at Golden Gate National Recreation Area. Although the Park Service contained an impressive planning division, the experience of agency planners came from more traditional park areas. The nature of Golden Gate National Recreation Area more closely mirrored the holdings of state and city parks than prior national park areas, making conventional agency planning seem misdirected at GGNRA. Douglas Cornell, who showed the new superintendent around the park as 1972 ended, led the initial planning team. Whalen quickly became dissatisfied; Cornell, in his estimation, "had his mind made up the way things were gonna be, and didn't want to listen to the people." Sensitive to the need for strong local support and already in the process of developing ties to San Francisco mayor Joseph Alioto's office and his parks department, headed by Joseph Caverly, Whalen recognized that his planners had to hear the voices of the public more clearly than had been expected of prior NPS planners. He dismissed Cornell and assembled a new team.[8]

Prominent among the new Golden Gate National Recreation Area planners were Doug Nadeau and Ron Treabess. Nadeau arrived in 1974 from the Park Service's Denver Service Center as planning coordinator. A landscape architect by training, he had been selected to play the lead role in the development of a general management plan for the park. Until the 1970s, general management plans and their predecessors, park master plans, were typically in-house projects, debuted to the public when completely finished. The tenor of the 1970s made such a strategy undesirable. Following the environmental revolution of the late 1960s, the Park Service faced a public that frequently sought to influence agency policy. Often public sentiments confounded the agency; the public knew what it wanted, but advocates rarely grasped policy goals, statutory obligations, and other constraints. The result was a decade in which the friends of the Park Service attacked it with more vigor than did its opponents. The prospect of alienating the very people whom the park was to serve was daunting. Nadeau recalled planning Golden Gate National Recreation Area as "a scary prospect."[9]

The situation at Golden Gate National Recreation Area almost guaranteed conflict and potentially could become one of the worst examples of public antipathy for the Park Service and its plans. Not only did every part of the park hold prior uses and constituencies that sought to protect existing and sometimes conflicting prerogatives, but GGNRA's establishment also depended on local activism. Even worse, the park was a "national recreation area," largely without boundary signs or markers. It was easy to overlook its national status, and Bay Area residents did not defer to park managers the way they might have at Yosemite or Yellowstone. Whalen and Nadeau clearly recognized that standard agency practice simply would not work. If the Park Service proceeded as it did in remote national parks, the community-park bonds necessary to success in the Bay Area would certainly become frayed. A new strategy was essential.[10]

The essence of the system was public participation. In a step that was new in Park Service history, Nadeau and Treabess were "assigned to live with the project they are planning," wrote Anne Hanley in *Westways*, the monthly magazine of the Automobile Club of Southern California, "and for yet another first, the planners have no plans." Nadeau and Treabus were committed to listening to the park's constituencies for nearly a full year before they began to develop plans for the park. In a two-stage process of collecting information, which began with more than 100 workshops and continued with focus groups, the boundaries of park management at Golden Gate National Recreation Area began to become clear. Before completion, the park undertook more than 400 workshops and meetings, easily the most comprehensive planning ever accomplished by the Park Service.

The million-dollar process was "extensive, intensive, and effective," Nadeau wrote many years later, but it was more than worth the investment. The planners found out that many of the diverse constituencies for the park shared objectives. Instead of the typical park amenities that the planners expected urban constituencies to request—baseball fields and basketball courts—the low-income and minority neighborhoods sought the same park attributes as their more upscale neighbors. "Just give us a way to get there," one African-American group in the East Bay told the park planners, pointing to the transportation difficulties of the Bay Area as an obstacle to wider participation in the park. This information alone suggested that listening widely was the best strategy.[11]

By the time Nadeau and the planning team formulated its initial ideas, Whalen's staff at Golden Gate National Recreation Area was ready to proceed beyond reactive administration. The only antidote to the situation was to formulate a strategy with specific objectives and goals that park personnel could rely on to stave off the demands of the broad array of constituencies. The document that resulted from the planning process, the Golden Gate National Recreation Area and Point Reyes National Seashore General Management Plan (GMP) of 1980, reflected the ongoing joint planning of the two parks that persisted even after their administrations diverged. The plan's debut marked an important watershed in park history. After the GMP, the agency proceeded with a set of guidelines, a proactive strategy rather than a loosely connected set of responses to circumstances. After nearly a decade in the Bay Area, the GMP gave Golden Gate National Recreation Area a map of its objectives, a rationale for its decisions, and a strategy for approaching the future. Ideally, it meant that the agency could now exercise a greater degree of control over the park's destiny.

The final Golden Gate Point Reyes General Management Plan, approved in September 1980, was one of the most comprehensive plans ever enacted by the Park Service. The process of listening to the public yielded tremendously valuable information. Even as public hearings dragged on past the time the agency allotted, park staff were sanguine. They recognized that the time spent in the process allowed them to digest the information they acquired and shape it in meaningful ways. The political minefield of a changing Bay Area lent that patience even greater significance. Not only did the plan's environmental analysis fulfill the dictates of the National Environmental Policy Act, but it also assessed available options and laid the groundwork for implementation of policies that would produce viable and widely shared objectives. "GGNRA/Point Reyes is many parks," the plan read, and this acknowledgment was a significant concession to the difficulty of managing Golden Gate National Recreation Area.[12]

One of the most daunting tasks in planning the park was assessing the remarkable range of resources it contained. Golden Gate National Recreation Area was so diverse that its land had to be divided into categories before ongoing management could begin. A zoning scheme created different land classifications, called land management zones, within the park. This recognition of the differences between the park's many resources enabled decentralized management to take shape. The idea of zones in the park came from NPS precedent. The agency often created zones within park areas to further management goals, but at Golden Gate National Recreation Area, the idea had very different implications. Semiautonomous park units remained within the park, and the diversity of resources required many management strategies. Decentralized management seemed the only real option. Although it offered many advantages, it could lead to a fracturing of the conceptualization of Golden Gate National Recreation Area as one park.

The land management zones formed by the GMP included one category called "intensive management zones," divided into three subcategories: natural resource zones, historic resource zones, and special-use zones. The natural resource zones were subdivided into two subcategories, a Natural Appearance Subzone that included Ocean Beach, Fort Funston, Lands End, Baker Beach, and the Rodeo Lagoon picnic area and an Urban Landscape Subzone including Crissy Field, West Fort Mason, the Fort Baker waterfront, the Fort Barry parade ground, and the developed area at Stinson Beach. A Pastoral Landscape Management Zone containing the northern Olema Valley and the northern Point Reyes Peninsula constituted another subheading. A Natural Landscape Management Zone, including the Marin Headlands, the southern Olema Valley, and a few areas in Point Reyes National Seashore, further subdivided the park. The natural resource category included Special Protection Zones, designated wilderness and other lands that had received legislative or special administrative recognition of exceptional values. These included a wilderness subzone in Point Reyes National Seashore, a national monument subzone at Muir Woods, a Marine Reserves Subzone at Point Reyes and Limantour Estero, and a Biotic Sensitivity Subzone composed of shoreline and stream courses.

Historic resource zones included a Preservation Zone, an Enhancement Zone, an Adaptive Use Zone, and a Special Use Zone. The Preservation

Zone included Fort Point, the historic buildings on Alcatraz Island, the historic ships, lighthouses, and fortifications under agency administration, and other historic structures. The Enhancement Zone included the Sutro Baths, Sutro Heights, Cliff House, and Aquatic Park, all originally used for recreational purposes. The Adaptive Use Zone included structures and spaces of historic value that were slated for recreational use or park management. The grounds at Alcatraz Island, most of Fort Mason, East Fort Miley, and parts of the Marin Headlands fell into this grouping. The Special Use Zone comprised lands within the boundaries of the two parks that belonged to other entities, public or private, and that the Park Service did not foresee managing in the immediate future.[13]

In one important step, the Park Service solved a major problem at Golden Gate National Recreation Area. In any situation, the park's diversity of resources drew attention away from comprehensive solutions to the questions of management. Faced with trying to manage historic buildings, urban populations, wilderness and other undeveloped rural land, historic ships, and a whole host of other resources, agency officials tended to compartmentalize issues and treat them in discrete ways. The Land Management Zones simultaneously allowed managers to think about solutions to localized problems while forcing them to regard their actions as interrelated pieces of a larger puzzle. After the publication of the plan, many could see the park as a whole rather than a series of parts. The division into land management zones was an essential precursor to comprehensive, integrated administration.

The GMP also laid out plans for development of facilities at Golden Gate National Recreation Area. The park contained eleven major development areas, six of which were former military sites. Eight of the eleven were clustered around the park in San Francisco; the other three were located in Marin County. In particular, the military areas were popular with the public. They were also in serious disrepair. Alcatraz Island, Fort Mason, Crissy Field, Fort Baker, and Rodeo Valley required extensive restoration and adaptation to recreational use. Aquatic Park and Cliff House also needed extensive care, and other areas of the park, including Muir Woods and Stinson Beach, were also slated for improvement. The plan recognized that Alcatraz offered a spectacular view of San Francisco Bay that visitors would continue to crave. Historic preservation and restoration of its parklike qualities became the priorities for Alcatraz Island. The agency projected Aquatic Park as an interpretive lens through which to experience San Francisco's waterfront.[14]

Transportation became a crucial issue in shaping the future of Golden Gate National Recreation Area. The quality of visitor experience depended on being able to reach the park and its resources, and the combination of Bay Area travel patterns, especially commuter traffic, and the demands of the public to use the park required intensive attention. Beginning with the Golden Gate Recreational Travel Survey in 1976, the Park Service devoted much of its planning initiative to finding out what the public sought both in terms of access and for transportation within the park. Although Golden Gate National Recreation Area was an integral part of the city, its ability to limit the impact of traffic was minimal. As traffic problems became ever more prominent, the limitations of Park Service power in this respect became ever more clear. The agency simply lacked the tools, resources, and control to do more than provide services to its day-use visitors.[15]

Park officials were sanguine about the limitations of their policies. They recognized that park decisions were only a small piece of a much larger question and that successful mitigation of transportation problems depended on a greater degree of cooperation than existed among the many local, county, state, and federal players. The predictable but fundamentally antisocial American attitude about cars—a sentiment the report termed, "I want to drive there, but everyone else should take the bus"—also made transportation planning more difficult. The uncertainties of modes of transportation in the aftermath of the 1973 OPEC oil embargo and the dramatic jump in gasoline prices in 1978 and 1979 also affected planning. Decisions made when gasoline was inexpensive might not be relevant in a climate during which fuel costs pushed people toward public transportation. The constraints they faced suggested to park officials that transportation was likely to become the most frequently revisited dimension of the planning process.[16]

The Park Service approached transportation with an eye to both long- and short-term solutions. During the early 1980s, the agency expected that it could improve transit service to the park, provide transportation within the park, expand ferry service to Marin County and create a Marin Head-lands staging area with parking for as many as 700 vehicles, improve auto-mobile access and parking capacity throughout the park, offer transit service to relieve congestion at Cliff House, Stinson Beach, and other overcrowded areas, and promote the new transportation options to the public. Most of the short-term goals could be accomplished by the Park Service alone, with minimal need for cooperation with other government and nongovernmental agencies. Longer term considerations posited wider involvement in transportation and looked at regional solutions to the problems vexing the Bay Area. The Park Service's role in these circumstances was focused but crucial. The park seemed to sit directly in the path of the onslaught of commuter and local traffic, and its resource management concerns had already become a critical factor in local planning. By 1980, the transportation problems of the Bay Area clearly required significant regional involvement and cooperation. For the park, the water ferry system was a primary concern, as was expanded shuttle service and remote staging areas for park visitors.

If the park could keep some of the vehicles that visitors brought to it out-side park boundaries, it could certainly improve the quality of visitor experience within park boundaries.[17]

Cultural resources presented another challenge for park managers. Golden Gate National Recreation Area possessed an amazing array of cultural resources that represented prehistory and more than 200 years of recorded human history and included themes such as the history of Spanish California, American westward expansion, and the Gold Rush of 1849. Its structures illustrated a number of American wars and revealed military history and architecture, agriculture, commerce, transportation, and natural disasters. Military forts and fortifications, the crumbling prison on Alcatraz Island, old ranches, century-old recreational facilities, lighthouses, and archaeological resources beneath the park all contributed to this compendium of human experience along the Pacific Ocean.[18]

The park's cultural resource management strategy consisted of preservation and adaptive restoration. In 1980, GGNRA contained 410 historic structures, a number far in excess of most national parks, and guided by Section 106 of the National Historic Preservation Act of 1966, the park embraced a complicated, time-consuming, and expensive cultural resources management mission. Many historic structures were decaying, forcing the park to develop a plan to first protect and preserve and then determine viable use. Stabilization to slow and stop decay provided one primary means of achieving this end, as did "mothballing," in essence protecting the structure by halting activity in and around it. The prison and fortifications on Alcatraz Island offered a location to implement preservation strategy, as did the historic ships at Aquatic Park, the artillery batteries and fire control stations throughout the park, outbuildings in the Olema Valley, and various archaeological sites scattered through the park. These places could be held in time for the benefit of the visitor and the resource.

Another important local need that the park had to fulfill was the demand for usable public space. The cost of property in San Francisco had become astronomical, a real burden for low-income people, small businesses, and any other renters. Adaptive reuse, a strategy that preserved historic fabric as well as the qualities that gave a place historic significance but accommodated modern needs, offered another means of managing cultural resources. A significant number of historic properties in the park were in use or slated to be used to house a range of cultural activities from community program space to hostels. Turning historic structures into usable 1980s space required a significant investment of capital and thought. Safety codes, structural standards, and disability access all impacted adaptive reuse, often raising the cost of such renovation, but the inclusion of the idea in the GMP gave planners and managers considerable leeway in managing the enormous number of structures in the park.[19]

Adaptive reuse had limitations, but conceptually it made the most sense in Golden Gate National Recreation Area. This strategy did not require complete historical restoration. Instead it suggested a historic mise-en-scène, a retention of the historic fabric to achieve a feeling of the past in the structures while renovations allowed the structures to accommodate new uses and constituencies, such as disabled people, that historic structures often inadvertently exclude. Actual restoration of every historic structure in the park was neither economically feasible nor necessarily desirable. Some of the buildings posed management problems; rubble and the remains of older utility systems dotted many locations. Leaving such places alone or restoring them to a historic time period served fewer purposes than either sealing them off from visitors or converting the useable areas into visitor space. Although the National Historic Preservation Act and Park Service policy governed such situations, the law did not require restoration or preservation. It only assured documentation of historic properties before destruction. Park Service policy heartily encouraged adaptive reuse, permitting many structures to be saved that might otherwise have been demolished. In most places, use of the strategy turned on questions of visitor need as well as the most efficacious use of historic properties.

Natural resource management was perhaps the mostly fully evolved dimension of the 1980 GMP. More than fifteen years of NPS emphasis on ecology and the relative ease of making natural resource policy at Golden Gate National Recreation Area contributed to the comprehensive nature of this section of planning. The GMP provided a blueprint for the future of the park's natural resources. It described objectives and management goals in clear precise terms, looked broadly at the impacts of various decisions, and suggested a number of necessary future studies. A vegetation management plan topped the list of needs, followed by a grazing plan and a shoreline management program. The plan also recognized the need for an endangered species management program.

The plan for management for natural resources had as its basis the protection of the native environment whenever possible. The southern section in San Francisco, including resources at Ocean Beach, Fort Funston, East and West Fort Miley, Lands End, and Baker Beach, was to be maintained in its natural setting. The wooded areas from the Golden Gate Bridge to the south were slated for protection, and the dunes and the rest of the ocean environment were to be restored wherever possible. Crissy Field, Fort Mason, Aquatic Park, Sutro Heights, and Alcatraz were designated as urban park settings, allowing historic values to play a larger role than in areas designated to be natural settings. This decision created de facto recreational use and ecological zones within the San Francisco section of the park. Among the recommendations for historic management, Sutro Heights Park was to be restored, and Crissy Field was to be reseeded and planted with trees. In

Marin County, natural values again took precedence. South of the Olema Valley, a zone was established in which the maintenance of the ecological features such as coastal environments and grasslands predominated; at Muir Woods, the stunning redwoods remained the focus of management. North of the Olema Valley, an emphasis on the rural past and the dairy industry led to a strategy to preserve the balance between woodland and grass. At GGNRA, the natural setting was part and parcel of cultural uses of the land, a fine combination as the Park Service began to recognize and interpret the concept of cultural landscapes.

At Golden Gate National Recreation Area, natural resource management more readily lent itself to this structured approach. A powerful local constituency supported natural resource activities, providing the Park Service with outspoken and influential supporters. Its issues were clear and at least similar; they changed with the ecology of the various segments of the park and as a result of prior human use of the lands in question. The problems that natural resource managers faced included the invasion of exotic and sometimes noxious species, human impact on land, and the ecological consequences of development. Natural resource management questions were familiar to the Park Service, compatible with park goals, and readily focused, making the evolution of natural resource planning an easier process than nearly any other area of park management.

By the end of 1979, when the General Management Plan had begun to circulate, Golden Gate National Recreation Area had become a model for national parks in urban areas. Its diverse resources catered to many publics in countless ways, and its location forced it into the difficult realm of local and regional politics. With the approval of the GMP in September 1980, the park completed its move from reactive to proactive planning. Its needs were clearly defined. Following the initiation of the subsequent cultural resource management plan, approved in 1982, and the natural resource management plan, a draft of which was circulated in 1981 and approved in 1987, park staff had the management tools necessary to develop its programs and procedures and a clear idea of the issues the many constituencies of the park felt were critical. A plethora of area- and issue-specific plans followed throughout the 1980s and 1990s, each tied to goals established in the GMP. Many of these addressed ongoing themes and problems that special interests brought to the table time and again, and the Park Service continually sought to find consensus.[20]

The approval of the General Management Plan changed the way the Park Service responded to public suggestions concerning the use of the park. Before the plan, Golden Gate National Recreation Area operated on a case-by-case basis, as park staff responded to individual queries, requests, and demands. After the plan, the agency had clearly established priorities and reasons that it could use to buttress its claims in the competitive environment in the Bay Area. Managing by program and directive firmed up agency objectives and provided rationales for opposing outside plans for parkland and resources.

The park's subsequent land-use planning decisions always attempted to reference the general prescriptions of the GMP—or were "tiered off" from them, as the planners would say. Among the major efforts were the delicate process of balancing agricultural interests with the cause of wetlands restoration at Giacomini Ranch near Point Reyes Station; the contentious but "interesting" planning for visitor use at Sweeny Ridge, where the community had somewhat unrealistic expectations of commercial benefit from a national park; Aquatic Park, where the park's initiative adjacent to Fisherman's Wharf helped it to become established as a player in the region; and the decades-long struggle to achieve a balance of nature, history, and recreation at Crissy Field.[21]

But the first test of the GMP and the power such a management directive contained came in 1982. Veterans Administration officials decided to build a two-story parking garage at Fort Miley and needed six acres of National Park Service land for the project. Fort Miley had been the genesis of Golden Gate National Recreation Area; the proposal to build a national archives facility there had ignited Amy Meyer and led to the founding of PFGGNRA. A decade later, the commitment to the neighborhood and what longtime San Francisco civic leader John Jacobs called its "nearly pristine" character remained powerful. Reflecting the tendencies of the time, response to the proposal was uniformly negative. The Park Service took a public stand against a project of another agency for one of the first times in the history of Golden Gate National Recreation Area. Pointing to the GMP, William Whalen, back at GGNRA after his stint as director of the National Park Service, promised the Outer Clement Neighborhood Association that the land in question would be turned "from parking into parkland." Whalen was able to keep his promise; Congress terminated the proposal in 1984.

Alcatraz Island also became a focal point for the implementation of the GMP. Because of its popularity, Alcatraz required much of the park's energy. It consistently drew people, attracted filmmakers, and more than any other part of the park captured a place in the public imagination, in the process making prodigious demands on park staff and priorities. Alcatraz required planning from the moment the NPS assumed responsibility for the island. The Indian Occupation left debris scattered across the island, and transforming the old prison into a visitor site required considerable ingenuity. The island, Ron Treabess remarked in a phone conversation with PFGGNRA's Amy Meyer in 1973, was "in a sad state of disrepair." The public clamored to visit the island, and the Park Service sought to accommodate them. Within months of park establishment, staff members at Golden Gate National Recreation Area prepared an interim management plan and a transportation concession prospectus to offer boat service to the island. Both documents were preliminary in their nature; both illustrated the problems of managing a place that attracted the public before a full-scale planning process had begun.[22]

When the island opened to visitors at the end of 1973, nothing prepared the Park Service for the intensity of demand. Park planners expected tours of the island to lay its image as America's Devil's Island to rest and quench the public's interest in The Rock; within a few years, they anticipated, demand would level off. Within weeks of the beginning of ticket sales, the Park Service recognized that it clearly underestimated the public's interest. Tours sold out months in advance, and a ticket on the Alcatraz ferry was one of hottest items in the Bay Area.[23] Only the firm control of arrival and departure gave the Park Service the opportunity to manage visitor flow and minimize severe impact on the cultural resources of the island.

During the next few years, the Park Service reassessed its initial plans for management of Alcatraz and sought to develop a consensus with other affected entities. In the context of the planning process that was to shape the entire future of the park, the agency encouraged public input to accompany its plans. In May 1977, the park debuted its *Assessment of Alternatives for the General Management Plan, May 1977: Golden Gate National Recreation Area, Point Reyes National Seashore*. The assessment offered three different scenarios for Alcatraz. The first would clean up the rubble and leave the historic buildings intact; the second proposed removing all but key historic structures and landscaping the remaining open space, and the third recommended stabilizing historic structures and offering self-guided tours and other educational programs.[24] All three closely followed the Park Service's plans for the island and did little to encourage other potential uses.

As a visitor destination, Alcatraz Island offered many management advantages. Most important, the Park Service could limit the number of visitors and control ingress and egress. No one could simply drive up to the island and walk in. Everyone—or nearly everyone—had to purchase passage on a concessionaire's ferry, and, initially, uniformed rangers gave guided tours to groups of twenty-five or fewer visitors. The guided tours were essential to the Park Service's initial scheme. Tours prevented injury in the sometimes dangerous and always crumbling structures on the island, and they assured that visitors did not damage the facilities. Initial plans also limited the number of visitors on the island to fifty at a time, a figure that quickly proved impossibly low.[25]

By the late 1970s, the growth in demand required reevaluation of the policies for the island. Alcatraz was a difficult place to work. Interpreters often experienced burnout, the facilities were inundated, and although the ranger-guided tours were widely acclaimed, they drained not only staff members but also park resources. Low morale that resulted from a combination of harsh weather and limited amenities plagued the Alcatroopers, as they labeled themselves, and turnover was high. Nor was a guided tour for every visitor feasible. By the late 1970s, the labor-intensive operations that had been the hallmark of the U.S. economy before 1970 had become expensive and unwieldy, and at Alcatraz, park staff needed to rethink management strategies.[26]

In 1978, the agency approved a development concept for the island and, soon after, a structural safety study. In the 1980 GMP, historic preservation remained the key goal at Alcatraz, but the Park Service committed itself to creating a "pleasant landscaped setting" to which the "stark prison and military structures will stand in honest contrast." But with "twice the visitors and half the rangers," as one staff member described the situation to a reporter, the island was becoming a different place, one that had to be managed as clearly for visitors as for preservation purposes. As demand increased, the agency catered to visitors in new ways.[27]

In 1985, the new policy was finally implemented. Visitors were no longer restricted to tours led by rangers, instead experiencing what one reporter, Judy Field of the *Salinas Californian*, called "free exploration" of the island. Rangers continued to give tours, but visitors could also rent Walkman-style cassette players with an interpretive tape that contained a cell block tour narrated by a number of people connected to Alcatraz, including former prisoners Jim Quillen and Whitey Thompson. The change in method of interpretation altered the experience of visitors on the island. Roaming about with their aural interpretive material, visitors experienced physical freedom and had greater impact on the island and its structures. Their freedom also cost them something. The visitor's tour acquired a new and markedly different feel. At the end of the guided tour, interpretive rangers asked for quiet and then clanged a cell door. The eerie sound reverberated through the crumbling halls of the windswept rock. The awesome quiet spoke for itself, mute testimony to a complicated and intriguing past that thrilled visitors. The self-guided tours changed the special sense of discovery that came with the silence of the guided tours. Delivered on headsets, the talks were excellent, well thought out, informative, and, with Quillen's and Thompson's voices telling a personal story, real. The tapes became a favorite of visitors. Crowded together, they jostled each other for position to better hear the words, the recorded "clang" of jailhouse doors, and the silence of the airwaves in their ears. Tuned to their headsets, their "excuse me's" as they maneuvered echoed where silence once awed the public and interpreters alike.[28]

The management advantages of the new program were many and varied, and support for implementation of this new management concept came from Golden Gate National Recreation Area Superintendent Brian O'Neill. Using his connections in the community and his skill as a leader, O'Neill promoted the lessening of visitor control on Alcatraz. Under the new system, the Park Service could accommodate many more visitors and could still maintain some measure of management of their actions. The Alacatroopers offered a mixed response to the new program. Many thought that the headsets offered high-quality interpretation, at least equal to that of live rangers; others saw the new system as a serious decline in the quality of experience. The new program offered one clear advantage: it made work on the island far less difficult. Inclement weather was one of the sources of low morale. Alcatraz was cold, and rangers who gave guided tours spent much of their time outside. Exposure took a heavy toll on park personnel, who were often ill. After visitors were allowed to roam the island without guides, rangers could spend more of their time indoors. Not only did they experience better health as a result, but it also provided an opportunity for staff to develop other aspects of the island's history.

Clearly the new program was a response to demand, a harbinger of more change. "We're trying to convert Alcatraz from a prison to a park," observed Rich Weideman, the supervisory ranger for Alcatraz, in the clearest description of the program's goal. The development of a management program illustrated a variety of previously overlooked resources on the island. As was nearly always the case in the Bay Area, each newly considered resource soon acquired a vocal constituency. The demands for Alcatraz became broader and more varied. The national public saw a prison on the island, a place of memory, history, and myth. After documentation of sea caves and the nesting of Heermann's gulls, local and vocal environmental groups regarded the island as a wildlife refuge.[29] The many demands on the island required further planning as well as more discussion.

In 1988, the distinguished architect Lawrence Halprin came to the park to help develop Alcatraz as a destination for visitors. The Golden Gate National Parks Association (GGNPA), the park's nonprofit cooperating association, sponsored Halprin's work, and the architect brought an impressive track record of community-oriented design. Born in 1916 and a resident of San Francisco since the 1940s, Halprin was widely revered for his attention to the human scale of large design projects and closely associated with the idea of environmental design. One of his prominent projects, Ghirardelli Square on the edge of San Francisco's waterfront, catapulted him to architectural prominence, and he continued for more than three decades as one of the nation's leading landscape architects. Among his important projects were the Lovejoy and Auditorium Forecourt Plazas in Portland, Oregon, Freeway Park in Seattle, Washington, the Haas Promenade in Jerusalem, Israel, and later the FDR Memorial in Washington, D.C. Near the end of a long and significant career, he sought to transform Alcatraz Island as he had so many other places.[30]

With funds from GGNPA, Halprin developed a series of new concepts for the island. On-site workshops and other similar mechanisms brought feedback from the public, and he worked these ideas into his vision of Alcatraz. Published by the association, "Alcatraz the Future: A Concept Plan and Guidelines" envisioned a very different island than existed in the 1980s. Building on a 1984 conception, Halprin's work sought to create an open island, with shoreline walks, overlooks, and picnic areas. The plan also suggested restoring the parade grounds and other public areas. Halprin's island looked more like a nature preserve than a historic prison.[31] Many in the Park Service thought this version of making the prison a park went too far.

The Halprin plan served to announce the emergence of the Golden Gate National Parks Association as an important influence. The association submitted Halprin's plan to the Park Service as an illustration of the goals of two of the park's most important planning documents, the General Management Plan and the interpretive prospectus. Gregory Moore, director of GGNPA, expressed support for the goals of the park and prepared for "the 'next era' of community participation in the park—when the goals of the General Management Plan are pursued through a program of contributed support." GGNPA saw its role as assisting the park by providing resources; it extended that to offering ideas and programs. The Park Service enacted only the Agave Trail from the "Alcatraz the Future" plan, but the association further established itself as an important asset for the park.[32]

After the Halprin plan, the Park Service worked toward a comprehensive program for Alcatraz Island. In the early 1990s, the island's role as a bird refuge grew in significance to the Park Service, melding natural and cultural resource management. This new emphasis served agency goals. If the Park Service wanted people to pay less attention to the prison and more to other features of the island, programs that focused on other dimensions of the island furthered its end. Following new interest in Heermann's gulls, the predominant western gulls, and other species and with growing interest in tide pools on the island, the park put together a new plan, the *Alcatraz Development Concept Plan and Environmental Assessment*, which it unveiled in 1993. The plan was a measure of the park's commitment to integrate natural and cultural resource management and to create a multifaceted plan to manage the various resources of the park. At the same time, it furthered the park's objective of turning Alcatraz from a prison to a park, increasingly reflecting the Park Service's long-standing predisposition for natural resources ahead of cultural resources. In a national recreation area devoted to public enjoyment, with local sentiment in favor of natural resources and historic preservation valued more highly by out-of-town visitors, that predisposition was strong, even enhanced.[33]

The 1993 plan also let the Park Service set a firm balance between use, history, and nature on the island. In it, the park codified the principle of an open island, a decade after its introduction. The plan gave the birds equal standing with historic resources on the island, a decision that made some cultural resources managers uncomfortable. Yet the Bay Area environmental community was powerful and wide-reaching, and the Park Service often bent to its influence. In this case, the park's many mandates coincided in a way that furthered resource protection, albeit some thought at the expense of the primary features of the island. The 1993 Alcatraz plan represented a step toward integrated management.[34]

An important synergy developed between Alcatraz and GGNPA that had powerful implications for park planning and management. According to Rich Weideman, the sales of gifts and souvenirs on Alcatraz facilitated the growth of GGNPA, which in turn created more resources for the park. As the association's coffers filled with revenue from Alcatraz, GGNPA, once a small cadre of enthusiasts, hired countless employees. The association was able to turn over large sums of revenue to the park each year and was able to support Golden Gate National Recreation Area in new and impressive ways.[35] The attraction of Alcatraz Island helped GGNPA attain a significance that far exceeded most other cooperating associations at individual park areas.

Yet the potential for tension existed with the growing significance of GGNPA and other similar entities throughout the park system. Even though close ties between GGNPA and Golden Gate National Recreation Area helped foster cooperation, GGNPA also could function as another of the seemingly infinite constituencies of the park. Under the unique circumstances at Alcatraz, the tension was muted. Weideman, the supervisory ranger at Alcatraz, regarded the park and the association as parallel organizations that pursued similar goals in different ways.[36] Since Alcatraz received much of its development money from GGNPA, and because visitation on the island was controlled—the boat trip remained the only way to reach the island, although demand compelled the Park Service to exceed the carrying capacity set in the GMP and later in the 1993 Alcatraz Plan—and the island required so much stabilization and reconstruction, the partnership worked well. The goals of the Park Service and of the association meshed smoothly at Alcatraz.

By the early 1990s, Alcatraz provided a precursor to the looming question of the management of the Presidio. On the island, where Weideman, a talented and energetic manager who showed great creativity, remained committed to the idea that increases in use and better protection of habitat were not mutually exclusive, GGNPA influence facilitated both historic preservation and natural protection. The Presidio clearly demanded something similar and by the early 1990s just as certainly would involve a public-private management structure. But Alcatraz, with its controlled ingress and egress, may be an exception. Visitors continue to regard the island as a prison and do not feel entitled to go where they choose as they do in other parts of Golden Gate National Recreation Area. As a result, planners and managers have a freer hand on the island than elsewhere in the park. It is possible to experiment at Alcatraz, and if the program fails, to simply section off that part of the island until the program can be redesigned. In park management, as the new century approached, such control remained a luxury that muted tension and created possibilities.

By the 1990s, planning at Golden Gate National Recreation Area had become an integral part of park management. A decade of preparation led to the General Management Plan, which became the point of departure for future changes. With the GMP in place, the park was able to move from simple reaction to planned response aimed at long-term goals. More detailed plans within overall context could be made and considered without devoting as much time to the broad array of unfeasible proposals that consumed much park time during its first years. In a park surrounded by powerful constituencies, each with not only valid claims to parklands for their purposes but also significant political influence, planning became the Park Service's defense against the heavy weight of special interests. The commitment to planning and to park goals has often slowed the agency's ability to move forward; it has also protected the GGNRA from being overrun by its friends.

Administering Golden Gate National Recreation Area: "There's a Constituency for Everything and Each Has a Voice"

The defining feature of Golden Gate National Recreation Area remained the power of the people who felt strongly about the park and who used it in all kinds of ways. Even with planning in place and with the park's clearly articulated resource management mission, the Park Service found that its constituencies not only ignored agency planning but also sometimes used blatant pressure to attempt to circumvent park goals. In such circumstances, the agency trod very carefully, using skillful negotiation and long-standing friendships to allay concerns, to reshape the goals of constituent groups, and, in some circumstances, to outwardly resist actions that either statute, policy, or the planning documents for the park excluded. The GMP became a working document, an argument for specific goals that had to be hashed out with the public. In the complicated terrain of the Bay Area, each situation reassessed the efficacy of planning at the park. Each time agency goals held, the Park Service took a step toward the kind of integrated management it sought; each time public pressure overwhelmed the agency or swayed its decision-making, management slipped back toward the reactiveness of the 1970s.

These more sophisticated responses to the social and political environments in which Golden Gate National Recreation Area operated presaged an essential versatility that all federal agencies sought in the 1980s and 1990s. After the 1980 election of Ronald Reagan, the federal bureaucracy found itself on the defensive. Government-bashing became sport, encouraged by the White House and administration officials such as James Watt, Reagan's first secretary of the interior. Federal agencies struggled to find a place in a cultural climate that increasingly disparaged their activities and, in some cases, their very existence. The Park Service was rocked in the same way as nearly every other federal agency, and in the new environment, the agency fell back on its time-honored practices. Management documents served two purposes: as a baseline for interaction with a multitude of competing constituencies and as a barometer of the agency perspective. Instead of dictating policy, the documents shaped and guided it into a form that was acceptable both to the Park Service and to the many publics it served.[1]

During the late 1980s, the General Management Plan at Golden Gate National Recreation Area helped inaugurate a third phase by permitting new dimensions in the relationship between the park and its publics. Because of the stunning amount of citizen participation in the planning process, most constituencies found themselves with a stake, sometimes a very strong one, in plan implementation. Simply put, the GMP gave most users much of what they wanted, providing them with an investment in its success, sometimes at the expense of the clearly articulated goals of the various management plans. As a result, the GMP was transformed from a way to circumvent unwanted use into a tool to promote a more comprehensive and more cooperative future. By the end of the 1990s, time had transformed the initial interest groups, the park had become a well-established entity in the region, and the range of users had greatly expanded. The plan became a blueprint, a road map, an integral part of the interaction not only between the Park Service and its constituents but among those constituents as well.

Stakeholder relationships at Golden Gate National Recreation Area frequently turned on issues with which the Park Service had little experience. One major issue was the proprietary reactions of those groups and individuals who lived near the park. They sought to enjoy the advantages of the park status without experiencing any of its drawbacks and wanted to retain their prerogatives after the park came into being. The struggles over use that ensued were titanic in nature, ongoing, and to a certain degree unsolvable. They reflected the inherent tension between resource management goals and constituency desires.

The use of the park by dogs and their owners became one of the fulcrums that articulated the tension between management policies and constituent goals. The park managed much of the open space in the city, and people had walked their dogs on its property long before 1972. Park establishment led to conflicts between users with pets—especially those not on a leash or other physical restraint—and people without pets. Pet owners believed that since they walked their dogs without a leash before the establishment of the park, their rights should be grandfathered in. "I must protest against the unreasonable enforcement of canine leash laws," wrote Muriel T. French, a fifty-year resident of the Bay Area, in a letter typical of the people who favored dogs. "We've walked our dogs down there for years," Richard Nason added, "long before anyone thought of a Rec. Area." Others disagreed; people without pets wanted to know why a national park area did not have rules to restrict animals. "I do not believe that dogs should be allowed on a national parklands, unless in designated areas set aside for dog owners," a Marin County resident told the superintendent. Another averred that "dog owners believe the areas are for animal enjoyment rather than people enjoyment." Caught between two vocal constituencies, the Park Service struggled for a response. The agency needed to take action, but as late as 1976, no specific policy existed. In April of that year, Whalen sent his staff a copy of the federal guidelines for pet management on federal property, the only official regulation applied to the situation. The document was explicit and concise, but it had little bearing on Golden Gate National Recreation Area.[2]

Dog control asked a fundamental, persistent, and always vexing question about Golden Gate National Recreation Area: was it a national park, an icon of American society, and thus worthy of the same reverence and parallel restrictions that governed places such as Yellowstone and Yosemite, or was it urban recreational space? The issue had been pushed aside throughout the park system between 1953 and 1964, Conrad Wirth's directorship. That great advocate of parkways and recreational space wisely confined such development to remote areas used mostly by overnight visitors. Only with the creation of Golden Gate and Gateway National Recreation Areas in the 1970s did the agency have to answer this question.[3]

Dogs and their control typified the first phase of administrative issues at Golden Gate National Recreation Area and illustrated the way such issues persisted despite the implementation of comprehensive planning. The park offered countless opportunities to engage in uses that were typically outlawed in national parks but remained unregulated in national recreation areas. The absence of rules did not stem from a lack of concern. Instead, the shortage of experience with questions such as hang gliding, pets on leashes, hiker-biker-horseback trail issues, and the lack of firm resource management plans confounded the Park Service. Again, the issues of an urban recreation area with a range of features and possible uses took the agency's existing rules and structures and forced rethinking not only of concepts but also of means of implementation. For the NPS, in the process of building relationships, conflicting claims meant that the agency had to take a side and required it to elevate some kinds of visitor experiences over others.

Animal control issues at beaches and elsewhere remained the dominant stakeholder issue in the 1970s, and Marin County provided its primary flash point. County residents long enjoyed recreational activities on what in 1972 became parklands. Many of them also owned dogs, and they were accustomed to having their animals accompany them while hiking, horseback riding, running, and pursuing other activities. At the same time, unencumbered dogs threatened the tenets of resource management. Dogs aggressively attacked the deer population in Marin County. Reports of deer killed by dogs abounded, inciting other stakeholders, wildlife advocates and even those who simply thought deer more attractive than dogs in creating a natural-looking vista. As early as the mid-1970s, complaints of feral dogs attacking and killing deer reached the Park Service. After a summerlong drought in 1976, Ray Murphy, chief of resource management and visitor services, reported that the "dog situation is getting out of hand."[4] He estimated that one deer was killed each day in the Tennessee Valley–Rodeo Beach area. The drought forced deer out of the sheltered valleys they favored and into open terrain, where they became targets for pets and feral dogs. Until that summer, the Park Service had been timid about enforcing dog policy in rural Marin County. Although some observed that dogs had been killing deer in Marin County since before the establishment of the park, national parks were not regarded as hunting grounds for either feral or domestic animals. The situation became a public relations problem, a challenge to the image of controlled resource management that the Park Service sought to project. The agency needed a forceful response, but without a plan, the options were limited.[5]

Protecting and preserving wildlife, a classic resource management objective, turned into a question of people management rather than animal control. In October 1976, the Park Service placed "Dogs Prohibited" signs in open areas of its Marin County properties, where the problem stemmed not from feral animals but from domestic pets. Local residents responded with a variety of perspectives, usually reflecting enlightened or even base self-interest. People who did not own dogs cheered the decision, people with dogs opposed the change, and a significant number showed their proprietary feelings about the region when they tried to wrangle specific exceptions to park rules.[6]

Dogs and their domestic peers, cats, became the test case, the issue that the Park Service used to try to define both its administrative obligations and the limits of its reach. The park's lack of a written policy gave the agency few ways to rule out the actions of any constituency, and existing rules offered little to help resolve the situation. Prepared for intense debate that might anger some constituencies, the staff at Golden Gate National Recreation Area initiated the dialogue. In 1977, Rolf Diamant, the park's environmental coordinator, circulated a draft dog policy for the San Francisco portions of the park. "This is a thankless task," Diamant admitted as he tried to negotiate the questions that stemmed from people's perception of their rights in public space. The issues were subtle and often confused. Even wild dogs were sympathetic creatures, shaggy canines who reminded many of the dogs in the stories of Jack London, one of the Bay Area's most well-known writers. Others saw the animals in different terms. "There is a world of difference between a well-fed dog killing a deer in Marin County and a coyote killing a deer in Yosemite," chief of resource management and visitor services Ray Murphy observed. "The coyote is earning his living; the dog is not."[7]

Pet management forced the Park Service to consider the separation of people and their animals from other users of Golden Gate National Recreation Area. The results illustrated another of the ongoing tensions of park management, the proprietary feeling that many neighbors held about parklands. In late 1977, the Park Service considered a trail in Marin County exclusively for obedience school–trained dogs certified by a local kennel club. Marin unit manager Richard B. Hardin thought such a program would encourage responsible pet owners and allow the Park Service to exclude unruly pets and to cite their owners. Since the governing policy, the federal code for pets, required all pets to be restrained by leash or other mechanism, the Park Service felt that allowing obedience-trained dogs to roam off leash on specific trails represented an enormous concession to pet owners. Dog owners felt otherwise, seeing in the attempt to restrict their access the curtailment of their long-established prerogative.[8] Local ire persuaded the Park Service to reconsider and eventually abandon the proposal. Staff members learned that ad hoc approaches that did not involve the community as a whole were unlikely to succeed. The best, and most likely only, solution to the Park Service's dilemma was a clear and well-defined policy shaped through dialogue with the many sectors of the public concerned about pets in the park.

Recognizing that the Park Service would benefit from the participation of intermediaries, Whalen enlisted the Citizens' Advisory Commission for Golden Gate National Recreation Area to mitigate the fray. This intermediary role had become one of the hallmarks of the CAC. The organization had been designed to undertake precisely such a task: to simultaneously stand in for the agency and facilitate citizen input as the planning process took shape and to absorb any negative aftershocks. After a slow start, the CAC came into its own as a valuable entity. It held public hearings on disputed issues, trying to create a climate in which passionate but civil discourse could take place and to simultaneously discern public sentiment and placate the most adamant advocates on both sides. In essence, the CAC quickly assumed the role of broker, listening, summarizing, and providing feedback for park staff on a wide range of questions as policy developed.[9]

By the time cats and dogs became an issue in the mid-1970s, CAC members had considerable experience at creating constructive feedback out of the chaos of competing interests. The pet discussions continued for more than two years. The initial efforts required much tinkering, as the various interests sought to achieve as much of their objectives as they could. As was typical of such arrangements, many ideas were offered and most were rejected when one or more of the stakeholders opposed them. For example, dogs under "voice control" initially seemed viable, but Richard Hardin pointed out that the language was too vague for any kind of systematic enforcement.[10] The Park Service ultimately rejected the suggestion.

In January 1978, the CAC formed a pet policy committee with Amy Meyer, one of the founders of PFGGNRA, at its head. The committee held hearings in San Francisco and Marin County in the spring and early summer to simultaneously collect information and disseminate ideas to which the public responded. In the end, these ongoing discussions shifted the terrain on which the debate took place. As the talks continued, everyone involved recognized that firm policy governing animals was the goal, and the longer the dialogue persisted, the more everyone understood that a policy decision was imminent. Giving up dreams of getting every desire, each group scrambled to carve out a position its members could tolerate.

The results of the process set a pattern for Golden Gate National Recreation Area: different subunits of the park were managed in different ways for different constituencies, suggesting that GGNRA was not one park, but many under one rubric. After public hearings on May 23 and June 14, 1978, the CAC drafted a proposed policy, describing specific regulations for each part of the park. The proposal for San Francisco required leashes for dogs at Sutro Heights, the Golden Gate Promenade near Crissy Field, at Fort Mason, and at Aquatic Park and Victorian Park. Dogs were excluded from Alcatraz and the historic ships. Elsewhere, dogs were expected to be under voice control. Leashes were required on weekends, holidays, and other crowded days, and signs that read "Please Pick Up Dog Litter" were placed along most trails and paths. The commission approved the report with a unanimous vote, establishing principles for administration and paving the way for a permanent policy.[11]

Early in 1979, the CAC finalized its policy for San Francisco; Marin County followed soon after. The pet regulations created three categories of domestic animals: unmanaged, managed, and voice or leash control. Unmanaged animals were not permitted in the park. Managed animals, those controlled by voice or leash, were permitted at specific times in most of the park. Voice or leash control provided a flexible system. Although dogs were the obvious target of policy in Marin County, pets in San Francisco were considerably more diverse. All kinds of pets lived in the city, and the CAC determined that with two exceptions, any pet that was uncontrolled was banned from the park. The lexicon "unmanaged pets" was a little clumsy but clearly understood. Only the existing cat colonies, which enjoyed powerful public support, the cats who kept down the rodent population around the historic ships, and animals who assisted the disabled were excepted from the rule. The policy was cheered; the unanimous vote signaled consensus. A month later, the recommendations for Marin County passed on another unanimous vote, and in May 1979, following the trend, similar recommendations were approved for Point Reyes National Seashore.[12]

Policies did not resolve hard feelings or deter persistent advocates, and throughout 1979 a parade of speakers appeared at CAC meetings to urge further changes in pet policy. Several groups, including the San Francisco Dog Owners Group, applauded the process and supported the new policies. John Kipping, a biologist at the Audubon Canyon Ranch, advocated even greater restrictions, a point of view echoed by Superintendent John L.

Sansing of Point Reyes National Seashore, who noted that one of the park's purposes was to permit people to see wildlife, a traditional use of national parks. They were far more likely to do so when dogs were not present. In August, Kathy Reid of Marin County supervisor Gary Giacomini's office recommended stricter enforcement of leash laws. Others advocated new limits on animals, on or off leash. Self-interest continued to be the measure for some. Park patron Christine Hoff of San Francisco favored new areas for dogs; she preferred hiking with her dog. Others suggested dogs intimidated criminals and made park patrons feel more safe, while some thought humans were a greater threat to wildlife than domestic or feral animals.[13] Special interest groups of all kinds proposed a number of exceptions to the policy, asking in effect to overrule it on a case-by-case basis. The CAC once again found itself in the familiar position of listening, its members fully aware they could not make everyone happy.

The General Management Plan, approved in 1980, did not specifically address pet policy, but it did present a blueprint for public use of Golden Gate National Recreation Area. By defining the desired purposes of every park sector, the plan simultaneously illustrated a vision and drew clear and distinct boundaries. Although imperfect, the plan offered the beginning of a firm and consistently defensible policy.[14] Throughout the 1980s and 1990s, however, dog control remained the archetypal urban park administrative issue. When it came to people and their pets, the intersection between urban and rural, between preservation and use, between resource management and individual prerogative, remained unclear at Golden Gate National Recreation Area.

Managing the many beaches included in Golden Gate National Recreation Area led to similar kinds of issues. Only a very few parks in the system offered beaches, limiting the Park Service's experience. Those that did, such as Lake Mead National Recreation Area, enjoyed greater control of ingress and egress than did the former city beaches included in Golden Gate National Recreation Area. Cape Cod National Seashore, which entered the park system in 1966, shared issues with Golden Gate National Recreation Area. Before 1970, parks with beaches were not a priority of policy makers. Their very attractions precluded a primary position in agency strategy in a time when the parks reflected cultural impulses more thoroughly than recreational ones. As they did in so many other ways, urban park areas forced a reassessment of agency emphasis. Golden Gate National Recreation Area included a number of widely used beaches. Ocean Beach, Muir Beach, Stinson Beach, Rodeo Beach, Phelan Beach (now called China Beach), Baker Beach, and many other coastal areas were a recreational responsibility. The park filled a function previously offered by other entities, diminishing the conceptual distance and managerial distinctions between Golden Gate National Recreation Area and the state and local park areas that preceded it.

Beaches offered another of the innumerable situations in which different users were bound to intrude upon each other's experience. The finite space at any beach and the range of possible uses exacerbated the problems that such situations presented. In the small spaces of most beaches, the demand was consistently great, and the Park Service's primary obligation became people management. The possible problems were endless. Too many people made the beach a congested experience, not pleasurable and hardly different from typical daily urban endeavors such as driving in traffic. Unleashed animals at the beach interfered with other patrons. "It is not conducive to picnicking at the beach," San Francisco resident Douglas Weinkauf wrote to William Whalen, "when a loose dog defecates nearby."[15] Beaches also held powerful symbolic status as the representation of leisure for all. Their management presented a series of issues far more like those of beaches elsewhere than of most national parks.

Typically surrounded by homes and other private property and reached by narrow, winding two-lane roads, the beaches became sources of tension between local communities, park managers, and the enormous constituency for their use throughout the Bay Area. Communities next to beaches often held proprietary feelings about the waterfront, and they organized active groups to further their ends. In some cases, they regarded nearby public beaches as de facto private property. Planning became the catalytic factor in balancing the demands of various constituencies. Again the Park Service shaped its policies after receiving input from the entire spectrum of users and residents. Policy making was the first step in an ongoing reevaluation of agency management goals, practices, and sometimes standards. Once again, the realities of urban park management dictated that no decision was ever final; reassessment was a crucial feature of managing beaches at Golden Gate National Recreation Area.

San Francisco's diverse cultural climate made the Park Service beaches symbolic of the complicated process of bringing agency standards in line with local norms. The Bay Area easily accepted practices that would have been thought offensive elsewhere. One of these, clothing-optional beaches, illustrated the region's degree of tolerance and the Park Service's ability to be flexible. In Marin County before the park's establishment, policy allowed people to swim without attire at some beaches. That pattern of behavior, essentially a cultural choice, spread from Marin County south to Baker Beach and Lands End.[16] The agency was again forced to address an issue that was well beyond the experience of most park managers, and it fashioned a Solomonic response. In a policy that evolved over a decade, the Park Service determined that it would respond to complaints about clothing-optional beaches, but without a complaint park workers would not initiate action against nude bathers. This decision reflected the Bay Area's openness, a growing cultural tolerance, and the sensibilities of individual freedom that dominated the last quarter of the twentieth century. It sanctioned diplomacy as policy, an ethic that served the agency well in the region's convoluted politics.

The growth of recreation as an industry in the 1970s and 1980s also challenged resource management goals and policy at Golden Gate National Recreation Area. Park Service history again did not provide a blueprint. "Demand for recreation at the park is divided between people who want structured activities and facilities," one observer wrote in a succinct assessment of the issues in 1979, "and those who want to go their own way."[17] Creating rules for hikers, bikers, and horseback riders was no easier than negotiating pet policies or the various constituencies of beach users. A variety of issues, including personal security, competition for trails and other resources, sanctioned and unsanctioned activities, and permitted uses by the military and others, forced the Park Service to broaden the role to which it was generally accustomed.

Hiking had been one of the most important recreational activities in Park Service history, and the inclination of people in the Bay Area spurred the importance of trail management and development. Hiking had always been a staple park activity. In the Bay Area, the tradition of recreational walking dated back nearly a century to John Muir and the founding of the Sierra Club. To the people of the region, this activity stood out as one that defined the special local relationship to the physical world that so many claimed as one of the distinctive features of Bay Area life. Between 1972 and 1979, the Park Service developed trails throughout the park, adding links between different areas, improving existing pathways, and generally facilitating hiking and walking in urban and rural parts of the park. It also participated in the development of the Pacific Coast Trail, the Bay Trail, and the Golden Gate Promenade, taking the lead role in countless situations.

The popularity of regional trails required vigilance, and beginning in 1979, security for hikers became a pivotal local issue. A sociopath called the "Trailside Killer" stalked the Bay Area. After killing a woman and wounding her male companion in a Santa Cruz state park, the killer became one of the many hazards of city life. Unlike the city's Zodiac Killer of the decade before, the Trailside Killer seemed somehow predictable. His killings appeared planned instead of random; they followed a pattern that included parks and trail locales. Lincoln Park near Lands End was the location of one of his murders; he killed two women in Point Reyes National Seashore late in 1980. In response, advisories that warned people, especially women, not to hike alone were everywhere. The Park Service significantly increased security for hikers but faced the problem of a limited ranger force and an enormous area to patrol. When David Carpenter, a fifty-year-old industrial arts teacher with a speech impediment and a history of sexual crime, was finally apprehended late in 1981, he had maps of Mount Tamalpais in his possession.[18] After Carpenter's capture and eventual conviction, the perceived need for trail security diminished but remained an ever-present concern. In the Bay Area, home at the time to more than three million people, security for hikers who sought solitude required a strategic response from the Park Service.

Hiking remained a favored activity of park users, leading to a proposal for a "Bay Area Ridge Trail," which surfaced during the late 1980s. The trail proposal accomplished a number of important political goals as well as promoting an interlocking network of trails throughout the Bay Area. The idea came from neighborhood activists, prominent among them Doris Lindfors, a retired schoolteacher who previously led the Sweeney Ridge Trail Committee, and Dave Sutton of the South Bay Trails Committee. Enthusiasts envisioned a complete network of trails inside Golden Gate National Recreation Area that would join with trails outside the park to create a ring around the Bay. The trails were expected to extend more than 400 miles, to nearly every corner of the three-county region, and allow easy access to hiking trails from almost anywhere in the Bay Area.[19]

The combination of dedicated activists, a powerful federal presence, and the sense that trails improved the quality of life made the project hard to resist. "Quality of life" environmentalism became an issue of considerable significance, both as an indicator of the area's attractiveness as well as a source of positive identity for communities. The Bay Area Ridge Trail meant considerably more than a place to hike, ride a horse, or walk a dog. It also signaled a commitment to the region's population to provide the kinds of amenities that made urban space pleasurable. After the trail system's dedication in September 1989, it received acclaim from a number of sources. "It's a wonderful project," opined the *Marin Independent Journal* when the project was dedicated. "With the advent of the Ridge Trail, there's something to look forward to."[20]

The Ridge Trail also gave equestrians, long a presence in Golden Gate National Recreation Area, another opportunity for a continued presence. Private organizations had stables within the park, some preceding the establishment of the park. The Golden Gate Stables at Muir Beach, the Presidio Stables at Rodeo Valley, the Miwok Valley Association Stable in the Tennessee Valley, and other buildings meant that horses were a frequent presence on park trails. The Park Service and the U.S. Park Police also used horses for their patrols, and the park police kept a stable at Fort Miley. The result was a typical situation for the Park Service, another of the endless situations of managing competing claims and constituencies.

Horses represented precisely the kind of class-based recreation that could influence park policy. Elites comprised much of the riding population; many were longtime friends of the Park Service, and horse riding enjoyed a long history in national parks. Equestrian clubs engaged in the kind of activity that the Park Service recognized, validated, and understood, and in most circumstances, horse riders enjoyed an easy camaraderie with the agency. Even though horses could severely damage trails, leave mountains of waste, and intimidate hikers and other users of the park, a combination of NPS predisposition for the activity, historic use of the park by horses, and the class, power, and status of many riders made the Park Service unlikely to sanction horses. The agency could embrace horses and their riders because they shared a value system and a vision, and it was easy for park managers to see the impact of horses as part of the cost of running an urban area park. As a result, horses found a place in the various management documents of the park and the agency assiduously cultivated equestrians.[21]

The park's recreational features were attractive to another constituency, bicyclists, who used the roads and later the trails for recreation, transportation, and exercise. When Golden Gate National Recreation Area was established in 1972, bicyclists made up only a small percentage of park users. The advent of mountain biking in the early 1980s revolutionized bicycling and created a new sport with much symbolic cachet. Mountain bike races became cultural events that expressed a heightened individualism, and the races helped build constituency. Mountain bikes were carefree and even anarchic, and they allowed baby boomers a taste of the freedom of their youth, symbolically located in the carefree and antiauthoritarian 1960s. To the generation raised on environmentalism, mountain bikes offered another advantage; they gave riders a claim to environmental responsibility as well.

At Golden Gate National Recreation Area, mountain bikes presented a new dimension to the ongoing questions of park and constituency management. Adjacent to Mount Tamalpais and with the state park in its legislative boundaries, Golden Gate National Recreation Area was close to the center of the mountain-biking universe; bikers quickly discovered the park and their presence challenged other users. Their new technology visibly redefined outdoor experience and etiquette; instead of being green, brown, and understated, the Generation-X mountain bikers seemed loud and adorned in bright blues, reds, and yellows. Mountain bikes freed cyclists from the roads, allowing them to ride the same trails where people rode horses or hiked. To those who had long enjoyed the trails, mountain bikers seemed to crash through the woods without respect for others. This situation led to the inevitable, a series of ongoing conflicts between users with equally valid claims to park trails but little tolerance for one another. Another clash of cultures in which the Park Service was to serve as referee began.

The hikers and horse riders quickly gained the upper hand in the hiker-biker wars, as they came to be called. Hikers and equestrians were a familiar constituency to the Park Service, and they tended to be far more sedate than bikers. They were quiet and moved at a pace to which the Park Service—and each other—were accustomed. Hikers and equestrians seemed to be of the age and class of the people who set park policy, who served on the CAC, and who attended meetings. Mountain bikers by contrast seemed out of control. They were young and raced around with abandon. The parallel between mountain bikers and Generation-X skateboarders, with their plaintive "skateboarding is not a crime" slogan was clear; the difference between constituencies was age and inclination. If hikers in their lightweight garb represented the back-to-nature ethos of appropriate technology that stemmed from the 1960s, best exemplified by Stewart Brand and the Whole Earth Catalogue, mountain bikers represented a new future, the embrace of technology to free the self in nature.[22]

It was little surprise that the Park Service found affinity with the hikers and equestrians. A little staid by the 1980s and unsure of itself during the Reagan-era assault on the federal bureaucracy, the Park Service held close its oldest friends, those who fashioned the park system and who prized it for its democratic purposes, which they casually translated as their own perspective. In a social and technological climate that tilted toward new values, the Park Service possessed few of the intellectual and cultural tools to sort out the new terrain. Despite its efforts to shape a future in urban parks, much of agency policy still focused on the crown jewels, the expansive national parks of lore. When faced with new and adamant constituencies, the Park Service relied on its past. Only its old friends, the ones who had always saved it, could bring the agency back from the morass into which it appeared to slide.[23]

Golden Gate National Recreation Area was different, a test case for the development of a new park ideal, and the existing formulas did not apply as well with the regional neighbors of the Bay Area. The tensions that the hiker-biker conflict created illustrated one of the primary issues that always seemed to return to haunt park managers: at Golden Gate National Recreation Area, the Park Service continuously faced the uncomfortable situation of having to divide up different kinds of uses on essentially qualitative, that is to say value-based, terms. Although the Park Service closely measured the impact of activities on park resources, the qualitative nature of decisions, the simple ranking of values, intruded. As long as American society accepted specific ideas about the hierarchy of values—when common culture asserted that a certain kind of experience was expected from national park areas—these distinctions were easily made and upheld. As cultural relativism, the idea that values were all the same, became one of the by-products of the 1960s upheavals, the certainty of earlier definitions became much harder to sustain. A national recreation area had many of the same features as a national park, but its purpose was different.

Public response revealed this fundamental difference in perception. By 1985, Mount Tamalpais had become a battleground between mountain bikers, the state park system, and other park users. The conflict spilled over into Golden Gate National Recreation Area. Harold Gilliam, a Bay Area columnist, agreed that bicycles should be allowed in Golden Gate National Recreation Area but advocated excluding mountain bikes from the designated wilderness in Point Reyes National Seashore. The Wilderness Act of 1964 banned mechanical traffic in wilderness areas, but the original 1965 U.S. Forest Service regulations defined "mechanical" as not powered by a living source. As a result, bicycling was permitted in wilderness areas, and bicycles did travel wilderness trails in Point Reyes National Seashore until 1985. That year, the Park Service followed a Forest Service revision of the rules that banned all "mechanical transport" from designated wilderness. The ruling set off a storm; administrative discretion ruled out an activity with twenty years of legal sanction, it seemed to biking advocates, precisely because the activity became more popular. The number of off-road bikes, as mountain bicycles were then called, changed the terrain, Gilliam averred, and bikers needed to abide by the rules and restrictions that governed public conduct.[24]

Gilliam's columns took the battle from the state park to Golden Gate National Recreation Area. Although his perspective reflected a legitimate interpretation of the statute, biking enthusiasts responded as if their very sport was under attack. Despite the official designation, "Point Reyes and Golden Gate National Recreation Area are not wilderness areas in any sense," observed June L. Legler of Oakland in a response. "You have mountain bikes confused with motorcycles," Bob Shenker pointed out in a sentiment typical of biking advocates. "We are not a group of oil drillers," another averred, linking the mountain bikers to the environmentalist ethic of the park.[25] The lines were clearly drawn; despite support for the bikers in the newspaper, the Park Service had uneasy relations with a constituency that was crucial—in its demography and future voting patterns—to the future of open space in the United States.

Most mountain bikers were law-abiding adults who enjoyed the sport as recreation, but like any technology that promoted speed and daring, the new bikes appealed to youth, especially young males, the prototypes of Generation X. They could be found careening down the roads of Marin County at breakneck speeds and soon were riding "single-track" trails and paths in Golden Gate National Recreation Area as well as Mount Tamalpais. The etiquette and culture of Generation X were different from those of the baby boomers and became a source of contention that illustrated the difficulties of managing a national park area in an urban setting. To many of the park's conventional users, mountain bikers did not respect nature or other users of the resource.

By the mid-1980s, however, bicycling had been reinvented as a widespread pastime. As cyclists spread through the population, a series of decisions cast their activity out of one of the primary open spaces in the Bay

Area. In 1987, the National Park Service ruled that all trails in national park areas were closed to bicycles unless park officials designated them as open. The Park Service had long been a centralized agency, and this ruling gave park administrators considerably greater leeway than before on an important policy issue, allowing them to respond to local needs but simultaneously creating inconsistency in the national park system. It left Golden Gate National Recreation Area in one of the circumstances that management plans did not address. Worse, two active and vital constituencies disagreed, and resource management and other guidelines did not offer a clear solution.

At Golden Gate National Recreation Area, in the heart of mountain-biking country, park staff made a concerted effort to fairly assess the impacts of different kinds of use. In a series of meetings and memos in early 1988, the natural resources staff assessed the impacts that they believed they could attribute to different kinds of use. Dogs chased and killed wildlife, marked territory and possibly affected wildlife behavior, bothered people, and left waste. Horses started new trails off of formalized trails, left manure on trails and in other use areas, accelerated erosion on and off trails, and deteriorated riparian areas. Bicycles and their riders widened and deepened minor social trails, made their own trails, caused ruts and water channeling in tire tracks, rode through endangered and rare plant habitats, scarred areas too steep for other users, and caused severe loss of top soil. Hikers and other pedestrians also created social trails, disturbed sensitive flora, initiated erosion, poached, and left garbage.[26] Assessing the collective impacts from a resource management perspective and regulating use presented an enormous challenge.

Local discretion forced the Park Service's hand. Despite the efforts to broadly assess impact, the park remained a captive of its most powerful constituencies, the environmental groups that had been its mainstay since PFGGNRA helped found the park in 1972. These were the single most consistent supporters of the park, the ones who backed it year after year. After three years of assessing possible programs, the Park Service followed history and the tacit inclinations of park personnel. In the Marin Trail Use Designation Environmental Assessment Staff Report of October 24, 1990, Golden Gate National Recreation Area banned bicycles from all but designated trails in the Marin Headlands and Point Reyes National Seashore. The response was entirely predictable. Protests abounded. Bikers and their friends howled at the ruling, seeing it as class and cultural warfare. "Dog owners: the GGNRA staff plans to restrict you next! Help us stop them!" read one mountain biker broadside that sought to identify other constituencies threatened by the ruling. Mountain bikers thought that they were persecuted by a confederation of older, wealthier users. "Some hikers and equestrians can't get used to a new user group," observed Tim Blumenthal of the International Mountain Bicycling Association (IMBA), an organization formed in 1988 in Bishop, California, to promote responsible riding. "Bikes go faster and are more colorful, so it's easy to see how they can be unsettling." Statistics failed to demonstrate to Blumenthal's satisfaction that mountain bikes were hazards on the trails, and he could not accept the restrictions. The lines were drawn, as clearly as ever.[27]

The resolution of this issue became another question of politics instead of management by objective. Again the letters poured in; again a combination of self-interest, enlightened and otherwise, and concern for the condition of the resource dominated the perspectives. Hikers felt threatened by mountain bikers, and many of those who sought limits on bicycle use were people of power and influence. Their complaints addressed to the park usually were forwarded to U.S. representatives, senators, and other political leaders. Hikers also used bicycles in the park. Many of their letters supported the new policies but asked for specific exceptions for the writer's favorite biking trail. Equally as many angry letters from bike advocates reached the agency, and the ban put the Park Service in the position of siding with one constituency against another, anathema in the complicated politics of the Bay Area.[28]

The sheer volume of concern forced Golden Gate National Recreation Area officials to reevaluate their policy. After long and tortured deliberations, in December 1992, the final mountain bike policy at GGNRA was announced. The policy kept much of the park closed to mountain bikes. In the view of Jim Hasenauer, IMBA president, the final policy was "virtually unchanged" from the original proposal. "It cuts existing riding opportunities by half," he observed. The Park Service offered its decision as a compromise, but many among the mountain bikers regarded the policy as a victory of privilege over ordinary people. Although PFGGNRA and the Park Service showed that 64 percent of the 72.6 miles of trails in Golden Gate National Recreation Area were open to biking, mountain bikers pointed out that every single-track trail, the narrow tracks mountain bikers favored, in the park was closed to them. Mountain bikers thought that the rules discriminated against them; they were even excluded from some fire roads that NPS trucks traveled, eliminating even the widest trails within the park. The Park Service countered by pointing to erosion that bikes caused on fire roads. "There's no good reason to ban bikes in the GGNRA," Hasenauer exclaimed, rallying the mountain-biking constituency.[29]

The different sides had become polarized during the fray, and the final policy, an attempt at compromise, satisfied no one. Golden Gate National Recreation Area and Mount Tamalpais evolved into the "most extreme mountain biking conflict ever," Gary Sprung, IMBA communications director, recalled a decade after the scrape. "It was ironic that it happened in the birthplace of mountain biking." The Bicycle Trails Council of Marin (BTCM), which in 1989 organized volunteer mountain bicycle patrols to help educate bikers in Mount Tamalpais State Park and also developed a "Trips for Kids" program to take inner-city children on bicycle trips, took the lead in battling the new policy. Working with IMBA, the Bicycle Trails Council of the East Bay, and other bicycling organizations, BTCM spearheaded a lawsuit that charged that the "Designated Bicycles Routes Plan" violated the National Environmental Policy Act (NEPA) and the Golden Gate National Recreation Area authorizing act. According to the suit, the decision was reached with insufficient public involvement and did not meet the demands of statute, and it requested an injunction to prevent implementation of the plan. The contention of the suit was rejected by the courts, reaffirming that, in a legal sense, there is no significant difference between a national park and a national recreation area.[30]

The mountain-biking community was split into three broad categories: radical riders who flouted the system, mainstream riders who sought to work within the system, and bikers who engaged in other activities and sought to bridge gaps between the different groups. Responses to the park policy varied according to each group's political stance. Angry cyclists cut "guerrilla trails," unauthorized paths through areas that the park designated as off-limits to cyclists. The pinnacle of this activity was the "New Paradigm Trail," a trail initiated in 1994 that was an overtly political statement. It was built in secret without government authorization and kept hidden from all but those in the mountain-biking community. Cyclists used the trail for two or three years until Marin Municipal Water District discovered and destroyed it. The trail became a cause célèbre for Bay Area cyclists, who regarded its development as civil disobedience and its destruction as perfidy. Wilderness Trail Bikes, which built its own bicycles, had been involved in bicycle advocacy since the beginning of fat tire bicycling. The company issued a widely reproduced broadside that championed the cyclists' cause, arguing for a strong relationship between cycling and environmental ethics.[31]

The New Paradigm Trail was guerrilla theater as well as a bike trail; the energy, enthusiasm, and clearly articulated perspective of its advocates signaled a constituency that the Park Service could and likely should have cultivated. The link between cyclists and environmentalism offered a new and potentially powerful constituency for the Park Service, but the agency and its friends rejected the concept. In response, the Sierra Club joined the agency against the renegade mountain bikers, further polarizing the situation and alienating mountain bikers. Although the bicycling groups lost their lawsuit against the park, the implications for park management were clear.[32] At Golden Gate National Recreation Area, the Park Service could expect challenges from activity constituencies it chose not to accommodate. Anywhere in the park system such a situation presented a political risk, but in the politics of the Bay Area, its dimensions were accentuated.

The mountain-biking situation represented the limits of policy. In part because the GMP did not address bicycling and in part because mountain bikers did not form the kinds of groups that other constituencies did, the agency could not bring enough mountain bikers into the process to achieve the kind of buy-in that made planning a success at Golden Gate National Recreation Area. Even though Commissioner Rich Bartke remembered the mountain bike issue as a "simple decision of what roads and trails could be specified for bike use by the Superintendent under national park policies without damaging the resource," the tension continued. Unlike the conservation and environmental groups and even the kennel clubs, mountain bikers did not respond to the invitations to participate that the agency offered. Their reticence and the close ties between the Park Service and mountain-biking opponents left the cyclists outside the loop. "After four public hearings, two-thirds of the park's roads and trails were designated for mountain biking," Bartke remembered. "Most bikers accepted that. A handful continued their polemics, to little effect."[33] Some mountain bikers were happy outside the system; they could engage in Edward Abbey–like anarchism, challenging the system in a sophomoric manner without any responsibility for the results. But the disintegration of relationships meant that the issue continued in an adversarial fashion, a less than optimal result.

The Park Service felt the need to sanction only one activity other than mountain biking that took place in the park, hang gliding. This new sport resembled mountain biking, for its genesis came from new technologies and seemed to the Park Service to flout the conventions of the park system. Like mountain biking, hang gliding had a sense of reckless individual daring about it. It too could be seen as irreverent and maybe even disrespectful of the park and the values for which it stood. Hang gliding was also dangerous; fliers strapped in metal-framed contraptions with brightly colored fabric wings ran downhill and caught a favorable wind that carried them out over the ocean. They sailed down in front of the sandstone cliffs at Fort Funston, angling for a landing on the beach; sometimes they reached it. In comparison with another similar activity the Park Service long sanctioned, rock climbing, hang gliding seemed arbitrary. When a rock climber fell, it usually resulted from his or her own shortcoming; when a hang glider got into trouble, mere fate often seemed the cause. Although legal and permissible, hang gliding required the deployment of agency resources in case of accident or emergency. It had been forbidden in national forest wilderness by the Forest Service's 1984 policy statement, establishing a precedent for barring the activity from the park. After considerable protest, the Park Service negotiated restrictions with hang-gliding associations, yielding to their needs but exacting promises that the activity would be run safely and that the organizations would police their own members. By 1987, the process worked so well that in plans for East Fort Baker, the Park Service proposed that sailboarders, windsurfers, sea kayakers, and other water sports organizations be enticed into similar arrangements.[34]

Golden Gate National Recreation Area also experienced another kind of use with the potential to impact park values. The military retained a close relationship that included a significant number of ongoing uses of the park for training purposes. Initially, the military continued its activities as if there had been no transfer of Presidio and other former military land. Although military activities usually remained low profile during the six years that followed the park's establishment in 1972, some park officials found the prospect of a continuing military presence unnerving. In no small part, this tension resulted from the cultural struggle between antiwar advocates and aging veterans groups for the intellectual control of the former military lands. On June 17 and 18, 1978, several military branches staged a mock amphibious assault, MINIWAREX-78, also called Operation Surf and Turf, on the Marin Headlands. Two units, named the "Blue" and "Orange" forces, battled each other as visitors watched in astonishment. Park rangers warned some visitors on the headlands and restricted the movement of others. Although the event took place with both the consent and cooperation of the Park Service, the arrival of reserve units from the Marine Corps, the navy, the army, the National Guard, and the Coast Guard became a source of consternation. Most of the operation took place at night in the Rodeo Valley subdistrict. By midmorning the following day, the operation was over and the Park Service reported little damage to its property.[35]

Yet cultural differences persisted, making it hard for the NPS to implement its objectives. "To me, the tensions that existed were based upon the 'culture' of the two agencies involved," Rich Bartke remembered. "Park Service employees were professional 'nice guys' who were trained to negotiate, and cooperate. The military, particularly Army brass, were trained 'tough guys' whose mission was to take and control land, and who took no heed of public opinion other than congressional appropriations committees." In the aftermath of Operation Surf and Turf, Associate Regional Director John H. Davis decided that the time had come to "lay some ground rules" about military endeavors inside the park.[36] Clearly the relationship between the Park Service and the military had begun to change. At the inception of the park, the army and the other branches retained primacy in the relationship with the Park Service. As the decade ended, the Park Service no longer simply accepted a junior role and seemed willing to confront the military in new ways.

Military training operations continued inside park boundaries, in part in a spirit of cooperation and in part the result of the cold reality of the power disparity between the two organizations. The park encouraged the military to stay, "partly to help pay the bills," Bartke recalled, "and partly because the park was made up of former military bases whose cultural resources were deep in military history. The presence of uniforms on the former bases was seen as a real plus by many involved in park planning." This sentiment reflected only one point of view. Some NPS people were glad to still see uniforms, but many preferred uniforms to real soldiers with their real issues. In the recollection of one longtime park employee, "Manikins with uniforms might have been preferable as long as they could fire the salute cannon at 5:00."

Golden Gate National Recreation Area contained, reflected, and interpreted the military past through its operation of various former army posts. Also, each October a navy festival, Fleet Week, took place, which typically included an aerial demonstration by the Blue Angels, the service's flight demonstration team. The pattern of occasional land use also continued. In 1979, the Marin Headlands were closed for another amphibious landing exercise; in 1981 at Fort Cronkhite, intentional explosions and tear gas were used during training.[37] As late as 1999, the Marine Corps planned a landing at Baker Beach or Crissy Field, both heavily used by visitors. What had been military land in 1971 had become a park resource in 1999, and the Department of Defense had to seek a permit for its action. The Presidio Trust denied permission, but military use of the park continued to be one of the recurring issues at Golden Gate National Recreation Area.

The park also grandfathered in vestiges of the military era, including practices and other functions that existed before the founding of the park. East Fort Baker had long been used for Army Reserve functions. This activity continued until 2000, and the military's final departure was expected as the new century began. Officers' quarters remained in use at Fort Mason, its officers' club remained in service as late as December 1998, and the army chapel at the fort only closed its doors in 1997. Beginning in 1998, planning for the transformation of the central post of Fort Baker to park use became a major project of Golden Gate National Recreation Area and GGNPA.

Golden Gate National Recreation Area also contained numerous inholdings, areas of private property located within the park boundaries. These privately held lands were typically anathema to the Park Service, a source of management difficulty because owners could make individual decisions about their lands and could impact not only the experience of park visitors but in many circumstances the ecology, natural setting, and sometimes even the viability of portions of parks. In many situations, inholdings became the single most vexatious issue for park managers, the sole set of circumstances that many parks could not manage to their satisfaction.[38] But inholdings at Golden Gate National Recreation Area were less troublesome to managers than at parks without a recreational mission. In the Bay Area park, designed to accommodate many uses at the same time, the conflicts about landownership became a question of constituent needs and desires. Often, despite the diversity of their perspectives, inholders were less problematic than competing interest groups.

Golden Gate National Recreation Area surrounded perhaps the most unique inholding in the national park system, the Green Gulch Ranch, a Zen Buddhist retreat. The ranch had been the property of George Wheelwright III, the scion of a Massachusetts family who worked with Edwin Land on the invention of the Polaroid Land camera in 1948. Wheelwright and his wife, Hope, came to Marin County in 1945, bought the Green Gulch Ranch, and started a boy's riding school. They raised cattle, supplementing their income with money George Wheelwright earned by consulting. In 1966, they became involved in Synanon, a system for living founded by Chuck Dederich that showed remarkable success treating drug addicts. When Hope Wheelwright was stricken by cancer, her will included a gift of Green Gulch Ranch to Synanon. After her death, Dederich and Synanon planned to sell the lower portion of the ranch to raise money for another project, an eventuality that made Wheelwright rethink the bequest. In a complicated series of maneuvers, he and his attorney, Richard Sanders, were able to nullify the gift.[39]

After the nullification, Wheelwright sought an appropriate recipient for the ranch he loved. Determined to make a gift of the ranch, he considered many offers. At one point, he planned to give it to the local school district; but one of the school board members made what a close confidant of the Wheelwrights, Yvonne Rand, described as "uncharitable" comments about Wheelwright, and that arrangement came to an end. In another often told story, a group of Native Americans sought the property, but after a disagreement among themselves, they failed to sign the transfer papers. Soon after, Wheelwright departed on an extended trip, and Sanders was left to arrange the gift of the property. Sanders sought advice from a number of people involved in land conservation in the Bay Area. Both Huey Johnson, then the western region director of the Nature Conservancy and founder of the Trust for Public Land, and Stewart Brand of the Whole Earth Catalog suggested the San Francisco Zen Center. Suzuki Roshi, the founder and moving spirit behind the center, died in December 1971 after a brief illness, and his successor, Richard Baker, recognized the Green Gulch Ranch as the embodiment of Roshi's principles. Baker spearheaded a drive to purchase the ranch, which occurred with Johnson's guidance. In the end, the upper part of the ranch went to the Park Service for Golden Gate National Recreation Area and the lower part to the Zen Center. Wheelwright found the precepts of Buddhism appealing; the faith was, he often said, the rare major religion that "didn't make war on nonbelievers."[40] The only Zen Buddhist retreat inside a national park area in the United States, the Green Gulch Ranch became a fixture.

The Green Gulch Ranch represented an array of similar entities inside the park and once more illustrated the complicated precepts of management at Golden Gate National Recreation Area. More than at any traditional national park area, GGNRA staff spent their time managing constituencies of all kinds, meeting, discussing, negotiating, cajoling, responding, and otherwise seeking to shape the terms of discourse to reflect the values of the park system and its managers, the National Park Service. The degree of difficulty involved in this crucial endeavor was enormous. Even as the park moved from reactive response to planned, proactive initiative following the approval of the GMP in 1980, the pull of the vast number of constituencies and their desires remained the single most powerful influence on day-to-day park management.

The GMP gave the Park Service a set of plans, but even the formalized participatory planning process could not always yield the respect for its goals that the agency sought. The most tendentious question the agency faced remained the definition of the purpose of a national recreation area. Because GGNRA could truly be all things to all people all of the time, the most difficult task the Park Service faced was to define appropriate and inappropriate uses of the park. In its interaction with constituent groups, the agency repeatedly encountered individuals and organizations that could define their activity as recreation and muster political and often grassroots support for their perspective. In the age of weakening federal institutions that followed the election of 1980, the realities of this situation prompted the Park Service in sometimes uncomfortable ways. Even statutory obligations and agency policies such as resource management did not always provide the Park Service with cover from the desires of constituents. With the diminishing clarity of mission for the agency as a whole and with the least clearly defined category of area, the managers at Golden Gate National Recreation Area grappled with the purpose of their park on a daily basis.

By the mid-1970s, the Park Service faced challenges to its discretion on a number of fronts. In the decade since George Hartzog Jr. installed the tripartite management structure that defined each park as natural, historic, or recreational, the Park Service lost considerable autonomy. New federal legislation and a changing cultural climate hamstrung the agency. NEPA, the Endangered Species Act, and other pieces of environmental legislation curtailed agency management prerogative, compelling the Park Service to document and defend its actions while proscribing specific patterns of management. The Park Service had counted on its friends in the public since the days of Stephen T. Mather, but the cultural revolution of the late 1960s created and empowered a more critical public. Private citizens and even organizations such as the National Parks and Conservation Association increasingly criticized agency policy and opposed decisions. Dependent on its public, the Park Service needed to reevaluate its policies and practices.[41]

Even as the agency undertook such measures, the very nature of what constituted a national park was changing. The Park Service remained ambivalent about recreation but increasingly found it thrust upon the agency. It ultimately emerged victorious from its battle with the Bureau of Outdoor Recreation during Stewart Udall's tenure as secretary of the interior in the 1960s, but in winning made itself the federal agency in charge of recreation by default. This triumph yielded a problem: having claimed recreation as its turf and having successfully battled to prove it, the agency had to do something with it. Recreation had been an afterthought since the creation of Boulder Dam Recreation Area, now Lake Mead National Recreation Area, in 1936, and as late as 1970, remained peripheral to main currents of agency policy. As the nation grappled with urban uprisings, and empowered constituencies, and as the need for outdoor space of all kinds became dire, recreation finally demanded the agency's full attention.

This combination of factors made the tripartite management that George Hartzog embraced obsolete. The Park Service had lost much of its power with its supporters and a great deal of its cachet. It needed to prove its worth to its old friends, make new ones, and maintain its relationships with Congress. The Park Service recognized that the faux wilderness parks were more a part of its past than its future and embraced the urban mission at the core of the "parks to the people, where the people are" ethos when it found itself with a large recreational component among its parks. Policy had to respond, and the codification of the three management books into one, in which all park areas were governed by the same doctrine, followed. The agency maintained flexibility by allowing management by zone within parks, so that areas that had obvious primary values could be managed in accordance with those features.

At Golden Gate National Recreation Area, the new mandate contributed to a change in the park's management philosophy. Despite its many natural attributes, Golden Gate had been managed as recreational space since its establishment. The new directives demanded more comprehensive management of the park, much more attention to resource management, and far greater cognizance of the difference between various areas of the park. Master planning at GGNRA quickly reflected the decentralized management by zone at the core of the new program. The park was spread out and diverse, and no Park Service policy better suited it than the ability to divide GGNRA into discrete areas and manage it accordingly. The new program simultaneously increased the importance of Golden Gate National Recreation Area and helped create a management structure that reflected its needs. The end to the isolation of the recreational category helped prepare the park for its role as a premier urban national park area.

Thus, the remarkable public interest—indeed investment—in the park also yielded great benefits. The uproar could pillory the Park Service, its managers, their policies and plans, and even statutes; it could just as easily back them against all manner of outside threats. In the complicated and sometimes precarious management situation in the Bay Area, the Park Service experienced and recognized circumstances that could work for and against it. The agency's remedy—planning and the implementation of its results—helped create the basis of ongoing management by principle and goal. In as many ways as the variety of constituencies challenged the park, they supported its goals with equal vigor.

CHAPTER SIX

Natural Resource Management
in a National Recreation Area

Among the many obligations of the Park Service at Golden Gate National Recreation Area, natural resource management is remarkable for the incredible array of responsibilities it encompassed and for the vast amount of time and attention it required. The park's wide expanse, different natural and built settings, myriad purposes, and sheer unwieldiness compelled a series of connected yet simultaneously discrete patterns of management. The park contained diverse natural features, including more threatened and endangered species than Yosemite, coastal and underwater resources, and typical natural resources such as scenic vistas and shorelines. Conventional management issues and themes such as visitor impact, grazing, and exotic species demanded constituency management. The unique array of features that the park encompassed compelled a broader approach to natural resource management than was typical in other similar park areas as well as more sophisticated planning to accommodate park constituencies.

Natural resource management at Golden Gate National Recreation Area became the boldest attempt in federal history to manage nature in an urban context. Unlike the large national parks in remote areas, at Golden Gate National Recreation Area the Park Service had little control over the impact of people on natural resources. The many park holdings created contradictory responsibilities. Just as accommodating diverse constituencies involved persuading the public to see the virtues of the park in new ways, natural resource management demanded sensitivity to public needs as well as to the physical environment. Compliance with the statutes that governed agency practice loomed equally large. Golden Gate National Recreation Area seemed to contain everything: open spaces that included wildland with little evident human impact and recreational space, urban flora, exotic species, beaches, marshes, tide pools, the ocean, grasslands and grazing, and the complicated impact of people on land and water. Any form of management was a daunting task, one that required both compliance with regulations and an effort to persuade the public of the value of the goals that underpinned policy.

Finding a balance between use and protection became the defining goal of natural resource management at Golden Gate National Recreation Area. The Park Service historically erred on the side of protection, but this orientation proved a frustrating task in a park devoted to use. The natural features that the Park Service typically preserved were only part of a much greater integrated whole at Golden Gate National Recreation Area. As a result of the park's national recreation area designation, the public did not always recognize justification for restricting use anywhere in GGNRA. No single category illustrated the complications of Golden Gate National Recreation Area better than natural resource management.

The difference between a national recreation area and a traditional national park, and the public's perception of their different purposes, again intruded not only on the process of making decisions about natural resources but equally on the assessment of the value of those resources. Even after recognition of the park's significance as a natural resource in 1988, when Golden Gate National Recreation Area received the designation of International Biosphere Reserve from the United Nations, the historic distinctions between categories of areas in the park system still influenced perception if not policy. Despite a generation of managing all park units under the same policies, park managers still reacted to a resource management issue in an urban park in a different way than they might at one of the traditional national parks.

Management questions at Golden Gate National Recreation Area were intrinsically tied to questions of use in a manner that would have shocked park managers at Yellowstone or Glacier National Parks. At the recreation area, the Park Service engaged in a delicate balancing act within the constraints created by an active and powerful community. Golden Gate National Recreation Area managed more people and their impact on natural resources than any other park unit in the system. The consequences of the many kinds of daily use, such as running, bicycling, dog walking, and countless other activities, combined with the mandates of natural resource management required great attention.

The transformation of the legal structure in which parks operated catapulted resource management to a position of greater importance in the national park system following World War II. During the first three decades of the Park Service's existence, resource management had been an uneven and sometimes haphazard process. Prior to the 1940s, the agency's primary concern had been constructing facilities to accommodate its growing constituency. Landscape architects played an enormously important role in the Park Service during this time, and their efforts culminating in "parkitecture," the protoenvironmental design that characterized New Deal construction in the parks. Beginning in 1945, the Park Service moved toward more integrated park management, using scientific principles as the basis for management decisions, and capitalized on the availability of newly minted college graduates to professionalize its staff.

Science and scientists became increasingly significant to the Park Service and its direction. The Leopold Report of 1963 solidified the position of scientific management in the agency, giving the discipline of ecology a much greater claim on policy making. As the 1960s continued, the Park Service became much more interested in managing natural and cultural resources, and by the following decade, legislative changes such as the National Environmental Policy Act (NEPA) and the Endangered Species Act of 1973 added legal obligations to its administrative responsibilities in resource management.[1] By the time Golden Gate National Recreation Area was established in 1972, the agency had a full-fledged mission in natural resource management, policies to govern its actions, and clearly defined institutional responses to categories of issues.

The development of Golden Gate National Recreation Area paralleled the increasing sophistication of resource management and the sometimes cumbersome weight of new statutory and administrative responsibilities. Unlike earlier parks, Golden Gate National Recreation Area developed its policies in close association with the demands of a post-NEPA society. After NEPA, environmental impact statements and other mechanisms to permit public oversight of agency functions became an integral part of the management terrain. In resource management, as in every other area of park endeavor, the agency enjoyed less leeway at Golden Gate National Recreation Area. In the Bay Area, the Park Service managed in close concert with the public, other levels of government, and other federal agencies. While this diminished the autonomy that park managers long enjoyed elsewhere, it also created a strong basis for cooperation with surrounding entities.

The development of natural resource management at Golden Gate National Recreation Area mirrored other park practices. Initially, the Park Service reacted to the demands of its many constituencies. Between 1972 and 1978, the agency collected data to support planning. The process yielded insight, shaped agency perspectives, and left a clear impression of the community's goals and values. In this context, the Park Service could create a resource management plan even as it planned and discussed the general management plan. The two documents sprang from the same sources. Between 1978 and 1982, in a second phase that paralleled other park developments, the Park Service moved to create a full-fledged natural resource management plan. Following its approval in 1982, the agency implemented comprehensive plans to manage the many park resources, running headlong into the diverse values of its communities and the new demands of a rapidly changing society. Planning became an important baseline, but a constant redefining process followed, in which the park redesigned management policies in an effort to assuage constituencies.

Although natural and cultural resource management at Golden Gate National Recreation Area were intrinsically linked, the agency separated their management functions out of necessity. In part as a result of the patterns of agency management and equally because of the fundamental diversity of resources and the ungainly sprawl from Marin County to San Mateo County, centralized administration of resources was unfeasible. The park could plan at the macro level, but decisions had to play out in a local context in a manner that resembled the early U.S. Forest Service more than the Park Service.[2] The sheer variety of resources and concomitant concerns mitigated against a parkwide natural resource management strategy and encouraged the development of a grassroots autonomy peculiar to its situation.

Perhaps the single most difficult task at Golden Gate National Recreation Area was trying to grasp the park's broad and various dimensions and finding a way to categorize them for management purposes. The process mirrored the pattern established earlier at the park; as the planners forging the GMP listened to the public, they learned a great deal about natural resource management needs as well. At the same time, the planning process articulated the park's general goals about natural resources. In 1975, the first studies that attempted to catalog the park's attributes were released. By 1977, a new document, Assessment of Alternatives for the General Management Plan for the Golden Gate National Recreation Area and Point Reyes National Seashore, began to establish patterns that could become practice at the park. As in other areas of park management, the agency determined that a multifaceted park needed different management tactics and techniques in different areas.[3]

The first Natural Resource Management Plan (NRMP), approved in 1982, typified the tension between the park as a series of interconnected entities and as discrete units managed semi-independently. Self-definition was crucial. "Most natural resource problems," the report continued, "have never been addressed." That succinct statement described the promise and the problem of natural resource management at Golden Gate National Recreation Area. The park had a natural resource history that in many ways ran counter to the experience of the Park Service. The circumstances demanded a strategy that simultaneously defined, assessed, organized, and presented a plan for management.[4] Building off the GMP's structure, the natural resource management plan reflected almost a decade of collecting information, responding to situations in the park, and listening to the public.

The plan was designed to promote the rehabilitation of Golden Gate National Recreation Area's ecosystems. Natural resource specialist Judd Howell's introduction to the NRMP described the document as an action plan, a guide to restore, conserve, and protect the park's natural resources. Only scientific research could serve as the basis for making decisions, the report averred, and the park lacked sufficient data about its resources. The report pointed to academics and outside institutions as the source for much of that baseline data. The next major natural resource need was a program to monitor changes in natural resources. The report envisioned that park staff would accomplish much of this day-to-day work, collecting data and monitoring specific situations. Combined with outside studies, the collected data could be used to achieve the third objective, active natural resource management.[5]

Understanding the park's many and varied resources required systematic division of parklands into categories that could be thought of as separate but interrelated entities. The NRMP began with the divisions created in the General Management Plan, focused on the natural resource zones, and used them as a template for managing nature in the park. The division into zones sorted landscapes first by use. An Intensive Landscape Management Zone, where exotic vegetation predominated, included the park's southern parts. A Natural Appearance Subzone, encompassing Ocean Beach, Fort Funston, Lands End, Baker Beach, and Rodeo Lagoon picnic area, offered a subset in which vistas were a primary value, but intensive management was prescribed for stabilization of the sand dune system. A Biotic Sensitivity Subzone, comprising the shoreline, ocean and underwater resources, and stream courses and riparian areas, complicated geographic organization.

An Urban Landscape Subzone, constituting the park's most heavily trafficked areas, places such as Crissy Field, Fort Mason, Fort Baker, the Fort Barry parade ground, and the developed area of Stinson Beach, illustrated the most comprehensive human impacts. The Pastoral Landscape Management Zone, comprising the Northern Olema Valley, revealed the setting and history of rural endeavor in the Bay Area. A Natural Landscape Management Zone that included the Marin Headlands, most of the Stinson Beach area, and the southern Olema Valley, allowed for the protection of the kinds of vistas that hikers and other recreational users most favored. Special Protection Zones, areas with legislative or special administrative recognition of exceptional natural qualities such as Muir Woods and Fort Point, where the intertidal ecosystem was of considerable interest, also were grouped separately. The division translated into the difference between the urban landscapes of San Francisco and semirural Marin County. With these distinctions, the NRMP created plans for specific areas within the scope of the overall direction established for Golden Gate National Recreation Area.[6]

The NRMP initiated management by definition, a process of using categorical subdivisions as the means to create flexible policy at Golden Gate National Recreation Area. Natural resource management plans at most parks treated resources as parts of a whole. At Golden Gate National Recreation Area, this strategy simply did not reflect existing conditions. The enormous population pressure on the park, the diversity of the many units, the differences in topography and terrain, and the fundamental ecological, cultural, and social differences demanded new management considerations.

Management by definition offered clear and proactive strategies, defined by the needs of the resource and often demonstrated by scientific research. The plan proposed to guarantee the general protection of resources by assessing, monitoring, and implementing policy based on information collected at the park. The impact of visitors on resources, erosion, the protection of water quality, and the close observation of development to prevent severe impact became the basis of policy. Plant management proceeded on a localized basis; decisions for each zone were based on the needs of that specific area. In one instance in 1982, animals grazed on seventeen leased tracts in Marin County, an activity that was only appropriate in the formerly pastoral areas north of the Golden Gate Bridge. Open space in the Marin Headlands or in the city of San Francisco clearly would not have been appropriate for such a use. In addition to proscribing strategy, the plan made possible localized decisions about issues such as pesticide use and prescribed burning, confirming grassroots needs as the overarching factor in decision-making.

The drawbacks to a policy of management by definition stemmed from the same sources as its advantages. Localized management goals and themes worked against integrated management of the natural resources of the entire park. Different areas were treated in a discrete manner; natural resources were separated from cultural resources and other issues. The division into categories compelled a hierarchical ranking of resources, creating priorities and sometimes obscuring and even devaluing other features of the same land. These rigid forms of management for specific purposes ran the risk of limiting professional and public perceptions of individual park areas.

Despite the best intentions of park managers, resource management retained a haphazard quality. In some areas, remarkable omissions jumped out. In 1980, the park lacked a fire management plan, an essential part of the program at most major park areas by this time. The threat of catastrophic fire from built-up fuel loads had become a growing concern, and the Park Service scrambled to prepare for the consequences. Golden Gate National Recreation Area, a likely candidate for such a document because of the devastating history of fires in the Bay Area, had not even begun the research. The oft-repeated phrase that the park managed people rather than resources seemed an accurate description of the state of resource management after nearly a decade of Park Service presence.[7]

When the agency instituted resource management programs, the same sort of local resistance emerged that had faced every other plan, program, idea, or concept put forward by park administrators. Particularly when the plans involved natural resource protection, the Park Service encountered a local public that often regarded use as a higher value. Even the process of collecting information and monitoring resources could engender local hostility. Constituency building and agency mandate clashed. The Park Service remained in the complicated position of seeking the support of people whose uses of the park were not always in concert with agency goals, standards, and policies.

Notable successes were achieved with park programs for community stewardship and environmental restoration. At Wolfback Ridge, Milagra Ridge, and Oakwood Valley, the Park Service was able to fuse its values with those of the public in community stewardship programs that encouraged the public to regard the park's resources as their own. This approach bridged the eternal gap created by nomenclature designation; no matter what the park was labeled, when communities invested in the ecology of the park, the agency needed to do considerably less to persuade people of the value of resources. Restoration projects also benefited from the close attention. At places such as Serpentine Bluffs in the Presidio, ecological restoration re-created natural environments. Flora and wetlands throughout the park were part of a comprehensive program to restore park ecology.

In a variety of instances, including the removal of exotic species such as feral pigs and axis and fallow deer, the controversy over mountain biking, the reintroduction of the tule elk, and efforts to combat oil spills on the coast, the NRMP served as a set of guidelines that gave the Park Service a clear path to implement its goals. In each circumstance, the response of the public demanded refinement of agency values and indeed prerogatives, and the agency reassessed its planning and adroitly conceived of new and often parallel strategies that could be implemented with less resistance. In the process, it implemented goals and satisfied the constituencies it needed by accommodating their demands.

By the 1980s, exotic species management had become a flash point for the Park Service. The 1963 Leopold Report argued that the park system should preserve "vignettes of primitive America," and by the 1980s, the agency had a firm policy of ridding parks of exotic animals and plants. In most parks, such management took place quietly; the removal of tamarisk and other noxious plants typified the easiest kinds of exotic plant eradication. Few strongly identified with salt cedar or other opportunistic xeric plants. Animals provided a more complicated scenario, and eradication programs had a long and checkered history in the park system. The first eradication programs began as the 1930s ended. Burros at Death Valley National Monument were the first animals hunted by park rangers, establishing removal or eradication as the dominant policy for exotic species. During the following three decades, the standard established by the Leopold Report held. But the shift in American values and the increasing tendency of friends of the Park Service to question agency resource management decisions meant that by the middle of the 1970s, "burro shoots," the colloquial term for eradication by gunfire, came under scrutiny. Organizations such as the Fund for Animals (FFA) advocated other means of animal removal. Although the FFA succeeded in safely removing animals in some situations, hunting exotic species remained an integral part of natural resource management policy in the park system.[8]

The nature of exotic species in question often determined the response. The feral pigs of Marin County, "Marin's Huge, Hungry, Hairy Marauders," one newspaper headline called them, became the premier exotic species management question at Golden Gate National Recreation Area. European boars had first been brought to the Bay Area by William Randolph Hearst and others during the 1920s so that the wealthy landowners could hunt these exotic animals. As was the case with most stock introductions, a few of the animals escaped, and over time, communities of escaped boars spread throughout north-central California. No one knew how the animals migrated from Hearst's San Simeon grounds, but by 1970, feral pigs lived in nearly thirty counties in the area. They made their initial appearance in the Lagunitas Creek watershed between 1976 and 1980, where they were typically found on Marin Municipal Water District lands and on the slopes of Mount Tamalpais. Researchers determined that the core area, the base from which the pigs spread in Marin County, was located within a legislated fish and game reserve on state land. Until the early 1980s and the codification of the NRMP, Golden Gate National Recreation Area largely observed the pigs from a distance. They were a county problem or in some circumstances an issue for Point Reyes National Seashore, but with all the other concerns at the park, feral pigs were something that staff could treat secondarily.[9]

By 1982, however, some animals had left the slopes of Mount Tamalpais and entered the recreation area. Pigs presented a clear hazard; in the wild, they developed some of the traits of the famed Arkansas razorbacks, the feared hogs of American folklore. They had powerful tusks, were low to the ground, and moved very quickly while weighing as much as 300 pounds. They were "very strong, wild animals," Skip Schwartz of the Audubon Canyon Ranch observed. "Anything that can't get out of their way gets eaten." The pigs demolished landscapes, leading one park ranger to observe that the lands they covered looked like they had been plowed by a tractor. In one instance, the pigs rooted up most of the habitat of the Calypso orchid, an increasingly endangered plant. Pig populations could double in as little as four months, and they seemed to be everywhere in West Marin. In 1985, a motorist hit a 300-pound hog on Highway 1. The car was demolished, the driver escaped unhurt, and the pig had to be put to sleep.[10]

As feral pigs became a regional boogeyman, an eradication program was widely embraced. With every other agency that managed land in Marin County, including the Marin Municipal Water District (MMWD), the California Department of Parks and Recreation, which administered Mount Tamalpais State Park, and the Audubon Canyon Ranch (ACR), the Park Service forged a Memorandum of Understanding that was signed in 1985. The agencies agreed to a two-pronged approach to pig management. One goal, containment, was an attempt to keep the animals in existing terrain. During the next two years, the Park Service built a $90,000 fence on Bolinas Ridge in an attempt to confine the feral pigs. The other goal was extermination. The agencies agreed to hunt, trap, and otherwise eliminate the boars wherever they could find them and devised a set of rules to govern their interaction.[11]

The Park Service responded with special aggressiveness to the threat of resource destruction by feral pigs. In 1985, the agency applied for a $104,000 grant from the San Francisco Foundation through GGNPA to trap and eliminate the pigs and to rehabilitate the lands they damaged. One year later, more than sixty pigs, estimated at about 20 percent of the park's population, had been killed within the park, and the beginning of comprehensive management of this exotic species began.[12]

As in many similar situations in the national park system, feral exotic species established a toehold, and while the agency had the will to dislodge the animals, they lacked both the resources and the ability to control what happened beyond park boundaries. As a result, Golden Gate National Recreation Area could contain feral pigs, could even slow or stop the growth of their numbers within the park, but could not genuinely expect to eradicate them or even under most conditions entirely rid the park of them.

Fallow and axis deer provided another of the endless series of tests of the principles of natural resource management, for these introduced species enjoyed some public support. The fallow deer was a native of the Near East; the axis deer came from Sri Lanka and India. Eight fallow deer and eleven axis deer had been introduced by a surgeon/rancher, Millard "Doc" Ottinger, in 1947 and 1948. As did many introduced animals in the Americas, both species of deer successfully carved out an ecological niche at the expense of similar native species. By 1972, there were at least 300 fallow deer and 350 axis deer within the Point Reyes National Seashore. As long as hunting continued, the nonnative deer population remained in stasis. When Point Reyes National Seashore was created, followed by Golden Gate National Recreation Area, and finally, when the Park Service acquired numerous dairy farms in the Olema Valley, hunting came to an end. The number of fallow and axis deer mushroomed after their primary predator, humans, gave up the chase, and species populations proliferated. The Park Service faced a crisis.[13]

Point Reyes National Seashore had begun an exotic deer management program in 1973 that sent rangers to hunt the species. Facing criticism, the Park Service held a series of hearings in 1976 that addressed exotic deer removal. The comments revealed little public consensus, and the agency proceeded with an elimination plan. Between 1977 and 1983, the park eliminated

576 fallow deer and 227 axis deer. In 1981, the peak year for hunting exotic deer, 440 animals were taken. Before that year, rangers necropsied and field-dressed each kill, requiring an investment of workpower that slowed the take. Beginning in 1981, rangers shot deer and departed without removing the carcass or, in some cases, even checking to see if the deer was killed or wounded. In others, the agency dressed the deer and gave the carcasses to local Miwok people or other agencies that could use them as food.[14]

California State Fish and Game officials, pursuing an agenda of their own, challenged park policy. They rejected the NPS explanation, trumpeted their own management policy as a better alternative, and attempted to marshal public support to affect Golden Gate National Recreation Area policy. The state agencies still harbored some resentment toward the Park Service's acquisition of the remarkable array of resources that became Golden Gate National Recreation Area, especially after 1978, when Proposition 13's aftermath crippled the state's ability to finance programs. Only powerful support for park goals among organizations such as PFGGNRA allowed the Park Service to implement its plans, but even successful implementation did not end efforts by California Fish and Game to influence the park.[15]

The Park Service proceeded with its policy, but successful culling of the deer herds depended on a range of factors, including budget, weather, and workpower. In the early 1990s, fallow and axis deer again jumped to the forefront at Golden Gate National Recreation Area. Angry letters about agency actions dotted the letters to the editor columns of Marin County newspapers after a management plan for the reintroduction of the native tule elk recommended the exotic deer's elimination. In 1992, a headline in the *Point Reyes Light* read, "Rangers Again Shooting Deer in Seashore: Some Carcasses Left to Rot," putting the Park Service in the position of justifying the twenty-year-old practice of hunting as well as the more noxious abandonment of carcasses.[16]

The Park Service continued with its policy, offering in 1993 to let the public monitor its activities. When the *Point Reyes Light* assessed Park Service actions, it found that the agency conducted four hunts beginning in summer 1993 and planned another for February 14, 1994. The choice of date was ominous, and the newspaper trumpeted the headline, "Valentine's Day Massacre of Exotic Deer Planned."[17] Adhering to the dictates of the natural resource management plan provoked an involved public.

Another natural resource management question, the presence of native and introduced predators, complicated relations with the public. The Park Service regarded predators as indicators of the ecosystem's health, and the growing prevalence of bobcats in the Marin Headlands meant that the Park Service needed a research program to track the species. The necessity to track other predators also became evident. The park was home to grey foxes, mountain lions, and coyotes as well, demanding baseline data to understand the predators, manage their population, and utilize their native instincts to further the goals of resource management. A memorandum of agreement with the state was the first step, followed by a research proposal to monitor and assess predators in the park.[18]

The Park Service also sought to reintroduce missing avian species to the park. An important step in this direction began in 1983 when three fledgling peregrine falcons were brought to a nest at Muir Beach. Peregrine falcons had been common in California until the use of pesticides spread. DDT especially affected the birds, thinning the shells of their eggs and limiting their reproductive capabilities. By the 1970s, few residents could recall seeing the falcons. At the end of the decade, the bird was listed as an endangered species. The Peregrine Fund's Santa Cruz Predatory Bird Research Group, which raised the birds from eggs, provided fledglings for the 1983 program. Within a few weeks, nine fledglings were nesting near Muir Beach, and another pair were installed at Point Reyes National Seashore. To further the reintroduction, the Park Service requested that the Federal Aviation Administration limit flights that passed over Muir Beach and Tennessee Cove in an effort to help the birds acclimate to the new location. The program continued until 1989, when park funding became unavailable.[19]

Golden Gate National Recreation Area provided a haven for a number of avian species, including a range of hawks and other raptors. The birds migrated north across the Golden Gate each year, providing a popular activity for regional bird-watchers. Both the National Wildlife Federation and the Audubon Society participated in annual counts. In 1983, the park began a volunteer raptor observation program based on the project statements in the NRMP. Woefully underfunded, the program received only $1,035.44 in the first year and slightly less during the second. In 1985, the Golden Gate Raptor Observatory was formed. This volunteer program, jointly sponsored by the Park Service and the Golden Gate National Park Association and financed with a $97,500 grant from the San Francisco Foundation, was designed to track the roughly 10,000 migratory raptors that crossed the Golden Gate between September and December of each year. From Hawk Hill, the hilltop of the abandoned Battery Construction no. 129 in the Marin Headlands, volunteer "hawk watchers" observed thousands of birds pass overhead. The birds were counted, and through a wildlife-oriented Volunteer in the Parks program, significant numbers were banded for future tracking. By 1986, the program made it possible to track the hawks as they migrated.[20]

The raptor program illustrated the results of the planning process and the Natural Resource Management Plan in dramatic ways. Before the program, bird-watching was a recreational hobby, but bird counting occurred in an idiosyncratic fashion, usually when interested people took the time to count birds during the fall. Using a project statement from the NRMP, Judd

Howell was able to integrate existing activities within park boundaries into agency goals. With the help of concerned activists such as Carter Faust, who counted hawks beginning in 1982, the Park Service was able to create support for agency goals, fit management objectives with public desires, and collect important baseline data to support future decision-making. It also inspired volunteers to undertake other related activities. In 1987, Buzz Hull, a volunteer raptor bander, initiated his own study of great horned owls of the Marin Headlands under the volunteer program's auspices. The Park Service embraced the project, clearing the way for Hull's research. Again the objectives of park managers and the public coincided in a way that benefited both.[21]

Other endangered, threatened, or unusual avian species benefited from the implementation of the natural resource management plan. The agency was able to monitor species such as Heermann's gull, first observed nesting in the United States on Alcatraz Island in 1980. Smaller than the more common western gull, Heermann's gull was common along the West Coast, but until the nesting pair were discovered on Alcatraz, the species had never been recorded as nesting outside of Mexico. Located near cell block 1 on the island, the gulls failed to breed in 1982. Disappointed staff observed that the absence of human interference in the area set aside for Heermann's gulls appeared to allow western gulls to multiply at their expense. Western gulls became the dominant population, but Heermann's gulls remained a visible presence. Black-crowned night herons, threatened in the Bay Area, pelagic cormorants, and common murres also found an opportunity to breed on Alcatraz Island.[22]

Plants, too, became part of the agency's NRMP. Beginning in the mid-1980s, the eucalyptus removal program became another of the countless hot issues that defined Golden Gate National Recreation Area. Again, a well-planned, professional natural resource management objective encountered the kind of resistance that typified NPS experience at the park. Public constituencies with an interest in the trees and increasingly suspicious of government agencies fought implementation. Despite the clarity of planning and policy and a preponderance of scientific data, the public saw the eucalyptus as a symbol of their region.

The eucalyptus, a native of Australia, came to California with the Gold Rush and American settlement. The popular tree was first noted in the Golden State in 1856. Because it grew quickly, it was a popular replacement for areas that had been clear-cut of redwoods and Douglas fir. Prized for its qualities as fast-spreading ground cover, and possible timber as well as its role as an insectrifuge, the eucalyptus became widely used. The army also valued the eucalyptus and planted countless trees between 1883 and 1910 in an attempt to "beautify" the windswept uplands of the Presidio. The trees were seen as ornamentals, as ground cover for scrub landscape, and as a windbreak to cut the fierce winds that made the scenic slopes of the Presidio almost inhabitable. As was often the case with transplants in the New World, the eucalyptus overwhelmed any competitors and spread wildly, becoming one of the dominant trees around the Golden Gate. They were so common that in the 1970s and early 1980s, the army initiated a removal program at the Presidio. As with other military decisions, the removal program was not subject to public comment, and the military cut its trees in relative quiet.[23]

For the Park Service, the terrain in which decision-making took place was a great deal more contested. During its first decade, Golden Gate National Recreation Area simply overlooked the eucalyptus. Park staff faced myriad issues with vocal publics, many of them far more pressing than the removal of exotic trees that had become so much a part of the regional landscape that few regarded them as nonnative. Although natural resource management documents always pointed out that the eucalyptus were intruders on the landscape, the Park Service did little more than nod toward the idea of removal. On its list of natural resource priorities in 1984, eucalyptus removal ranked fourth, along with broom grass and other exotics.[24]

In 1985, Thomas M. Gavin, plant ecologist in the Park Service's Western Region, brought the eucalyptus to the forefront of regional attention. "Every morning and evening, I stare at the eucalyptus groves which dot the landscape to the west of Highway 101," he observed in a widely circulated memo to the regional director, "and am confronted with the same question: as a principle natural resources management staff to the regional director, why have I not taken upon myself to recommend to him that we begin to remove this exotic species?" Gavin recognized that the Bay Area was a volatile place and any attempt to remove the trees was a guaranteed prelude to controversy, but agency policy dictated the removal of exotics. To initiate a program of removal meant negotiating the complicated social and cultural minefields of the Bay Area and especially Marin County.[25]

Gavin recognized that his memo had the potential to thoroughly disrupt the agency's practices in the Bay Area. The Park Service alone could not initiate a program, he believed, and the recommended scope and scale of removal—a total of 632 acres—stretched the imagination of park staff. Gavin sought to open up eucalyptus stands in both Golden Gate National Recreation Area and Point Reyes National Seashore to a Forest Service–style timber sale. Frankly controversial, the proposal presented a pragmatic option that eliminated the myriad problems of control as well as the immense fire hazard that eucalyptus presented. In Gavin's estimation, the Park Service could solve a difficult ecological management problem, have the solution pay for itself, and promote the overall ecological health of parklands. Park staff supported the proposal, seeing in it same ecological advantages as Gavin did. Only convincing the public remained; to successfully implement such an eradication program, the agency needed the public to understand its mission and goals. Gavin understood that the implementation of such a plan required time, energy, and capital to promote.[26]

The Park Service announced its removal plan on Arbor Day, a holiday set aside for the planting of trees, and inflamed opponents. A drawn-out public scrape followed, with advocates of the eucalyptus assailing the park at every opportunity. Some formed a group called Preserve Our Eucalyptus Trees (POET), devoted to stopping the Park Service. In a particularly outspoken opinion-editorial piece, San Rafael surgeon Ed Miller called the Park Service "short-sighted and downright foolish" for seeking to remove the trees. To Miller, trees—any trees—were better than a lack of them. Others countered his view, using ecological, scientific, and other rationale. Throughout 1986 and 1987, the issue remained controversial in Marin County, and as late as 1988, the Park Service trod lightly when it presented eucalyptus removal plans to the public. "No large eucalyptus trees will be removed," a typical announcement from 1988 revealed. "The program is part of an ongoing project to contain the eucalyptus groves within the area of the original plantings." The choice of language suggested the tentative nature of the agency's stance.[27]

When it came to public controversy, animal and plant removal could not compare to fire management. No activity had greater potential to make the public uncomfortable. In the Bay Area, the very mention of fire invoked the specter of the conflagration that swept the town in the aftermath of the Earthquake of 1906.[28] San Francisco ever after feared fire, a situation exacerbated by wildland fires in Berkeley in 1923 and Mill Valley in 1929 (and eventually in Oakland in 1991).

The National Park Service and the rest of the nation shared the same sentiments for better than fifty years. Fire was anathema to anyone who lived in open land; before sophisticated systems of pumping and the infrastructure to deliver water, fire was the single most threatening menace to communities and land managers alike. Generations of park rangers spent their careers viewing fire as the enemy. Beginning with the Leopold Report in 1963, the rise of scientific management in the park system sought to change that perception. In many parks, fire suppression created thick understories with enormous fuel loads around trees, a precondition of powerful and hard-to-stop forest fires. Many species of trees depended upon fire to initiate seed germination, a process blocked by the intense flames that resulted from long-term fire suppression. Some plants and trees also depended upon fire to keep competitors away. Science offered a new method to address this issue, the implementation of programs of prescribed burning. By the mid-1970s, the Park Service began such programs in more than a dozen parks, and in some wildland parks allowed a policy of letting natural fires, typically started by lightning, burn themselves out without human intervention.[29]

At Golden Gate National Recreation Area, fire management began slowly and quietly. Controlled "Let Burn" policies remained controversial, and in an urban area with a history of fire such as that in the San Francisco Bay Area, any talk of permitting fires to burn received a predictably quick and negative response. Fire suppression created an equally dangerous situation, and despite the knowledge that the region would fear any program of controlled burning, the agency quietly began one. As the planning process yielded the management plans, Judd Howell, instrumental in Golden Gate National Recreation Area's development of natural resource planning, studied fire management in the park's coastal plant communities as part of his master's degree program. He served as the point person for scientific management, organizing meetings to discuss strategy and goals, planning a daylong workshop for other interested agencies, and generally promoting the fire concept. Howell temporarily left the park to undertake Ph.D. work at the University of California, Davis. When he returned in 1983, he implemented a fire management program as research for his doctoral dissertation. Howell's work influenced park policy. The Natural Resource Management Plan noted the need for a fire management program. Doug Nadeau, chief of the Division of Resource Management and Planning, advocated such a program, informing the general superintendent that fire management presented "the most effective and economical way of restoring and maintaining the park's vegetation communities in a desirable condition."[30]

Prescribed burning had numerous advantages as a management tool. It helped reduce the accumulated fuel load, an ongoing danger to resources and people. This benefit was particularly important because, as a result of the combination of Proposition 13 and the Watt administration at the Department of the Interior, neither the California State Parks Department nor the National Park Service possessed the workpower to effectively fight major conflagrations. Prescribed burning was a small step toward lessening the danger of extensive wildfire compounded by built-up fuel loads. In addition, prescribed fire helped clear exotic plant species, making room for native plants and restoring habitat for species such as the tule elk.[31] From a manager's perspective, prescribed burning was good science and good policy.

As Golden Gate National Recreation Area moved toward putting its fire management program in place, the concept of managed fire received negative local publicity. High winds and greater than expected quantities of dry brush pushed a prescribed wilderness burn in Point Reyes National Seashore out of control. Before the fire was contained, it burnt fifty acres more than anticipated. Because the burn took place within a wilderness area, the Park Service response was limited by law. Wilderness designation forbade mechanized equipment, and the entire fire crew consisted of six men with hand tools. They could not successfully contain the spread of the fire.[32] Although the event did no lasting damage to either the land or the concept of managed fire, it did put a segment of the general population on alert for subsequent park endeavors.

Marin County became the initial focus of fire management programs. In March 1984, the Park Service informed nearby property owners that small-scale prescribed burning would commence the following month. A 1.5-acre research burn in Oakwood Valley near the Tennessee Valley Road was the initial endeavor. The fire was designed to provide information about fuel-load reduction, the response of eucalyptus to fire, and seed germination of plants. April was chosen because the grass remained wet and the danger of the fire's spread was low.[33] As the program became an integral part of park strategy, the Park Service worked to keep the local community informed.

Developing a fire strategy for the San Francisco portions of the park offered another of the murky situations for which Golden Gate National Recreation Area had become renowned. The Park Service and the city and county of San Francisco had never entered into an agreement about firefighting within the park. The city and county fire departments always responded to calls within park boundaries but had no obligation to continue the practice. The Park Service also relied on the Presidio Fire Department at Forts Mason, Baker, Barry, and Cronkhite. As the Park Service contemplated specific fire planning, this question demanded resolution. Although prescribed burns were unlikely except under stringently controlled situations in the city and even though the fire departments treated the park as their obligation, the lack of an agreement posed an issue for the park.[34]

The Park Service enacted comprehensive fire management guidelines in 1983. In light of those guidelines, the agency devised its own strategy, which culminated in the Fire Management Plan, a 1985 addendum to the Natural Resource Management Plan. The agency addressed two very different dimensions of fire management: suppression, which had been de facto practice for most of the century, and prescribed burning. The plan provided the justification for controlled burning, articulating the problems of long-term suppression. Under the plan, lightning fires and other conflagrations would continue to be suppressed. Prescribed burning would begin with small areas, initial burns of one to twenty-five acres, in an effort to gather information before attempting any larger endeavors.[35]

The Fire Management Plan offered both a rationale for fire management and a strategy of cooperation with other agencies. The process accelerated quickly; within two years of the Golden Gate National Recreation Area fire plan, the Park Service and California State Parks Department and Recreation signed a memorandum of agreement concerning fire management. By 1987, a full-fledged memorandum of understanding (MOU) had been implemented, describing the responsibilities of both state parks and the NPS along the Mount Tamalpais–Muir Woods boundary.[36]

Segments of the public remained more difficult to persuade. Although controlled burning continued through the mid-1980s, most years the number of acres burned was minuscule. In 1986, the park burned a total of forty-four acres: eight acres of eucalyptus community in Oakwood Valley and fifteen acres of eucalyptus on Smith Road in Mill Valley in March and April, seventeen acres of redwood and mixed woodland in Muir Woods, and four acres of grassland in the Tennessee Valley in September and October.[37] When the Park Service announced its 1987 program of controlled burning, park staff expected few objections to the total of twenty-nine acres in three Marin County locations. The Park Service simply continued the pattern established since prescribed burning began in the early 1980s.[38]

A campaign headed by Sandy Ross of the Tamalpais Conservation Club, an avowed opponent of controlled burning, made managed fire into a regional issue. Ross complained that even prescribed fires scarred the hillsides, pointing to the consequences of a controlled burn on Mount Tamalpais in 1984. She beseeched Golden Gate National Recreation Area superintendent Brian O'Neill to stop the planned burns, using scientific articles that denigrated controlled burns as rationale for ending the program. Ross's objections caught the attention of the press, and area home owners followed her and articulated their own fears. Even though sixty years had passed since the last major fire on Mount Tamalpais and the consequences of an accumulated fuel load of such proportions could be devastating, a visible portion of the public argued that fire suppression ought to continue.[39]

Much of the anti–controlled burning sentiment focused on Mount Tamalpais rather than Golden Gate National Recreation Area. A series of hearings in 1988 attacked plans for managed fire within the state park. "I think the Water District [which managed lands in question] ought to forget it," former Mill Valley mayor and Water District board member Jean Barnard opined in a typical expression of opposition. Although the scientific evidence indicated that controlled burning was a necessity, an energized public was able to slow the process of implementation.[40] Prescribed burn policy remained an issue that pitted agency prerogative against public sentiment as well as science against belief.

Grazing also illustrated the tension between planning and implementation. Grazing had been one of the predominant features of Marin County in the nineteenth and early twentieth centuries. Although the Park Service typically excluded grazing from national parks, other kinds of areas in the system were open to grazing. Historical instances of grazing in the national parks did occur, but they were few and usually associated with emergencies such as war. National monuments and national recreation areas permitted restricted grazing, and with the establishment of Golden Gate National Recreation Area, grazing leases became an important way to keep longtime Marin County residents happy with their new park.[41]

Grazing had visible impact on the park's landscape. After a Soil Conservation Service study first showed significant impact on parklands in 1974, the Park Service began to restrict grazing two years later. After a subsequent 1977 study showed conditions worsening, the agency refused to renew grazing permits on ecologically fragile lands. The Tennessee Valley, heavily grazed, revealed severe impact by 1981. Judd Howell noted erosion of stream banks, a thistle invasion that resulted from the trampling of native species in open meadows, clogging of ponds from sediment and animal waste, severe trampling and grazing of the freshwater marsh and lagoon, and cattle excrement on a beach that visitors frequented. Proposed short-term solutions included new fencing and proper management, but Howell believed that cows should be excluded from the Tennessee Valley at the "next available opportunity," likely the end of existing grazing leases.[42]

Even if science strongly indicated that grazing would destroy parkland, exclusion of stock was a difficult political goal to attain. Grazing was an integral part of Marin County, an ongoing activity that created a cultural landscape of historic import. Objections to the practice grew more frequent throughout the 1980s. On one side stood environmental groups, led by the Sierra Club; opposing them was a cluster of interests that could have only come together in a complicated metropolitan area: old-time ranching interests and conservation and science specialists who did not really favor grazing but who did not approve of the Park Service's methods, strategies, or principles. The agency responded in the fashion it had established at the park; planners listened to public sentiment and crafted a document designed to provide as many constituencies with satisfactory outcomes as the condition of land permitted. As in nearly every other circumstance in the Bay Area, such an objective remained elusive. In 1987, after a study showed that one-quarter of Point Reyes National Seashore was overgrazed, the Draft Range Management Guidelines for Golden Gate National Recreation Area and Point Reyes National Seashore proposed new, more restrictive standards for grazing. Its stated goals were to slow erosion and continue to keep ranching in the park economically viable, but its release set off a struggle about the use of parklands for grazing.[43]

Even though many opposed grazing, their reasons differed greatly. Anne West of the Marin County chapter of the Sierra Club recognized the value of local ranching but regarded the draft as an economic preservation document rather than national park area guidelines. "There is no clear statement," she observed in a letter to the editor of the *Point Reyes Light*, "that protection of national park values . . . must be the backbone of each decision for our national parks." Other environmental groups challenged her perspective; Carl Munger of the Environmental Action Committee of West Marin suggested that "we have too much at stake to permit her the luxury of absolutism." Others seconded the sentiment, calling the draft a model program for managing conflicting interests.[44]

The causes of erosion inspired the disagreements among opponents. West especially saw great and dangerous erosion as a result of grazing, a belief echoed by other observers. As erosion became the focus of sentiment that opposed the plan, the political terrain became even more complicated. Columnist David V. Mitchell pointed out that the Park Service's own figures dispelled the notion that grazing caused the erosion that silted Tomales Bay, questioning the premise that erosion concerns underpinned the draft document.[45] The multiplicity of perspectives confused the issue. Erosion was real; was grazing the primary catalyst? As grazing opponents argued nuance in an exchange in the newspapers, they promoted misunderstanding and conflict.

When the *San Francisco Examiner* published the headline "New Marin Range War: Birders vs. Cows," the existing rift deepened. Framed as a battle between Marin County's "environmental movement" and ranchers and the conservation groups that supported them, the newspaper story heightened tensions. Cows trampled sensitive marshlands and bird habitat, prompting Don Dimitratos, head of the Marin County Parks Department, to assert that "there's no room for cows anymore." Ranchers argued that they abided by the terms of their leases. They once owned the land they now leased, selling it with the stipulation that they could lease the properties back for grazing. James Tacherra, a fifth-generation rancher, lamented the decline in ranching. Of the twenty-four dairy ranches he remembered from childhood, only three remained. "The park is a national treasure," an editorial in the *Coastal Post* averred, "[and] ranching . . . is a part of that treasure."[46] The emotions on both sides obscured the important issues. Grazing on state and county land was endangered, leaving Golden Gate National Recreation Area, Point Reyes National Seashore, and private land as the only locations for this historic activity in Marin County.

The Park Service and local ranchers reached accommodation over the plan, straining ties between the park and environmental groups such as the Sierra Club. The GMP had given de facto approval to grazing in 1980, but the changing impact on the land required revisiting the issue. In a hearing on February 10, 1988, Point Reyes National Seashore geologist Ed Margason suggested that rainstorms, not grazing, accounted for most of the erosion that silted Tomales Bay. Although geologist Gene Kojan, a resident of Point Reyes Station affiliated with the Sierra Club, angrily opposed Margason's views, the idea that rainstorms and not grazing caused erosion had much political heft. Marin County supervisors and residents were happy with the plan; rancher George Grossi called the guidelines "fair and reasonable," and ranchers agreed to reduce their herds to facilitate study of the causes of erosion. When the principals worked closely with one another, the tension of public venues was reduced.

Many environmentalists were sympathetic to the needs of ranchers. Jerry Friedman, chairman of the Advisory Committee of Golden Gate National Recreation Area and a Marin County supervisor, agreed. "Agriculture is in the park to stay," he observed during the meeting in a tacit acknowledgment of the cultural landscapes of the region. Consensus governed resolution at Golden Gate National Recreation Area. When the Citizens' Advisory Commission adopted the seashore's new Range Management Guidelines after a four-hour meeting in May 1993, the ranchers in attendance applauded loudly. Marin County supervisor Gary Giacomini, a member of a ranching family and a vociferous supporter of continued agricultural activity in the county, pronounced himself pleased with the results.[47]

In subsequent years, the stance of the Park Service became crucial to preserving agriculture in Marin County. The agency recognized this natural resource as a cultural landscape, permitting both the continuation of grazing and the preservation of the natural features of the area. The combination of park-supported research that monitored land conditions and grazing leases helped build strong ties between ranchers and the Park Service. From the ranchers' perspective, the Park Service enjoyed independence from special interests that the county parks department did not. As a result, Point Reyes National Seashore and Golden Gate National Recreation Area became protectors of historic agriculture in Marin County. The success of these relationships proved to be a triumph of resource management over the strident points of view so common in the Bay Area.

Managing the coastline required the same kind of cooperative vigilance, political alliance, and public relations focus as any other activity in the Bay Area. The Park Service again needed other agencies and entities to achieve its mandate and again needed to structure its relationships for common objectives much larger than the park to attain its resource management goals. Surfers, windsurfers, and bathers; whale watchers; and fishermen described a triangle of coastal use within park boundaries; a combination of federal legislation and local activism was crucial to assuring that the resources necessary for all three uses were available to the public.

Increased prosperity in California and the sense of loss that accompanied rapid postwar growth prompted concern for environmental issues. The Planning and Conservation League, a grassroots group that sought to manage growth, was established in 1965, inspiring a series of bills designed to protect the environment. One of these, Assembly Bill 1391, introduced by Assemblyman William Bagley, a Republican from Marin County and a friend of Phil Burton, created the Coastline Conservation Study Commission. It foreshadowed the California Coastal Zone Conservation Commission's 1975 California Coastal Plan, prepared under the provisions of the

Federal Coastal Zone Management Act of 1972.[48] The National Park Service and Golden Gate National Recreation Area were instantly sympathetic to the coastal plan. It promoted goals and outcomes very similar to those of the park, articulating balance as a primary end, advocating restrictive management of the coast, and promoting viable communities and productive agriculture.[49]

The major coastal issue for Golden Gate National Recreation Area became the threat of impact from increased offshore oil drilling, a direct by-product of the Reagan-era Department of the Interior. Early in the 1980s, Secretary James Watt sought to unlock federal resources and make them available for development in a fashion not attempted since the Teapot Dome scandals of the 1920s. Watt's agenda included opening the entire California coast, including the oil-rich waters off the Bay Area, to drilling. He focused on the Bodega and Santa Cruz basins, both closed to drilling by Watt's predecessor, Cecil Andrus. Watt had his defenders. In an era in which OPEC had reached agreement on production capacities, forcing the cost of oil skyward, domestic production—even at the expense of long-accepted conservation goals—seemed possible in the world of politics.[50]

Conservation retained many of its champions, and one of the more vocal among them was John Burton. The younger brother of the powerful Phil Burton represented Marin County beginning in the mid-1970s, generally following his powerful brother's lead. Watt's ruling to open the area between the Golden Gate and the Farallon Islands to drilling initiated paroxysms of outrage in the Bay Area. When Watt's office announced that the new regulations for marine sanctuaries did not include a ban on drilling for oil and gas, John Burton pounded the table in front of the U.S. House Interior Subcommittee on the Panama Canal and the Outer Continental Shelf, charging that "lock, stock, and barrel, [Watt] is in the pocket of the oil industry." Watt's regulations were egregious, Burton claimed. They opened valuable offshore lands with little oil near the Bay Area and ignored far more oil-rich lands in the Santa Maria Basin near Santa Barbara. A majority of Congress lined up behind John Burton, as did organized conservation and environmental movements.[51] Opponents obtained a preliminary injunction against thirty-two leases in the Santa Maria Basin the day before the tracts were slated to be auctioned. Marin County supervisor Gary Giacomini, whose district was directly affected by the leases, was ecstatic at the ruling. "This is the first glimmer of hope," he observed afterward. "I'd like to think it's more than a glimmer."[52]

Even the combination of high oil prices, enthusiasm for the new Reagan administration, and the support of the oil industry could not stem the powerful forces allied against drilling. Although the Park Service kept quiet during the fray, its leaders in Washington, D.C., and at Golden Gate National Recreation Area secretly cheered the opposition. As a Department of the Interior agency, the Park Service needed its friends in the conservation and environmental community to fight its fight and grapple with Watt. The secretary was a clumsy political operator, frequently wielding a cudgel instead of more delicate instruments. As a result, his regulations were frequently challenged in court and overturned. In a situation entirely typical of the Watt regime, the California congressional delegation succeeded in imposing a moratorium that halted drilling off the coast of the Golden State; the moratorium was extended three times and eventually was applied to the entire California coast.[53]

Watt's influence persisted throughout the tenure of the Reagan administration. His successor in 1983, William Clark, followed the same policies with little of the rancor that accompanied Watt's pronouncements. Clark's successor, Donald Hodel, sought a compromise in 1985, proposing the opening of only 150 leases to drilling, but withdrew the offer when the oil industry balked at his choice of tracts. When Hodel offered a proposal for a five-year leasing plan in 1987, U.S. Representative Barbara Boxer and Mel Levine of California responded with a bill that banned drilling within 200 miles of the California coast. "They're back with the same old story," Boxer told the press, "and we want to close this show down for good." Only after the election of George H. Bush in 1988 did the administration agree to a ban on drilling off Point Reyes, and only when the president, himself a veteran of the beleaguered domestic oil industry, desperately needed California's fifty-four electoral votes for his reelection did the administration come out in support of a marine sanctuary that permanently protected much of the coast.[54]

The offshore drilling issue illustrated that the Park Service could manage its resources perfectly well but could not assure their protection without consideration of the larger political questions as well as the decisions of other federal, state, and local agencies. A positive consequence of the presence of so many government agencies in the Bay Area was the development of multiagency planning for emergency situations. Beginning in 1983, the Park Service looked to create a multiagency contingency plan to address possible consequences of a severe oil spill in the Bay Area because it simply could not respond to such a threat on its own. Not only did the agency lack the resource base to combat an oil spill of even one-tenth the magnitude of the 1969 Santa Barbara spill, but it had no control over the movement of oil tankers and other transportation mechanisms in the Bay Area. In short, the Park Service faced a classic situation; when it came to protecting resources against an oil spill, the agency had legally mandated responsibilities but had neither the budget to develop self-contained programs nor the authority to control activities that might lead to such an event. When the Sierra Club initiated a proposal to develop an oil spill contingency plan for Marin County, the Park Service enthusiastically seconded the proposal and helped the club find financing.[55]

Although the public perception of an oil spill focused on the huge damage that ensued from the three million gallons spilled in the Santa Barbara disaster, for the Park Service, smaller-scale, frequent spills and slicks presented a significant natural resource management threat. Nearly every year, Golden Gate National Recreation Area faced some kind of small spill that damaged ecological resources. Tide pools in most of the coastal regions were particularly delicate, and even small amounts of oil disrupted these ecological communities. Events such as the February 1986 Rodeo Lagoon spill temporarily disrupted tidewater goby habitat, causing the Park Service to closely monitor the situation. Heavy rains in subsequent months mitigated much of the damage, limiting population loss. At Aquatic Park, nearby shipping was a constant source of small leaks and spills that continually threatened the historic setting.[56]

Large oil spills remained the single greatest threat to natural resource management on the Golden Gate National Recreation Area coastline. The danger was always present, and every so often a major spill presented a challenge to the entire structure set up to manage such events. On Halloween 1984, a 632-foot oil tanker, the *Puerto Rican*, burst into flames shortly after passing under the Golden Gate Bridge. The Coast Guard responded by towing the boat out to sea to a point about eleven miles south of the Farallon Islands and almost thirty miles from the continental coast. The direction of the currents indicated that from that point, the seeping light lubrication oil from the tanker would be carried out into the Pacific Ocean, where it would dissipate. Instead, on November 3, the ship tore in half, and the stern section containing more than one million gallons of oil sank. Almost 100,000 gallons of oil spread out across a wide area, precipitating the first major oil spill inside the park's coastal waters.[57]

Although nowhere near the magnitude of major oil spills, the *Puerto Rican* created significant natural resource management issues for the Park Service. Once a dumping ground for waste of all kinds, the Farallon Islands had been revived after the establishment of Point Reyes National Seashore in 1962, and by the time Golden Gate National Recreation Area was established in 1972, efforts to protect the islands were under way. In 1973, the islands received national wildlife refuge designation; a decade later, just before the *Puerto Rican* spill, the waters around the island were labeled the Point Reyes–Farallon Islands National Marine Sanctuary. After the spill, waterfowl were covered with oil, precipitating a widespread cooperative effort among federal and state agencies and regional environmental groups to save the birds. As dead birds washed up on the beaches of Point Reyes National Seashore, groups of volunteers worked to clean the oil from other birds. Although more than 1,000 birds were covered in oil and hundreds died as a result, the efforts of volunteers helped save countless birds and minimize the ecological consequences of the spill.[58] Even though successful natural resource management depended on factors beyond the Park Service's control, the pattern of joint management and cooperation again yielded dividends. The impact of the spill could not be avoided, but mitigation proceeded quickly and effectively.

Such concerns illustrated a number of ongoing natural resource issues for the Park Service. In a populated area, natural resources were susceptible to pressure from the needs of surrounding communities. In some cases, the agency could successfully resist pressure from the community, and its chances improved when other entities shared its opposition to a project or plan. In other cases, cooperation was essential if the agency was to achieve its mission. When the Park Service and other area agencies worked together, the consequences of anything from an oil spill to a sewage project could be lessened. Managers at Golden Gate National Recreation Area quickly learned to keep their friends close and to let them know of objections to proposals for development. The circumstances placed the Park Service in a tricky position. It had to defend its resources carefully, and that care sometimes required a pronounced dimension of tact.

With this complicated collection of planning instruments, strategies, and constituencies to manage natural resources, the Park Service faced the new century. The implementation of natural resource management planning in the early 1980s signaled a new era, one in which the agency moved beyond reaction and into the implementation of plans designed to preserve park resources. Planning created a framework that gave the Park Service clear reasons for its actions and sanctioned objectives in even the most difficult circumstances. The road from objectives to implementation continued to be fraught with the same perils that existed before the agency conceived of a direction for the park. The public still held its proprietary view, still largely regarded the park as play space, and even those elements of the public that recognized the intrinsic natural resource value of Golden Gate National Recreation Area lands sought to implement group-specific agendas to park planning. The biosphere designation changed global perception of the value of the park's resources and may have opened the way to a different perception of national recreation areas as a whole. The designation compelled not only the park's supporters but land managers in general to see Golden Gate National Recreation Area's lands in new ways. Yet on the whole, the planning process and designations that affirmed the significance of the park's natural resources were only part of a larger, more complicated picture of competing desires. Planning gave the park a blueprint, but constituency issues continued to be paramount.

Constituencies may have respected the park and its plans, but that did not diminish their desire to shape policy to their ends, which were not necessarily the ends that planning and NPS policy dictated. Implementing programs still encountered the very same kind of resistance that characterized the park's early years. Natural resource management had become an institutionalized process, but it could not always make the step from process to program. The issues that vexed natural resource management were at the core of the management dilemma of Golden Gate National Recreation Area: people's proprietary feelings for parklands stood in the way of implementing policy too often to ignore. The Park Service could fashion policy with public support, but it could not always count on the public to support the implementation of the policy.

CHAPTER SEVEN

Cultural Resource Management

The Nixon-era concept of "parks for the people, where the people are," the genesis of urban recreation in the park system, did not naturally include conventional cultural resources, nor were historic and cultural features considered primary assets by those who battled for Golden Gate National Recreation Area's establishment. Hailing from the Sierra Club tradition, advocates such as Edgar Wayburn focused on the open spaces and natural features of the region; Amy Meyer and other proponents had been energized by the environmental movement as they harnessed the power of San Francisco's neighborhood groups. They sought to protect open space and enhance local and regional quality of life, a common theme in the environmentalism of their day.[1]

In cultural resource management more than natural resource management, the Park Service undertook an enormous responsibility that the public only peripherally understood as part of the mission of Golden Gate National Recreation Area. In this initial formulation, the recreation area's forts and other historic features were afterthoughts, a series of structures that had intrinsic value but were included because of their location. Yet when the boundaries were finally drawn and the park signed into law, the Park Service inherited a complex historic fabric at the moment when a 1974 amendment to the National Historic Preservation Act of 1966 formalized the management of such resources and demanded procedures and practices for their administration.

Golden Gate National Recreation Area was home to a remarkable constellation of historic resources, among the most diverse in the entire national park system. Historic and cultural resources included military buildings from the Spanish/Mexican and American eras, remnants of the history of San Francisco and the Bay Area, archaeological features that predated European contact, and a range of other features. Alcatraz alone presented a major cultural resource management question; its crumbling exterior, multifaceted history, and the Indian Occupation of the late 1960s all demanded significant management of cultural resources. The arrangement that assured that the Presidio would eventually become part of the park added more than 470 National Register structures and as many as 700 other National Register–eligible structures to Golden Gate National Recreation Area, a larger number than in any other national park area. Even as public perceptions of the park focused on natural attributes, the Park Service acquired vast cultural resource management obligations.

By 1972, cultural resource management was subjected to its own set of dictates, most of which derived directly or indirectly from the National Historic Preservation Act of 1966, later amended in 1974 and 1980. The demands of this set of laws and regulations—different from NEPA, the Endangered Species Act, and other legal mechanisms that governed natural resource management—created a parallel structure that mandated two essentially separate administrative structures for the different kinds of resources. Statutory obligations such as compliance with sections 106 and 110 of the amended National Historic Preservation Act and, later, the American Indian Religious Freedom Act of 1977, the Archaeological Resources Protection Act of 1979, the Native American Graves and Repatriation Act of 1991, and a host of other laws and rulings demanded constant attention from park managers. They also consumed an enormous proportion of park resources. At the same time, cultural resource management required the same attention to park use by its many constituents as did natural resource management.

At Golden Gate National Recreation Area's inception, a number of the components were already managed for their cultural resource value, while other areas easily lent themselves to this management. Fort Point, established as a national historic site in 1970, provided the most obvious cultural resource management setting. It preceded Golden Gate National Recreation Area and retained a separate superintendency until 1977. With the support of the Fort Point Museum Association, the Park Service began an extensive program to renovate the fort after inclusion in the park system. The chief ranger of the new park, Charles Hawkins, was a retired master sergeant who was a veteran of World War II's Battle of the Bulge. He had worked for both the Presidio Public Affairs Office and the Fort Point Museum Association and played an instrumental role in the new site's early operations. Charlie, or "The Hawk," as he was known, exemplified the characteristics of the "old Army" and effectively applied those methods to the NPS. He had a superb knowledge of the resource and a uniquely effective way with bureaucracy. He was also a mentor to a generation of Park Service professionals who cut their teeth at old Fort Point.

By 1971, the Fort Point Museum Association had become a cooperating agency of the National Park Service, one of the many support organizations that assisted parks by providing volunteer labor, running bookstores, and coordinating other fund-raising activities. Its members served as guides at Fort Point and undertook small physical improvements. Architects and historians planned extensive renovation under Park Service auspices, and within three years, the decaying property became far more attractive. Iron balustrades and columns were sandblasted and repainted, ironwork rails for the casemate and gorge faces and along the barbette tier were reproduced, the lighthouse that was first constructed in 1864 was rebuilt, and examples of the historic cannon that had been in the fort were located and brought to the Bay Area.[2]

Where Fort Point typified conventional historic approaches, Fort Mason represented a different dimension of cultural resource management. Fort Mason had powerful historic significance. It included a 1797 gun battery and structures from the Gold Rush and Civil War eras. Along with the Presidio, it served as a training center and campground for Americans sailing west in their attempts at empire in the Pacific Ocean during the Spanish-American War in 1898 and thereafter. Fort Mason was a principal embarkation station for the Pacific-bound troops of World War II, but by the 1970s, the military determined that it no longer needed parts of the fort. In 1971, after Representative William Mailliard had begun the initial efforts to create a national park area in the Bay Area, the army released twenty-two of the sixty-nine acres of the fort to the General Services Administration (GSA) for disposition. Immediately, a range of claimants rushed forward.

Representative Manuel Lujan of New Mexico wanted to trade the lands to private developers for forested land in his home state. The GSA sought to build a new federal building and planned to sell the excess land for $25 million to developers to finance the project. Nearby Galileo High School, which used some of the fort's buildings for overflow classes, sought to relocate its tiny campus to the more spacious waterfront. A proposal to turn the fort into a prison for youthful offenders also circulated. Mailliard and Representative Phil Burton protested loudly, Mailliard pressuring the GSA for a commitment to keep the land until a Golden Gate National Recreation Area bill became law, and Burton—in an irony that no one could have perceived in 1971—insisting that a prison facility on the fort was akin to building one next door to the Watergate Hotel. On the local front, Amy Meyer and PFGGNRA battled against using the fort for anything but a park, and when Golden Gate National Recreation Area was established, the Park Service set up its administrative headquarters at Fort Mason.[3]

The perception of national recreation areas and the particular situation in the Bay Area played a large role in determining the future of Fort Mason. The Bay Area needed more public space and buildings devoted to community development and public programs. The Park Service's strategy of creating an identity for itself and developing a support base easily encouraged the development of community projects within the park's physical and social boundaries. Nothing about the national recreation area category forbid such endeavors, and with the new pressure on the Park Service to be relevant to urban needs, community projects in historic space made considerable sense.

Fort Mason became the home of such programs. Although San Francisco supervisor John L. Molinari asked the Park Service to include an ice-skating rink and an indoor tennis facility in the fort, Whalen held firm to his plans. He wanted the fort to become a cultural center. Late in 1974, the Park Service requested public proposals for use of the space and by January 1975 had received twenty-nine suggestions, far more than the agency had room to accommodate. Whalen turned to the Citizens' Advisory Commission, which created a subcommittee that initiated regulations for use of the fort. Whalen offered parameters for use: programs could not be "predominantly commercial or lack . . . significant visitor appeal." The commission recommended that three categories of activity—performing arts, fine arts and crafts, and education and research—constitute the initial lessees.[4]

The kind of daily, hands-on management that such a cultural center demanded was the forte neither of the Citizens' Advisory Commission nor Golden Gate National Recreation Area. The Park Service actively sought one organization to oversee the entire cultural center; dividing responsibility among a number of interests assured countless headaches and a complicated and tendentious administration. With the recommendation of the advisory commission, the Park Service entered into an eight-year cooperative agreement with the nonprofit Fort Mason Foundation in May 1976. The foundation established the Fort Mason Center to create and administer a broad, many-faceted center for the arts, humanities, recreation, education, and ecology. A community-based entity, the foundation drew support from many constituencies and because of its nonprofit status could seek outside funding. The foundation and the new center opened their doors in May 1976.[5]

The dilapidated condition of much of Fort Mason made the first years of the cultural center difficult. The pier area, called Lower Fort Mason, had become a cluster of vacant warehouses, left to the shoreline's harsh elements. "The place was a mess. Nothing worked," Mark Kasky, who became executive director of the center, later observed. For historic structures, the questions of renovation loomed large, and the Fort Mason Center, with Park Service help, followed the guidelines of adaptive reuse. Once the cleanup was complete, six tenants moved in, and about 125,000 people came to the center during its first year. Grants and money from San Francisco's hotel tax helped support the foundation and its activities, the Department of the Interior added $1 million for renovation, and within a few years, the programs and offerings of the center were widely acclaimed. By 1979, 36 groups were in residence and as many as 120 used the facility. The center struggled with its budget at times, but by 1981, the project was heralded as a success. Fort Mason Center had become a model for urban planning across the globe, described by one Bay Area newspaper as an "eclectic cultural park" that served a local audience in myriad ways.[6]

The Fort Mason Center was the prelude to numerous agreements with other park partners, nonprofit organizations with specific goals that coincided in some fashion with those of the Park Service. By the 1990s, such arrangements were commonplace. They included entities as diverse as the Bay Area Discovery Museum, the Point Bonita YMCA, the Headlands Center for the Arts, and the Deep Ecology Center in the Marin Headlands. Collectively, the agreements with such organizations reflected the park's commitment to the local community as well as its desire to communicate with the diverse publics of the Bay Area.

Lower Fort Mason and its cultural center never presented a conventional cultural resource management situation. Adaptive use of historic structures created a different definition of cultural resources, one that included more than preservation and spoke to community and regional needs. It also prevented historic space from deteriorating, even though it altered that space. On occasion, some expressed concern that the activities of the center were too local—that it served a local audience at the expense of a national one that enjoyed as powerful a theoretical claim to the space—but the initiation of events such as the San Francisco Blues Festival, which enticed out-of-town visitors, also became standard fare. The center became one of the places that visitors sought precisely because it reflected local culture. By the mid-1980s, it attracted almost two million people a year, proving that the versatility of national recreation areas offered a tremendous asset for urban areas and that public-private partnerships such as the one between the Park Service and the Fort Mason Foundation could contribute greatly to the cultural environment of cities.[7]

Alcatraz Island presented another dimension of cultural resource management. In many ways the catalyst for establishment of Golden Gate National Recreation Area, Alcatraz had the greatest command on the American public of any cultural feature in the park. The drawback was that its popular perception as "The Rock" reflected aspects of culture with which the Park Service felt uncomfortable; combined with the decaying condition of much of the island's physical plant and the aftermath of the Indian Occupation, Alcatraz Island appeared a difficult and expensive place for the Park Service to manage. Perhaps the only intrinsic advantage the agency perceived was its ability to control the ingress and egress of visitors, preventing the island from being inundated by demand.[8]

In April 1973, the Park Service decided to open the island to the public for the first time, but much work had to be undertaken before visitors could come to the island. Two crucial circumstances needed to be resolved: the island had to be made safe for visitors and a transportation system to convey them across the bay had to be developed. Concessioners vied for the right to transport visitors, who offered a captive and likely very lucrative market. The General Services Administration and the Park Service undertook cleanup, maintenance, and improvement on the island. The initial efforts were designed to make the property safe, not to articulate its cultural resource significance. One of the crucial themes of NPS management of Alcatraz Island, the struggle between presenting a cultural resource to a public that thought it understood the island's value and maintaining its historic fabric, began almost from the instant the Park Service considered allowing visitors on the island. The agency grappled with how to best present the resource, and, as a result, what resources to preserve and in what manner.[9]

Alcatraz Island retained powerful symbolic standing, and a number of groups were not prepared to readily consign the island to conventional cultural resource management. At the Citizens' Advisory Commission meeting on November 19, 1977, the public was invited to comment on the three proposed options and to offer additional suggestions. Among the new proposals were a number of time-worn ideas. The World Island Committee sought to have Alcatraz become a symbol of the aspirations of humans to live in peace. Spokeswoman Lucille Green beseeched the commission to convert it to a place of "dignity and beauty." The United Nations Association proffered a museum about the United Nations on the island to commemorate its role in seeking world peace; other ideas included a 240-foot high monument to peace, a proposal to turn the island back to the state of California, and another to turn it into a source of alternative energy. There were countless others. The city of San Francisco also offered its perspective. The director of city planning, Rai Okamoto, announced that the city supervisors favored the strengthening and rehabilitation of historic structures, continued public access, and the removal of rubble.[10]

Even with this complicated input and with the ongoing clamor to visit the island, the Park Service hewed to a conservative line at Alcatraz. The agency focused on the island's natural and parklike features, accentuating its spectacular view of the Bay Area and its natural setting. Historic preservation and its attendant objectives were obvious goals, and the agency focused on creating an attractive environment on the island. Aware that "the majority of future visitors . . . will continue to be attracted by the intrigue of the prison," the agency worked to shift attention to the island's natural features.[11] This compromise meant that the Park Service determined to undertake two possibly mutually exclusive objectives on Alcatraz: to give the public the prison history it wanted and to point to other interesting dimensions that visitors may not have considered.

An even more difficult cultural resource dilemma for the Park Service was Cliff House, above the remains of Sutro Baths. Graced by a fabulous five-story Gothic structure that was completed in 1896, the restaurants, dining rooms, art gallery, and a veranda that overlooked the water made Cliff House the center of San Francisco's recreational waterfront in the late nineteenth and early twentieth centuries. After that property burned in a fire in 1907, a new building was constructed in 1909, far less lavish and impressive.

As public expectations of leisure and patterns of movement and transportation changed, the area became an anachronism, declining and crumbling. By the 1970s, with the closure and demolition of the amusement park Playland at the Beach, the area reeked of urban blight. None of the fine nineteenth-century structures remained; Sutro Baths, the last building standing, burned to the ground in 1966. A few smaller structures, one often called a "tacky Cliff House" and described by author John Hart as "less than an echo, squat and blocky," replaced the grandiose structures of the early century.[12]

The new Cliff House had potential to be historic; begun in 1908 through the patronage of Sutro's daughter, it was designed by the Reid Brothers, famous San Francisco architects, and repeatedly renovated as late as the 1970s. The building reflected the history of the area and its transformation—and some said decline—in clear detail; it just did not contain the physical structures that revealed the high points of that history. As a result, the battles over Cliff House forced the Park Service to weigh a restrictive reading of the National Historic Preservation Act against a conception of a more glorious, more spectacular, and likely more attractive history. Much of the architectural community and the CAC opposed the Park Service's perspective, citing the additional language in the NHPA that illustrated the lack of historic integrity and pointed out that there were better examples of the Reid brothers' work.[13] It took the Park Service almost twenty years to fashion a program that reflected its belief that the structure was eligible for the National Register of Historic Places; even then, the California State Historic Preservation Office (SHPO) did not agree with the agency's assessment.

At the old San Francisco Maritime State Historical Park on the Hyde Street Pier, which was added to Golden Gate National Recreation Area in 1977 and became the independent San Francisco Maritime National Historical Park in 1988, the Park Service inherited another conventional cultural resource management situation. The maritime park suffered from a lack of financing. It had bounced from one underfunded branch of state government to another for more than a decade, all the while its floating stock of eight historic ships decaying. At its establishment, the new park acquired all museum collections held by Golden Gate National Recreation Area that were maritime in nature. Only artifacts that directly pertained to parklands, such as lighthouses, and shipwrecks were retained. This intellectual/property interpark agreement transferred the Golden Gate National Recreation Area collections and all the museum staff to San Francisco Maritime National Historical Park.

Maintenance and funding for upkeep remained the primary issues at the museum. NPS regional director Howard Chapman persuaded Phil Burton to include in the legislation a clause that let the revenues that accrued from rent at Haslett Warehouse and Cliff House fund the ships and the Fort Mason Foundation. Burton also arranged for an admission fee for the *Bal-*

clutha, the primary attraction among the historic ships. After Burton's death in 1983, his wife, Sala, who succeeded him in the House of Representatives, extended the admission charge to the park's entire fleet of historic ships.[14] Yet the maintenance costs of the ships were exorbitant, and even with the addition of new revenues, money for upkeep remained scarce. As occurred throughout the park system, maintenance was deferred on the ships, creating a situation that meant that sometime in the future, the consequences of an established pattern of inadequate care would have to be faced.

The ships were an afterthought at Golden Gate National Recreation Area, illustrating the precarious position of cultural resources in the park. Again, the national recreation area designation loomed large. Even though the Park Service managed all of its units by the same set of standards, the idea of significant cultural resource management within a national recreation area remained hard for the public, and sometimes for the agency, to fathom. Even more, the public perception of Golden Gate National Recreation Area as a series of individual units presented an enormous barrier to an appreciation of integrated cultural resource management. The Maritime Museum was the most extreme example of such a perception, a difficult marriage of objectives and personnel that reflected the complexity characteristic of the park. When visitors toured the ships or climbed the parapet at Fort Point, they perceived themselves as being in independent park units, decidedly not the same park as when they hiked in the Olema Valley or watched the sunset from the Marin Headlands. Cultural resource management underscored the diversity of the park's themes and the difficulty of communicating them as a whole to the public.

Among the many tasks of the GMP was an effort to reconcile the various dimensions of park management into a coherent overall strategy. Cultural resource management played an integral role in the planning process and was clearly represented in the final product. At the same time, a 1980 amendment to the National Historic Preservation Act of 1966 added new expectations regarding cultural properties. In section 110 of the amended document, every federal agency was assigned responsibility for the historic properties under its jurisdiction, an obligation that had been implied in the original legislation but not made explicit until 1980. The result added complex new responsibilities at Golden Gate National Recreation Area and focused considerably greater attention on cultural resources.[15]

The GMP introduced the historic resource land management zones concept, creating a Preservation Zone, an Enhancement Zone, and an Adaptive Use Zone. Resources in the Preservation Zone were to be managed for their historic qualities, those in the Enhancement Zone were historic but had always been devoted to recreational purposes, and those resources in the Adaptive Use Zone were historic in character but were already adapted or likely to be adapted for park purposes.[16] Although an imperfect set of designations, the zone concept tried to put a framework around the previous unit-by-unit responses.

In the Park Service, adaptive use of historic properties remained controversial. The agency had always uncomfortably mixed protection and use, beginning with the Antiquities Act of 1906 and continuing with federal statutes governing historic preservation in the 1930s. Especially after the advent of Mission 66, the postwar era muted preservationist tendencies, but historic preservation again gained agency attention after 1960. The cultural climate of the 1960s and the emphasis on preserving vignettes of the natural past in the 1963 Leopold Report added momentum to an existing and already powerful strain of thought in the agency.[17] Even in an era when the Park Service actively accommodated the public's desires, programs such as adaptive use inspired resentment in some quarters. Cultural resource managers were initially reticent about such uses, but with the incredible number of structures in Golden Gate National Recreation Area, and especially as a result of the abandoned ones at lower Fort Mason, rehabilitation seemed the only viable solution. Some within the agency grimaced, but in a national recreation area in an urban area, adaptive use was destined to become a cornerstone of cultural resource management.

At about the same time, the Park Service became concerned with external threats to the national park system. As a result of the legislative matrix that surrounded the National Environmental Policy Act and increased pressure for energy development in response to the OPEC oil crisis of the mid-1970s, park managers found that the once remote character of major natural national parks had become compromised and that activities outside park boundaries possessed colossal implications for the lands within. Air pollution that marred vistas at the Grand Canyon became symbolic of the problem, but the threats were even more widespread and diverse. Late in the 1970s, at the behest of two former NPS officials who were working for the U.S. House of Representatives Interior Committee National Parks subcommittee, the agency undertook a survey of threats to the parks. Each unit responded to a questionnaire that sought to discern not only what the threats to the parks were but how the Park Service expected to address them.[18]

At Golden Gate National Recreation Area, the response to this query revealed a great deal of information about the state of cultural resource management. The urban industrial character of the Bay Area combined with its oceanside setting to create significant threats, especially to the park's cultural resources. Smog, smoke, and dust as well as salt air affected outside displays such as Hyde Street Pier, the historic ships, gun batteries, and even the coastal fortifications. Alcatraz Island appeared particularly vulnerable, as did the west face of Fort Point, where brick facades routinely deteriorated from the ongoing pounding of wind and surf. Air and water pollution and soil erosion at historic structures at both Fort Funston and Fort Baker presented obstacles to maintaining park resources. Nor was the park prepared to manage the endemic vandalism that occurred in a metropolitan area. Graffiti on seacoast fortifications and visitors trampling archaeological middens posed another category of threats to cultural resources.[19]

The army presence created another uncertainty for the Park Service; while the military "displayed careful preservation management" for the Presidio's occupied structures within the context of its desire to modernize, the report observed that its habit of abandoning structures no longer useful posed cultural resource management problems. Once military buildings were no longer in use, all maintenance ceased—generally including heat. Worse, the park feared that the army would point to the dilapidated condition of older buildings as a reason to replace them with new construction. If employed, this strategy posed a threat to historic resources in general.

The solution to these problems was planning, park officials believed, and the planning process, which had been formalized with the GMP in 1980, continued. In June 1982, the Cultural Resource Management (CRM) Plan for the park debuted. A candid document, it tried to set the tone for planning and felt no compunction about pointing out the numerous difficulties associated with cultural resource management. The plan followed the lead of the GMP, using the concept of historic resource land management zones and further elaborating on them. By the terms of the CRM plan, Fort Point and the ships, lighthouses, fortifications, and historic buildings on Alcatraz were located in the Preservation Zone and were to be managed for the complicated and sometimes contradictory goals of facilitating public enjoyment and appreciation of their historic values. In practice, this strategy meant that within these areas, historic preservation efforts focused on the protection of structures from deterioration. In the Enhancement Zone, consisting of Sutro Heights, Cliff House, and Aquatic Park, management practice preserved the basic integrity of the settings as well as specific structures. In the Adaptive Use Zone, which included Alcatraz's grounds, Upper Fort Mason, Haslett Warehouse, East Fort Miley, and portions of the Marin Headlands, historic space was to be redesigned and adapted for recreational use while its integrity was maintained and if possible enhanced.[20]

Although a historic preservation purist might scoff at such a set of goals, the plan made considerable sense at Golden Gate National Recreation Area. With 340 properties on the list of classified structures and twenty-six areas on the National Register of Historic Places, a fleet of historic ships, as well as a huge inventory of written, graphic, and photographic resources, the park had an enormous cultural resource mission, but it was not the only management obligation at Golden Gate National Recreation Area. The CRM plan attempted to bridge the park's many-faceted mission, with its obligations in legislation and to the public, and to satisfy the countless constituencies that felt strongly about Golden Gate National Recreation area and its resources.

The plan also more clearly delineated the dimensions of cultural resource management at the park. It built from the historic resource studies of NPS historians Anna Coxe Toogood and Erwin Thompson, synthesizing their detailed historical work into a series of themes for the park to preserve. Prehistoric Native American peoples and their lives, primarily the Coast Miwok and the Ohlone—once called Costanoans by Europeans—who preceded Europeans and Americans in the region, formed one theme. The plan noted the presence of a number of sites inside the park, attributing their predominance in the San Francisco unit to the development on that side of the bay. The less-disturbed nature of west Marin County, in particular, meant that many more archaeological sites were likely to be found.

Cultural resources from the Spanish-Mexican period were divided among three locations, Fort Point, Fort Mason, and the Olema Valley. The first two likely held archaeological remains of that era, as certainly did the nineteenth-century adobe walls that had been enclosed in the Presidio officers' club, and the Olema Valley contained ranchos that reflected the culture and social organization of the Mexican era as well as the dairy farming culture of the twentieth century. The plan acknowledged a lack of historical research focusing on this period and the need for further evaluation of park resources. The American period was divided into two time frames, one focusing on acquisition and the Gold Rush and the second focusing on the military period. The park had only a few cultural resources to reflect the first era. The four Gold Rush–era structures at Fort Mason were administered by the army, and the National Maritime Museum, with its ships and related artifacts, served as the primary illustration of this history. Submerged cultural resources, an activity in which the Park Service in 1980 had only recently begun to engage, also merited attention.[21]

The most visible and best collection of cultural resources in the park illustrated the military experience in the Bay Area and the Pacific Rim. The park contained an outstanding collection of military and seacoast defense architecture and engineering, spanning the evolution not only of Americans' military prowess but also of the Spanish and Mexicans who preceded them. This remarkable collection included the remnants of Spanish fortifications and every subsequent stage in the development of defense capabilities through the NIKE antiaircraft missiles of the 1950s. With myriad physical structures and equipment, the park offered an outstanding opportunity to preserve the military past and to illustrate the history it preserved.[22]

The GMP recognized maritime resources as the park's last major category of cultural resource fabric. The historic fleet, which included eight major ships and sixty smaller vessels, constituted an enormous cultural resource as well as a challenging set of preservation and protection issues. The park also contained three historic lighthouses, all listed on the National Register of Historic Places, on Alcatraz Island, atop Fort Point, and at Point Bonita. Wharves, piers, docks, and other shoreside embarkation points also qualified as cultural resources, as did shipwrecks and other submerged artifacts.[23]

Other cultural resources demanded agency attention. These included transportation resources, agrarian resources, engineering resources, and remnants of various urban lifestyles. An urban lifestyles theme articulated in the plan permitted two innovations that were more difficult to establish in other park areas. This theme reflected ethnic history and accentuated the complex and multifaceted ethnic and racial history of San Francisco. By 1980, the Park Service sought such cultural resources as part of its serious attempt to reach more broadly into American society and reflect the history of the nation's growing diversity. Recreation also presented a theme that the park could preserve and interpret. The structures that revealed its history, in places such as Cliff House, Sutro Heights, Playland, and Aquatic Park, also fell within park boundaries.[24]

The authors of the plan recognized significant gaps in research that impeded the management of cultural resources. By 1980, the Park Service had compiled a significant amount of information about park resources in its basic research reports and inherited a great deal of maritime history from the library at the San Francisco Maritime Museum, but the breadth of features meant that a considerable number of themes and resources remained largely unexplored. The deficiencies were most pronounced in knowledge of prehistoric peoples and for submerged cultural resources. With a park as complicated as Golden Gate National Recreation Area, the report averred, "continued and detailed historical research needs to be continued at all times." Only with such an effort could the agency keep abreast of its cultural resource management obligations.[25]

The difficulty in implementation stemmed from two disparate points of origin. Distinctly different segments comprised the historic preservation community in the Bay Area. One, military enthusiasts, focused closely on the buildings, structures, and landscapes associated with the martial presence. Many were military retirees who became the intellectual descendants of the Fort Point Museum Association, far better positioned and better organized than their predecessors, but their concerns were confined to the preservation of army, navy, and Coast Guard sites. Other cultural resources in the park had specific constituencies as well. The historic ships at Hyde Street Pier had a particularly vocal group of supporters, as did Cliff House, Alcatraz, and other features. All supported their individual causes, but a few supported cultural resource management in general. The groups that did promote a general historic preservation agenda did so as a secondary concern. As did PFGGNRA, groups such as Headlands Inc. included historic preservation among their concerns, but only in concert with larger natural resource preservation issues. The national historic preservation organizations such as the National Trust only reluctantly got involved in local issues, preferring instead to influence policy. Even state historic preservation officers found themselves tightly constrained by legal and institutional procedures and could rarely offer much help.[26]

Another obstacle to successful management was the shortage of resources for management at the crucial moment that the plans were adopted. In 1982, the year the cultural resource management plan was completed, Golden Gate National Recreation Area faced a reduction in full-time positions. At precisely the moment the park needed personnel to begin the process of implementing planning and persuading the public of the value of those decisions, existing staff had to do more with fewer resources.[27] The most viable strategy was to rely on the prescriptions of the General Management Plan. The historic resource land management zones developed in the GMP became the basis for cultural resource management. The intensive use zones such as Alcatraz Island and Sutro Heights were defined as urban parkland and managed in that fashion. Although this approach did not necessarily compromise the integrity of cultural resources, it did mean that resources in these areas would be subjected to considerable use and the consequent impacts. The question of heavy use guaranteed that cultural resource management in intensive use areas would consistently require the investment of resources.

Section 106 compliance, the assessment of federal undertakings on historic properties, demanded an enormous proportion of park attention. The number of properties that fell under the act was so great that Golden Gate National Recreation Area simply could not be expected to handle compliance with the available staff. Regional office personnel reviewed undertakings submitted by parks under a programmatic agreement signed by the Park Service, the National Council of State Historic Preservation Officers, and the Advisory Council on Historic Preservation, colloquially called the Triple X because it required three signatures. Regional office personnel reviewed the form to determine if the undertaking fell under the jurisdiction of the programmatic agreement. If so, the park received notification that it met its section 106 compliance requirements. If the agreement did not cover the undertaking, the regional office followed with a full consultation with the applicable State Historic Preservation Office and the Advisory Council on Historic Preservation to keep the agency in compliance.

The oversight of Golden Gate undertakings unraveled over a building replacement at the Julius Kahn Playground on the Presidio grounds. In 1922, the San Francisco Parks and Recreation Department and the U.S. Army created the playground, and a local institution was born. Early in 1990, the transition of the Presidio from the army to the park began, and the national historic landmark status of the Presidio was being revised. At this juncture,

Richard and Rhoda Goldman, two important supporters of Golden Gate National Recreation Area and GGNPA, offered to donate the funds to build a new clubhouse at the playground in memory of their deceased son. Governed by the "one up, one down" rule that kept the number of structures on the Presidio constant, the replacement of a building was permissible. Since the army owned the land, but the city of San Francisco owned the building, not one but two other agencies held some jurisdiction. The army asked for NPS assistance in assessing the impact of a replacement building on the property.

The question hinged on the status of the old clubhouse. If it was a historic structure or a contributing structure to the national historic landmark, then section 106 would be invoked and the process changed. Park Service historical architect Ric Borjes observed that since the building was in the Presidio, it was likely to be a contributing structure, but the national historic landmark (NHL) revision team, updating the Presidio's status, assured him that civilian properties inside the Presidio were not being considered as contributing structures. The decision seemed clear and headed for an easy route to resolution. Then the NHL revision team changed its determination and located the playground as a contributing structure to the national historic landmark. The decision created a new tone in the debate, which became simultaneously political and rancorous. When the NHL determination included the playground, the Park Service backed away from the section 106 process, ceding the lead role to the military. The army still administered the Presidio; the transfer was slated but had not yet occurred, and the military's claim to lead agency status was easily made. At the recommendation of Golden Gate National Recreation Area, the military hired a former park staff member, Glennie Wall, who had started a consulting firm that specialized in historic preservation, to undertake the compliance action. The assessment eventually determined that the Kahn playground was ineligible for inclusion as a contributing structure to the national historic landmark, and the state historic preservation office concurred.[28]

The State Historic Preservation Office's concurrence ended the grappling. When the existing playground was determined not to be an eligible property, the construction became a "no effect" action under section 106. At an October 10, 1991, Citizen's Advisory Commission public hearing, David Warner, chief of planning in real estate at the Presidio, announced that he believed the new clubhouse was "simple and well thought out." Deborah Learner of the San Francisco Parks and Recreation Department seconded Warner's perspective, and with little objection from the public, the commission passed favorably on the recommendation of "no adverse impact."[29]

The section 106 struggle over the Julius Kahn Playground became a seminal event for cultural resource management at Golden Gate National Recreation Area. It made historic preservation seem as if it were a roadblock in the process of a change, an obstacle rather than the inventory and collection process required by law. Both Golden Gate National Recreation Area and the Goldmans were incensed at the delays caused by compliance process. Instead of a preservation tool, opponents began to see the law as a hindrance to viable objectives, a sentiment that had an ongoing and largely negative effect on historic preservation programs at the park.

The Kahn playground struggle also changed the Park Service's section 106 procedure. Golden Gate National Recreation Area administered a greater number of historic structures than the rest of the Western Region combined. The Presidio was already slated for transfer to the Park Service. Golden Gate National Recreation Area possessed a sufficiently large professional staff to make determinations about National Register eligibility and sought its own programmatic agreement. In 1992, the park entered into the National Park Service's first comprehensive programmatic agreement for park-level review at less than "adverse effect" level; instead of passing the decision to the regional office, Golden Gate National Recreation Area staff made regional-level decisions at the park level. This decision simplified agency procedure and practice.

Section 110 of the National Historic Preservation Act also required park action, expressing the intent of the act to assure that historic preservation was integrated into all federal agency programs. Included as a concept in the preamble to the original 1966 act and incorporating Executive Order 11593 from 1972, the ideas became section 110 in the 1980 amendment to the act. In 1992, additions to section 110 set out specific benchmarks to assure that historic and cultural resources were given adequate protection by federal agencies. Properties were to be managed and maintained to preserve their cultural value. Cultural properties that federal agencies did not control but that could be affected by their actions had to be addressed in agency planning. Preservation activities had to be carried out in consultation with other affected groups, as well as other federal, state, and local agencies. To comply with section 110, agency procedures for addressing section 106 had to be consistent with the guidelines of the Advisory Council on Historic Preservation, and agencies had to hold permits accountable under section 106. In addition, agencies were instructed to look to historic structures for adaptive uses before new construction when planning expansion.[30]

Although on the surface it appeared that the 1992 amendments to section 110 raised the standards for park management of cultural resources, in reality the park had practiced the new standards at least since the GMP and CRM plan in the early 1980s. With the large number of structures and the tremendous demand for adaptive use, Golden Gate National Recreation Area took the lead in resolving countless situations, providing a blueprint for implementation of these policies elsewhere in the park system. The park helped move historic preservation from the strict mode of the 1950s and

1960s, characterized by some as making historic buildings into museums, toward more interactive uses. Again, the complicated nature of resource management in an urban area, the quantity and variety of historic structures and other cultural resources, and the demands of policy and statute combined to put Golden Gate National Recreation Area into a leading position in implementing the new statutory obligations.

The evidence of this prescience showed in management situations across the park. Especially in the intensive use areas, the dictates of section 110 came to the forefront. In each such situation, the concerns of new users, typically not federal agencies, had to be melded with the statutory demands of resource management. In these circumstances, the major check on compromising cultural resource management became the intensity of concern for statutory obligation. In most situations, Golden Gate National Recreation Area provided outstanding care of historic properties even when they were designated for adaptive use. Operating under the principle that a structure in use is a structure being maintained, and well aware that the agency was unlikely to receive adequate resources for all its cultural resources, park managers pursued adaptive use as a protection strategy.[31]

Fort Mason, where adaptive use gave historic preservation a different character, illustrated the range of section 110 issues. The fort itself was divided between two different kinds of areas. The lower fort became the Fort Mason Center, and its use skyrocketed as the events became "real cultural happenings." Adaptive reuse was of the essence, guided by the precepts of a historic structure report in 1991. In 1978, 45,000 people came to center events. The following year that figure rose to more than 180,000, a harbinger of even more increases in future use. Also in 1979, the city began a long process of renovating the Great Meadow in Upper Fort Mason. Dirt was brought in and left for a number of years. Landscaping came later, allowing recreational space in the upper fort. The physical structures in the upper fort, both the old headquarters of the Army of the West, which the Park Service turned into its headquarters, and the nearby residences, in which military personnel still lived, were treated as a historic scene. The result was a fusion of historic preservation and adaptive use that anticipated the demands of statute in the same sector of the park. In 1992, Borjes attested to the success of Lower Fort Mason when the historical architect called it one of the first examples of creative management of historic structures to preserve them and use them.[32]

Section 110 questions were muted at Fort Point, which remained a premier historic resource as it had been since its addition to the national park system in 1970. By 1981, more than one million visitors per year reached the old brick fort, creating resource management issues that stemmed from their impact. The Golden Gate National Recreation Area maintenance staff played a crucial role in maintaining the structure, and Fort Point site managers gratefully acknowledged their efforts. As growing numbers of visitors reached the fort by public transportation, the trails to the fort from Battery East on the cliff above it were inundated with visitors; at the same time, the continuous impact of ocean waves contributed to the deterioration of the fort's brick walls.[33] Management of the structure remained consistent with the goals of cultural resource management, for the fort—alone among the different units of Golden Gate National Recreation Area—had one and only one clearly defined purpose. It was historic, the public treated it as such, and the Park Service managed it in that manner. Its issues remained far less complicated than in other units of the park, where competing interests vied to define cultural resource features.

Decommissioned NIKE missile sites offered another window into cultural resource management. The park contained a number of these sites, vestiges of the recent past and heirs to a long tradition of coastal military defense around the Bay Area. Yet the missiles illustrated a classic Park Service and historic preservation dilemma: the history they offered was too recent when the park was established, and it was hard for the agency to see the recent past as historic. Since the missiles were not fifty years old, the age required for assessment under the National Historic Preservation Act, the agency did not initially treat the NIKE sites as historic. After the Strategic Arms Limitation Treaty and the swords-into-plowshares program of the early 1970s, the NIKE missiles were the first weapons to be dismantled. As the last missile launchers in the Bay Area were being taken out of operation in 1974, NIKE Site SF-88L in Fort Barry was offered to the Park Service in a nearly intact demilitarized condition, but the agency declined. As was the case with many other cultural resources recent in time, the agency did not recognize the resource as valuable to its mission. Superintendent William Whalen felt the park lacked the capability to manage the site, and in 1976, no chief of interpretation had been appointed, leaving no advocate for the idea. Whalen accepted the lands, but without the missile equipment.[34]

This situation illustrated a typical conundrum for the Park Service, one repeated across the country with the advent of new parks. Very often, cultural resources in the parks did not illustrate the themes that the Park Service recognized as the reason for establishment. Equally often, the agency devalued existing resources so as to draw attention away from prior uses of the park. From Bandelier National Monument, where the Park Service removed historic structures in the 1930s only to wish they were still there in the 1980s, to Golden Gate National Recreation Area, the agency evinced a narrow approach to the range of cultural resources. In countless circumstances, the Bay Area included among them, it later regretted decisions and wished for the resources it had declined, removed, or altered.

As a cultural resource, NIKE Site SF-88L followed a common pattern, and its significance increased over time. The cold war became part of history, and Americans recognized historic values in the places that reflected it. Once the Park Service acknowledged the historic and interpretive importance of the missile site, preserving it served a broader and neatly historic purpose as the interpretation of a kind of military defense that no longer seemed real, but instead was an anachronism from an increasingly distant past. As a commemoration, the missile site worked well; it told a story about coastal defense and the evolution of strategy, techniques, and weapons that could be linked to other histories of the area precisely because a changing political climate had made them historic in the most distant sense of the word. In the 1970s, the NIKE site was too close to the present; in the 1990s, it had quickly become a relic of something far in the past.

Yet the NIKE site, Fort Point, and other purely cultural areas within the park were anomalies of management. At Golden Gate National Recreation Area, adaptive use and multiple-purpose intensive use situations dominated. Visitor demand turned the intensive use areas from cultural resource issues into something far more convoluted under statute. In situations of overwhelming visitor use, complying with the terms of section 110 was most difficult.

Alcatraz Island presented the most complex set of cultural resource management questions and as a result became the most difficult site regarding compliance. The island's history was varied, but the public's interest concentrated on one time and one specific kind of use, the federal prison that so captured the American imagination. The Park Service regarded the island as a series of historic resources with wonderful vistas and natural resources added, linked together by time, but the public remained focused on the stories of the federal prison, of inmates such as Al Capone, and on the idea that no one ever escaped from the island. Public demand stretched the Park Service's sense of the historic resources on Alcatraz Island, and for a number of years, the agency had difficulty recognizing that no matter what it did, to the public, Alcatraz was a notorious prison.[35]

By 1977, the San Francisco Visitors and Convention Bureau regarded the island as San Francisco's most popular visitor attraction. In 1980, 524,000 visitors saw the island in more than 10,000 personalized tours. No amount of fixing, cleaning, or rehabilitating could guarantee safety. The structures on the island were old and had experienced all kinds of use as well as being subjected to a harsh climate. In 1979, a structural safety study pointed to countless hazards, and during the 1980s, cultural resource management and maintenance on the island were closely aligned.[36] Compliance with section 110 meant that safety measures intruded on the historic scene, continuing the pattern of straddling conflicting demands that characterized management of the island.

Section 110 also drove the process of submerged cultural resource management. Coastal waters under NPS jurisdiction contained a broad array of historic resources, but until 1980, when both the GMP at the park was approved and the amended National Historic Preservation Act passed Congress, submerged resources rarely found a place in the reactive patterns of the park. Only the massive Westside Transport project, with its enormous sewer box under Sloat Avenue, threatened submerged cultural resources and inspired NPS response. After the amendments to section 110, the Park Service began proactive management. The first project statement in the 1982 CRM plan pushed for a survey of submerged resources. The founding of the Submerged Cultural Resource Unit (SCRU), located in the Santa Fe Regional Office Cultural Resource Management Center, followed. SCRU was one of the few projects in the center staffed by permanent Park Service personnel instead of seasonals, giving it a stronger claim on longevity than many similar operations.

Submerged resources at Golden Gate National Recreation Area benefited from the interest of an enthusiastic and knowledgeable staff member, James P. Delgado, a park historian who became affiliated with SCRU and whose activities drove the process.[37] At Golden Gate National Recreation Area and in the Bay Area, SCRU focused on section 110–based survey work. Delgado's efforts led to more sophisticated management of shipwrecks and other underwater resources. Many were better managed by a conservation archaeology regime than by any kind of intrusive action, and the preemptive work of SCRU helped acquire greater knowledge and simultaneously preserve resources. In 1982, the unit undertook a survey of submerged resources in the Gulf of the Farallones National Marine Sanctuary and Point Reyes National Seashore and in 1989 completed the Golden Gate National Recreation Area Submerged Cultural Resource Assessment. The study was an outgrowth of the Southeast Sewer Outfall construction, El Niño in 1982 and 1983 and its impact on resources, and the personal interest of Delgado. The report documented 97 shipwrecks in park waters; in the areas including the Gulf of the Farallones, the total reached 148. With its close attention to an often overlooked facet of cultural resource management, the report became the basis for resource management decisions along the shoreline and under the water.

The Park Service embraced the idea of cultural landscapes in the early 1980s, and they abounded at Golden Gate National Recreation Area. As the concept became an important trend in resource management, the park again became a testing ground for new ideas and policies. Robert Page, the person in the Washington Office responsible for cultural landscapes, set up meetings to orchestrate the park's ability to lead agency thinking in this new category. The original national parks were conceived to be devoid of humans, tributes to nature. The idea persisted in the park system that places people inhabited could not be sufficiently significant for national park status. As late as 1963, when ecology was on the rise in the park system and the Leopold Report, with its image of parks as "vignettes of primitive America," was released, cultural landscapes remained secondary to the Park Service's traditional mission. The move to be inclusive that led to urban parks shifted the focus from landscapes without people to landscapes that could serve nearby people and, not incidentally, in which other people lived. By the time Golden Gate National Recreation Area was founded in 1972, cultural landscapes had become a consideration for the Park Service.

The concept evolved further, from a description of a landscape to a way to analyze and categorize resources. In the late 1990s, *NPS-28*, the governing handbook for cultural resource management, included cultural landscapes among its categories of analysis. The idea evolved into a sort of organic theory, arguing for the historicity and significance of evolving landscapes of human and natural interaction instead of freezing them in a moment of time. The Cultural Landscape Assessment Inventory and Management System (CLAIMS) developed a four-stage process with each level providing progressively more information. The fourth level mirrored an implementation plan. At Golden Gate National Recreation Area, park staffers Patricia Quintero and Nick Weeks worked closely with Cathy Gilbert of the Seattle office and Robert Melnick of the University of Oregon and Land and Community Associates to develop the concept. By the late 1990s, cultural landscapes had become an important tool for resource management. The concept allowed a kind of flexibility, arguing for both growth and change in the landscape as well as its whole over any specific part. CLAIMS and cultural landscapes made the Park Service significantly more able to include inhabited landscapes within park boundaries.

The emergence of the concept had powerful implications at Golden Gate National Recreation Area. The park was very simply one enormous cultural landscape, a laboratory for the implementation of this idea; human habitation of the area stretched back at least 5,000 years. Every feature of the park had been used by humanity in some way, and the entire park reflected those uses. Its urban location meant that expansion of the park necessarily affected people and often included them in the park. Unlike most national parks, Golden Gate National Recreation Area had been acquired from other agencies or by purchase from private owners, not selected from the public domain. As a result, human use and humans were ever present in the park. Everyone, especially PFGGNRA and the other groups that lobbied for the park, recognized this reality. In its early newsletters, PFGGNRA referred to the proposed park as a "greenbelt," recognizing that conceptually it was different. Unlike other parks, Golden Gate National Recreation Area would have to accommodate human activity and continued presence in ways that other national parks did not.[38]

For the Park Service at the onset of the 1980s, the cultural landscapes concept presented important opportunities. After the Alaskan National

Interest Lands Conservation Act (ANILCA), and President Jimmy Carter's lame-duck proclamation of national monuments throughout Alaska in 1980, expansion of the park system seemed limited to historic properties in the lower forty-eight states.[39] Large expanses of land suitable for park purposes no longer existed except in private holdings, and the agency needed a way to add new areas to improve both its base budget and to maintain its standing among federal agencies. An urban park such as Golden Gate National Recreation Area provided ample opportunities to try out the new strategy even if follow-through did not always occur. No place in Golden Gate National Recreation Area was better suited to the cultural landscape concept than the Olema Valley. This collection of old ranches and grazing areas included in the park offered not only the American past in the form of ranches, dairy farms, and other agricultural enterprises but also the more distant past. Part of the area had been a Mexican-era land grant called the Rancho Tomales Y Baulenes, given to Rafael Garcia. After the Gold Rush of 1849, Italian-Swiss and Portuguese immigrants ranched the region, leaving not only historic fabric but also strong local identification with the place. The CRM plan in 1982, which followed from the GMP, noted this presence and suggested its interpretation.[40]

The cultural landscape concept remained a viable idea for park management, but selling it beyond the agency became problematic in some circumstances. The Park Service sought to use the concept to create a Sutro Historic District. Almost from the establishment of the park, advocates were split over whether the existing historic fabric ought to be preserved or whether an attempt should be made to upgrade the property. The GMP laid the basis to "rejuvenate the unsightly development and recapture the spirit of another era." In the decade following its passage, the Park Service planned that transformation.[41] After almost twelve years, on July 30, 1992, the agency brought its plans for the district to the Citizens' Advisory Commission. Again, a long and involved period of public discussion followed, with numerous viewpoints heard and a variety of options considered. The results demonstrated the consensus. As Doug Nadeau, chief of resource management and planning at Golden Gate National Recreation Area, noted in 1992, the Sutro District still needed polish. Unlike other intensive-use cultural resource areas, the Sutro District had not been significantly improved in the preceding decade. The plan proposed restoration of the 1908 Cliff House, making the ruins of the Sutro Baths safe but not tidy—comments suggested that the public valued the ruinlike quality of the baths—and a partial restoration of the gardens on Sutro Heights to retain their character as a neighborhood park. "We are now beginning to scratch the surface," Nadeau opined, of presenting the cultural and natural resources of the Sutro District.[42]

The major departure from the GMP in this formulation involved the construction of a new visitor center at Cliff House. The visitor center proposal was an acknowledgment of much more than growing demand. It signaled no less than the acceptance of the concept of cultural landscapes in both natural and cultural resource management and the need to interpret these features of the park. Nadeau affirmed this change in perspective in front of the commission. "Our appreciation and understanding of the natural resources of the site have increased tremendously," he told the commission. "We all love the ruins. And we felt, based on some early studies we did, that they had no historical value. Now we know they do."[43]

The introduction of the cultural landscape concept provided an impetus to leave things closer to the way they evolved, to respect the past as the past in ways that planning generally eschewed. "Leave the ruins the way they are," intoned Cheryl Barton of EDAW, the consulting firm that assisted in the design of the proposal. "Let them be ruins and let them continue to ruin and interpret them."[44] The cultural landscape idea allowed greater fealty to the past by permitting a broader assessment of significance than other forms of cultural resource management. One drawback is that a cultural landscape typically offered a lens into an ordinary past. Even a full generation after the creation of historic preservation law, Americans still focused preservation efforts on the places and structures associated with the prominent. "Historical" meant great political and social leaders and their homes, the locations of important events such as battlefields, but not the places where ordinary people did ordinary things. As a result, the cultural landscape concept was always vulnerable to charges that its features were not significant. Eventually, the California State Historic Preservation Office rejected the Sutro District as a historic district because it did not convey a turn-of-the-twentieth-century scene.

No place more comprehensively embodied the range of issues in cultural resource management than the Presidio. Home to 662 contributing structures, the Presidio National Historic Landmark included every possible category of management. Much of the post had been intensively used, and the pattern seemed likely to continue. With the army's departure, parts of it were likely to be unattended, a situation that the Park Service experienced at Fort Mason in the 1970s. Structures with tremendous historic significance were included in the post. The officers' club contained the adobe remnants of the Spanish and Mexican Presidio, and Lieutenant General John L. DeWitt administered the order for the internment of Japanese-Americans after Pearl Harbor in one of the post buildings. Some have suggested that the Presidio offered the best museum of American military architecture between 1853 and 1941. All of these issues required management, and meeting the obligations of sections 106 and 110 demanded an exceptional investment of resources.[45]

Relations between the Park Service and the army were uneven between the passage of the Omnibus Bill in 1978 that gave the Park Service veto power over construction in the Presidio and the decision to transfer the post to the park. The military had been accustomed to much greater leeway in its compliance activities. Its immense power and its ability to claim national defense as a reason for its actions gave it both cachet and the ability to make the system work in ways that other agencies could not. As the Park Service often noted, the army served as an excellent steward of historic resources as long as it occupied structures. When it determined that areas no longer met its needs, much historic space suffered neglect.

With a clause that biographer John Jacobs observed was "indecipherable to anyone but Burton," the congressman included in the Omnibus Bill of 1978 a provision that declared that the square footage of the buildings in the Presidio and on any other military lands slated for inclusion in Golden Gate National Recreation Area must remain constant. This stipulation meant that the military had to tear down square footage equal to anything it chose to build, needed the approval of the Department of the Interior, and in most circumstances, assured that the military would comply with section 106 of the amended National Historic Preservation Act.[46]

The army might have been legally bound by the Omnibus Bill of 1978, but the statute did not often encroach upon military planning. The construction of a post office in the middle of Crissy Field and a Burger King by the Presidio's parade ground contributed to the realignment of the relationship between the military and the Park Service. On October 10, 1985, Golden Gate National Recreation Area announced a $5 million to $7 million plan to restore Crissy Field. The announcement followed by one day a report in the *San Francisco Examiner* that the army planned a $100 million development in the Presidio. Sierra Club members found a sign that announced a large post office and a concrete pad that had already been poured in the middle of the old airfield, a clear violation of the governing legislation. The Sierra Club learned that the planned post office was part of a one-stop shopping center that included the post office, which the army leased to the U.S. Postal Service as a public facility, a Burger King, a child-care center, a convenience shop, several barracks, and other buildings on the edge of the Park Service portion of Crissy Field and onto the adjacent Presidio. An outburst from park supporters was immediate. The Park Service, the advisory commission, and Congresswoman Sala Burton received a deluge of mail protesting the military's plans.[47]

The pressure had an immediate effect. On November 1, 1985, Representative Burton announced that the army had suspended construction plans. "Many of our mutual friends and neighbors are both concerned over some elements of the construction program," Superintendent Brian O'Neill wrote Colonel Robert Rose, Presidio commander, "and with a perceived incompleteness of the coordination and public review processes." The military recognized the power of public opinion allied against its action. "Let me assure you of our genuine interest in continuing the positive and valued relationship that has existed through the years between the Presidio, the National Park Service and the community at large," Rose responded.[48]

The army found itself in a difficult position and retrenched. In January 1986, two federal reports, one by an army judge and the second by the American Law Division of the Library of Congress, found that the Presidio military construction program violated federal legislation. Calls for a congressional hearing followed, but the army continued to maintain that it was within the law. The Sierra Club and PFGGNRA filed a lawsuit, charging the army with improper public notice and hearing for a federal undertaking, violation of the clause in the Golden Gate National Recreation Area enabling legislation that gave any excess military land at the Presidio to the Park Service because the army did not intend to operate the post office for its own purposes, and violation of the "one up, one down" provision of the Omnibus Bill of 1978. A February 14, 1986, injunction halted post office construction. Finally, the army relented. In April 1986, the Sierra Club and the Sierra Club Legal Defense Fund reached an agreement with the army and the U.S. Postal Service that led to the demolition of the partly constructed post office and relocation of the rest of the project away from Crissy Field.[49]

The environmental community rejoiced. A concerned group of citizens could assure that federal legislation applied even to the army, and a decision that would have had vast implications for the eventual transfer of the Presidio was reversed. Dr. Edgar Wayburn, the Sierra Club's vice president for national parks and a founder of PFGGNRA, announced, "As has been said of liberty, the price of a national park system is eternal vigilance." The military had been stopped and the primacy of Golden Gate National Recreation Area had been achieved, albeit in the most unlikely arena. "Because our legislation was so protective, the lawsuit was successful," Amy Meyer reflected nearly a decade later. With the support of its constituencies, Golden Gate National Recreation Area successfully grappled with one of its larger rivals in the Bay Area.[50]

Although the legislation that defeated the post office was designed to protect cultural resources, the historic fabric of the Presidio proved ancillary to resolution of the controversy. The issue mobilized the basic Golden Gate National Recreation Area constituency, the very group whose prime interests focused on nature and recreation. Cultural resource support groups were only peripherally in evidence. Although the statute that the groups used to fight the construction served cultural resource ends, the intent of the struggle was much larger than mere cultural resource management. The struggle addressed the questions of the ultimate transfer of the Presidio and of the power of advocates, special interest groups, the army, and the Park Service.

It also pointed out one of the larger difficulties of cultural resource management at Golden Gate National Recreation Area, the issues that stemmed from trying to manage such resources within the context of a national recreation area. In the end, managing cultural resources in Golden Gate National Recreation Area worked best for visitors when the cultural resources were discrete from other park functions. Fort Point and Alcatraz, even with the designation for the birds, were clearly managed as cultural resources. The public identified their primary purpose as cultural, and even when faced with incredible numbers of visitors, the agency could fulfill its function because it and the public recognized the same values in the resources in question. Adaptive use worked well. As long as the tenants and their operations respected the resources and took an active role in managing them, adaptive use served as a way to simultaneously protect cultural resources and provide services for the community. Still, when people thought of Golden Gate National Recreation Area, they did not generally think first of cultural resources. The marvelous variety of military architecture, the Native American, Spanish, and Mexican-era sites, and the array of locations that reflected local and regional history were secondary to other values. Despite sections 106 and 110, cultural resource management at Golden Gate National Recreation Area remained a secondary concern. The combination of public perception, limited resources, and the variety of statutory obligations meant that cultural resources management remained a struggle.

CHAPTER EIGHT

What Stories? Why Stories at All?
Interpreting an Urban Park

Interpreting Golden Gate National Recreation Area pointed the way not only to better understanding of the park's past but also to a better grasp of the meaning and role of the park in the Bay Area. Astride a powerful national image of the Golden Gate, a vista that graces the national imagination and carries great meaning, the park held many layers of historical and natural significance. It became the home to an almost infinite variety of local cultural representations that taught values of all kinds as it offered the opportunity not only to interpret the natural world but also the human relationship to it and the possibilities and problems of managing it. In many ways, interpretation became the linchpin of the park, its way of communicating with the endless constituencies that it served.

As a result, the interpretation mission at Golden Gate National Recreation Area required a level of dexterity uncommon elsewhere in the park system. Interpretation had long been the key feature of Park Service communication, the way the agency both cultivated its public and enhanced respect for the parks. The task was easiest and most evident at the crown jewels—the great national scenic parks such as Yellowstone and the Grand Canyon—and at the places that reflected human and especially American history, such as Civil War battlefields and Philadelphia's Independence Hall. Few parks included all of these features as well as the mandate to provide public recreation. Fewer still experienced the incredible day use that consistently put Golden Gate National Recreation Area at the top of park system visitation statistics. This combination of factors assured that park staff faced myriad responsibilities, especially in regard to visitor safety and resource protection, that distributed NPS personnel and resources across a wider spectrum than at most national park areas. Interpreting became another of the park's balancing acts, a way to maintain constituencies, make new friends, prove the value of the park to a national audience, and support local goals. This complex mission required consistent and intense management.

Interpretation also became crucial to the park's identity. At Yellowstone or Yosemite, visitors instinctively recognize that they are in a national park. All the signs and symbols that surround them reflect their image of a national park. At Golden Gate National Recreation Area, the distinction was

149

always less clear and sometimes entirely murky. Nomenclature contributed to this ongoing identity crisis. The multiple entry points into the park defied NPS efforts to define visitor activities. Myriad uses, many of which preceded the park, further complicated definitions, and the dual status of law enforcement, assigned to both Park Service rangers and U.S. Park Police officers, made it difficult to clearly delineate the agency's presence. Golden Gate National Recreation Area was difficult to distinguish from the nearby city-owned Golden Gate Park, the subject of so much San Francisco folklore. As a result, interpretation's crucial role at the park extended its significance beyond the role it played in remote natural parks and indeed in most park areas. Instead of merely explaining the features, interpretation at Golden Gate National Recreation Area explained the very presence of the Park Service as well.

The roots of interpretation in the Park Service dated to the 1920s, when the agency sought to extend its reach by becoming the purveyor of information to the public. Beginning with museums as vehicles for its communication, the agency branched into interpretive walks and hikes, lectures, and other forms of personal communication with the public. Although by 1933 agency interpretation focused on natural areas at the expense of archaeology, the influx of historic sites into the park system during the New Deal gave the agency ready access to a set of areas with which the public could easily identify. By the end of World War II, interpretation had been institutionalized in the park system as one of the many representations of the value of national parks.[1]

After World War II, Mission 66 provided the Park Service with a level of financial resources that it had never before experienced. This change upgraded not only the caliber of interpretation, because the agency could better benefit from existing research and could in some circumstances engage in its own research about the parks, but also the facilities and technological expectations of interpretation. Museums became more numerous, and more complex exhibits aimed to reach a broader variety of visitors with familiar types of media. New visitor centers offered introductory films, slides, and eventually videotapes that described and interpreted the resources of the park even before a visitor saw them. In this endeavor, interpretation began to serve a twofold role: not only did it enlighten visitors about the park in question but it also promoted Park Service capabilities.

By the time Golden Gate National Recreation Area entered the park system in 1972, interpretation was a sophisticated process that followed set agency patterns. As was typically the case, the new urban national recreation areas fit uncomfortably within the existing Park Service framework. Interpretation had been largely confined to parks with historical or natural significance, places where Americans came, in the older framing of national park values, to be in touch with the beauty of American nature or the heritage of the nation, not where they came for relaxation, leisure, and recreation. In 1972, the question of whether a national recreation area should engage in conventional interpretation loomed large.

In the extraordinary array of tasks that needed to be accomplished during the early years of Golden Gate National Recreation Area, traditional interpretation was put aside. During the 1970s, interpretation focused on education for children and on recreational values. Fort Point provided one of the park's primary locations for reaching younger audiences. Its established position as a cultural resource guaranteed frequent visits from school groups, and its natural setting provided other interpretation opportunities. By 1977, fort personnel had developed a consistent methodology for connecting with youthful visitors. Interpreters structured their presentations to the educational objectives of teachers who brought their students to the site, and they had become skilled at involving students. The Fort Point Environmental Living Program, aimed at grades four, five, and six, allowed students to play the role of soldiers as they stayed overnight. It was consistently oversubscribed, and site managers scrambled to meet demand. The Fort Point Ecowalk, Bay Marine Ecowalk, and other similar shoreside programs functioned with the input of the San Francisco Unified School District. At a time when the Park Service had few programs to counter claims of its neglect of younger visitors, Fort Point and by extension Golden Gate National Recreation Area provided high-quality interpretation that targeted this much sought constituency.[2]

"Parks for the people, where the people are" continued as the primary theme of much of the park, and accessibility and recreation took precedence over interpretation. Fort Point and the other major interpretive areas, such as the Maritime Museum, remained anomalous and easier to interpret because of the inherent focus on cultural resources at such places. These areas fit the conventional definitions of interpretive areas better than the rest of the park, and they functioned with considerable autonomy. As a result, interpretation played a greater role in these subareas of the park than elsewhere. Only Alcatraz Island stood out for the introduction of an interpretive program, but in many ways, the unique characteristics of the island drove the process. The controlled access and safety issues on the island meant that rangers needed to guide visitors around Alcatraz. With rangers' presence, the number of visitors that tour boats brought to the island, and the peculiar place of Alcatraz in the national imagination, an interpretive program needed to be developed.

By the early 1980s, a shift to more traditional interpretive programs began throughout the park. Equally driven by the planning process and by the beginning of a clear definition of a broader purpose for the park, interpretation needed resources. Most interpretive activities were expensive. Museum design and the acquisition of artifacts cost money, and to achieve the ends the Park Service wanted, interpreters had to be employed. During the early years of the Reagan administration, finding resources for anything in the park system was a chore; when the answer was personnel, the chances of receiving adequate financing diminished even further. Golden Gate National Recreation Area needed an entity that could assist its burgeoning interpretive program.

The Golden Gate National Park Association filled that niche. Since its founding, Golden Gate National Recreation Area had participated in a group called the Coastal Parks Association, the only one of the many nonprofit groups associated with the park that had achieved cooperating association status with the National Park Service. The Coastal Parks Association had its roots in Point Reyes National Seashore. By 1980, some staff members at Golden Gate National Recreation Area felt that the association focused too narrowly on the national seashore at the expense of the larger recreation area. Allocation of resources dogged the relationship; most of the funds that the Coastal Parks Association generated went to Point Reyes National Seashore. Although chief of interpretation Greg Moore noted that part of the lack of interest stemmed from inaction by Golden Gate National Recreation Area, the Park Service recognized that the situation did not serve its best interests. Beginning in 1979, the agency explored creating a different relationship with a nonprofit group. The first effort assessed the feasibility of making the National Maritime Museum Association into the cooperating association for Golden Gate National Recreation Area. Both the Park Service and the association had reservations, and in the middle of 1980, Golden Gate National Recreation Area still searched for the best alternative for a cooperating entity.[3]

The agency considered three options, and each possessed advantages and drawbacks. The Coastal Parks Association presented the difficulty of focus. For it to function as well for Golden Gate National Recreation Area as for Point Reyes National Seashore, the Park Service needed to commit sizable amounts of staff time. The National Maritime Museum Association presented similar issues. Its board was committed to the park's maritime resources and feared dilution of its mission. The third option, a new cooperating association designed specifically for Golden Gate National Recreation Area and geared to focusing its impact on interpretive activities, entailed a great deal of work for the park but offered the best opportunity to meet the park's needs. In a bold executive decision, General Superintendent William Whalen opted for a new association.[4]

The Golden Gate National Parks Association (GGNPA) started with a cadre of people with park experience. A former park ranger who had worked for the Denver Service Center and become chief of interpretation at Golden Gate National Recreation Area, Greg Moore, took a leave of absence to play a role in establishing the new organization. Founded in 1982 by a "handful of us," as Moore remembered, and spearheaded by Judy Walsh, the association began to gather momentum. The impetus from the park was unusual; although cooperating associations often developed through parks, there were few cases in which the decision to start an organization came from the park superintendent and a number of park personnel took leave or left the agency to follow through. In 1982, Walsh was hired as a part-time director for the organization and remained in that position for about three years. By 1985, GGNPA had done well enough to hire a full-time director, and Greg Moore was hired in that capacity.[5]

When Moore took on the leadership, GGNPA was a small operation. Three employees comprised the staff, and small bookstores in the various visitor centers around the park provided most of its revenue. The material GGNPA offered was interpretive in nature. In the subsequent fifteen years, as a result of what Moore called the association's "comparative advantage" of being located in an urban park that enjoyed strong public support, GGNPA grew into the largest cooperating association for any single national park area. Its value to the park's programs far exceeded its enormous financial contribution, which by the late 1990s was more than $4 million per annum. GGNPA served as a community liaison, a public relations entity for the park, a fund-raising division, and a supporter of interpretive and resource management programs. It also expanded the role of park cooperative associations, becoming a partner in major development and adaptive reuse projects at Crissy Field and Fort Baker. No other cooperative association had played such a significant role in any park area.[6]

The shift to developing more traditional interpretation programs began as the new cooperative association took shape. Interpretation programs at Golden Gate National Recreation Area served a broader variety of purposes than at most national park areas. The park system developed its interpretation from the context of cultural tourism, an affirmation of the triumph of American society as people of the first three decades of the twentieth century recognized it. By the 1980s, two decades after the great cultural upheaval of the 1960s and its transformation of American values, the tone of much park interpretation seemed stale and hackneyed, tied to an earlier vision of progress that post-Watergate Americans viewed dubiously.[7]

At Golden Gate National Recreation Area, the complicated local ethnic history set atop the military fabric provided one venue for redesigning the way interpretation reached many publics. The park's abundant natural resources and the strong local environmental community tradition added another dimension. Native Americans, African Americans, Japanese Americans, Chinese Americans, the Spanish and their descendants, Russians, and Italian Americans constituted important components of the regional story. In addition, the park had to deliver different varieties of interpretation in widely disparate places. The San Francisco unit contained tremendous urban fabric; Marin County revealed rural themes. Interpretation for the enormous day-use constituency of recreational users consisted largely of user information. As it did in many parks, such information might include a listing of available trails, hazards, and traffic information as well as more conventional forms of interpretation. Again, the incredible variety of audiences and resources at Golden Gate National Recreation Area meant that the mission of interpretation had to expand.

The General Management Plan illustrated the position of interpretation in the park. This comprehensive planning document, designed to guide the park's future, described interpretation very generally in the larger conceptualization of the park. Although the management objectives for Point Reyes National Seashore discussed interpretation in passing, the plan's management objectives for Golden Gate National Recreation Area failed to mention interpretation as a discrete category. Despite many themes that clearly called for some kind of communication with the public, interpretation planning paled in comparison to other goals, such as integrating park functions with San Francisco and other Bay Area communities, and natural resource management. Cultural resources provided an important subsection, and the objective to "Provision a Broad Variety of Park Experiences" could be construed as including interpretation, but the implication of the absence of a clearly defined and specific goal was stunning.[8]

In the GMP, interpretation remained closely tied to recreation, an unusual pairing that reflected the recreational dimensions of the park. The park was to become a laboratory for public education. Interpretation was to focus on discovery of the park's attributes, creating a sense of ownership and responsibility for the park among the public, understanding the social and natural history of the region, and increasing awareness of the regional environment. Ultimately, the experience was supposed to increase visitor enjoyment of park resources. Compared to conventional park interpretation and especially considering the remarkable historic fabric in existence, these were modest goals. The details of interpretation programs were melded into the development section of the plan, maintaining the autonomous character of each subarea within the park.[9]

Despite a growing agency desire to manage all park areas in the same fashion, the predisposition of planners and managers continued to regard national recreation areas as different from national parks and other named categories in the system. Because of the unusual creation of Golden Gate National Recreation Area, which subsumed Fort Point, Muir Woods, and other areas with traditions of self-management into one large and sometimes unwieldy entity, these internal units functioned with great autonomy. Both Muir Woods and Fort Point developed interpretation programs before the plan, and in the larger context of planning an enormous and complex regional entity, it was easy to leave interpretation to grassroots management.

The division of the park into ranger districts, also autonomous, impeded the implementation of larger interpretation objectives. In 1980, eight years after park establishment, the Park Service had yet to become sure of its obligations to the public at Golden Gate National Recreation Area.

Much of the interpretation the Park Service offered began in visitor centers, the key structure in most national park areas. Most parks had one major visitor center; a few had two or more, usually when there were two distinctly different and heavily traveled entrances to the park. At Golden Gate National Recreation Area, the centralized structures to which the agency was accustomed did not work. There were as many as twenty-five entrances to the park, so the function of a centrally located visitor center had to be spread out to many possible entry points. Nor did a large portion of the potential users of Golden Gate National Recreation Area fit the profile of visitors who used a visitor center. Day users, repeat outdoor users, and countless others sought the park's resources but seemed unlikely candidates for the information imparted in a visitor center.

The Park Service understood visitor centers as integral to its mission, and plans for Golden Gate National Recreation Area included the construction of a number of them as ways to facilitate public interaction and interpretation. The first Golden Gate National Recreation Area visitor center was established in a historic structure at the Marin Headlands in 1974; before its renovation, only Fort Point and Muir Woods, still independent units, had separate visitor centers.

That summer, the Park Service took administrative control of much of Fort Barry and Fort Cronkhite; and among the first things the staff established was a combination visitor contact station/ranger station/visitor center in Building 1050 at Fort Cronkhite. The army still occupied most of the other buildings at the fort, and Building 1050 was selected because it was available and near the beach, which park managers correctly assumed would be the primary visitor destination in the new area. The tiny building contained offices, search and rescue equipment, an information desk, embryonic displays, and a minuscule bookstore. Interpreters set up a display of historic photos of coast defense batteries, and the Headlands Visitor Center was in full operation.[10]

In 1975, the park tried to establish a visitor center at park headquarters in Fort Mason that would serve the function of the large visitor centers common at the entry of most national parks. The Fort Mason location posed problems. Although the fort served as the administrative headquarters of the park and in many ways became its social center with the development of the Fort Mason Center, it was not a place that many of the users of recreational resources in the park encountered. As an attempt at a parkwide visitor center, the Fort Mason effort illustrated that reaching the wide variety of visitors to the park was far more difficult than anticipated. The timing of the Fort Mason Visitor Center was fortuitous. It started as a weekends-only facility that consisted of movable display panels that park staff rolled into the ground floor hallways on Saturdays and Sundays and then stowed in a back room during the work week. In 1976, the facility expanded into the large downstairs room now used for public meetings, both as a place to install expanded park-related displays and also as a location for traveling exhibits, common during the bicentennial year of 1976. But location doomed the effectiveness of this visitor center, for Fort Mason did not routinely draw the constituencies that used the park. By the early 1980s, it had become the Western Region's Information Center, a repository of information from parks around the West placed there to fulfill the outreach mission for the San Francisco–based regional office.[11]

The Cliff House Visitor Center followed in 1978. Although park staff recognized that the space was not optimal for visitor contact, the agency had few options. As in the headlands, the structure was the only one made available. The first NPS ranger to operate the new facility found it wanting not only in location but in convenience. Complaining that during the entire planning process no one had ever considered a staff bathroom, she had to close the Visitor Center and go into the Cliff House, a trip that involved climbing up three flights of stairs and then descending two more. The short-comings of relying on existing space were never more apparent.[12]

At the Maritime Museum, the "visitor center" consisted of a tiny desk with an attached chair where the ranger staff sat while on duty, surrounded by the museum's exhibits. Not technically a visitor center, the post served to advertise the Park Service's presence. Prior to Park Service administration of the Maritime Museum in 1977, the Museum Association ran a bookstore there, and the salesperson offered some information to visitors. The NPS sought to establish its presence, and supervisor John Martini decided to put in a formal information desk that would be similar in design to, but separate from, the bookstore. Curator Karl Kortum, who did not like either the NPS or its rangers and who assigned park staff just one antique desk, battled the concept. "I don't know if this counts as a true Visitor Center," Martini recalled, "but we did manage to cram the desk with the mandatory brochures and maps, as well as an information board announcing when the next tour would start."[13] Once again the agency found obstacles to the implementation of its primary strategy for reaching visitors.

In a move that reflected long-standing Park Service conventions, visitor centers became the way the agency measured the success of early inter-pretation. The agency initially regarded the number of visitors who used the visitor centers as its bellwether, reporting that the park's three visitor centers served 153,744 visitors in 1977, an increase of 10 percent over the previous year.[14] This concession to the modes of more traditional national parks simultaneously acknowledged that the Park Service saw interpretation at Golden Gate National Recreation Area in the same terms as it did everywhere else and also meant that the way it regarded the topic guaranteed that many—maybe even most—park users were unlikely to encounter interpretation.

The drive to expand the number and reach of visitor centers continued after the approval of the GMP. In 1988, Muir Woods received a new visitor center, as did Fort Funston and the headlands.[15] Section 110 governed each area, compelling the agency to look first at existing resources before planning new construction. The Fort Funston facility came to fruition in the early 1990s. The recommendation to set up a ranger station/visitor center at Fort Funston, because the existing station at East Fort Miley was totally inaccessible to the public, had been under consideration for at least a decade. The South District law enforcement rangers vociferously opposed the move, observing that even a visitor center would not bring anyone to remote Fort Funston. From the headquarters Interpretive Division staff, John Martini felt that the move could be a good one if the facility was sited in an accessible and appealing location. The former NIKE assembly building adjacent to the parking lot seemed perfect, as every vehicle that entered Fort Funston had to pass the structure. Only one obstacle stood in the way: a hanggliding organization called Fellow Feathers held a permit to use the structure as a hangar. Park management remained sensitive to constituency questions, and, in the end, Golden Gate National Recreation Area determined not to evict or relocate the tenant to make way for staff use. The visitor center and ranger offices were eventually established in a former NIKE-era building at the extreme southern end of Fort Funston, far from most vehicular traffic. Despite signs and other enticements, most visitors mistakenly headed for the hang-gliding area and adjacent parking lot. The visitor center only operated for four years, closing on September 30, 2000.[16]

In 1992, the original Fort Cronkhite Visitor Center was relocated to the refurbished Fort Barry Chapel. In the mid-1980s, an interpretive prospectus for the headlands had been prepared by the Park Service's main interpretation support center at Harpers Ferry that recommended the move to the former chapel. Although a huge percentage of visitors never left Conzelman Road, the main artery through the headlands, all those who did venture further into the headlands had to pass near the chapel, and park staff decided its highly visible location fit the criteria for an expanded visitor center. The building required considerable work to comply with federal statute and to be safe for visitors. Issues such as accessibility and historic preservation loomed during renovation, and planning for design exhibits and information facilities for the center were costly. In a reflection of one of its prime goals, GGNPA financed the design and rehabilitation work, including the interpretive planning. The headlands ranger staff were deeply involved in planning at all levels, negating any sense that GGNPA replaced the park's functions. The new Marin Headlands Visitor Center served as a model of the kinds of partnerships crucial to Golden Gate National Recreation Area. At the grand opening, Superintendent Brian O'Neill announced that he hoped to repeat the process of updating visitor centers throughout the park in partnership with GGNPA.[17]

Despite the reliance on cultural resources, the drive for visitor centers as central cogs in park interpretation illustrated the dilemma of NPS planning at Golden Gate National Recreation Area. Agency history dictated that parks funneled visitors through a central location before guiding them to the resource, and the visitor center was institutionalized in agency culture. Unlike the situation at most park areas, the park's many audiences needed a broader range of information at a wider array of locations. If Golden Gate National Recreation Area could not build a single central visitor center that reached the vast majority of its audience, then the park needed another way to accomplish its goals. Conversely, the lack of perception of Golden Gate National Recreation Area as one park made the visitor centers even more important as ways to reach people.

By the early 1980s, the park's Division of Interpretation had begun to implement interpretation programs throughout Golden Gate National Recreation Area. Outdoor signs at all kinds of locations provided a medium well-suited to the park. Working with Harpers Ferry Center, the division coordinated an information program that produced graphics and text for more than 100 wayside exhibit and information-kiosk panels. Park staff and at least fifteen organizations contributed time to the project. The division also supported the work of the Headlands Institute, in particular by reviewing plans for environmental education and the Headlands Art Center, transportation proposals, and programs for special populations. Park staff members also stepped up research and interpretation of ethnic history and coordinated a draft scope of collections for the National Maritime Museum. They also developed interpretive training for park interpreters, provided technical assistance to permittees and outside organizations, and maintained assistance for exhibits in a number of areas.[18]

Much of the success of the Division of Interpretation came not from facilities development, but from interactive programs such as community outreach and site stewardship programs, enhanced by the cooperation of GGNPA. Many of the functions of the division more closely resembled the kinds of activities that entities such as the Harpers Ferry Service Center typically undertook. The complex nature of the park made interpretation more than just communication with visitors. Planning, the development of open houses to bring new organizations in touch with the park and its facilities, cooperative arrangements with outside groups that used parklands and facilities, and other similar programs comprised a significant percentage of interpretation efforts.[19]

The NPS urban initiative provided one of the best examples of the expanded role of interpretation at Golden Gate National Recreation Area. In 1979, with William Whalen still serving as agency director, the premium on service to urban constituencies remained high. Whalen challenged the park system to better serve urban constituencies, a role for which Golden Gate National Recreation Area was very well suited. During 1979, the Division of Interpretation planned, coordinated, and evaluated a broad range of programs for this purpose. These included Great Explorations, an environmental awareness outreach program that served 12,100 people in 1979 alone. The Cultural Heritage program included summer festivals celebrating Native American, African-American, Asian, Latino, and European cultures, reaching more than 70,000 people. The Energy Awareness program created a "Conservation Household," a former military residence next to park headquarters that was being developed as a model for energy conservation in private residences, and a series of energy education programs were developed for specific areas of the park, including Alcatraz, Hyde Street Pier, Fort Point, Fort Funston, and the Marin Headlands. The Wilderness Dance Concert brought more than 2,000 people to a series of twenty multimedia dance performances throughout the Bay Area. The dances emphasized the relationship of people to wilderness, furthering one of the goals of NPS environmental programs.[20]

Although the GMP called for an interpretive prospectus as the next step in interpretive planning, individual subunits were asked to design theme-specific prospecti for their areas prior to a parkwide document. The time and money to undertake this project had to come from existing budgets, so the process was slow and cumbersome. Although the Alcatraz Interpretive Prospectus was published in 1987 and other areas developed their own, as late as the end of the 1990s, a Golden Gate National Recreation Area comprehensive interpretive plan had not been completed.[21]

The lack of definition provided flexibility, which meant that interpretation could be responsive to community needs in a way that a fixed planning process might not permit. On one level, the visitor center–based interpretation, aimed at people who came to the park to see cultural and natural history, served its goals well. The other dimension, interpretation that aimed at constituency building, often by promoting the concept of stewardship, enjoyed the room to grow.

GGNPA played an essential role in that growth. By 1983, the new cooperating organization had become an important contributor to the park. It brought in more than $100,000 in grants for projects, designed a new bookstore for Hyde Street Pier, expanded the items it offered for sale, and planned a major fund-raising campaign. It also began to shape the direction of interpretation, promoting both the development of interpretation programs for cultural and natural resource management and the constituency-building programs that were the hallmark of Golden Gate National Recreation Area. Among the most successful was the Site Stewardship program, a blend of cultural and natural resource management that attracted the public in impressive ways.[22] As a nonprofit organization, GGNPA enjoyed options that the Park Service could not match. Not governed by the same kind of statutory regulations, it could function with greater flexibility. The funds it generated were not designated for the narrow budgetary categories of government; GGNPA could apply especially the revenues it earned from sales in any way that fit its charter. It also had the ability to hire people quickly and to compensate them at market rates. Equally important, GGNPA could more easily let unsuitable personnel go than a government agency could.

In some ways the organization functioned much like any other cooperating association, but its size, reach, fund-raising ability, and skill at negotiating the Bay Area made it an invaluable partner for Golden Gate National Recreation Area. GGNPA played a more prominent role at Golden Gate National Recreation Area than any other cooperative agency in the park system. Its evolution into an entity that assisted the Park Service in planning and development suggested an evolution into more than mere partnership. GGNPA became part and parcel of the park's future. In the Bay Area, the Park Service worked through emissaries even before the founding of the park, and GGNPA, closely tied to the park but without the restrictions of government policy, reached into important places in the community that the Park Service could not. GGNPA had grown out of the interpretive division of the park, and the synergy between the association and the Division of Interpretation became a defining feature of Golden Gate National Recreation Area.

As GGNPA took a leading role in supporting interpretation in the mid-1980s, the emphasis shifted from conventional cultural resource sites such as Fort Point to the natural features of the park. This change in direction stemmed from many sources. Environmental groups and open space advocacy organizations had been instrumental in the founding of the park, and their influence persisted. Thus, despite the outstanding military architecture of the park, natural resource management received a relatively large share of interpretive attention and resources. In this respect, interpretation mirrored the ongoing set of issues that characterized Golden Gate National Recreation Area and pointed it toward the future. Not only did the definition of the park as a "national recreation area" leave the question of interpretation more open than in national parks and other conventionally labeled park areas, but constituency building, regional partnerships, and the diffuse location of park resources also contributed to a complex management arrangement.

The relationship between GGNPA and Golden Gate National Recreation Area came to define the park. Governed by a board of trustees who stood out for their expertise and determination, "a bunch of fireballs," as Doug Nadeau referred to them, GGNPA retained an innovative and creative spirit, accomplishing remarkable goals for Golden Gate National Recreation Area. Its leaders included some of the most influential and civic-minded citizens of the Bay Area, among them Roy Eisenhardt, president of the Oakland A's, who was elected president of the GGNPA board in 1985.[23] In most situations, the association and the Park Service smoothly worked together; in a few instances, incomplete communication and a differing assessment of the issues led to tension in the relationship. GGNPA's flexibility and creativity were sometimes the envy of park staff who found the means to achieve their goals blocked by federal rules, regulations, and the cumbersome nature of government. Even though GGNPA only engaged in projects with the Park Service's concurrence, in some quarters the feeling grew that the power in the relationship resided with the cooperating association.[24]

The advantages of GGNPA were numerous, and as the 1990s progressed, its role became the subject of debates among park staff. Alcatraz became the focus of much of this tension. As visitor demand for the island grew, providing interpretation became an increasingly tendentious management question that involved GGNPA. Although the association contributed to a number of important projects at Alcatraz, several of its efforts seemed to some observers to overtake the park. One, "Alcatraz: The Future," a plan designed for GGNPA by noted landscape architect Lawrence Halprin in 1988, exacerbated the tension.[25]

Even though the plan had been developed at the request of Golden Gate National Recreation Area, its style and goals seemed a little quirky to park staff. With the superintendent's permission, GGNPA gave Halprin a free hand, and in his quest to open all of the island to visitors, he ignored existing regulations and resource management obligations. In one often retold story, Halprin "blithely waved his hands" as he walked the island when confronted with questions such as the nesting area for Heermann's gulls and impacts on historic structures that required compliance with sections 106 and 110. The park appreciated the visionary conceptualization, but in the minds of many resource managers, his approach did not pay sufficient attention to legislation and other constraints.[26] Rightly or wrongly, some in the park felt that GGNPA had become bigger than the park, and Halprin contributed to the spread of that sentiment.

The issue came to a head over interpretation at Alcatraz. In 1984, the open island concept debuted for Alcatraz, a management strategy that gave visitors far more leeway than ever before. In 1987, the Park Service instituted self-guided tours of islands with headsets. The new system provoked a firestorm of controversy, and interpreters revolted. Faced with a new technology that they believed performed their job without them, some rangers feared being consigned to the scrap heap of island history. In the highly controlled environment on the island, the headsets could replace them forever, becoming a precursor of the end of the role of the interpreter—coveted by so many—elsewhere in the park system. The headsets became a defining moment that summer for the fifteen permanent and seven seasonal interpreters and reinforced the oppositional feelings of Alcatraz rangers. Even after the headset system was installed, the tension remained palpable. Two different modes of interpretation competed. The headsets won the Director's Award for best piece of interpretation and even garnered praise from *Preservation* magazine, always a tough critic of Park Service activities. Yet the interpreters on the island were not excited about the change. At least one interpreter left and has refused to set foot on the island since.[27]

To a greater degree than opponents of the headsets realized, budget questions drove the transformation. After 1980, when Park Service budgets stagnated as a result of the Reagan administration, visitors' demand for Alcatraz tours continued to grow, and the need for interpreters increased as part of the management strategy for the island. Short of funds and positions, the Park Service used revenue from the concessionaires to hire fifteen summer interpretive staff, an egregious violation of NPS policy. Even as demand escalated, no other financing became available. In 1986, NPS director William Penn Mott, a former head of the California State Parks system, ordered the practice stopped. For all of its controversy about the role of interpreters, the self-guided tour resulted from financial realities that dictated diminishing ranger staff, a prelude to denying countless visitors access to the island.

The self-guided tour materials at Alcatraz became exceedingly popular. Between 80 and 95 percent of visitors use the headsets, compared to an average of 30 percent in other museum settings. The authentic voices—a former corrections officer narrated the tape, and Jim Quillen, a convicted kidnapper who spent time on The Rock, is interviewed—the controlled flow inside the cell block, and the easy pattern of movement combined to make self-guided tours a far higher-quality interpretive experience than in many other circumstances. By the mid-1990s, when shrinking budgets considerably decreased the interpretive staff and the reliance on self-guided tours increased, most interpreters conceded that the headset program offered a high-caliber experience, and the awards it won confirmed that impression.

The Park Service faced even rougher times in the mid-1990s, and heightened tension on Alcatraz was one of many results. The election of the Republican Congress in 1994 initiated an attempt to diminish the role of government; some of the proponents of the "Contract with America," Representative Helen Chenoweth of Idaho prominent among them, regarded the Park Service as a villain and sought to dismember it. Efforts to decertify some national parks emanated from Congress and contributed to increased tensions between it and the Department of the Interior.[28] In 1995, a General Accounting Office report on the national park system suggested that doing more with less had never yielded optimal results for the park system. The Park Service, the report recommended, should reduce services or seek more comprehensive partnerships with private entities. At about the same time, the agency and GGNPA began to explore the possibility of keeping Alcatraz open at night with an interpretive staff hired by GGNPA.

The proposal set off a rancorous debate with ramifications for the entire national park system. The Alcatroopers responded with a fury derived from a combination of protectionism and powerful allegiance to the historical goals of the agency. Their numbers had already diminished since the beginning of audio tours in 1987; from a peak of as many as thirty summer interpreters, the Alcatraz staff shrank to six in the middle of the 1990s. Nor did they regard the opening of the island at night with GGNPA interpreters as analogous to the beginning of self-guided tours. In 1987, the agency did not have the staff to meet the demand for its posted schedule; in 1996, the night program represented an expansion of service without an agency presence. GGNPA placed hiring advertisements for employees with job descriptions nearly identical to NPS interpreters and interpretation supervisors even before the program was approved. The rangers felt undermined and fought back. Hewing to reasoning that they traced back to the second director of the Park Service, Horace M. Albright, and quoting the vaunted director's words—"Be ever on the alert to detect and defeat attempts to exploit commercially the resources of the national parks. Often projects will be formulated and come to you sugarcoated with an alluring argument that the park will be benefited by its adoption"—the Alcatroopers blasted the proposal as an abdication of the history and values of the Park Service. "The shifting of program responsibility from a 'public' agency to a private nonprofit that does not have to answer to the public is wrong," a widely circulated position paper by the Alcatroopers insisted.[29]

The Alcatroopers' resistance struck a nerve in the Park Service, for the issue on the island reflected larger trends that frightened Park Service personnel across the country. "Congratulations to the Alcatraz Rangers!" one e-mail posted to the NPS Interpretation Division's electronic bulletin board read, reflecting a level of discontent that stemmed not only from change but also from the ways in which the new circumstances demoralized staff and diminished the values for which the Park Service stood. Even as NPS director Roger Kennedy championed protecting the parks "above visitor convenience and income generation," a visible proportion of Park Service line staff felt compromised. The job they had to do was enormous and the resources scant. "We are here to conserve the parks' resources, provide for the public's enjoyment of them, and leave them unimpaired for the future," observed John Martini in a March 1997 e-mail that offered a clear articulation of the agency's creed tinged with reality. "Don't we wish we had the funds and FTE to do all that by ourselves?"[30]

After protracted opposition, the GGNPA tour guides began work in July 1997. Their uniform looked enough like that of a park interpreter to confuse an unwitting public but was sufficiently different to be distinguished by more than casual observers. Even some very difficult visitors enjoyed their experience with the GGNPA guides. "That evening at Alcatraz they showed me a side of history I'd never before seen," observed Dwight Adams of *Preservation* magazine. "And gave me goosebumps in the process. When was the last time a federal agency did that for you?" Adams's observation also illustrated a dilemma for the Park Service. Their presence became a reflection of the changes that the agency faced nationally as well as a crystal-clear image of the future of park management. Even in the best of times, the government was likely to contract out services that it previously provided with full-time staff. For many federal bureaus with far less viable and meaningful agency culture than the Park Service, this was not as problematic. For the National Park Service, with "service" in its title and a nearly eighty-year tradition of special pride in its activities with visitors, GGNPA interpretive tour guides served as a harbinger of a complicated future that demanded reorientation of agency values along with practices. Even though the Alcatroopers lost the battle, they asked powerful questions about the direction of the agency and about Golden Gate National Recreation Area. Chief among their issues was the relationship between the GGNPA and the park.

By the mid-1990s, Golden Gate National Recreation Area needed a clearer articulation of its message to the local as well as the national public, and GGNPA set out to find a solution to the park's lack of a clear identity. Executive Director Greg Moore envied the strong identity of places such as Yosemite and Yellowstone National Parks and, with the consent of the park, sought a similar powerful image for Golden Gate National Recreation Area. Moore enlisted Rich Silverstein, a trustee of the park association and one of the principals in Goodby, Silverstein, and Partners, one of the largest advertising agencies in San Francisco, to help create a new image for the park. Moore sought to bring the ad agency's creative energy to the park's dilemma, to develop a symbol and a name—a brand—that the public could connect to the physical location. Goodby, Silverstein excelled in developing identity for products; the famed "Got Milk?" campaign was only one of their notable successes. Silverstein himself regarded Golden Gate National Recreation Area as a "magical greenbelt" and sought a strategy for communicating that idea to the public. Silverstein and Moore settled on something they described as small but revolutionary: they relabeled Golden Gate National Recreation Area "the Golden Gate National Parks," creating imagery as part of an effort to articulate the distinctive nature of the area. Instead of individual units, Silverstein positioned the park as a family of sites allied together. "Don't tell anybody we did that," Silverstein, tongue firmly in cheek, beseeched countless audiences in subsequent years.[31]

The decision to change the name in promotional materials did a great deal more than simply create identity. It transformed an ongoing question for the park: the meaning and purpose of national recreation areas. This category had always been amorphous, implying a different manner of management than the flagship national parks despite regulations that insisted on identical management policies for all categories of park areas. When Golden Gate National Recreation Area boldly adopted the name Golden Gate National Parks, it made a claim to the public for a different kind of status—and a different kind of treatment by the public and management by the Park Service. The subtle name change had profound impact. It gave credence to a transformed mission for the park, one that fell more in line with the mainstream traditions of the Park Service and simultaneously engendered more respect from the local and regional public.

The name change was the first step in a multidimensional campaign to promote the park and its features. San Francisco artist Michael Schwab designed a set of images of places in the park, similar in style but emphasizing different areas—Alcatraz, Olema Valley, Fort Mason, and Muir Woods among them—to illustrate the shared management of the park and promote its resources. These images became a signature; easily recognizable, they connoted a sense of shared destiny. The park also had more than fifty different entrances, graced by thirty-six different styles of signs. The campaign replaced the variety with new Golden Gate National Parks markers, uniform signage distinct from the Schwab images that let the public know when they entered the park. The defining artwork and the signs became cornerstones of a consistent visual package. GGNPA also opened a national parks store on the Embarcadero and enhanced its network of park friends. Goodby, Silverstein designed a Web site in three languages: English, Spanish, and Chinese. Through the *San Francisco Chronicle* and direct mail, 15,000 people joined to support the park. To emphasize belonging to the organization and the park, GGNPA produced and sold stickers that created identification for user groups: "I bike the Golden Gate National Parks" read one; others promoted hikers, horse riders, and other activities.[32]

The identification campaign helped create the context for the most ambitious project GGNPA had ever undertaken—the ecological restoration and interpretation of Crissy Field. The project, conceived late in the 1990s and started in 1996 after characteristically fractious public hearings, was a joint effort of Golden Gate National Recreation Area and GGNPA with minor assistance from the Presidio Trust, established in 1994 to administer the built-up areas of the Presidio. GGNPA's fund-raising skills made the project feasible. The Campaign for Crissy Field began in 1998 with a target of $27 million. A lead gift of $16 million, $12 million of which came from the Evelyn and Walter Haas Jr. Fund and the remainder from the Colleen and Robert Haas Fund, seeded the project. By 2001, more than $34 million had been raised for a project that had the ability to re-create nature and reinvent the role of Golden Gate National Recreation Area in the Bay Area. San Francisco Airport contributed large sums to the restoration as part of the requirements that allowed it to expand its runways by developing wetlands elsewhere. Goodby, Silverstein coined the slogan for the campaign, "Help Grow Crissy Field," juxtaposed with the silhouette of a child holding a plant. The advertisements were everywhere in the Bay Area, in the newspapers, on television, on billboards, and on the Internet. Even a city bus was covered with the Crissy Field image. The goal was simple. The public could psychically invest in the project and help to restore the natural habitat at Crissy Field simply by planting one plant in the restored marsh. Hands-on participation guaranteed a sense of proprietary ownership, precisely the kind of public sentiment necessary for the park to serve the community and the nation.[33]

The plan for Crissy Field envisioned nothing less than a comprehensive interpretive, recreational, and natural space in 100 acres along San Francisco Bay. Visionary in every respect, the new Crissy Field was slated to include every dimension of park experience: a promenade with trails, boardwalks, and amenities such as seating areas and picnic tables, open space at the location of the old grass airfield for recreational activities and small public events, a restored twenty-acre marsh that included interpretation and live demonstrations from the Ohlone people, the original inhabitants of the Bay Area, a community environmental center, and much more. Archaeological discoveries led to a memorandum of understanding and a general agreement with area Native Americans that assured archaeological monitoring, compliance with legislative requirements, and interpretation of this important dimension of regional history.

The Crissy Field renovation was an enormous construction project. At the inception, crews removed more than 230,000 cubic yards of soil and rubble and opened a forty-foot-wide channel to the bay. Dune and marsh planning began in November 1999, complete with Ohlone rituals; by early 2000, a smaller version of the historical marsh had begun to take shape, and the waterfront region attained a special feel. The expanded promenade was completed late in 1999, the grass airfield reseeded early in 2000, and the project moved toward completion. As construction of the marsh was finished and its outlet opened to the bay in November 1999, freshwater and seawater mixed in the Crissy Field tidelands for the first time in nearly 100 years.[34]

One of the most impressive green space projects in Bay Area history, the Crissy Field renovation, one of the largest restoration projects the Park Service had ever undertaken, represented the fulfillment of the park's single most difficult mission, the need to be all things to all people all of the time. The new marshland project included nature, culture, and recreation, interpreted the past and the space, and left room just to play. The restoration of the airfield provided both open space and a historic scene. Visitors who wanted a natural experience along the waterfront, those who sought to learn about the Ohlone people or about environmental issues, and those who simply wanted to walk, run, or hike all found the space accommodating. In a way that no previous Park Service project had accomplished, Crissy Field melded all the uses and all the park's constituencies. In a little more than 100 acres, it answered the myriad questions about interpreting Golden Gate National Recreation Area and fulfilled each and every one of the complicated mandates of the park's mission.

Crissy Field revealed the complicated tension between uses that characterized Golden Gate National Recreation Area. The plan was supposed to be a historic restoration of a grass airfield where it had been covered by buildings. The airfield clearly had a wider variety of uses as a meadow than as historic space, but the area was still a valuable historic resource. Even though the Crissy plan and the GMP Amendment for the Presidio called for historic restoration, the recreational and environmental dimensions of the plan took precedence. When the Ohlone middens and the historic archaeological areas of Crissy Field were discovered, some felt that the historic resources competed with the marsh restoration and the attempts to promote recreational pastimes such as windsurfing. Addressing the archaeological component also threatened to delay completion of the project. Again, the competing goals of the park pushed against one another.

Crissy Field also illustrated the crucial nature of relationships in the Bay Area. Without GGNPA's outstanding fund-raising experience and capability, without the support of its talented board and volunteers, without the resources it could bring to bear on the process of renovation and the association's acute decision-making, the Park Service could never have succeeded with the project. The agency lacked the resources that GGNPA could muster, further illustrating the significance of the partnership with an association that contributed more than $52 million to park projects during its history. The synergy between Golden Gate National Recreation Area and GGNPA was never more clear or pronounced; the entities were intertwined for the benefit of both. The public could only benefit from the close ties, but in certain circumstances, the boundaries between the park and the association could blur.

To visitors, such a distinction often seemed immaterial. Although in any group of Park Service employees, park interpreters most strongly identified with the values of the agency, outside guides such as those provided by GGNPA could also provide visitors with an excellent experience. In situations such as Alcatraz and to a lesser degree Crissy Field, NPS interpreters saw themselves as beleaguered, swarmed over by an unappreciative public and recalcitrant funding. "We old-timers always felt the best time for both interpreters and visitors at Golden Gate National Recreation Area were those first years [between 1973 and 1977]," observed John Martini, "when everyone who went to Alcatraz received a guided program AND the groups were still small enough to maintain a sense of intimacy with both the interpreter and the resource."[35] During this era, control of visitation numbers at Alcatraz meant that the resources devoted to management of interpretation on the island equaled the demand, a situation that changed as the park and its interpretive mission expanded after 1978. In many ways, the path to the GGNPA interpreters began with the growth of the park twenty years before, and each step, from the Reagan administration's attempts to privatize public holdings to the reinventing of government of the 1990s, had the same composite effect: they forced the Park Service to do more with the same resources. With every increasing demand and level of funding and staffing resources, the shift to other kinds of service providers—even in specialized areas such as interpretation—seemed preordained.

Nowhere did this conundrum become more clear than at the Presidio. By the time the transfer of the former army base to the Park Service took place, the questions of resource distribution and the challenges to the agency's ability to manage its domain were frontline issues. As a result, the addition of the Presidio followed the public-private partnership model increasingly common in the park system. Much of the administration of the Presidio fell to a congressionally created governing body, the Presidio Trust. In the establishing legislation, interpretation at the Presidio remained the responsibility of the Park Service.

The Presidio presented an enormous interpretation challenge, an amalgamation of the entire history of interpretation at Golden Gate National Recreation Area. Its diverse themes, including a Native American presence and Spanish, Mexican, and American military themes, and its 470 contributing historic structures as well as a variety of natural habitats and species presented clear avenues for interpretation. The Presidio contained 1,480 acres of green space and historic setting, managed by the army for more than a century, which as part of the park became one of the most valuable pieces of urban green space in the nation. The crowded Bay Area coveted the space, and to much of the public, the highest and best use of the Presidio was recreational.

The establishment of the Presidio Trust, with its clear financial mandate, both created opportunities and complicated the possibilities for interpretation. At the core of the trust's mission was financial self-sufficiency, for the Presidio's unique mandate—being able to pay its own way by 2013 at a cost of as much as $36 million per year—was daunting. Although the GMP amendment, the document created by the park service in 1994 to guide the Presidio's transition from military post to national park, clearly identified natural and cultural interpretive themes, the need to generate revenue from the former post pushed real estate and leasing to the fore and interpretation and resource protection to the peripheries of the planning process during the late 1990s. Even though the written agreements stipulated that each tenant make a contribution to the interpretation of the Presidio as a condition of their lease, in early 2000, the effort was not yet comprehensive. The organization of interpretation at the Presidio had not evolved far enough to create cohesiveness.

In an effort to accelerate the emphasis on interpretation, the park, the trust, and GGNPA convened a conference in April 2000. A brainchild of Colonel Whitney Hall, former post commander of the Presidio, and Redmond Kernan of the Fort Point and Presidio Historical Association, the descendant of the Fort Point Museum Association that lobbied for the national historic site in the 1960s, the Park Service and the trust brought together almost seventy scholars and educators from the museum community with expertise in cultural and natural interpretation. For two and a half days, the participants formulated ideas about planning and interpretation for the Presidio, seeking a balance between the visible structures and spaces of the post and the needs and ideas of different cultural groups with a stake in the park. As the conference ended, the participants expressed hope that their ideas would be integrated into the process of planning and interpreting the Presidio.

The attempts to interpret the Presidio illustrated the changing nature of interpretation not only at Golden Gate National Recreation Area but also in American society as a whole. As late as the 1970s, the themes of a place such as the Presidio or Alcatraz followed a clearly delineated narrative derived from the dominant course of American history. The 1960s changed forever the way Americans looked at their past. What had once been a story of certainty became terrain that was contested for its symbolic meaning.

As the twenty-first century dawned, interpretation filled many roles at Golden Gate National Recreation Area. It served as education, explaining nature and natural history and telling stories about the diverse human past. Interpretation also defined the presence of the Park Service in the region, explaining to the public the limits on behavior in recreational lands, and let it reach new constituencies. Multilingual interpretation material and multilingual staff members became crucial as visitation patterns brought broader numbers of visitors who did not speak English. Interpretation served as a constituency-building forum for the agency, bringing local and regional groups into the park's sphere and enabling them to broaden the message the park offered. With the support of a powerful association,

GGNPA, the agency had the resources to initiate and maintain a publication program that did a great deal to interpret the park and define its role in the Bay Area.

Yet challenges remained, both at the Presidio and in the rest of the park. Interpretation had made great strides in fulfilling the park's many-faceted missions. Examples such as Crissy Field really did become all things to all people nearly all of the time, but questions of priorities such as those on Alcatraz, questions of power such as those in the relationships between the Park Service, GGNPA, and the Presidio Trust, and questions of significance—what kind of interpretation a national recreation area needed—cropped up with regularity. As the public face of the park and as its primary constituency-building endeavor, interpretation served much more complicated functions than did other areas of park administration. Under the circumstances, the ways in which interpretation seemed diffuse and contradictory testified more to the many missions and masters the park had to serve than to any shortcoming.

CHAPTER NINE

The Presidio and the Future

As the twentieth century ended, the most beautiful spaces in the nation increasingly felt like private property. Especially along American coasts, the dollar value of real estate grew exponentially and public space on the coasts became harder to find. Some states, such as Hawaii, declared all beaches public property, but access to the shore became difficult to find and even harder to preserve. A dimension of exclusivity rose around coastal areas; more and more, the beauty of the shoreline became a status symbol of distance from the mainstream in American society. This transformation accentuated a rising class division in the United States, much exacerbated by the unbridled economic climate of the 1980s, best labeled with the ethos "greed is good" of the fictional Gordon Gekko in Oliver Stone's 1987 film *Wall Street*, and made into national dogma with the enormous stock market run-up of the 1990s.[1]

Public open space was the only hedge against the privatization of the coast. Just as the national park had been the American contribution to the idea of democracy, public spaces of all kinds remained one of the perceivable levelers in American society, one of the few mechanisms left to dispel growing notions of the perquisites of privilege. By the end of the 1980s in the always expensive, increasingly redeveloped, and class-riven Bay Area, open public space often meant one of the units of Golden Gate National Recreation Area. The park symbolized the concept of public space, firmly placing public over private, a genuine obstacle to the privatization of the region's most cherished features. From the Marin Headlands to Sweeney Ridge, the park included not only coast and beach but also a range of green space, places where the public could enjoy the region's beauty in shared space. It had become the place where people interacted, a multifaceted space that held great significance for not only the privileged but also nearly everyone in the Bay Area.

Against that backdrop, the announcement of the closing of the army base at the Presidio and its transfer by law to Golden Gate National Recreation Area served as a pivotal moment in the history of the Bay Area park and indeed the national park system. Often described as one of the finest pieces of property in the United States, the Presidio was spectacular urban recreational space filled with valuable cultural resources as well as prime territory for commercial and high-end residential development. Estimates of its private-sector value ranged from $500 million to $20 billion, leaving the growth coalition, that sector of the business community that benefited from development, salivating. The military presence at the Presidio was the sole reason it had not been developed long before the 1990s. Its status as public land made it more than simply desirable space along the coast of the Pacific Ocean. It also became a symbolic antidote to the problems of American society, to the class and cultural differences that increasingly tore at the nation's social fabric.

At the moment of the announcement of its transfer to the Park Service, the Presidio became an emblem of nearly everything important about the cultural past in a changing society. It simultaneously represented the end of the cold war, the fundamental alteration of the Bay Area's economy, the commitment to public endeavor in the region and beyond, the idea of shared public space for recreation and preservation, and in many ways the concept of democracy in a postindustrial society. In its transformation from "post to park," a phrase coined by the Presidio planning team, the Presidio truly seemed poised to become all things to all people. "When the historic Presidio's 1,480 acres of strikingly beautiful headlands are turned to civilian use," the *San Francisco Chronicle* observed, "San Francisco will enjoy a gift unmatched by any other city on the globe."[2]

Astride the Golden Gate, the Presidio seemed to be a canvas on which the wonderfully fractious and politically astute communities of San Francisco and the Bay Area could paint their desires. It was beautiful and lush, full of stunning and even breathtaking views, with a remarkable array of historic structures, native and exotic plants, wildlife, bicycle trails, and roads. Two major commuter routes bisected the post, making it a focus of urban traffic planning as well as park preparation. The nearly 1,500-acre enclave was an anomaly, its development fixed in time by the transformation of the army and Phil Burton's far-sighted legislative action that had prevented new construction. In one of the nation's most expensive cities, the Presidio offered a safety valve of the kind Frederick Jackson Turner envisioned when he talked of the closing of the frontier a century before. Its location in the heart of a densely populated region and its potential definition as a combination of urban green space and community living and working space could serve as a way to ease the tension of a packed urban area. The reinvention of the Presidio also served as a powerful symbol of what San Francisco could become, and everyone who sought to define the space simultaneously attempted to put their stamp on the city as well.

Yet the military's departure from the Presidio left an enormous hole in the Bay Area's economy. During the 1980s, military expenditures increased dramatically, adding to a sense of well-being for communities in which the military had an extensive presence. The end of the cold war provided an enormous shock; from Los Alamos, New Mexico, to San Francisco, many communities found that the lifeline that had long supported them first diminished and sometimes disappeared. Large segments of the Bay Area were outraged when news came that the Presidio would be closed along with more than fifty other bases across the nation. The Defense Department's Base Realignment and Closure Commission (BRAC) estimated that the closing of the Presidio would save $50.2 million each year and yield an additional one-time savings of more than $313 million.[3] By any measure, these numbers represented significant economic activity in the Bay Area, a genuine loss for the community and region—even if the resulting transfer helped alleviate regional open-space and quality of life issues.

The former U.S. Army base had the potential for equally grand administrative problems for the Park Service. Its significance and cost dwarfed any previous Park Service endeavor, even the parks that resulted from the implementation of the famous Alaskan Native Interest Land Claims Act in 1980. Because of its location in urban San Francisco, the transformation of the Presidio into a park provided an opportunity to redefine the intellectual boundaries of the Park Service at a moment when the agency struggled to fulfill the many facets of its mission. By the late 1980s, the agency was in disarray, pulled between competing goals and stripped of its powerful ties to its heroic past by external threats. The Park Service had always been the public's favorite federal agency; to hear itself called "an empire designed to eliminate all private property in the United States" by wise-user Ron Arnold, a sentiment later echoed by Idaho congresswoman Helen Chenoweth, shocked an agency that believed its mission and values were at the core of American culture. Such attacks startled the agency and made it question its purpose. Many felt that its principles, so carefully articulated by Stephen T. Mather and Horace M. Albright and implemented for most of the century, had become subsumed in the quest to please a fickle Congress and an irate public.[4] The Presidio was both salve and salt in the wounds of the Park Service.

Although many in the agency relished the prospect of transforming the Presidio into a national park, the project demanded expertise and resources far greater than those available. The Park Service had little experience with the kind of economic management that the transformation of the post demanded. The agency had a long history of developing parks from public land but far less experience with transfiguring large plots of urban and suburban real estate. Some questioned whether the Presidio ought to be a park at all. Park Service director James M. Ridenour, a George H. Bush administration appointee, felt particular qualms about the addition. This "economic development project," in Ridenour's view, had the potential to redefine the meaning of national parks, drain agency resources, and become a key park for shaping the future of the agency in the twenty-first century. The Presidio project possessed the scope and scale to redefine the management of the park system and, even more, the potential for altering the meaning of national park areas in American society.[5] Much was at stake as preparation for the transfer began.

Equally challenging was the sheer cost of running the Presidio. An initial estimate of the operating costs topped $45 million annually, more than twice the line-item budget of Yellowstone National Park; by the late 1990s, the budget had been cut to the $25 million range, still an extraordinary sum by agency standards. One unnamed Park Service official called the entire project a "$50 million a year maintenance sinkhole."[6] Besides maintenance, the management of the cleanup of hazardous and toxic waste and the enormous cost of rehabilitation, already a strategy to lobby for funding as much as a preservation tool, posed threats to the agency. In the most basic of terms, the Park Service lacked the resources to run the new park. Facing staff shortages throughout the park system and with more than $1 billion in deferred maintenance, the agency needed help with the capital outlay that the new park required. The project's expenses, in a time when Congress regarded government spending as a vice rather than a civic virtue, compelled different tactics at the Presidio than at any other national park. From the start, most people understood that some kind of public-private arrangement would be necessary to assist in the transformation and to manage the many assets of the Presidio that could be made to pay for its public spaces. The countless structures offered an opportunity to raise funds to offset the enormous cost of historic preservation and of running the post-as-park.

But the Park Service was a resource management agency, not a commercial real estate leasing company, and Presidio management demanded reorientation of agency perspective. The Presidio was part of a park, but in a way no previous national park area had ever been: it was to be run in a pay-for-itself manner. In some fashion, the agency would need to be able to use the Presidio's many and varied structures to generate revenue to fund programs. Almost from the moment the transfer was slated to take place, it was clear that the Park Service would either run an enormous leasing service or would have to engage in some kind of partnership with an entity that could manage commercial and residential space. In an agency accustomed to autonomy and still reeling from the change in practice that managing urban parks demanded, this eventuality meant reassessment of internal values. Could the Park Service maintain its mission and become landlord of 6.3 million square feet of prime space on market basis?

This complicated conception lay at the heart of the tension that surrounded the transfer and its aftermath; clearly for some more traditional Park Service people, the unique situation at the Presidio threatened to redefine what national parks were and how they were funded. The tacit guarantees that had stood since 1916—national parks for the people, paid for by their taxes, and reserved for their enjoyment and use—were challenged by the creation of the Presidio Trust. Many lamented the creation of the trust, worried that it meant the end of this ideal. "The Presidio is public land," wrote Huey D. Johnson, director of the Western Region of the Nature Conservancy in the 1960s, founder of the Trust for Public Land in 1972, secretary of the California Resources Agency under Governor Jerry Brown from 1978 to 1982, and president of the Resources Renewal Institute, in 1996 in a clear articulation of the conventional value of public land. "The nation's parks and wilderness areas belong to all the people of the United States and are meant to be reserved for use by the people, not turned into profit-making ventures. How we deal with them is a measure of the state of American culture."[7] In the late 1980s and early 1990s, American culture had morphed into liberal consumerism, which shed any notion of community and common space and placed a dollar value on everything.

The timing of the transfer added markedly to the demands on the Park Service and to the already enormous pressure to reenvision the Presidio as a park that included nonresidential space. Although it was widely acknowledged that the army would one day depart and that the organic legislation for Golden Gate National Recreation Area stipulated that the post would be incorporated into the GGNRA, the closing had enormous ramifications for the Bay Area. On the heels of the debilitating California recession of the late 1980s and early 1990s, the closing of the Presidio military base and countless other installations in the area dented the regional economy. Closure created a gap in civilian employment in San Francisco, and nonmilitary workers were transferred or "riffed"—governmentese for laid off by a "reduction in force." The influx of capital from the military also dried up; it left no more contracts for the Presidio, and even the paychecks that soldiers stationed there spent in the community ceased to cycle through the regional economy. On more than one level, the Park Service was expected to help bridge the gap left by the military.

The agency had never faced such an enormous task. For most of its history, the Park Service managed parks far from urban centers. Only since the 1970s had urban management been a significant dimension of the Park Service, but in the more than twenty years that followed, no park ever faced the promise and responsibility of an economic development project of this scope and size. With public-private partnerships one of the foci of efforts to change government's role in American society, the idea of bringing other entities into the management process became both politically viable and attractive to many constituencies. The Park Service appeared initially overmatched at the Presidio; its experience did not seem applicable to many of the issues it faced. The combination of not-for-profits such as GGNPA and commissions similar to the Citizens' Advisory Commission added to the expertise of professional managers seemed likely to offer a redefined Presidio that best accommodated the needs of the public. No situation lent itself more to utilization of the alliances that the Park Service nurtured for the previous twenty years in the Bay Area. In the convoluted atmosphere of the Bay Area, Golden Gate National Recreation Area unwittingly forged a base for relationships that was to prove crucial when the Presidio dropped into its lap. The combination of outreach, public hearings, conciliatory behavior, recruitment of constituent groups, and nearly every other step that the Park Service took at Golden Gate National Recreation Area all seemed to lead directly to the Presidio.

The task was daunting, as all involved remembered. Despite the optimism of the initial moment, Amy Meyer recognized that the alliances so valuable elsewhere in the park and the CAC's public processes were insufficient to the task. Given fifteen years, and in need of at least $100 million for environmental remediation and roughly $600 million for capital expenses ranging from seismic protection to meeting codes and compliance, the trust faced the largest task ever allotted to a public park.[8]

The 1972 bill that included the Presidio in Golden Gate National Recreation Area began to reverse the typical distribution of power among federal agencies in the Bay Area. After the Omnibus Bill of 1978, when the army was forbidden from engaging in the construction or demolition of structures on the Presidio or other military lands slated to become part of the park without permission from the secretary of the interior, the army learned that it no longer had sole jurisdiction over the future of the Presidio.[9] The aging post was not sufficiently large to meet any of the needs of modern military practice, lacking the storage capabilities, space, and airport facilities that supported army missions in the post–cold war military. Nor could the post provide adequate training space for modern warfare. Despite its important location, spectacular scenery, and historical position as the point of departure for Pacific activities, in the post–cold war world, the Presidio was an expensive anachronism.

The Presidio's predesignated status as part of a national park meant that while the economic impact of the closure remained large, the community in which the post stood was caught between its desire for park space and its economic health. The Bay Area retained a strong regional economy that needed military expenditure, but to a much greater degree than in most other cases of base closure, the military was only one component of the regional economy. By the end of the 1980s, San Francisco had reinvented itself as a convention and tourism destination as well as a regional and Pacific Rim financial center. Nearby, the economic engine of the future, Silicon Valley, gathered momentum. The military was important, but unlike circumstances in other communities, it alone did not drive the economy, and even the closure of other bases did not portend economic doom for the Bay Area. Once Congress confirmed the closure, the transfer of the Presidio from post to park began. The Department of Defense envisioned a five-year transition period, with the army leaving by the end of 1994. The question of what the Presidio would become loomed large in the Bay Area, and no shortage of claimants for the space came forward after the decision to close the post.

The proposals took many forms and represented many points of view. The Bay Area seemed engaged in a contest with the goal to find an appropriate use for the Presidio, leading to a variety of unsolicited proposals. The *San Francisco Chronicle* ran a four-page spread entitled "The All-New Presidio: 1001 Ideas on What to Do with It Now." The *San Francisco Independent* trumpeted "Help Shape the Presidio." Even Mikhail Gorbachev weighed in, calling the Presidio the ideal place for the headquarters of the U.S. chapter of his Gorbachev Foundation. Robert Corrigan, president of San Francisco State University, envisioned "an Education Park," while Kevin Starr, California state historian, saw "a prophetic place, where the future is evoked and struggled for in ways at once symbolic and practical." Others envisioned a space that could provide solutions to urban ills; one such proposal sought an AIDS hospice, another, a homeless shelter, and a third, a recovery center for drug addicts. Visions of the Presidio as one large space or broken up into many small ones competed. As the proposals streamed in, William Penn Mott, who stepped down from the National Park Service's director's post in April 1989, encapsulated the issue. The Presidio was "a global resource," he intoned. "Where is the vision that will stir our blood?"[10]

The energized public embraced the idea of the transfer. To many in the Bay Area, the Presidio seemed an ideal of public space in an age when publicly oriented programs and the values they embodied fought against the spreading concept that private entities functioned better than public services. To the public, the question focused not on park status, but on the nature of the park. The Presidio was difficult to define as space. Military structures did not completely define it; natural habitat, earlier history, and urban recreational space offered other themes for exploration. Even with the bold ideas advanced at the earliest planning stages, the final disposition remained entirely open to debate. No idea yet captured everyone's imagination. As 1990 began, Mott was correct. No one had come forward with an idea worthy of the magnificent space in the shadow of the Golden Gate Bridge.

The opposition to closure compelled the Park Service to keep its plans for development out of the public eye. The Bay Area congressional delegation made it clear to the Park Service that its main objective was to keep the base open, and Golden Gate National Recreation Area staff clearly recognized the consequences of anything that thwarted the delegation's goals or embarrassed its members in public. "They didn't want us out there trying to lead the community organization to define its future," Superintendent Brian O'Neill remembered. "We lost a year of valuable time in thinking through the transition" to park status as much of California's congressional delegation tried to reverse BRAC's decision. The Park Service did not even publicly announce the formation of its planning and transition teams, preferring to keep the groups and their members away from the public gaze until the congressional delegation finished its maneuvering. "We didn't send out press releases saying we were organizing," O'Neill remembered.[11] The park had learned its lessons of local politics well, avoiding any hint of discord as Pelosi and Boxer attempted to diminish the impact of the closure.

Although the Park Service was merely one of many stakeholders at the Presidio, it held the land. Developing a new relationship with the army was paramount. Existing relationships from Whalen's era persisted, but the Presidio demanded new emphasis. The transfer could go easily or badly, and the process depended on how the two agencies regarded each other and whether they could reach accommodation. Superintendent O'Neill felt "both excitement and a sinking feeling in my own stomach" when he heard the news of the transfer. "We knew that we were going to be working under a magnifying glass," he remembered.[12] The two agencies had very different cultures, and both sides had to learn better how the other operated in order to achieve the best results. In one early encounter, O'Neill requested a meeting with Lieutenant General William Harrison, commander of the Sixth Army. When asked its subject, O'Neill replied that it would cover general issues. Army protocol required more detail, as military officials were accustomed to being informed of the topics to be discussed so that they could be prepared. Park Service representatives soon found that if they wore their Class As, the standard Park Service dress uniform, they received a better response from military officers than if they wore civilian business clothing. Mike Savage, head of the Park Service's transition team, displayed a cool professionalism that helped the process. With some protocol training for park personnel by the army's public affairs office, the Park Service and the army were able to develop a solid working relationship.[13]

The military remained ambivalent about the transfer. From one perspective, it ceded a place of importance and history, and for some of its leaders, relinquishing control was difficult. Yet the Presidio had become an expensive headache, the terms of its management changed greatly by Phil Burton's "one-up, one-down" rule and especially by the cessation of construction on the post office in 1986. The army experienced a level of scrutiny to which it was unaccustomed, as newspapers and magazines trumpeted accounts of its management practices. *National Parks*, the National Parks and Conservation Association's magazine, took an aggressive stance that caught the army unawares. The association charged that the army failed to adequately assess the condition of the Presidio and provide steps to mitigate its issues in a draft environmental impact statement on the transfer. Accustomed to proceeding without watchdogs, the army found life in the court of public opinion uncomfortable. Although notable exceptions, such as Lieu-

tenant General Glynn C. Mallory, Harrison's successor, had difficulty accept-
ing civilian control of the Presidio, many in the command structure recognized that greater public scrutiny highlighted the administrative strengths
of other agencies. The Park Service worked to be sensitive to the concerns
of military personnel who found their lives transformed by the decision to
close the Presidio.[14] The transition began as smoothly as could a reversal of
roles of such proportion.

The time line for the military's departure was very short. In retrospect,
some NPS officials wished they been given fifteen years to plan the transition, but five was all they received. "I always felt that because the timeline
for the Army's departure was so precipitous, we should really simplify our
planning for the Presidio," recalled Doug Nadeau, chief of resource management at Golden Gate National Recreation Area at the time. He advocated concentrating on the structures, the more than 500 buildings that
contributed to the national historic landmark designation, and deferring
natural resource issues such as forest management. Instead the agency
opted for a more conventional approach, "by the book," Nadeau described
it, that placed heavy demands on park staff and on the planning process
and contributed to the growing distance between the Presidio and the rest
of the park.[15]

To meet the challenges of the Presidio, the Park Service utilized its
friends and established the kind of relationships for the Presidio that had
been successful at Golden Gate National Recreation Area. The Park Service
needed influential friends if it was to affect Congress and the Department
of Defense as they appropriated funds for the Presidio; even local uproar
was not sufficient. The park's cooperating association, the Golden Gate
National Park Association, entered the process. At the request of the Park
Service, GGNPA developed a concept for the Presidio Council, an advisory
group similar to the CAC, as a way to bring volunteers into the planning
process. The Park Service wanted "to pull together some of the greatest
minds in the country in an advisory role," Craig Middleton remembered,
"to try to get some ideas about what should the vision be for this place." In
the Bay Area, this was a tried and true strategy that created a proprietary
feeling about the resource in question.

As a solution to the management of the Presidio, GGNPA offered the
CAC, the single most successful community advisory board in the park system, as the organizational model. GGNPA envisioned the Presidio Council
along similar lines, an entity that could bring the benefit of professionals in
various areas as well as a national context to Presidio deliberations, but the
council was never intended to be a public body like the CAC. "It simply
wasn't going to happen," O'Neill recalled, "unless we had a very strong
voice from a national constituency." There were few more high-powered
entities than the Presidio Council. Included among the earliest members

was James Harvey, chairman of the board of the Transamerica Corporation, a charismatic leader who accepted the chair of the council. John Bryson, CEO of Southern California Edison, and Richard Clarke, CEO of Pacific Gas and Electric, headed a diverse group of civic leaders, business professionals, conservation professionals, and even movie directors on the Presidio Council. Architect Maya Lin, known for her design of the Vietnam War Memorial in Washington, D.C., also was a member. A real synergy developed among the group, and many remembered their discussions as fruitful and enlightening.[16]

The Presidio Council soon included an array of powerful and influential people who donated their time to help create a Presidio plan and raise funds to implement it. The council and GGNPA together raised almost $1 million and received a similar sum in donated time and services to conduct economic analysis. GGNPA used part of the money to hire professional staff to assist the council, to commission consulting projects to further the planning effort, and to create and disseminate newsletters, promotional brochures, and other communication materials. Composed of powerful and influential individuals, the council could not help appearing as if it favored privatization. "I never felt that the Council overstepped its bounds," O'Neill observed as a counterpoint. At the same time, the Citizens' Advisory Commission was enlisted to support the planning effort.[17] The assembled influence, experience, and resources seemed perfect for the task of redefining the Presidio as a national park.

Planning the Presidio was a Park Service endeavor, too large a task for the staff at Golden Gate National Recreation Area alone. Both the regional office and the Denver Service Center, one of the Park Service's specialized support units, vied for control of the process, and in the end, the agency assembled two teams to assist in the process. The General Management Plan Amendment (GMPA) planning team reported to the Denver Service Center and was charged with creating an amendment to the Golden Gate National Recreation Area GMP for the Presidio. The management transition team reported to the park and planned for the actual transfer of the Presidio. From the Denver Service Center and duty-stationed at Golden Gate National Recreation Area, the seven-person core team was headed by Roger Kelly Brown, who was succeeded by Don Neubacher, both longtime NPS veterans. Both had experience with complicated projects. Differences in management style led to Neubacher's succession; advocates such as Amy Meyer thought Brown was "in over his head." Neubacher experienced considerably more success; he was "really smart," Craig Middleton remembered. "I was amazed at how they could pull together an extraordinary amount of workshops and an extraordinary amount of public comment into something that turned into a plan." The complete twenty-person planning team included experts in historic preservation, landscape architecture, park planning, law, finance, and community development from all over the Park Service and consulted park staff on numerous occasions. The Park Service financed a position for a San Francisco city planner to serve on the team, adding valuable urban input.[18]

Neubacher brought two decades of Park Service experience when he succeeded Roger Kelly Brown. As chief of interpretation at Point Reyes National Seashore from 1985 to 1992 and with a background in planning, he was close to the area and its issues. Regional director Stanley Albright asked Neubacher to step into what everyone knew was a tough assignment.[19] Creating a master plan in the form of an amendment to the GMP required the same kind of comprehensive participation as did every similar endeavor at Golden Gate National Recreation Area. In the case of the Presidio, the stakes were much higher.

The staff at Golden Gate National Recreation Area understood the need for public involvement, and one of the best features of the park was the ability to let the public weigh in on proposals. The planning team followed the Park Service's long-standing pattern of outreach, utilizing frequent public meetings and workshops as ways to assure that the agency received the community's input and to allay any fears that a group might be excluded from the process. The public was enthused and participated in myriad ways. The disposition of the Presidio clearly was crucial to the locals' public sense of well-being in their city. At one public forum at Marina Middle School, 400 people sat in the audience. The typical array of Bay Area organizations appeared; neighborhood groups, community organizations, grassroots environmental groups, and other similar entities voiced their strong and distinct perspectives. Despite these inputs, a cohesive vision continued to elude planners, and as an answer, the Park Service and San Francisco State University sponsored a two-day "Think Big" conference in November 1989. Presidio "Visions" workshops followed, and by the spring of 1990, an open participatory process had been established.[20]

The planning process yielded the Presidio Planning Guidelines, introduced to the public in May 1990. Its ten principles affirmed the historic fabric, natural features, and visual integrity of the Presidio, articulated a commitment to national park values and to maintaining open space in the former post, and promised the clean-up of hazardous waste, long-term thinking to underpin planning, and ample public input. The guidelines also allowed the agency to dispense with some of the more bizarre public proposals that cropped up in an entirely open proceeding. After eighteen years in the Bay Area, the Park Service had learned its lessons well. Everyone, however ephemeral, had to have their say, and the agency listened. The only downside of the wide-open process was the cost in time. Fringe ideas, largely irrelevant but that did comply with federal laws and regulations, extended the procedure, but in the end, the conscious effort to assure widespread involvement kept interested groups in the process and prevented opponents from thwarting the complicated plans.

The planning guidelines completed the initial phase of creating a vision for the old post, the first step in a Presidio master plan. This segment took place between 1989, when the closure was announced, and the end of the public input process in 1991. Media attention and countless hearings defined the period and two separate publications, suggesting different perspectives, reflected a number of points of view. *Reveille,* the planning team's newsletter, and *Presidio Update,* a newsletter from GGNPA, both described the process to the public. By the time the planning guidelines were announced, the Park Service could affirm with certainty that no agency endeavor had ever been so carefully and publicly scrutinized.

The transition from ideas to plans revealed the complicated synergy of integrating the public, the Presidio Council, the Park Service, and the army in the planning process. The planning team led the way, with support from GGNPA and the Presidio Council. They distributed a "Presidio Visions Kit" to the public, held Visions workshops in a town meeting format in 1990 and early 1991, organized a trade show in June 1991 called the Presidio Forum to publicize ideas, and encouraged proposals. The release of the Presidio Concepts Workbook in December 1991, full of sample plans, reiterated the Park Service's commitment to include a wide range of activities. The process moved forward. In November 1991, James Harvey, leader of the Presidio Council, observed that the council's task seemed to be about halfway complete. It was a "turning point," Harvey told the council, "concluding our advice on visions and moving on to identification and analysis of future uses." Primary among these objectives was finding tenants who could pay for the combination of physical improvement and the interpretation and other park programs essential to converting the Presidio into a national park.[21]

As Harvey's memo indicated, from the end of the idea phase, conversion of the Presidio simultaneously proceeded on a series of different levels. In April 1992, the Park Service distributed "Calls for Interest" for prospective tenants and received more than 400 responses. As the agency sifted through the proposals, Neubacher's team tried to create focus from the diverse collection of ideas. Some tension between the planning team and the council ensued, and different kinds of objectives and time lines contributed. "I don't think at the time we felt they were very supportive," Neubacher recalled. "I think they wanted a plan to really move a lot faster."[22] The Presidio Council assumed the obligation to secure "practical revenue sources" to support implementation of the visions. The council's focus shifted to identifying prospective tenants and future sources of revenue. The planning process included a practical dimension from the outset, the ongoing need for financing to support the range of uses. Even as the planning team held a design workshop for the Presidio in June 1992 and continued to hold public hearings throughout the year, questions of finances loomed large.[23]

Finding the means to pay the enormous bills that the plan would generate was essential. As a range of groups sought to acquire Presidio space, the Park Service, the Presidio Council, and GGNPA recognized that unless someone took the initiative, financial resources were likely to be too scarce to accomplish most objectives. Without any conception of Congress's actions, an enormous effort to discern a practical basis for measuring the economic value of the Presidio took shape. Commissioned by GGNPA, Glenn Isaacson and Associates undertook a preliminary financial analysis that assessed the market value of medical and research facilities and housing as well as the viability of converting existing conference centers to revenue-generating use. The report also offered an analysis of maintenance and operations costs for the Presidio. This analysis laid the basis for the Presidio Building Leasing and Financing Implementation Strategy, one of the supplements to the eventual Presidio plan.[24] Clearly, the planning of the Presidio would proceed on more than one track.

The planning process encouraged a combination of vision and pragmatism. A draft plan was circulated internally beginning in March 1993, followed by a draft plan amendment released to the public for review. Hearings followed, the revision process began, and finally in October 1993, the grand vision for the Presidio was released in draft form, along with supplemental studies. "It's hard to get a vision of a place down into one page," Middleton remembered with a laugh, but "they ultimately did." With the debut of the draft plan, the council and the planning team found common ground. James Harvey, chair of the Presidio Council, telephoned Neubacher to congratulate him on the contents. The draft plan contained the kind of global vision that everyone sought for the Presidio, envisioning it as a linchpin in the park and a conduit for a vision of a sustainable future. "He was pretty happy with the report," Neubacher remembered, and the satisfied response to the plan helped clearly define different and complementary obligations.

The Final General Management Plan Amendment and Environmental Impact Statement was approved in July 1994. The Presidio would become a "great urban national park" and a "model for sustainability" under the plan.[25] Divided into thirteen planning units, the post became a series of areas drawn together by shared overarching management but likely to pursue independent destinies. They were established from existing patterns of use, topography, vistas, and public input, and they subdivided the Presidio into more manageable units from the National Park Service's perspective. At its most basic level, the plan seemed to replicate at the Presidio the grassroots structure of Golden Gate National Recreation Area. The hard-won lessons of the Bay Area yielded dividends.

The plan also showed the tension the Park Service felt over its ability to maintain administrative control of the Presidio. The project was of a scope so much greater than the agency had ever encountered that day-to-day administration of the planning process remained with the agency's Washington office. Park superintendent Brian O'Neill was characteristically philosophic about the circumstances. "It was becoming more and more apparent that a large number of very important decisions needed to be made at the highest levels of the Administration and Congress," he told an interviewer. "The future of the Presidio was going to be dependent on the ability to execute that sort of high level engagement."[26] The master plan revealed this tension as well as the Park Service's desire to maintain control.

By the time the plan was unveiled, the army's departure from the post had already begun. In March 1993, the army turned the Presidio Forest, Lobos Creek Valley, and Coastal Bluffs, the last managed by the park since the 1970s, over to the Park Service. In September 1993, the transfer continued. The Park Service assumed complete administration of Crissy Field, long divided by a fence down the center to differentiate the park's area from the army's, the army museum, and the cavalry stables.[27] The departure of the army added urgency to the planning process and made the transfer seem real. Until the army began to leave parts of the post, the entire project sometimes seemed to the Park Service like a hypothetical exercise in planning.

With the grand vision released to the public, the Park Service eagerly awaited responses. The debut began inauspiciously when, two days ahead of the official release, the *San Francisco Chronicle* featured a two-page story about the plan. Neither the mayor of San Francisco nor the city supervisors had seen the plan before the story appeared, creating a public relations problem for the Park Service. After this gaffe was smoothed over, the public response generally favored the plan. Bay Area politicians such as U.S. senators Dianne Feinstein and Barbara Boxer, who won a seat in the upper house in the 1992 election, and Representative Nancy Pelosi recognized that over time, the plan returned to the Bay Area much of the economic benefit that the closing of the post had cost it. It also offered new avenues of constituency building, and most of the remainder of the California delegation lined up behind the plan. San Francisco mayor Frank Jordan got over his shock at the early release to announce that the city would "stand firmly behind the proposal." Even vocal critics of the private-public dimensions of the transformation of the Presidio supported the plan.[28] Despite criticism of some of the plan's features, no lawsuits ensued, in itself a triumph. The Muwekma Ohlone raised concerns over what they regarded as the disposition of Indian land, and a fringe publication, the *San Francisco Bay Guardian*, questioned the transfer of electric power service to Pacific Gas and Electric, but in the larger scope of potential objections, these were relatively minor issues.

Only the army raised loud objections. Following BRAC's decision to keep 400 military soldier and civilian employees at the Presidio after the transfer, the army sought to reassert some forms of administrative control. The plan left out military needs, an army communiqué asserted, failing to ensure amenities that guaranteed quality of life for the remaining soldiers and their families. Housing was a primary military concern. More than 600 units were slated for demolition in the plan, and the army believed there would not be enough space to house its personnel. Presidio interim general manager (and former state park director) Russell Cahill believed the matter could be easily resolved, but in the meantime, the army used the problem to express some of its frustration over the transfer.[29]

At about the same time that the draft debuted, the reality of managing the Presidio became an issue. The two planning teams competed with one another, and by 1992, the relations between the two had become tense and counterproductive. The plan hinged on forging partnerships, securing investment capital, a full-blown leasing program, and philanthropic support. Factionalism within the Park Service working groups did not help further these goals, and at the behest of Jim Harvey and the Presidio Council as well as GGNPA, McKinsey and Company, one of the most significant management consulting firms in the country, developed the outlines of a system of joint management. McKinsey proposed implementing a public benefit corporation or a public-private partnership that would let the Park Service do what it did best—resource management, interpretation, planning—and provide specialists for the more technical economic dimensions of running the Presidio. McKinsey concluded that the arrangement could save as much as 30 percent of the cost of management. It was a merger of "economic reality with park stewardship."[30]

The Presidio Project Office, established in 1993, resulted. The office, headed initially by Robert Chandler, who had been superintendent of Grand Canyon National Park, and reporting directly to the Washington, D.C., office of the Park Service, completed the GMPA, handled the transition from the army, and initiated leasing of properties on the old post. "I realized the Presidio was going to be all-consuming for some period of time," Chandler recalled, "and so we just acknowledged the fact that it was going to be kind of a tough row for a while." He and his wife were the first civilians to move onto the post, and they confronted the rigid social structure of the military. Chandler's office was the first nonmilitary-related entity to open on the post, and it became the conduit for park management. In his three and a half years there, Chandler addressed the implications of a Congress hostile to the Presidio as a park, the demise of the Presidio Council, which stepped aside as he arrived, and the gradual dilution of Presidio legislation. Most difficult was the transition from conventional park status to self-sustaining free market entity. "It was a question of the economic imperatives as opposed to the programmatic goals that the Plan outlined," Chandler recalled, "and how that balance could be achieved."[31] Only after

December 31, 1999, did the lines of authority shift with the dissolution of the Presidio Project Office, after which the project reported to the Golden Gate National Recreation Area superintendent.

Weakened, the Park Service could not muster the support to retain greater control of the Presidio. During the early 1990s, the agency continued to flounder, whipped between an essentially supportive but ineffectual Democratic Congress and a vituperative minority buoyed by loud outcries from the Wise Use movement, the faux conservation organizations that began in the 1980s, and others who regarded national parks as a threat to private property. Although Director James Ridenour could reflect that "the negative attitude toward the Park Service gradually improved over the four years" he served, his optimism took longer to reach the park level.[32]

Political concerns also hampered the transfer of the post. As the 1994 congressional session ended, Presidio advocates found themselves stymied by the California Desert Protection Act. The Park Service had invested more than a decade in trying to protect the Mojave Desert, and when the chance finally came to pass the bill, it took priority over the Presidio project. The legislation passed just prior to the 1994 election, on October 31, 1994. Advocates were told that Congress could not pass two California park bills so close together in time, and the Presidio would have to wait till the next session.[33] To politicians in Washington, D.C., the Presidio seemed somehow less urgent than the long-standing battle in the desert.

The election of the "Contract with America" Republican majority–Congress in 1994 changed the calculus of the situation. Antigovernment at its core, this self-styled "New Right" sought to reform government by eliminating its functions. The Presidio came into focus for some of these reformers, and one, Representative John Duncan of Tennessee, proposed selling the post. Although Representative Nancy Pelosi blunted this objective, the very proposal suggested that Presidio advocates operated in a decidedly different environment. Without the support of the now wobbly bipartisan conservation coalition in Congress and absent a Democratic majority, the Presidio became part of larger discussions about the role of government in American society.[34]

The Park Service's position had become tenuous. Morale remained low, and the talk of government reorganization that began with the election of Bill Clinton did little to improve the climate. The pressure for some kind of paying proposition at the Presidio grew, and the Park Service lost control of the process. Even the agency's friends and partners denounced it in public forums. In one instance, the Park Service was undermined by criticism from the Presidio Council in front of Representative Pelosi. Some agency officials believed that the exchange damaged the quest for Park Service management of the Presidio. Without support, the agency could not resist pay-as-you-go proposals, much to the dismay of longtime supporters such as Rich Bartke and Amy Meyer. "It was evident," Meyer remembered, "that Congress bi-partisanly did not intend to continue to pay and would not pay a huge amount in perpetuity for the Presidio. . . . we got a very onerous bill and had to live with it." "Financial self-sufficiency, although it was considered pretty Draconian, galvanized a lot of support around the bill," Craig Middleton remembered. "And it wasn't only Republican support. It was bipartisan support. The bill passed by an extraordinary margin."[35]

As Congress set out to finally define the Presidio management structure, it sought to give such an entity legislative sanction. The initial bill to establish the partnership called it the "Presidio Corporation," but the Presidio Council advocated a name that connoted the public nature and responsibility of the entity, and Presidio Trust was selected instead. "One of the pivotal things was when we came up with the idea of this public benefit corporation," Craig Middleton recalled. "As people started to understand that through this kind of set-up, we might be able to actually do this thing without causing the taxpayer too much pain, it started to win acceptance." Despite the attempt to craft a way to protect the Presidio, criticism in the community followed almost immediately. Loud if scarce voices insisted that the legislation created an entity that served business needs ahead of the larger community. Some labeled the proposed entity "Presidio Inc.," charging that the post would become a business park free of San Francisco's stringent zoning restrictions and other regulations, a tax-free corporation running a redevelopment agency under the guise of a national park that would not be bound by open meeting statutes or state and local environmental laws.[36]

The January 1994 revelation of an almost clandestine arrangement between Pacific Gas and Electric and the Park Service offered powerful proof of suspicions about the idea of a public-private partnership. Without public hearings or a competitive bidding process, the Park Service planned to pay PG&E $4.43 million to take over the aging electrical system at the Presidio and an additional $5.5 million to bring the system up to standards. PG&E would then operate the system for profit. "This is a tremendous giveaway," Joel Ventresca, president of the Coalition for San Francisco Neighborhoods, observed. "It's a conversion of a government-owned system to a private-owned electrical utility, paid for by the taxpayers." Journalist Martin Espinoza tried to tie the decision, which he framed in the least flattering of terms, to the composition of the Presidio Council, largely composed of influential business leaders and others from the growth coalition. The Park Service recanted, issuing a call for bids for the operation, and PG&E won the bid anyway.[37]

Part investigation and part conspiracy theory, Espinoza's attack asked important questions about the Presidio's future. Although some of his claims were simply outrageous, he did point to an easily overlooked downside of public-private partnerships, that the private side might exercise undue control over the process of transformation. Powerful individuals and corporations evoked fears of exclusivity in planning, creating a de facto image of a park that operated on behalf of the few rather than the many, a direct counter to the role of public open space in the Bay Area and a legitimate threat to the public in an age of privatization. Espinoza's articles hinted strongly in that direction, but the evidence to support such a contention remained obscure. Still, his acerbic attacks compelled reassessment of legislative and agency plans for PG&E even if the eventual result was the same. Later in 1994, open meeting clauses and other similar public access mechanisms were included in the draft legislation.

Congressional opposition to the Presidio transformation also surfaced. At the same time that the Park Service readied the grand vision plan, Republican Congressman John Duncan of Tennessee added an amendment to the 1994 Department of the Interior appropriations bill that reduced the the Presidio appropriation from $25 million to $14 million. Duncan's attack came on strictly economic grounds; one of his staff members argued that the Park Service "can't afford to run the parks they have now" and under the circumstances could not possibly manage new ones. Duncan favored private solutions, selling features of the post to the highest bidder. Advocates of the transfer were outraged. Newspapers enlisted local support and began letter-writing campaigns, others scrutinized Duncan's record of pork-barreling for his district, and generally the community united behind the idea of a Presidio park.[38] The question of what kind of park was put aside.

Problems with Congress were not the only obstacle to moving forward. As the sixty-day review period for the draft plan began, the Park Service faced another area of concern, tension with the army about the mechanics of transition. One estimate suggested that bringing the structures of the Presidio up to building code standards would cost $660 million. At the core remained the question: Who would foot the bill? A joint operating budget of $45 million was allocated to finance the transfer. At the outset, the Pentagon funded the majority of the costs of the transfer, but as army operations diminished, the budget burden shifted to the Park Service. "The Army was trying to transition the Presidio at least cost to the military," Brian O'Neill observed. "The Park Service had everything to gain by trying to maximize the burden of responsibility that was placed on the defense budget. . . . We were at opposite ends of the spectrum about the future." Maintenance projects such as sewers, storm drains, and electrical systems came from the military budget, while the Park Service added public safety functions such as police and fire protection to its obligations. The commitment strained the Park Service allocation of $3 million a year for the Presidio between 1990 and 1992, and the community began to worry about the agency's ability to maintain historic structures in the post.[39]

The community had been worried about the army's commitment to maintaining the Presidio since the announcement of possible closure, and Amy Meyer and many others kept pressure on the military. "We met with Gen. Harrison, and his intention is to leave the Presidio in 'A-1' condition," Representatives Pelosi and Boxer wrote Meyer in 1989. Despite that assurance, the transition offered many opportunities to dispense with expenditures, and the public closely watched the military's actions for signs that it intended to fulfill its commitment. In April 1991, more than 100 people turned out to hear the U.S. Army Corps of Engineers explain the consequences of the environmental impact statement for the closure. The audience inquired about hazardous waste removal, the fate of Letterman Hospital, and other issues associated with making the Presidio ready to transfer. In 1992, the *San Francisco Chronicle* announced that the Pentagon planned to renege on a commitment to spend $10 million on repairs and upgrades to the post's infrastructure. The intervention of Representative Pelosi and public pressure forced the army to follow through on its commitment, and by the end of the year, the army publicly assured the community that it intended to maintain the condition of the Presidio until the day it departed.[40]

Environmental issues loomed over the transfer. Since the enactment of environmental regulations in the United States during the late 1960s and early 1970s, the military typically had been exempt from outside scrutiny. The cold war and claims of national security allowed the military to avoid public accounting for its environmental impact. After 1986, when President Ronald Reagan signed Executive Order 12580, which permitted the Department of Justice to disapprove any Environmental Protection Agency enforcement action against a federal facility, even the law effectively gutted civilian protection from federal as well as military toxicity. Beginning in 1987, Congress inquired into military mishandling of toxic and threatening substances, and the results shocked the public. The discovery of more than 4,500 contaminated sites at 761 military bases around the country began to pierce the veil that shrouded military action.[41]

Scrutiny of military environmental procedures and consequences began as BRAC contemplated the Presidio transfer. Federal law required the military to clean up hazardous waste prior to its departure from the post, and nearly a century of unregulated use of the lands left countless problems. Leaking underground gasoline storage tanks, one of the major civilian toxic issues of the late 1980s and early 1990s, landfills, asbestos in buildings, and innumerable other problems led to an estimated bill for cleanup that topped $90 million. The Pentagon had become accustomed to being unresponsive to civilian concerns on this issue. It operated largely without public scrutiny before 1990 and successfully fended off outside observers even after congressional hearings in the late 1980s. At the Presidio, the army relied on its longtime strategies and tried to defer the cleanup until after its departure. Its environmental assessment, one of the many National Environmental Policy Act requirements, indicated that the army might not have the resources and the time to successfully mitigate some areas of the Presidio before the scheduled 1994 departure.[42]

The public outcry in the Bay Area against the Department of Defense (DOD) strategy was instantaneous. Many regarded the attempt to defer the cost of mitigation as part of a convoluted strategy to impede the transfer. The enormous cost of the cleanup could have easily crippled the entire Presidio transfer. The Park Service could not muster the resources to accelerate the timetable for cleanup, and, some park advocates observed, the public acknowledgment of toxicity at the Presidio compromised its national park qualities. The military's public image suffered even more when after a series of surprise inspections in May 1994, EPA officials fined the DOD more than $560,000 for sloppy handling of waste at the post. Only after the formation of the Restoration Advisory Board for Environmental Cleanup, composed of volunteers from the Department of Defense, the Park Service, EPA, and citizen groups, did the public again begin to believe that the army intended to follow through on the promises given in conjunction with the closing of the post. By the beginning of the new century, the Presidio Trust had secured $100 million for environmental remediation and an additional $100 million insurance policy against future cleanup needs.[43]

Military reticence stemmed from a number of factors. Its long history at the Presidio invoked sentimental feelings about the place, for the military remained one of the very few institutions in American society with respect for the lessons of history. Defense policies had been formed in an earlier era, when the military safeguarded the nation against vivid external threats and could count on Congress and the public overlooking any hazards associated with its requirements. Nor was the military accustomed to functioning in the harsh light of public opinion. During much of its tenure in the Bay Area, military leaders could cloak their action in claims of national security and, in the odd case where such a strategy failed to sway opponents, could point to the sheer volume of dollars the military generated as a persuasive tool. Even in the new climate, defense officials sometimes evinced an arrogant tone that inspired local resentment. "Contrary to some public sentiment or comments from some local leaders that the U.S. Army has not been a great steward of the environment at the Presidio, this is not supported by historical records," Lieutenant Colonel David McClure opined at the height of the toxic crisis. Facing as much as a $90 million cleanup bill, the Park Service did not seem to grasp the immensity of the task it faced.[44] In the post–cold war world, the rules were different, and the military found itself accountable in new ways.

The tension of transfer manifested in other ways as well. Even though the eventual departure was a foregone conclusion, the army became increasingly reluctant to entirely evacuate the Presidio as the transfer date drew near. BRAC's summer 1993 announcement that 400 military employees of the Sixth Army would remain at the post after the scheduled closure date considerably altered the transfer. Recognizing that delayed departure was insignificant in the larger picture and aware of the need for cooperation, the Park Service initially supported the move. The measure that permitted the soldiers to stay also included a clause allowing the army to hold any land it considered necessary until the secretary of the army deemed it excess to defense purposes. In November 1993, Congress passed the bill without significant dissent.[45]

A small cadre in Congress recognized danger in the bill, but for different reasons. Representative Bruce Vento of Minnesota, chair of the House Interior Department Subcommittee on National Parks, Representative George Miller III of the East Bay, who depended on Phil Burton for support in his initial election to the House in 1974, and Representative Nancy Pelosi all thought that the legislation significantly revised the terms of the post closure. With the clause that left the change of administration to the secretary of the army, the Pentagon could halt the transfer without consultation. The three complained to Secretary of Defense Les Aspin in a private letter, but the story leaked to the San Francisco area press. Again public opinion assisted the transfer of the Presidio. The press loudly inveighed against the bill, claiming that the army sought to circumvent the transfer. In December 1993, the military confirmed the newspapers' fears. With quiet support from Representative Ron Dellums, the chair of the House Armed Services Committee, the army declared its intention to keep the headquarters at the Main Post, the commissary, swimming pool, Officers' Club, some housing, the youth service center, and the golf course. Dellums's maneuvering helped the army keep most of the amenities that the Presidio provided, retaining some of the choice advantages of the post for the military, its retirees, and its dependents alone. The Park Service also counted on the army's presence as a source of revenue in its financial assessments.[46]

The army's stated intentions opened a question that loomed large over the entire transfer: Whose Presidio was it really? The base golf course was one of the primary perquisites of the post, and in the golf-happy but golf course–shy Bay Area, the public coveted the exclusive links. When the army left the Presidio, Pat Sullivan of the *San Francisco Chronicle* quipped, "The Bay Area's legions of public-course golfers will be poised to storm the fort." Opening the course to the public had been an express goal of the Presidio planning document, which was formulated as an amendment to the general management plan. Howard Levitt, communications chief at Golden Gate National Recreation Area, announced that under the Park Service, "the doctrine of full public access and fairness will prevail" at the golf course.

The Park Service expected to lease it to a concessioner as it did with a similar course in Yosemite National Park; estimates of the revenue it would generate ranged from $800,000 to $1 million per year.[47] The army's decision to keep it under military administration was widely regarded as an act of bad faith. The golf course promised an important source of revenue for the Presidio as a park, and stripping it from the transfer seemed a declaration of war on the process, an attempt to use administrative fiat to hamstring the transfer. If such a decision stood, local observers believed, the Presidio would be compromised financially and in the end the Park Service could not meet its financial and management obligations.

The Department of Defense–Department of the Interior conflict over the golf course also highlighted another important impact of the transfer. If the decision stood, army control of the course would keep it exclusive, defying one of the most important community objectives for the Presidio and playing into the larger questions about access that continued to vex American society. By the mid-1990s, exclusivity in American society had become fashion; the run-up of the stock market in the 1990s accentuated the 1980s trend toward class definition, and the wealth it created sent people in search of all kind of amenities. Public spaces bore this burden. In some places they were transformed into private or semiprivate spaces; in others they received much greater use as a result of the closure of formerly open space. In the Bay Area, with its strong tradition of civil liberty and its emphasis on community and grassroots organization, keeping the golf course exclusive reflected a wider trend that many thought simply wrongheaded and even antidemocratic.

The always vocal Bay Area press focused on the attempt to keep the golf course in military hands. The struggle was dubbed "Operation Divot Storm," a tacit tongue-in-cheek critique of the use of military power and political capital for so nefarious and self-serving an objective. Retired army officers were adamant about continuing to receive preference on the golf course. The Presidio Golf Club assiduously fought to retain its prerogative, at one point hiring William Whalen to lobby its case. Public opinion was allied against the army, and even Whalen could not help. "It was less beneficial to the Presidio Golf Club to have him [Whalen] than if they had not had him," Pacific West regional director and former Presidio general manager John Reynolds recalled.[48] The army once again became the object of scorn and distrust; the ever-present Farley cartoon strip lambasted the military in a weeklong series. Pulled to the table by public opinion, the army began what became a year of negotiations that led to compromise. The agreement stipulated a five-year phase-in of public use of the golf course; at the end of the phase-in period, 50 percent of the tee times would be slated for public use. After the five-year interim period, the Park Service would assume administrative responsibility for the course, although some tee times would continue to be reserved for military use.[49]

The vast number of structures in the Presidio also attracted the attention of homeless advocates. The incredible cost of living in the Bay Area and the lack of available space contributed to increasing homelessness, and in the 1980s and 1990s, the homeless in many communities found a voice. In San Francisco, they attracted considerable sympathy. A 1991 *San Francisco Examiner*/KRON-TV survey indicated that the largest percentage of those polled, more than 35 percent, believed that the Presidio should be converted to homeless housing and job training. This number was twenty percentage points higher than those who thought the Presidio should become a park. "People have an urge to do something about [homelessness]," a *San Francisco Examiner* editorial opined. "Whether or not there is a realistic prospect for using the Presidio for homeless housing it will take something that dramatic to make real progress."[50]

Homeless housing was one of many options for the Presidio, and while it garnered some advocacy, it also generated antipathy and considerable indifference. In 1991, a Bay Area delegation to Congress included homelessness among the issues for which it sought support, but San Francisco mayor Art Agnos opposed using the Presidio for the homeless. One area of the post became the focus of efforts to create housing. The Wherry housing area, used for enlisted housing, was slated for demolition. After the GMP amendment, it was located in an area scheduled to be returned to coastal prairie and scrub. Homeless advocates sought the space for the disadvantaged but were rebuffed. In May 1994, just before the scheduled transfer, the California Homeless Network sponsored a protest in which homeless advocates occupied part of the Wherry housing area above Baker Beach. At least 100 people participated in the demonstration.[51]

Letterman Hospital and the Letterman Army Institute for Research (LAIR) also became the focus of controversy during the transfer. The hospital played an integral role in the community, serving military personnel, dependents, and all other Department of Defense beneficiaries. A total of 128,000 people in the Bay Area were eligible for care at Letterman, and its closure three years before the Park Service took control limited them to two other military hospitals in the area, one of which soon closed. As the transfer approached, veterans and their advocates pressured the Park Service to reopen the hospital. Despite this demand, agency planning proceeded in another direction. "The National Park Service is not in the business of running a veterans' hospital," said planning team captain Don Neubacher as the agency announced its plans. The change created a difficult situation, and the initial announcement of the transfer brought loud protest. But at the same time, many looked longingly at the hospital and LAIR, coveting the facilities for other purposes. "There's no doubt that the Letterman/LAIR complex is a very desirable asset," noted Kent Sims, deputy executive director of the San Francisco Redevelopment Agency. The Park Service desperately needed an anchor tenant for the facility, one that could significantly demonstrate that the Presidio transfer was more than an expensive boondoggle.[52] A paying tenant of stature granted the entire project a gravity it previously lacked, and the array of medical and research facilities in the Bay Area offered plenty of possibilities.

The Park Service rushed headlong into a process designed to yield a suitable tenant and soon found much community opposition. With special legislation that allowed the agency to enter into a long-term lease at Letterman, the Park Service selected two respondents for consideration from the sixteen who submitted proposals. The University of California–San Francisco (UCSF) entered into negotiations for the entire 1.2 million square feet of the Letterman complex, planning to rename it the Presidio Center for Health Science Research and Education. The university's significance was enormous. Former San Francisco mayor George Christopher regarded UCSF as the ideal tenant for the old hospital, and the *San Francisco Examiner* declared that "the Presidio and UCSF are a superb fit." The university did not want to be a full partner in the process, expecting the Park Service not only to accommodate its demands for renovation but also to waive rent for use of the space. Some believed UCSF was only interested in the federal dollars that administrators believed would come along with the project. As 1994 ended, the relationship between UCSF and the Park Service collapsed, and the university pulled out of the process. The Tides Foundation's 73,000-square-foot Thoreau Center for Sustainability took its place in the complex, a much smaller operation than the Park Service had hoped for.[53]

Despite conflict in these and more areas, the logistics of the transfer proceeded, if not easily, then at least with direction. Although a weary Secretary of the Interior Bruce Babbitt "learned that in San Francisco, there are 2 million experts on the future of the Presidio," momentum and skilled political maneuvering by Representative Pelosi carried the transfer forward despite the objections of Representative Duncan and others. Money to accomplish the transfer was not going to be easy to find, but "we can squeeze more productivity out of the Washington-based operation," the secretary insisted. In March 1994, the Park Service assumed control of Presidio housing. Obstacles to the process remained, and as October approached, Congress wrangled over the long-term fate of the post, neighbors worried about the impact of the changes, and the Park Service readied itself for the most formidable task in its history.[54]

On September 30, 1994, the army transferred all remaining parts of the Presidio to the Park Service. At 4:00 P.M., the Presidio's Sixth Army Garrison and Headquarters Battalion became inactivated, and the army conducted a formal retreat ceremony, lowering the flag for the last time. At 11:00 P.M., taps were sounded, and between that moment and sunrise, signs at the seven gates that announced entry to a military reservation were replaced with ones that read, "Welcome to the Presidio of San Francisco, Golden Gate National Recreation Area." At 12:00 P.M. on October 1, 1994, Vice President Al Gore presided over a post-to-park ceremony at the main parade ground. After 218 years of military service, the Presidio became part of the national park system.[55]

In the way that Golden Gate National Recreation Area symbolized what national parks could become, the Presidio encapsulated the issues and advantages of the entire park in one space. Small in comparison with the rest of Golden Gate National Recreation Area, the Presidio was enormous in the consequences that stemmed from decisions about it. The transfer forced everyone—the Park Service, GGNPA, the Presidio Council, the army, and the Bay Area community—to move beyond negotiations. It compelled the articulation of a vision for the city and the rest of the Bay Area, a way in which the region would function for decades to come, and it made every entity associated with it declare its position. Although many saw the road to the transfer as the battle, the real struggle began at the moment of the army's departure, when the amendment to the GMP became the governing policy for the Presidio and changes to the document signified power relationships that stretched all the way to Washington, D.C. The Presidio was no mere addition to a national park area; it was instead an embodiment of regional aspirations.

The process of transfer shaped the Presidio's future. Even though in some accounts the Park Service was beginning to reach an appropriate level of management when Congress gave responsibility to the Presidio Trust, the Presidio still strained Golden Gate National Recreation Area's resources. "We were out of control and in deep trouble before the Presidio came along," Doug Nadeau recounted in the least optimistic version of the moment. "The Presidio sucked up so much time, energy and commitment that it just set the park in a spin."[56] Although Nadeau's comments might have seemed extreme, they were widely echoed in more measured form. Superintendent Brian O'Neill tacitly agreed when he observed that "we were burnt out and overextended and there had been so many things we couldn't attend to" that the creation of the Trust "in one way was a blessing." O'Neill astutely assessed the crux of the problem in a discussion of the relationship between the park and the army during the transfer. "We knew that in the Army system very little is delegated down in terms of power to resource issues," he strategized. "I think clearly our ability to succeed was going to be dependent on our political access to the very highest levels of the Department of Defense." This capsule illustrated the Park Service's problem. It could have the Presidio, but without the resources to operate it, administration was an academic exercise. Securing the resources meant ceding some autonomy in management, a practice at which Golden Gate National Recreation Area had been skilled since the 1970s.

Securing the Presidio became much more than passage of a bill; it became a process of integrating a series of complicated relationships with political forces, social organizations, and the local community, all of whom were simultaneously benefactors but also had specific needs to which they felt their participation and contribution to the process entitled them. "No matter what Brian O'Neill, the Director of the Park Service, or Greg Moore [executive director of GGNPA] or anyone else who believed in the Presidio said," O'Neill insisted, "it simply wasn't going to happen unless we had a strong voice from a national constituency. . . . It was absolutely essential to the Park Service that its voice be echoed by a cross-section of Americans who had the credentials to be able to advance thinking." Such people uniformly came with ideas of their own.[57]

The agency developed relationships that it needed to sustain the Presidio and became part of a larger operation. O'Neill played a significant role in achieving that end. He had "always been a really good partner. He really does value not only the concept, but the actual working of partnerships—understanding that they can be difficult, understanding that there's give and take—but ultimately convinced that it's the best thing to do, not only for the park, but for the community that surrounds the park," Middleton observed. "He's a great advocate of pulling in community to help restore public assets."

What began as a park became a partnership, albeit an unequal one. Even though the Park Service and the Presidio Trust were "sister federal agencies," in the words of Amy Meyer, the trust eventually became the dominant partner. In that process, the Presidio became more than a hybrid. It pointed to a new definition of "national park area," one that differed greatly from the history of the national park system. Unlike every other unit in the system, the Presidio was compelled to pay its own way after a fixed date. Every decision that managers for the trust made was conditioned by that fact, and the weight of finances and the implied threat of sale of the former army post challenged the concept of "parks for the people where the people are," the original idea behind Golden Gate National Recreation Area.

As Golden Gate National Recreation Area survived by passing on costs to park partners such as GGNPA, the Presidio, with its combination of exceptional space and national cachet, might have been able to accomplish something similar. When survival hinged on financial leverage, power relationships dictated new values. In arguably the most liberal city in the nation, the "money talks" philosophy of postmodern America, a nation of markets driven to consume, seemed to have won out. When Regional Director John Reynolds called the Presidio "unique" in a speech to a 2000 interpretation conference, he correctly labeled this divergent part of Golden Gate National Recreation Area.[58]

The Park Service accomplished a great deal during its short stint of control of the Presidio. It developed the GMPA, attained and kept the support of a wide segment of the Bay Area public, and with the help of Representative Pelosi and Representative John Murtha, secured considerable funding for infrastructure and building renovation and rehabilitation and environmental cleanup. The Park Service also smoothly handled a complex transition from the military, secured annual operating budgets of upwards of $25 million as well as additional revenues from leasing, and successfully managed a transition to a smaller level of involvement after the establishment of the trust. Most important, the agency did not bend when it came to the implementation of its core values in resource management, sustainability, historic preservation, and other similar areas.[59] In short, the Park Service managed the Presidio as a park, passing it to the Presidio Trust under those terms. The subsequent tension between the Park Service and the trust resulted from differences in situation and philosophy. Was the Presidio going to feel like it was part of a national park? Was it a model for the future or an anomaly among national park partnerships?

For the national park system, the Presidio experience asked hard questions about public-private partnerships. National parks required outside support, and since 1919, organizations aided the parks. Rarely had they been partners, comanagers with status equal to the Park Service. In a changing America, one in which nearly everything else in the nation had become "pay for play" and in which national parks no longer held the kind of meaning that Huey Johnson, the founder of the Trust for Public Land, or Stephen T. Mather might grant them, an experiment with public-private management made social sense. It allowed the park system to accommodate a hostile Congress and an excited city simultaneously, and it appeared at least initially that the Park Service could maintain control. By the time the army marched out in 1994, that control was beginning to wane, and in its own park the agency seemed less and less the master of its destiny. "I consider the Trust/Park Service relationship to be akin to a marriage and we've had our ups and downs," Craig Middleton summed up the process. "Certainly some of the downs have been around the concern by Park Service people that this would become a model, and be used over and over, and it would be used by people who wanted to make the Park Service self-sufficient in some way. And it just doesn't apply. And I think that we've understood now that this is unique."[60] With the experience of the Presidio, it was easy to see why the Park Service might shy away from future opportunities in public-private partnerships.

In the end, after considerable grappling, the Presidio became an autonomous entity, separate from the rest of Golden Gate National Recreation Area in significant ways. In part that transformation stemmed from politics in Washington, D.C., but it came equally from the way the power relationships were set up in the Presidio Trust and the park. On the executive level, the Presidio remained part of the park; in its operations, it became an entity that espoused Park Service standards but answered directly to Washington through a series of mechanisms far different from agency protocol. As 2000 dawned, the result was perplexing. The Presidio was both part of Golden Gate National Recreation Area and a de facto redevelopment agency, both public open space and private facility, both recreational park and research park. Its complicated status stood astride the blurring line between public and private in the United States.

Epilogue

As the new century began, Golden Gate National Recreation Area had become one of the premier national park areas in the system. Its visitation numbers were among the highest of all parks, the Park Service had successfully negotiated countless resource management and constituency situations, and with the addition of the Presidio, Golden Gate National Recreation Area seemed poised to emerge from its designation as a national recreation area and was in position to be considered an important national park. The management challenges that remained were many and complex, while the strategies that the Park Service developed over nearly three decades testified to the commitment of management to agency goals and the flexibility of leadership in building support in the public and private sectors for the park.

Golden Gate National Recreation Area had much to teach the rest of the park system. In its twenty-eight-year history, the park had become one of the most important examples of urban national park areas, and it was among the few places that faced issues that foreshadowed the future of the park system. As a national recreation area, Golden Gate helped redefine the category in the public mind, raising the status and stature to match those of other categories of park areas. The park allowed people to enjoy recreation; its varied features taught about the many pasts of the Bay Area, about the seas and the coast, about life in northern California before the coming of Euro-Americans and their cities. With much more than recreation available, a new generation of visitors and Bay Area residents, especially those who were poorer or immigrant, thought of Golden Gate National Recreation Area as their national park.

A template for the rest of the park system, Golden Gate National Recreation Area had become a place to which staff of other parks looked as they sought to devise responses to changing contexts. In many instances, Golden Gate National Recreation Area planners had already addressed similar issues. Its remarkable variety of resources complicated management of the park and demanded coordinated responses from managers. Park planning yielded documents such as the General Management Plan of 1980 and subsequent natural and cultural resource management plans, which provided the tools to construct a park from the myriad features of Golden Gate National Recreation Area. The Park Service pioneered complex forms of management in its integration of cultural and natural resource objectives with the goals of an enormous day-use public and the interests of neighbor-

199

hoods, activists, ranchers, and interested parties. It led in creating public participation in the park system with the Citizens' Advisory Commission, and its cooperating association, Golden Gate National Parks Association, became one of the most significant contributors to the resource base of the park and easily the largest provider of funds of any cooperating association in the system. This close relationship between GGNPA and the park foreshadowed the creation of the Presidio Trust. Another public nonprofit organization that exercised considerable control and influence over the Presidio, the trust was easily the most significant urban addition to the national park system since the 1970s, an addition that required a different management philosophy. In this affiliation, the Park Service faced a series of administrative arrangements that demanded unparalleled dexterity.

In the Bay Area, the Park Service also had to deal with the concerns of an energized and involved public that had clear ideas about what it wanted from a national park area. In some circumstances, those ideas and the agency's goals and values did not mesh, forcing Golden Gate National Recreation Area into a series of ongoing negotiations. In the complicated political climate of the Bay Area, Golden Gate National Recreation Area found itself in a secondary position. The park's fate and the economic future of the Bay Area were related, but many other entities had much greater impact on the regional economy. A different approach was needed than was common in places where parks dominated the regional economy. From its inception, Golden Gate National Recreation Area assiduously cultivated the public, seeking its input into every major decision. The Park Service learned many lessons in this process; paramount among them was the understanding that just because the public agreed to an idea as part of a plan did not mean that it would support the implementation of that plan. The gap between planning and implementation remained one of the most vexing for the agency.

Close ties with the public yielded important community relationships. Golden Gate National Recreation Area developed important ties in the Bay Area with managers of all kinds. Community leaders, financial experts, and activists were among the many friends of the park. In situations when public support for the park was needed, the agency's consistent maintenance of relationships gave it strong and vocal backers. This support in turn allowed the Park Service to implement programs that might otherwise have been stalled. It could turn to its association, commission, or friends for cover, deflecting animosities to other quarters. Even though managing Golden Gate National Recreation Area was always contentious, park leaders often sighed with relief as powerful park supporters stepped forward.

The result was a complicated park that foreshadowed the needs of a demographically changing nation that interpreted its national parks in new ways. Golden Gate National Recreation Area crossed from a recreational park into a comprehensive one that was managed with the needs of its many constituencies in mind. In this approach, the Park Service was able to build strong alliances that could protect the agency from attack while also running the risk of letting its friends dictate terms to park managers. Golden Gate National Recreation Area required visionary but flexible leadership, a balancing act between firm adherence to federal, agency, and park policies and thoughtful decision-making that included the countless constituencies of the park.

The travails and successes of Golden Gate National Recreation Area offer an insight into the demands of park management in the twenty-first century. In the future, the traditional supporters of national parks and their elected officials will become fewer. The reaction of the larger public will determine whether national parks as Stephen T. Mather and Horace M. Albright envisioned them were a class-based creation of a moment in American history. As those constituencies and their representatives diminish as a percentage of the American population, the techniques and strategies of Golden Gate National Recreation Area will become increasingly necessary to protect the existing parks. As a leader in integrating the different facets of management with the needs of a wide range of constituencies, Golden Gate National Recreation Area will serve as a model for national parks of the coming century.

Chronology

1847, January 30	Yerba Buena renamed San Francisco by Lieutenant Washington Bartlett, U.S. Navy.
1847, March	Americans (7th New York Volunteers) take over Presidio.
1847, May	U.S. Army begins survey of Alcatraz Island as site for harbor defenses.
1848	Gold discovered at Sutter's Mill.
1848	Treaty of Guadalupe Hidalgo cedes California to the United States.
1850	President Millard Fillmore reserves Alcatraz Island and Angel Island for military purposes.
1850, November 6	President Fillmore proclaims the Presidio, Alcatraz, Angel Island, and other Bay Area sites as military reservations.
1850, December 31	Fillmore modifies reservation proclamation to reflect new boundaries.
1853	Army begins construction of Fort Point
1854	U.S. Army begins construction of fort on Alcatraz Island.
1854, June 1	Lighthouse on Alcatraz Island begins operating; first lighthouse on Pacific coast.
1859, July	Belt of stone and brick fortifications built around Alcatraz Island, with seventy-five guns mounted.
1861, February 15	Fort Point completed, army orders troops to garrison fort. Construction costs about $2.8 million.
1862	First true prison building built on Alcatraz Island, forming nucleus for development of "Lower Prison" complex.
1863, October 15	Original Cliff House opens for business.
1866, July 24	Army purchases land for Lime Point reservation (Forts Barry and Baker). Baker later named after Colonel Edward D. Baker, veteran of Mexican War killed in action during the Civil War.
1883	Major William Albert Jones, engineer at army department headquarters, develops comprehensive plan for afforestation of Presidio reservation.
1884, December 12	War Department designates former post cemetery and surrounding land as first national cemetery on West Coast.
1885	Sutro Heights opens for public use as park. (Adolph Sutro elected Populist mayor of San Francisco in 1894, serves 1895–1897.)

1890–1893	Army begins afforestation of Presidio, planting eucalyptus, pine, acacia, and other species, set in ordered rows on ridges and hills of reservation.
1890	Treasury Department establishes Fort Point Life Saving Station in Lower Presidio.
1892, May 1	U.S. Quarantine Station opens on Angel Island.
1893	Army declares Fort Point's guns obsolete and begins work on series of reinforced concrete installations, with building to continue for about fifteen years.
1892, January 23	Army acquires 200-acre land area through condemnation proceedings, calls site Fort Miley.
1894–1896	U.S. Army spends $10 million on twenty-six coast defense batteries around the Bay.
1895, July 1	Army designates Alcatraz Island as U.S. Disciplinary Barracks.
1897, July 7	First permanent garrison established at Fort Baker (Battery 1, 3d Artillery).
1898	Army establishes Laguna Merced Military Reservation, later becomes site of Fort Funston.
1900, April 14	Government establishes Veterans' Hospital at Fort Miley.
1904, December 27	Army divides Fort Baker reservation in half, creates Fort Barry.
1905	Army decides to abandon Alcatraz Island as defense site, designates island solely as military prison.
1905, July 8	Secretary of war allots land on Angel Island to Commerce and Labor Departments for Immigration Detention Station.
1906	William Kent purchases lands around Muir Woods to prevent logging.
1906, April 18	Earthquake hits San Francisco. Four refugee camps established on Presidio on order of General Frederick Funston, housing 16,000 refugees for ten days. Fort Mason also houses refugees and is site for Army Relief Headquarters for entire city.
1915	Panama-Pacific International Exposition held just east of Presidio on landfill. Marina built as yacht harbor for exposition.
1917	U.S. government buys ocean frontage portion of Fort Funston property from Spring Valley Water Company.
1917, June 26	Army names Fort Funston in honor of Major Gen. Frederick Funston.
1920–1930s	San Francisco Park Commissioners and state and federal assistance programs help improve marina. In 1930s, WPA crews build stone seawall, harbormaster's house, and lighthouse.
1921	Army designates Crissy Field as military airfield; first army coastal defense airfield on Pacific coast, built over site of Exposition's automobile race track. (Field is named

after Major Dana Crissy, who was killed in 1919 in transcontinental air race that started in San Francisco.)

1921	Design work starts on Julius Kahn Public Playground, 7.294-acre site on Presidio's south boundary.
1924	War Department gives consent for construction of Bay bridges.
1928	California establishes Mount Tamalpais State Park.
1932	Army releases 19.2 acres of land at Fort Miley to General Services Administration for construction of Veterans' Administration Hospital. Hospital opens in 1934; latest addition opens in 1965.
1933	Act of Congress transfers Alcatraz Island from Department of War to Department of Justice for prison.
1933	Golden Gate Bridge designer Joseph Strauss plans steel arch for approach over Fort Point, making it unnecessary to remove fort.
1934, July 12	Army abandons U.S. Disciplinary Barracks at Alcatraz.
1934, Aug. 15	First fifty prisoners arrive at Alcatraz Island. Convicts' railcars ferried across Bay to avoid risking transfer.
1937, May 27	Golden Gate Bridge dedicated and opened. Designers incorporate special arch in bridge to avoid destroying Fort Point.
1937, December	Army buys about 800 acres in Marin County and creates Fort Cronkhite, named in honor of Major Gen. Adelbert Cronkhite.
1940s	Ansel Adams and former Sierra Club president Ed Wayburn propose Golden Gate area be designated national monument.
1942	Army buys remaining land for Fort Funston from Spring Valley Water Company (this purchase is the eastern section; ocean section purchased in 1917. Land used as Nike missile base in 1950s).
1950	City of San Francisco receives northern fifty acres belonging to Fort Funston (originally 237 acres total).
1951, November	City voters approve $1.1 million bond issue to purchase 116 acres south of armory for recreation and park use. (Land offered by federal government as surplus property.)
1953	City leases seven acres of former Fort Funston property to state for National Guard Armory on ninety-nine-year lease.
1954	Nike Ajax missiles begin to be sited around San Francisco.
1958	National Park Service releases coastline study, includes report calling for creation of Point Reyes National Seashore.
1959	Fort Point Museum Association incorporated.
1960s	Idea develops in California to create "Parks for the People." Concept spreads to Washington, brought there by

	Interior Secretary Walter Hickle; becomes buzzword in National Park Service, leads to creation of Gateway National Recreation Area.
1961	Undeveloped areas of Fort Baker turned over to California for park purposes.
1962	Department of Defense declares Fort Mason "surplus military property," transfers remaining military functions to Oakland Army Base.
1962, June	U.S. Attorney General Robert Kennedy announces Alcatraz to be phased out of Federal Penitentiary System.
1962, June 13	Presidio designated National Historic Landmark.
1962, September 13	President Kennedy signs legislation establishing Point Reyes National Seashore.
1963, March 21	Alcatraz closes as prison, last prisoners transferred off island.
1963, April	Alcatraz Island reports to General Services Administration as excess property.
1964, March	President's Commission on Disposition of Alcatraz Island formed.
1964, May	Alcatraz commission recommends island be used to commemorate founding of United Nations in San Francisco. (No action taken on this proposal.)
1964, August	San Francisco Board of Supervisors passes Resolution no. 472-64, requesting secretary of interior and administrator of General Services establish Fort Mason as national historic site, or if such action proves impossible, requesting GSA make Fort Mason available to city as park and recreation area.
1964, November	Thomas Frouge and Gulf Oil Corporation unveil plans for Marincello, 18,000-person community to be built on Marin Headlands.
1965, June	State of California publishes *A History of San Francisco Harbor Defense Installations: Forts Baker, Barry, Cronkhite, and Funston.*
1966	Sutro Baths burn in fire.
1968	Federal and California agencies indicate to GSA they do not wish to acquire Alcatraz Island.
1968	San Francisco Bay Discovery Site designated National Historic Landmark.
1968	City of San Francisco expresses interest in acquiring Alcatraz Island, calls for development proposals; about 500 received.
1968	NPS releases *Fort Point National Historic Site, California: A Proposal.*
1969	Federal government (General Services Administration) proposes building football field–sized National Archives storage building on surplus U.S. Army land at Fort Miley. Amy Meyer, who lives across from Lincoln Park, begins

	organizing protest. (Building is eventually constructed in San Bruno.)
1969, November	Department of Interior Bureau of Outdoor Recreation recommends transfer of Alcatraz to National Park Service and inclusion of other surplus federal property as Park for the People. Committee recommends that lands be pulled together to form 8,000-acre park.
1969, November 29	Beginning of Indian occupation of Alcatraz Island, lasts nineteen months.
1969, December	San Francisco Board of Supervisors votes to lease Alcatraz Island to H. Lamar Hunt for commercial development.
1970	William Whalen named one of government's ten outstanding young men.
1970, April	Fire destroys lighthouse keeper's house, military buildings, post exchange, warden's residence, and surgeon's home on Alcatraz Island.
1970, Summer	Congressman Phil Burton introduces legislation to create GGNRA (H.R. 16444).
1970, October 16	President Nixon signs Public Law 91-457 creating Fort Point National Historic Site.
1971	U.S. Army turns twenty-two acres of Fort Mason over to General Services Administration for disposal.
1971, January	Protest group founded by Amy Meyer becomes People for a Golden Gate National Recreation Area.
1971, February	Nixon makes "Legacy of Parks" statement.
1971, June 16	Representative Phillip Burton introduces expansive proposal for national recreation area in Bay Area. Plan includes Park Service veto power over future Presidio developments by army.
1971, August 9	House Committee on Interior and Insular Affairs, Subcommittee on National Parks and Recreation holds hearings in San Francisco on H.R. 9498 and related bills.
1972, January 23	William J. Whalen named general manager, Bay Area Parks.
1972, May 11–12	House Committee on Interior and Insular Affairs, Subcommittee on National Parks and Recreation holds hearings in Washington, D.C., on H.R. 9498 and related bills.
1972	92d Congress publishes *Golden Gate National Recreation Area, Hearings,* on H.R. 9498 and related bills.
1972, July 28	House Subcommittee on National Parks and Recreation passes bill authored by Representative Phillip Burton to establish 20,000-acre Golden Gate National Urban Recreation Area.
1972, September 5	President Nixon visits proposed site of Golden Gate National Recreation Area to demonstrate his support.
1972, October 11	House approves bill establishing 34,000-acre Golden Gate National Recreation Area. (Bill passes without dissent.)

1972, October 27	President Nixon signs *An Act to Establish the Golden Gate National Recreation Area* (Public Law 92-589), which allocates $61,610,000 for land acquisition and $58,000,000 for development. On same day, Whalen given responsibility for administering Golden Gate National Recreation Area, Point Reyes National Seashore, Muir Woods National Monument, and Fort Point National Historic Site.
1972, December	Gulf Oil Corporation sells Marincello property to Nature Conservancy. Marin citizens form Marin Headlands Association, designed to persuade state to purchase all surplus lands along south rim for safekeeping. (This land would be combined with Alcatraz and San Francisco Headlands to form initial basis for park.)
1972	National Park Service acquires Alcatraz Island.
1972	NPS acquires Fort Mason, which army had used strictly for storage since 1962.
1973	NPS releases *Fort Point: Historic Data Section, Fort Point National Historic Site, California.*
1973, October	Alcatraz opens to public under Park Service management.
1974	Army closes Crissy Field to fixed-wing aircraft, restricts use to helicopters.
1974, August 4	Jerry L. Schober named superintendent of South Area.
1974, December 26	President Ford signs Public Law 93-544, adds 750 acres of contiguous private lands in Marin County to GGNRA.
1975	NPS releases *Preliminary Information Base Analysis, North Portion of Golden Gate National Recreation Area, Muir Woods National Monument, and Point Reyes National Seashore.*
1975	NPS releases *Preliminary Information Base Analysis, South Portion of Golden Gate National Recreation Area, California.*
1975	Visitor center established at park headquarters at Fort Mason.
1975, May	PFGGNRA and Park Service unveil plans for expanding Golden Gate National Recreation Area south into San Mateo County.
1975, June 10	City of San Francisco officially turns over 91.5 acres of city parklands to Golden Gate National Recreation Area. (Transaction involves lands around Fort Miley, Lands End, and portions of Lincoln Park excluding golf course.)
1975, September	GGNRA superintendent releases *Golden Gate Recreational Travel Study.*
1975, October 11	Title of Bay Area general superintendent changed to general manager of Bay Area parks.
1976	Congress declares about half of Point Reyes National Seashore as unit of National Wilderness Preservation System.
1976	NPS releases *Archeological Resources of Golden Gate National Recreation Area.*

1976	Outline of planning requirements approved.
1976, May	Fort Mason Foundation created, given responsibility for guiding and shaping development of abandoned warehouses and piers into cultural center.
1977	NPS acquires Cliff House for $3.79 million.
1977	NPS acquires Haslett Warehouse, located in center of Fisherman's Wharf/Ghirardelli Square tourist area. (Building acquired by State of California for railroad museum, but plans were derailed.)
1977, January	Fort Mason opens to public.
1977, May	NPS releases *Golden Gate National Recreation Area, Point Reyes National Seashore: Assessment of Alternatives for the General Management Plan.*
1977, July 3	Jerry Schober named acting general manager.
1977, September 16	San Francisco Maritime State Historical Park added to GGNRA.
1977, October 1	Point Reyes National Seashore separated from GGNRA.
1977, October 22	Title of general manager discontinued.
1977, November	NPS releases *Historic Resource Study: Alcatraz Island, Golden Gate National Recreation Area.*
1978	San Francisco Maritime Museum added to GGNRA.
1978	Cliff House Visitor Center opens at GGNRA.
1978	California voters approve Proposition 13.
1978, April 23	Lynn H. Thompson named superintendent.
1978, November 10	Public Law 96-625 expands park by adding nearly 3,000 acres in Marin County under *National Parks and Recreation Act of 1978.*
1979	NPS releases *Golden Gate National Recreation Area: Collection Management Plan.*
1979	NPS releases *Historic Resource Study: Seacoast Fortifications, San Francisco Harbor, Golden Gate National Recreation Area, California.*
1979	NPS releases *Inventory of Occupation Graffiti, 1969–1971: Alcatraz Island, Golden Gate National Recreation Area, California.*
1979, June	NPS releases *Golden Gate National Recreation Area, Point Reyes National Seashore, California: General Management Plan, Environmental Analysis.*
1979, November	NPS releases *Historic Resource Study: Forts Baker, Barry, Cronkhite of Golden Gate National Recreation Area, California.*
1980, March 5	Public Law 96-199 adds lands in Marin County to GGNRA by extending park boundaries eight miles north to include Samuel P. Taylor State Park (2,450 acres) and Gallagher, Ottinger, and Giacomini ranches (1,214 acres).
1980, March 5	Division of Museum Services, NPS, releases *Museum Storage Plan, Golden Gate National Recreation Area.*

1980, June	NPS releases *A Civil History of Golden Gate National Recreation Area and Point Reyes National Seashore, California.*
1980, June 1	William Whalen named superintendent.
1980, September	NPS releases *Golden Gate National Recreation Area/Point Reyes National Seashore: General Management Plan, Environmental Analysis.*
1980, September 8	Public Law 96-344 adds 1,096 acres to GGNRA in Marin County.
1980, September 19	General Management Plan, GGNRA and Point Reyes National Seashore, approved.
1980, December 28	Public Law 96-199 expands GGNRA into San Mateo County and along coast to Half Moon Bay (2,000 acres) by including 23,000 acres of Sweeney Ridge.
1981	NPS releases *Golden Gate National Recreation Area, California: Draft Natural Resources Management Plan and Environmental Assessment.*
1982	U.S. Air Force automates its radar tracking operations and releases all but 2.5 acres of its 106.4-acre site atop Mount Tamalpais in Marin County to NPS. Site contains fifty-three abandoned structures and complex utility system capable of supporting community of 300. Many buildings contain asbestos, hindering removal plans.
1982	Golden Gate National Park Association established.
1982	NPS releases *Golden Gate National Recreation Area, California: Draft Natural Resources Management Plan and Environmental Assessment.*
1982	National Maritime Museum completes first Scope of Collections Statement.
1982	Federal Emergency Management Agency moves into Barracks 105 at Presidio.
1982, January 10	John H. Davis appointed general superintendent of GGNRA.
1982, March	NPS moves Western Information Center to Fort Mason from 450 Golden Gate Ave.
1982, May 5	Mexican Museum opens in new quarters at Fort Mason Center.
1982, June 1	NPS releases *Cultural Resources Management Plan.*
1982, June 4	NPS releases *Addendum, Natural Resources Management Plan and Environmental Assessment, Golden Gate National Recreation Area.*
1983	NPS releases *Structural and Seismic Evaluation of the Structures in the Fort Mason Pier Area* (Phase I: study of structures; Phase II: recommendations for and costs of correcting deficiencies).
1983	Congressman Phillip Burton dies.
1983, March 17	Land Protection Plan approved.
1983	GGNRA prescribed burn program begins.

1984	Joe R. McBride writes Forest Management Plan for Presidio and East Fort Baker.
1984	NPS releases *Historic Structures Report: Fort Barry Buildings 960, 961, 962.*
1984, October	Tanker *Puerto Rican* burns after passing under Golden Gate Bridge. Ship sinks on November 3, resulting oil spill reaches GGNRA beaches.
1984, October 13	Revised Natural Resources Management Plan and Environmental Assessment approved.
1985	Golden Gate Raptor Observatory at GGNRA established.
1985	San Francisco Port of Embarkation designated a National Historic Landmark.
1985	*Balclutha* (only full-rigged ship in National Maritime Museum collection) designated a National Historic Landmark.
1985	NPS releases *Presidio of San Francisco, National Historic Landmark District: Historic American Building Survey Report.*
1985, January	Ferryboat *Eureka* designated a National Historic Landmark.
1985, March 12	Fire Management Plan approved.
1985, September 29	Brian O'Neill named acting superintendent.
1985, October 10	Park Service announces plans to restore Crissy Field.
1986	Alcatraz Island declared a National Historic Landmark.
1986, February 16	Brian O'Neill named superintendent.
1986, August	NPS releases *Marin Headlands, Golden Gate National Recreation Area: Interpretative Prospectus.*
1987	NPS releases *Interpretive Prospectus—Alcatraz.*
1987	Bicycles restricted to designated trails within GGNRA.
1987	Self-guided tours of Alcatraz Island begin.
1987, June	U.S. Coast Guard receives Park Service's permission to relocate search and rescue function from Station Fort Point near south end of Golden Gate Bridge to East Fort Baker, immediately northeast of bridge; frees up five-acre site surrounded by Crissy Field.
1988	United Nations designates GGNRA an International Biosphere Reserve.
1988	Golden Gate National Park Association sponsors "Alcatraz the Future—Concept Plan and Guidelines" (planning and design effort to visualize GMP and Interpretive Prospectus).
1988	New visitor center built at Muir Woods.
1988, June 27	Public Law 100-348 creates San Francisco Maritime National Historic Park and transfers museum and historic ships from GGNRA to new park. Measure intended to enhance ability of maritime park to compete for scarce funding within NPS and relieve GGNRA of expensive maintenance commitments to ships.

1988, December	Defense Department releases *Base Realignments and Closures: Report of the Defense Secretary's Commission.*
1988, December 29	Presidio of San Francisco on list of military bases recommended for realignment or closure under proposed Public Law 100-526, *Base Closure and Realignment Act.*
1989	Bay Area Ridge Trail dedicated.
1989	NPS releases *Submerged Cultural Resources Assessment: Golden Gate National Recreation Area, Gulf of the Farallones National Marine Sanctuary, and Point Reyes National Seashore.*
1989, April	Congress approves *Base Closure and Realignment Act,* with Presidio closure no later than September 1995.
1990	Coast Guard opens new lifesaving station at Fort Baker in Marin County.
1990	Federal prisoners begin working on Alcatraz Island projects under supervision of Federal Bureau of Prisons and National Park Service.
1990	NPS releases *Base Closure of the Presidio of San Francisco: Draft Environmental Impact Statement.*
1990	NPS releases *The Top of the Peninsula: A History of Sweeney Ridge and the San Francisco Watershed Lands, San Mateo County, California.*
1990, May	Presidio Planning Guidelines released to public.
1990	NPS initiates first phase of GMP on Alcatraz: opening of island's southern end, known as Agave Walk, and parade ground. After concerns expressed by two local Audubon Society chapters, NPS withdraws project.
1991	Scope of Collection Statement approved.
1991	NPS releases *San Francisco Point of Embarkation: Golden Gate National Recreation Area, National Park Service.*
1992	Golden Gate Operations and Maintenance Programmatic Agreement signed with Western Regional Office of NPS, California State Historic Preservation Office, and Advisory Council on Historic Preservation.
1992	NPS releases *Historic Resource Study: El Presidio de San Francisco, A History under Spain and Mexico, 1776–1846.*
1992	Visitor center at Fort Cronkhite relocated to rehabilitated Fort Barry chapel.
1992	GGNRA superintendent releases Alcatraz Cultural Landscape Report draft.
1992, April 22	Statement for Management, GGNRA, approved.
1992, June	NPS releases *Historic Gardens of Alcatraz.*
1992, June 9	Public Law 102-29 adds Phleger Estate to GGNRA.
1992, August	NPS releases *Presidio of San Francisco, Golden Gate National Recreation Area, California: Special History Study, Presidio of San Francisco, An Outline of Its Evolution as a U.S. Army Post, 1847–1990.*

1993	NPS releases *Draft General Management Plan Amendment, Presidio of San Francisco: Presidio Building Leasing and Financing Implementation Strategy, A Supplement to the Draft General Management Plan Amendment, Presidio of San Francisco.*
1993, March	Army relinquishes management of Presidio Forest, Lobos Creek Valley, and Coastal Bluffs to Park Service.
1993, April	Presidio becomes home to U.S. headquarters for Mikhail Gorbachev's Gorbachev Foundation.
1993, July 9	NPS releases *Alcatraz Development Concept Plan and Environmental Assessment.*
1993, September	NPS assumes complete control of Crissy Field.
1993, October	NPS releases *Creating a Park for the 21st Century: From Military Post to National Park, Draft General Management Plan Amendment, Presidio of San Francisco.*
1993, October	Update of Presidio National Historic Landmark approved.
1994	NPS releases *Golden Gate National Recreation Area: Collection Management Plan.*
1994, March	NPS assumes control of Presidio housing.
1994, July	NPS releases *Final General Management Plan Amendment, Environmental Impact Statement, Presidio of San Francisco.*
1994, July	NPS releases *Presidio of San Francisco, Golden Gate National Recreation Area: Comments and Responses, Final General Management Plan Amendment and Final Environmental Impact Statement.*
1994, September 30	U.S. Army transfers all remaining parts of Presidio to Park Service.
1995, May	NPS releases *A Good Life: Dairy Farming in the Olema Valley, A History of the Dairy and Beef Ranches of the Olema Valley and Lagunitas Canyon, Golden Gate National Recreation Area and Point Reyes National Seashore.*
1996, June	Jones and Stokes Associates publishes *Environmental Assessment for Crissy Field Plan* for NPS.
1996	GGNRA and GGNPA staffs begin work on restoration and interpretation of Crissy Field, one of largest restoration projects ever undertaken by Park Service.
1997, July	GGNPA guides begin leading tours of Alcatraz.
2000	More than $31 million raised for restoration of Crissy Field.
2000, April	Conference, led by Park Service, Presidio Trust, and GGNPA, discusses Presidio interpretation.

Appendix

Visitations to GGNRA, by Month, 1979–1999

Month	Year	Visits	Month	Year	Visits
January	1979	529,802	April	1982	1,816,131
February	1979	805,332	May	1982	1,939,585
March	1979	1,163,146	June	1982	1,993,261
April	1979	866,836	July	1982	2,324,124
May	1979	1,044,645	August	1982	2,317,151
June	1979	1,137,845	September	1982	1,598,361
July	1979	1,201,874	October	1982	1,230,142
August	1979	1,200,030	November	1982	1,384,466
September	1979	1,035,038	December	1982	1,257,499
October	1979	874,597	January	1983	1,218,631
November	1979	765,823	February	1983	1,022,888
December	1979	696,159	March	1983	1,273,427
January	1980	1,009,310	April	1983	1,499,164
February	1980	1,048,930	May	1983	1,700,522
March	1980	1,094,436	June	1983	2,686,294
April	1980	1,276,658	July	1983	1,730,789
May	1980	1,549,423	August	1983	1,746,359
June	1980	1,736,887	September	1983	1,699,660
July	1980	2,595,773	October	1983	1,285,890
August	1980	1,917,277	November	1983	983,043
September	1980	2,060,709	December	1983	757,884
October	1980	1,850,484	January	1984	1,030,439
November	1980	1,075,557	February	1984	1,063,706
December	1980	1,206,329	March	1984	1,222,122
January	1981	1,067,346	April	1984	1,303,760
February	1981	1,155,238	May	1984	1,332,716
March	1981	1,304,302	June	1984	1,464,281
April	1981	1,364,366	July	1984	1,945,851
May	1981	1,691,042	August	1984	1,925,716
June	1981	2,416,359	September	1984	1,923,758
July	1981	2,296,376	October	1984	1,535,673
August	1981	2,469,125	November	1984	1,001,118
September	1981	2,492,918	December	1984	982,566
October	1981	1,534,950	January	1985	1,125,982
November	1981	1,310,247	February	1985	1,220,659
December	1981	1,177,520	March	1985	1,138,352
January	1982	1,324,163	April	1985	1,476,035
February	1982	1,312,297	May	1985	1,502,803
March	1982	1,400,209	June	1985	1,787,375

Month	Year	Visits	Month	Year	Visits
July	1985	1,943,866	July	1989	2,467,759
August	1985	2,027,928	August	1989	1,636,678
September	1985	2,077,624	September	1989	1,425,279
October	1985	1,717,146	October	1989	1,592,487
November	1985	1,224,964	November	1989	996,690
December	1985	1,112,631	December	1989	904,329
January	1986	1,258,252	January	1990	1,043,598
February	1986	1,266,006	February	1990	979,342
March	1986	1,276,579	March	1990	1,098,731
April	1986	1,357,779	April	1990	1,361,166
May	1986	2,116,045	May	1990	1,131,377
June	1986	2,151,600	June	1990	1,468,856
July	1986	2,735,997	July	1990	1,471,350
August	1986	2,779,350	August	1990	1,468,567
September	1986	2,249,520	September	1990	1,336,655
October	1986	1,840,318	October	1990	1,341,237
November	1986	1,417,895	November	1990	1,110,429
December	1986	1,133,027	December	1990	838,905
January	1987	1,199,474	January	1991	1,043,598
February	1987	1,227,791	February	1991	979,342
March	1987	1,242,682	March	1991	1,098,731
April	1987	1,992,370	April	1991	1,361,166
May	1987	2,423,636	May	1991	1,131,377
June	1987	2,143,065	June	1991	1,468,856
July	1987	2,386,270	July	1991	1,471,350
August	1987	2,594,571	August	1991	1,468,567
September	1987	2,044,208	September	1991	1,336,655
October	1987	1,921,977	October	1991	1,341,237
November	1987	1,383,160	November	1991	1,110,429
December	1987	1,207,972	December	1991	884,463
January	1988	1,006,170	January	1992	1,009,567
February	1988	1,405,548	February	1992	924,760
March	1988	1,480,117	March	1992	1,058,138
April	1988	1,773,231	April	1992	1,130,026
May	1988	2,137,367	May	1992	1,254,631
June	1988	2,478,775	June	1992	1,376,558
July	1988	2,787,131	July	1992	1,496,267
August	1988	2,493,243	August	1992	1,409,272
September	1988	2,162,553	September	1992	1,447,701
October	1988	1,653,202	October	1992	1,878,507
November	1988	1,192,245	November	1992	1,332,805
December	1988	1,189,689	December	1992	991,106
January	1989	984,430	January	1993	1,043,598
February	1989	1,023,779	February	1993	979,342
March	1989	1,106,804	March	1993	1,098,731
April	1989	1,415,206	April	1993	1,361,166
May	1989	1,309,148	May	1993	1,131,377
June	1989	1,794,307	June	1993	1,468,856

Visitations to GGNRA, *continued*

Month	Year	Visits	Month	Year	Visits
July	1993	1,471,350	October	1996	1,109,012
August	1993	1,468,567	November	1996	1,039,460
September	1993	1,336,655	December	1996	940,389
October	1993	1,341,237	January	1997	973,083
November	1993	1,110,429	February	1997	1,081,129
December	1993	884,463	March	1997	1,113,382
January	1994	1,043,598	April	1997	1,198,736
February	1994	979,342	May	1997	1,296,246
March	1994	1,098,731	June	1997	1,240,357
April	1994	1,361,166	July	1997	1,269,101
May	1994	1,131,377	August	1997	1,254,808
June	1994	1,468,856	September	1997	1,165,448
July	1994	1,471,350	October	1997	1,214,818
August	1994	1,468,567	November	1997	1,066,352
September	1994	1,336,655	December	1997	929,922
October	1994	1,341,237	January	1998	949,556
November	1994	1,110,429	February	1998	1,016,357
December	1994	884,463	March	1998	1,125,410
January	1995	1,043,598	April	1998	1,220,318
February	1995	979,342	May	1998	1,258,958
March	1995	1,098,731	June	1998	1,337,678
April	1995	1,361,166	July	1998	1,350,034
May	1995	1,131,377	August	1998	1,188,875
June	1995	1,468,856	September	1998	1,251,288
July	1995	1,471,350	October	1998	1,267,198
August	1995	1,468,567	November	1998	1,024,980
September	1995	1,336,655	December	1998	1,055,938
October	1995	1,341,237	January	1999	972,474
November	1995	1,110,429	February	1999	1,070,058
December	1995	884,463	March	1999	1,132,792
January	1996	1,050,640	April	1999	1,302,790
February	1996	1,015,037	May	1999	1,179,726
March	1996	1,222,501	June	1999	1,327,761
April	1996	1,335,448	July	1999	1,167,544
May	1996	1,202,476	August	1999	1,209,249
June	1996	1,282,725	September	1999	1,264,156
July	1996	1,202,211	October	1999	1,186,212
August	1996	1,366,995	November	1999	1,091,638
September	1996	1,277,090	December	1999	1,143,685

Statistics courtesy of the National Park Service Public Use Statistics Office.

GGNRA Superintendents, 1972–2000

	Title	Years at GGNRA
William J. Whalen	General Manager Bay Area Parks[1]	1/23/1972 to 7/02/1977
Jerry L. Schober	Acting General Manager[2]	7/03/1977 to 10/22/1977
Jerry L. Schober	Superintendent	8/04/1974 to 2/10/1979
Lynn H. Thompson	Superintendent	4/23/1978 to 2/29/1980
William J. Whalen	Superintendent	6/01/1980 to 2/12/1981
John H. Davis	Superintendent	1/10/1982 to 9/28/1985
Brian O'Neill	Acting Superintendent	9/29/1985 to 2/15/1986
Brian O'Neill	Superintendent	2/16/1986 to Fall 2000

1. Assigned to Golden Gate National Recreation Area; administered GGNRA, Point Reyes National Seashore, Muir Woods National Monument, and Fort Point National Historic Site from 10/27/1972. A south area superintendent position was filled as of 8/4/1974 at GGNRA, and the north area and Point Reyes were assumed by the incumbent superintendent. The areas formerly supervised by the superintendent of Point Reyes, John Muir National Historic Site, and Muir Woods National Monument were then placed under the supervision of the south area superintendent. Title was changed on 10/11/1975 from Bay Area general superintendent to general manager of Bay Area parks.
2. Organizational change eliminated the north area (Point Reyes) from the Bay Area grouping on 10/1/1977, and the title of general manager was discontinued effective 10/22/1977.

PUBLIC LAW 87-657, authorizing Point Reyes National Seashore, was signed into law by President Kennedy on September 13, 1962.

PUBLIC LAW 92-589 (H.R. 16444) established the Golden Gate National Recreation Area and an Advisory Commission on October 27, 1972. It sanctioned the expenditure of $61,610,000 for the acquisition of lands and interests in lands. It also authorized inclusion of all army lands within the boundaries when these lands were declared excess by the army; immediately transferred administrative jurisdiction of Fort Mason, Crissy Field, Forts Cronkhite, Barry, and the westerly one-half of Fort Baker to the secretary of interior; and placed the Marina Green, including the railroad right-of-way, within park boundaries.

The establishment section read: "In order to preserve for public use and enjoyment certain areas of Marin and San Francisco Counties, California, possessing outstanding natural, historic, scenic, and recreational values, and in order to provide for the maintenance of needed recreational open space necessary to urban environment and planning, the Golden Gate National Recreation Area (hereinafter referred to as the 'recreation area' is hereby established. In the management of the recreation area the Secretary of the Interior (hereinafter referred to as the 'Secretary') shall utilize the resources in a manner which will provide for recreation and educational opportunities consistent with sound principles of land use planning and management. In carrying out the provisions of this Act, the Secretary shall preserve the recreation area, as far as possible, in its natural setting, and protect it from development and uses which would destroy the scenic beauty and natural character of the area."

PUBLIC LAW 1193-544, enacted in 1974, added several relatively small parcels of land to GGNRA's boundary in the Mill Valley/Sausalito area.

PUBLIC LAW 94-389 (H.R. 738), passed in 1976, provided for federal participation in preserving the tule elk population in California and suggested that Point Reyes National Seashore was one of the federal areas that offered a potential for use.

PUBLIC LAW 94-544 (H.R. 8002) and 94-567 (H.R. 13160), also passed in 1976, established the 25,370-acre Point Reyes Wilderness Area and a wilderness potential of 8,003 acres.

PUBLIC LAW 95-625 authorized the acquisition of 3,723.60 acres of private land in the Lagunitas Loop/Devil's Gulch area of Marin County in 1978, as well as the addition of Samuel P. Taylor State Park.

PUBLIC LAW 96-199, enacted in March 1980, extended the park boundary more than eight miles further northward, adding about 2,000 acres that encompassed most of the waters of Tomales Bay.

PUBLIC LAW 96-344, enacted in September 1980, modified P.L. 96-199 by adding eighteen more parcels, amounting to about 1,100 acres.

PUBLIC LAW 96-607, passed on December 28, 1980, authorized a boundary expansion of Golden Gate National Recreation Area by adding 26,000 acres in San Mateo County, including 1,047 acres of privately held land on Sweeney Ridge.

PUBLIC LAW 100-526, *The Base Closure and Realignment Act*, enacted October 24, 1988, required that the army installation at the Presidio of San Francisco close and that approximately 1,234 acres of the Presidio transfer to the jurisdiction of the U.S. Department of the Interior.

Notes

ABBREVIATIONS USED IN THE NOTES (ALL DOCUMENTS
HOUSED IN THE GGNRA ARCHIVES)

AD	Alcatraz Documents
CCF	Central Correspondence Files
CRMP	Cultural Resource Management Plan
DCR	*Daly City Record*
FPAR	Fort Point Administrative Records
GMP	General Management Plan
GMPA	General Management Plan Amendment
HDC	Historic Documents Collection (number)
KFC	Katharine Frankforter/Headlands, Inc. Collection
MIJ	*Marin Independent-Journal*
NRMP	Natural Resource Management Plan
NRMR	Natural Resource Management Records
OCPA	Office of Communications and Public Affairs Records
PAT	*Palo Alto Times*
PAC	*Petaluma Argus-Courier*
PARC	Park Archives and Records Center
PCC	Press Clippings Collection
PFGGNRA I	People for a Golden Gate National Recreation Area Archives, 1972–1984
PFGGNRA II	People for a Golden Gate National Recreation Area Archives, 1985–1994
PRL	*Point Reyes Light*
PS	*Pacific Sun*
PT	*Pacifica Tribune*
SCS	*Santa Cruz Sentinel*
SFBG	*San Francisco Bay Guardian*
SFC	*San Francisco Chronicle*
SFC&E	*San Francisco Chronicle and Examiner*
SFE	*San Francisco Examiner*
SFI	*San Francisco Independent*
SFP	*San Francisco Progress*
SJMN	*San Jose Mercury News*
SOA I	Superintendent's Office Archives, 1957–1977
SOA II	Superintendent's Office Archives, 1977–1998

CHAPTER 1. NATIONAL PARKS AND THE BAY AREA

1. Henry Gilbert, *Robin Hood* (New York: Blue Ribbon Books, 1912), 11–23.

2. Alfred Runte, *National Parks: The American Experience*, 3d ed. (Lincoln: University of Nebraska Press, 1997), 33–61; R. W. B. Lewis, *The American Adam: Innocence, Tragedy, and Tradition in the Nineteenth Century* (Chicago: University of Chicago Press, 1968); Henry Nash Smith, *Virgin Land: The American West as Myth and Symbol* (Cambridge: Harvard University Press, 1950), 3–50, 123–32.

3. This is not to discount the debunking of the famed creation of the myth of the national park idea at a Yellowstone campfire. The story of deciding that Yellowstone should be held as a national treasure did happen. The motives were hardly as pure as Nathaniel Pitt "National Park" Langford later claimed; for the mythic view, see Robert Shankland, *Steve Mather of the National Parks* (New York: Alfred A. Knopf, 1953), 43–44, and John Ise, *Our National Park Policy: A Critical History* (Baltimore: Johns Hopkins University Press, 1961), 15; for the revised view, see Runte, *National Parks*, 36–45, and Richard West Sellars, *Preserving Nature in the National Parks: A History* (New Haven: Yale University Press, 1997), 9.

4. T. J. Jackson Lears, *No Place of Grace: Antimodernism and the Transformation of American Culture, 1880–1920* (New York: Pantheon, 1981); Hal K. Rothman, *Devil's Bargains: Tourism in the Twentieth-Century American West* (Lawrence: University Press of Kansas, 1998), and *Conservation and Environmentalism in the American Century* (Chicago: Ivan R. Dee, 2000).

5. Shankland, *Steve Mather of the National Parks*, 6–11; Horace M. Albright and Marian Albright Schenck, *Creating the National Park Service: The Missing Years* (Norman: University of Oklahoma Press, 1999).

6. Horace M. Albright, as told to Robert Cahn, *The Birth of the National Park Service: The Founding Years, 1913–1933* (Salt Lake City: Howe Brothers Press, 1986), 69–73.

7. Alfred Runte, *Yosemite: The Embattled Wilderness* (Lincoln: University of Nebraska Press, 1990), 45–56; Michael P. Cohen, *The History of the Sierra Club, 1892–1970* (San Francisco: Sierra Club Books, 1988), 12–14.

8. Hal K. Rothman, *Preserving Different Pasts: The American National Monuments* (Urbana: University of Illinois Press, 1989), 59–60; Duane H. Hampton, *How the U.S. Cavalry Saved Our National Parks* (Bloomington: Indiana University Press, 1971).

9. William Issel and Robert W. Cherny, *San Francisco, 1865–1932: Politics, Power, and Urban Development* (Berkeley: University of California Press, 1986), 139–64.

10. Stephen R. Fox, *John Muir and His Legacy: The American Conservation Movement* (Boston; Little, Brown, 1981), 134–35; Rothman, *Preserving Different Pasts*, 61–64.

11. Rothman, *Preserving Different Pasts*, 61–64.

12. Ibid., 33–51.

13. Stephen J. Pyne, *How the Canyon Became Grand: A Short History* (New York: Viking, 1998); Rothman, *Devil's Bargains*.

14. Rothman, *Preserving Different Pasts*, 62–63.

15. Cohen, *The History of the Sierra Club*, 22–29; Roderick Nash, *Wilderness and the American Mind*, 3d ed. (New Haven: Yale University Press, 1982), 161–81.

16. Susan R. Schrepfer, *The Fight to Save the Redwoods: A History of Environmental Reform, 1917–1978* (Madison: University of Wisconsin Press, 1983).

17. John Hart, *San Francisco's Wilderness Next Door* (San Rafael, Calif.: Presidio Press, 1979), 31–37.

18. Gerald Nash, *World War II and the West: Reshaping the Economy* (Lincoln: Uni-

versity of Nebraska Press, 1990), 191–201; Roger Lotchin, *Fortress California, 1910–1961: From Warfare to Welfare* (New York: Oxford University Press, 1992), 19–21; Raymond F. Dasmann, *The Destruction of California* (New York: Macmillan, 1965), 200–202; John Jacobs, *A Rage for Justice: The Passion and Politics of Philip Burton* (Berkeley: University of California Press, 1995), 20–22; Marilynn S. Johnson, *Oakland and the East Bay in World War II* (Berkeley: University of California Press, 1993), 5–15.

19. Ronald A. Foresta, *America's National Parks and Their Keepers* (Washington, D.C.: Resources for the Future, 1984), 171; *Our Fourth Shore: Great Lakes Shoreline Recreation Study* (Washington, D.C.: National Park Service, 1959), 2–14; Sellars, *Preserving Nature in the National Parks*, 180–212.

20. Hart, *San Francisco's Wilderness Next Door*, 43–44.

21. Ibid., 44; Cohen, *The History of the Sierra Club*, 278; Sellars, *Preserving Nature in the National Parks*, 312.

22. Stewart Udall, *The Quiet Crisis* (New York: Holt, Rinehart and Winston, 1963).

23. Foresta, *America's National Parks and Their Keepers*, 64–65; Udall, *The Quiet Crisis*; James Bailey, "The Politics of Dunes, Redwoods, and Dams: Arizona's 'Brothers Udall' and America's National Parklands, 1961–1969" (Ph.D. diss., Arizona State University, 1999); Hal K. Rothman, "'A Regular Ding-Dong Fight': Agency Culture and Evolution in the Park Service–Forest Service Dispute, 1916–1937," *Western Historical Quarterly* 26, no. 2 (May 1989): 141–60.

24. "Congress Asked to Probe Action on Fort Property," *Haight-Cole Journal*, July 7, 1960; Cohen, *The History of the Sierra Club*, 277–83; Hart, *San Francisco's Wilderness Next Door*, 45–46; Foresta, *America's National Parks and Their Keepers*, 171–73; Judith Robinson, *"You're in Your Mother's Arms": The Life and Legacy of Congressman Phil Burton* (San Francisco: Mary Judith Robinson, 1994), 430–31. The Bodega Bay nuclear project has its own separate and contentious history. In the end, PG&E did not build a power plant there after local resistance and the discovery that the San Andreas Fault, the most significant earthquake zone in California, bisected the site. PG&E gave the land to the state as a state park for a token one dollar payment, and Bodega Head became part of the Sonoma Coast State Beaches.

25. Jane Jacobs, *The Death and Life of Great American Cities* (New York: Random House, 1961), is the classic attack on urban renewal and its mechanisms.

26. Chester Hartmann, *The Transformation of San Francisco* (Totowa, N.J.: Rowman and Allenheld, 1984), 7–11.

27. Richard E. DeLeon, *Left Coast City: Progressive Politics in San Francisco, 1975–1991* (Lawrence: University Press of Kansas, 1992), 41–43; Hartmann, *The Transformation of San Francisco*, 9–11, 19.

28. Lears, *No Place of Grace*, 3–16.

29. John A. Martini, *Fort Point: Sentry at the Golden Gate* (San Francisco: Golden Gate National Parks Association, 1991), 3–39.

30. Ibid., 40.

31. Lotchin, *Fortress California*, 340–41, 346–52; Nash, *World War II and the West*, 200–201; Martini, *Fort Point*, 47.

CHAPTER 2. A NATIONAL PARK FOR THE GOLDEN GATE

1. Chris Carlsson et. al., *Shaping San Francisco* (San Francisco: Bay Area Center for Art and Technology, 1998), CD-ROM, has an excellent section on the Freeway Revolt; Robinson, *"You're in Your Mother's Arms,"* 430; Tom Wolfe, *The Electric Kool-Aid*

Acid Test (New York: Farrar, Straus, and Giroux, 1968); Hal Rothman, *The Greening of a Nation? Environmentalism in the U.S. since 1945* (New York: Harcourt Brace, 1998).

2. David Farber, *The Age of Great Dreams: America in the 1960's* (New York: Hill and Wang, 1984); Morris Dickstein, *Gates of Eden: American Culture in the 1960s* (Cambridge: Harvard University Press, 1997); Terry H. Anderson, *The Movement and the Sixties* (New York: Oxford University Press, 1996).

3. Kenneth Jackson, *The Crabgrass Frontier: The Suburbanization of the United States* (New York: Oxford University Press, 1985).

4. Samuel P. Hays, *Beauty, Health, and Permanence: Environmental Politics in the United States, 1955–1985* (New York: Cambridge University Press, 1987); Hal Rothman, *Saving the Planet: The American Response to the Environment in the Twentieth Century* (Chicago: Ivan R. Dee, 2000).

5. Foresta, *America's National Parks and Their Keepers*, 53–54, 70–71; Sellars, *Preserving Nature in the National Parks*, 181–91; Rothman, *Preserving Different Pasts*, 89–118.

6. Lotchin, *Fortress California*, 335–45.

7. In one of the most dramatic of these situations, between the late 1940s and 1980 the Los Alamos National Laboratory gave away more than 60 percent of its nearly 60,000 acres in New Mexico; see Hal K. Rothman, *On Rims and Ridges: The Los Alamos Area since 1880* (Lincoln: University of Nebraska Press, 1992), 289–91.

8. As early as the 1940s, the island was considered as a state park, and efforts gained momentum in the 1960s. In 1966, the best opportunity for development came when state senator J. Eugene McAteer engineered $560,000 for development of the state park. The decision was widely lauded by the press and the public.

9. John A. Martini, *Fortress Alcatraz: Guardian of the Golden Gate* (Kailua, Hawaii: Pacific Monograph, 1990), 3–98; James P. Delgado, *Alcatraz: Island of Change* (San Francisco: Golden Gate National Parks Association, 1991), 7–38.

10. Delgado, *Alcatraz*, 36; James J. Jacobs, *Stateville: The Penitentiary in Mass Society* (Chicago: University of Chicago Press, 1977); Tom Wicker, *A Time to Die* (New York: Quadrangle Books, 1975).

11. Ramsey Clark to Sen. Edward V. Long, May 15, 1964, Box 1, H-14 Vol. 1, Alcatraz, January 1972–December 1972, Historical, CCF; Troy R. Johnson, *The Occupation of Alcatraz Island: Indian Self-Determination and the Rise of Indian Activism* (Urbana: University of Illinois Press, 1996), 16–25; Troy Johnson, Joane Nagel, and Duane Champagne, "American Indian Activism and Transformation: Lesson from Alcatraz," in *American Indian Activism: Alcatraz to the Longest Walk*, ed. Troy Johnson, Joane Nagel, and Duane Champagne (Urbana: University of Illinois Press, 1997), 25–27.

12. Delgado, *Alcatraz*, 39.

13. Bureau of Outdoor Recreation, *A New Look at Alcatraz* (Washington, D.C.: Bureau of Outdoor Recreation, 1969), 16; Ray Murray, interview with Sara Conklin, 1993, GGNRA Oral History Interview.

14. Adam Fortunate Eagle, "Urban Indians and the Occupation of Alcatraz," in *American Indian Activism*, ed. Johnson, Nagel, and Champagne, 55–57.

15. Ramsey Clark to Sen. Edward V. Long, May 15, 1964, Box 1, H-14 Vol. 1, Alcatraz, January 1972–December 1972, Historical, CCF; Johnson, *The Occupation of Alcatraz Island*, 16–25; Johnson, Nagel, and Champagne, "American Indian Activism and Transformation," in *American Indian Activism*, ed. Johnson, Nagel, and Champagne, 25–27.

16. John A. Hussey, *Fort McDowell, Angel Island, San Francisco Bay, California* (1949; reprint, San Francisco: National Park Service, 1981); Bureau of Outdoor Recre-

ation, *Golden Gate: A Matchless Opportunity* (San Francisco: Department of the Interior, 1969).

17. Doug Nadeau to Stephen Haller, January 23, 2002.

18. Amy Meyer, interview by Stephen Haller, February 25, 2002, 3, GENRA Archives, Nadeau to Haller, January 23, 2002.

19. Robinson, *"You're in Your Mother's Arms,"* 431; Jacobs, *A Rage for Justice,* 211; Meyer interview, February 25, 2002, 3–4.

20. Hartman, *The Transformation of San Francisco,* 121, 159.

21. Cohen, *History of the Sierra Club;* Edgar Wayburn, interview by Ann Lage and Susan Schrepfer, 1976–1981, 12, Bancroft Oral History Office, Bancroft Library, University of California, Berkeley.

22. The Nature Conservancy, "Marincello: Park Addition Proposal to the Gulf Oil Corporation," March 23, 1970, KFC, Box 7, File 45, Nature Conservancy; John Busterud to W. L. Henry, September 8, 1970, KFC, Box 8, File 34, Gulf Oil Correspondence; Wat Takeshita, "Marincello Plan Ruled Invalid," *MIJ,* November 2, 1970; Alice Yarish, "Marincello Is Back on the Front Burner," *PS,* September 29, 1971; Pat Angle, "A Conservation Victory: An Option on Marincello," May 12, 1972, *MIJ;* Hart, *San Francisco's Wilderness Next Door,* 54–61.

23. Hart, *San Francisco's Wilderness Next Door,* 28, 60–62; Wayburn interviews, 1976–1981, 19.

24. Jacobs, *A Rage for Justice,* 212. Wayburn offers a different perspective. He avers that Burton referred to him as "my guru" and tells that when he brought the park proposal to Burton, the congressman asked, "Is this what you want?" Wayburn responded that it was. See Wayburn comments to Stephen Haller, February 2002.

25. Robinson, *"You're in Your Mother's Arms,"* 405–6.

26. Wayburn interviews, 1976–1981, 129.

27. Jacobs, *A Rage For Justice,* 212–13; Robinson, *"You're in Your Mother's Arms,"* 431–32; Wayburn suggests that Mailliard's bill was the year before, but legislative records indicate that while Mailliard proposed a bill the year before, it was this bill to which Burton directly responded.

28. Jacobs, *A Rage for Justice,* 211; Robinson, *"You're in Your Mother's Arms,"* 433.

29. Robinson, *"You're in Your Mother's Arms,"* 432.

30. Jacobs, *A Rage for Justice,* 214–15.

31. Edgar Wayburn to Stephen Haller, February 2002; Wayburn interviews, 1976–1981, 128–29.

32. Joseph L. Alioto to Robert J. Dolan, May 12, 1972, Box 10, San Francisco Government—Office of the Mayor—Correspondence, Articles, PFGGNRA I; Jerry Burns, "Recreation Area Urged for Bay-Ocean Front," and "Supervisors Eye S.F. Beachheads," *SFC,* May 8, 1971; Hartman, *The Transformation of San Francisco,* 24–31, 139–40; Meyer interview, February 25, 2002, 8.

33. "Statement by Robert H. Mendelsohn, Member, Board of Supervisors, City and County of San Francisco, in Support of a Golden Gate National Recreation Area before the House of Representatives Subcommittee on National Parks and Recreation, August 9, 1971," and "Supervisor Robert E. Gonzales, Chairman: State and National Affairs Committee, Statement before House Subcommittee on National Parks and Recreation, August 9, 1971," both in Box 10, San Francisco Government, Board of Supervisors, PFGGNRA I.

34. Jacobs, *A Rage for Justice,* 214–15; Robinson, *"You're in Your Mother's Arms,"* 435.

35. Robinson, *"You're in Your Mother's Arms,"* 435–36; Jacobs, *A Rage for Justice,* 214.

CHAPTER 3. GOLDEN GATE NATIONAL RECREATION AREA AND
GROWTH

1. Foresta, *America's National Parks and Their Keepers*, 59–68; Sellars, *Preserving Nature in the National Parks*, 173–232.
2. Foresta, *America's National Parks and Their Keepers*, 177–79, 185; Jacobs, *A Rage for Justice*, 210.
3. Foresta, *America's National Parks and Their Keepers*, 68–73; Rothman, *The Greening of a Nation?* 52–61.
4. John Hart, *Farming on the Edge: Saving Family Farms in Marin County, California* (Berkeley: University of California Press, 1991); Samuel P. Hays and Barbara D. Hays, *Beauty, Health, and Permanence: Environmental Politics in the United States, 1955–1985* (New York: Cambridge University Press, 1987); Rothman, *Saving the Planet*.
5. Amy Meyer, "PFGGNRA and the Marin Countywide Plan," February 20, 1973, and Amy Meyer, Walter Mollison, and Robert C. Young to Board of Supervisors, Marin County, May 27, 1973, both in Box 15, PFGGNRA—Memos, PFGGNRA I; Edgar Wayburn and Amy Meyer to Nathaniel P. Reed, June 22, 1973, L-1417, Vol. 1, 12/1/72–7/31/73, Acquisition of Land, General, GGNRA, CCF.
6. William Thomas, "Setback for Gate Recreation Area," *SFC*, February 5, 1973; "Lawmakers Will Seek Park Funds," *SFC*, February 6, 1973; Dale Champion, "Big Bay Park—U.S. Finds Cash," *SFC*, February 27, 1973.
7. "Statement of the Honorable Peter Arrigoni, Member, Marin County Board of Supervisors to the Interior Subcommittee of the U.S. Senate Appropriations Committee, May 9, 1973," Box 9, Marin County Government—Board of Supervisors, PFGGNRA I.
8. William Penn Mott Jr. to Honorable Eugene A. Chappie, February 14, 1973, Box 18, Projects—State Park Land Transfer, PFGGNRA I; William Thomas, "Tough Mott Stand on Headlands Park," *SFC*, May 7, 1973.
9. Superintendent, Golden Gate National Recreation Area, to the Files, February 23, 1973, Box 1, L-1417, Vol. 1, 12/1/72–7/31/73, Acquisition of Land, CCF.
10. Edgar Wayburn and Amy Meyer to Nathaniel P. Reed, June 22, 1973, Nathaniel P. Reed to Edgar Wayburn and Amy Meyer, July 16, 1973, and "Proposed Boundary Revisions, Golden Gate National Recreation Area," all in Box 1, L-1417, Vol. 1, 12/1/72–7/31/73, Acquisition of Land, General, CCF; William J. Whalen, "Status Report, Golden Gate National Recreation Area," Box 1, L-1425, Vol. 1, November 1971–July 31, 1973, CCF; Douglas B. Cornell Jr, to Bernard C. Hartung, April 26, 1973, Box 1, L-1417, Vol. 1, 12/1/72–7/31/73, Acquisition of Land, General, CCF.
11. Associate Director, National Park Service, to Legislative Counsel, July 10, 1973; Richard A. Drever to William Mailliard, July 30, 1973, and William J. Whalen, "Status Report: Golden Gate National Recreation Area," ca. July 1973, all in Box 1, L-1425, Vol. 1, November 1972–July 31, 1973, CCF.
12. Whalen, "Status Report: Golden Gate National Recreation Area"; "Degree of Federal Jurisdiction," ca. 1973, Box 1, L1417, Vol. 2, 8/1/71–12/1/73, Boundary Changes, GGNRA, CCF.
13. "Ranch Tracts Bought for Recreation Area," *SFC*, August 4, 1973.
14. Huey Johnson to Joseph Rumberg, July 7, 1971, Box 1, June 1, 1970–December 31, 1972, H14 History—Formation, GGNRA, CCF; Hal Rothman, *America's National Monuments: The Politics of Preservation* (Lawrence: University Press of Kansas, 1994), 74–88, 212–32.

15. Assistant Secretary of the Interior Jack Horton to Carl Albert, November 12, 1973, Box 1, L-1417, Vol. 2, 8/1/71–12/1/73, Boundary Changes, CCF.

16. F. W. Warren and June Warren to William Mailliard and Phillip Burton, November 15, 1973, and "Statement of Congressman William S. Mailliard on Legislation to Amend the Act of October 27, 1972, to Establish the Golden Gate National Recreation Area in San Francisco and Marin Counties, California, submitted to Subcommittee on Parks and Recreation, House Committee on Interior and Insular Affairs, November 12, 1973," both in Box 1, L-1417, Vol. 2, 8/1/71–12/11/73, Boundary Changes, CCF; Jacobs, *A Rage for Justice*, 214.

17. Jacobs, *A Rage for Justice*, 250–54; Robinson, *"You're in Your Mother's Arms,"* 604–6; Richard Allan Baker, *Conservation Politics: The Senate Career of Clinton P. Anderson* (Albuquerque: University of New Mexico Press, 1985), 1–9; Gary E. Elliott, *Senator Alan Bible and the Politics of the New West* (Reno: University of Nevada Press, 1994).

18. Jack Horton to Carl Albert, November 12, 1973, Box 1, L-1417, Vol. 2, 8/1/71–12/173, Boundary Changes, CCF; "Park Land Completion Date Is Told," *MIJ*, December 11, 1973; "Recreation Area Bill Sent to Ford's Desk," *MIJ*, December 17, 1974; *The National Parks, Index 1997–1999* (Washington, D.C.: Department of the Interior, 1997), 27.

19. Department of Parks and Recreation, *The Golden Gate State Urban Park: A Special Study* (Sacramento: California Department of Parks and Recreation, 1975), vii, 4; Leonard M. Grimes Jr. to George R. Moscone, May 22, 1975, Box 18, Projects—State Land Transfer, PFGGNRA I.

20. Joanne Williams, "Not So Fast, GGNRA," *PS*, August 29, 1975; Michael Wornum to California State Park and Recreation Commission, September 19, 1975, Claude A. Look to Claire T. Dedrick, September 19, 1975, Leonore Bravo to George Moscone, October 24, 1975, and Herbert Rhodes to Robert F. Raab, October 29, 1975, all in Box 9, Marin County Government—Board of Supervisors, PFGGNRA I; Walter Schwartz, "Conservationists!" and "Commission Attacks Parks Plan," *SFC&E*, September 21, 1975, and "Brown Vetoes Park Transfer," *SFC*, October 2, 1975, all in Box 18, Projects—State Park Land, Transfer, PFGGNRA I.

21. Larry Liebert, "A Compromise on Bay Park Control," *PS*, June 15, 1976; "Brown Signs Bill to Shift Parks Control," *SFC*, July 10, 1976; "Feds to Take Over Stinson State Beach," *PRL*, July 22, 1976.

22. Homer Rouse to Associate Director, Legislation, April 5, 1973, Box 1, L-1417, Vol. 1, 12/1/72–7/3/73, Acquisition of Land, General, CCF; Dale Champion, "First Steps toward Huge Coastline Park," *SFC*, May 16, 1975.

23. "Two More Plans Tell How to Plan the Coast," *PT*, May 21, 1975.

24. Betty Hughes to Edgar Wayburn, May 23, 1975, Box 14, PFGGNRA—Legislative Proposals, Boundary Revisions, 1974–1976, PFGGNRA I.

25. "Warning: Your Land and Home Are in Danger of Being Confiscated for Use as a National Park," n.d., Box 14, PFGGNRA—Legislative Proposals, Boundary Revisions, 1974–1976, PFGGNRA I.

26. PFGGNRA, "Golden Gate National Recreation Area South," June 1, 1975, "Golden Gate National Recreation Area South," September 12, 1975, "Land—San Mateo County," ca. September 1975, "Golden Gate National Recreation Area South Proposal," ca. September 1975, all in Box 15, PFGGNRA—Regional Group—Articles, etc. Re: 1975 Expansion, PFGGNRA I; "Extend Golden Gate Area to the South?" *Country Almanac*, November 5, 1975; "Open Space Extension Rapped," *PAT*, November 1, 1975; "Golden Gate Recreation," *Country Almanac*, November 12, 1975.

27. "Ryan Introduces Bill to Study Mammoth Park for Coastside Area," *Half Moon Bay Review*, November 13, 1975.

28. William H. Whalen to Mrs. J. H. Poinsett, January 7, 1976, Box 3, GGNRA—Subjects—Correspondence, 1972–1984, PFGGNRA I; "How Many Parks?" *SCS*, November 28, 1975; "Unwise Proposal on Golden Gate National Recreation Area," *San Mateo Times*, November 28, 1975; R. Allen Zink, Kristin M. Clark, and William B. Grant, *An Analysis of Development and Counterdevelopment Pressures: A Study of California's Half Moon Bay Coastal Region* (Palo Alto, Calif.: Stanford Research Institute, 1975); "Park Expansion Bill Dropped," *MIJ*, February 5, 1976; "Too Much Land," *PRL*, February 5, 1976; Dave Mitchell, "Crowd Decries Land-Buy Plans," *PRL*, February 5, 1976; Alice Yarish, "GGNRA: Egg on the Face," *PS*, February 6–12, 1976.

29. Hartman, *The Transformation of San Francisco*, 135–37; DeLeon, *Left Coast City*, 13–22.

30. Dale Champion, "U.S. Takeover Planned for Aquatic Park Area," *SFC*, September 4, 1976.

31. Janis MacKenzie, "New Plans for Playland," *San Francisco Business*, October 1978; Russ Cone, "Feinstein Raps Playland Proposal," *SFE*, May 12, 1978.

32. Rothman, *Devil's Bargains*, 1–27; Fox, *John Muir and His Legacy*, 134–38.

33. Amy Meyer to Jerry Friedman, January 25, 1976, Box 14, PFGGNRA—Legislative Proposals, Boundary Revisions, 1974–1976, PFGGNRA I; Hartman, *The Transformation of San Francisco*, 139–40; Jacobs, *A Rage for Justice*, 211–14.

34. Amy Meyer and Bob Young, "Some Thoughts Reguarding [*sic*] the Marin RCA Properties," October 8, 1975; John H. Jacobs to Cong. John Burton, November 14, 1975, Anton Holter to Cong. John Burton, November 20, 1975, and Amy Meyer to Jerry Friedman, January 25, 1976, all in Box 14, PFGGNRA—Legislative Proposals, Boundary Revisions, 1974–1976, PFGGNRA I.

35. Amy Meyer to Jerry Friedman, January 25, 1976, Box 14, PFGGNRA—Legislative Proposals, Boundary Revisions, 1974–1976; PFGGNRA I; Dave Mitchell, "Crowd Decries Land-Buy Plans," *PRL*, February 5, 1976.

36. "Too Much Land," *PRL*, February 5, 1976; "Park Expansion Bill is Dropped," *MIJ*, February 5, 1976.

37. Alice Yarish, "GGNRA: Egg on the Face," *PS*, February 6, 1976.

38. George Nevin, "Conservationists' Proposal to Expand Federal Lands," *MIJ*, January 7, 1977; "Burton on Park Buy," *PRL*, January 13, 1977.

39. "What, No Argument?" *PS*, September 16, 1977; "More Park Debated," *PRL*, September 23, 1977.

40. Jacobs, *A Rage for Justice*, 295–326.

41. Ibid., 403–4; Hartman, *The Transformation of San Francisco*, 235–36; Mike Davis, *City of Quartz: Excavating the Future in Los Angeles* (New York: Verso, 1990), 180–86.

42. Carl Irving, "3 Redwood State Parks Worth $1 Billion Will Go to Feds," *SFE*, June 27, 1978.

43. Robinson, *"You're in Your Mother's Arms,"* 443–45.

44. "Park Bill Signed; 5,739 Acres for Marin," *MIJ*, November 11, 1978; John Fogarty, "House Unit Quickly Passes Burton's Record Parks Bill," and "Projects for State in Big Bill," *SFC*, May 11, 1978; Jacobs, *A Rage for Justice*, 363–79; Robinson, *"You're in Your Mother's Arms,"* 445–56.

45. Gary Giacomini to John Burton, November 29, 1977, and Gary Giacomini to John Burton, December 5, 1977, both in Box 9, Marin County Government—Board of Supervisors, PFGGNRA I.

46. Lawrence C. Hadley to Director, Western Region, May 3, 1973, Box 1, L-1425, Vol. 1, November 1972–July 31, 1973, General, CCF.

47. *Land Acquisition Plan, Golden Gate National Recreation Area*, April 1980, Land Acquisition, PFGGNRA I.

48. Jacobs, *A Rage for Justice*, 390–91; Robinson, *"You're in Your Mother's Arms,"* 440–41.

49. Foresta, *America's National Parks and Their Keepers*, 80–86. Foresta and Richard Sellars are both well-known for their criticism of Burton's work as "diluting the stock" of the national parks.

50. Laurie Itow and Carl Irving, "Reagan Budget Cuts: Shortage of Green for Bay Parklands," *SFE*, March 5, 1981; Dale Champion, "Budget Crunch Threatens National Park Service," *SFC*, February 11, 1981; Jacobs, *A Rage for Justice*, 400; Robinson, *"You're in Your Mother's Arms,"* 433.

51. Doug Nadeau to Gul Ramchandani, December 4, 1980, Box 3, GGNRA—Subjects, Correspondence, PFGGNRA I; Nadeau, Doug, interview by John Martini, October 6, 1998, Presidio Oral History Project.

52. Acting Chief, Division of Land Acquisition, Western Region, to Associate Director, Operations, Western Region, March 16, 1981, and John H. Davis to A. B. Pace, April 17, 1981, both in Land Acquisition, PFGGNRA I; Edward Flattau, "National Parks Money Unspent," *MIJ*, December 4, 1982; Steven Shelby, "Ridge Land Transfer to Park Service Approval," *DCR*, September 20, 1986.

53. "Addendum to Land Protection Plan for Golden Gate National Recreation Area, February 1986," Regional Director, Western Region, to Director, National Park Service, September 3, 1986, Box 55, L-14, Land Acquisition, Miscellaneous, 1986–1989, SOA II; Ken White, "Park Changes Priorities for Land Buys Here," *PRL*, August 21, 1986; "'Park Purchase' Powerful Friend," *MIJ*, August 21, 1986.

54. Ken White, "Park Buying Genazzi Ranch," *PRL*, September 15, 1988; Elaine Larsen, "Cattle Hill Transfer Almost Complete," *PT*, December 25, 1991; Elaine Larsen, "Cattle Hill to GGNRA; 'Last Hurrah' Vote Angers Some," *PT*, June 10, 1991; Bill Drake, "GGNRA Chief Anxious to Talk About Cattle Hill, But Not Road," *PT*, June 24, 1992.

CHAPTER 4. HOW TO BUILD AN URBAN PARK

1. John A. Godino, "Changing Tides at the Golden Gate: Management Policies of the Golden Gate National Recreation Area and the Role of the National Park Service in Urban America" (Master's thesis, University of California, Santa Cruz, 1988), 32–36; Mrs. Stuart H. (Katy) Johnson to Phillip Burton, June 15, 1972, Box 17, Projects—Citizens Advisory Commission Establishment, PFGGNRA I.

2. Scott Thurber, "GGNRA Advisory Board: What Advisory Board?" *PS*, November 8–14, 1973, 1–2; Howard H. Chapman to Edgar Wayburn, May 1973, Box 17, Projects—Citizens Advisory Commission Establishment, PFGGNRA I; Judith Weston, "Legislation Forming Citizens Advisory Committee for New Park and Seashore Being Pigeonholed," *PRL*, September 9, 1973.

3. Godino, "Changing Tides at the Golden Gate," 37–38; interestingly, the appointments inspired some controversy. From the board of supervisors, Dianne Feinstein sought to appoint Amy Meyer to one of the San Francisco seats. As the head of PFGGNRA, Meyer might have been expected to take one of its two undesignated seats; see Dianne Feinstein to Ronald Pelosi, May 10, 1973, Box 10, San Francisco Government—Board of Supervisors, PFGGNRA I.

4. William C. Everhart, *The National Park Service* (Boulder, Colo.: Westview Press, 1983), 149–51; John C. Miles, *Guardians of the Parks: A History of the National Parks and Conservation Association* (Washington, D.C.: Taylor and Francis, 1995), 237–48. Whalen's appointment as director in 1977 returned the Park Service to career

officials, albeit one with a comparatively short tenure. Whalen's successor, Russell Dickenson, came from the NPS mold; he first joined the agency in 1935, reaching the directorship in 1980. After Dickenson's retirement, three successive directors came from outside the agency. The appointment of Robert Stanton in 1996 returned the directorship to a career official.

5. Godino, "Changing Tides at Golden Gate," 39.

6. Ibid.

7. William Whalen to Frank Boerger, January 5, 1979, Box 7, Federal Government, NPS—Office of the Director, PFGGNRA I.

8. William J. Whalen, interview by Sara Conklin, March 27, 1993, GGNRA Oral History Interview.

9. Doug Nadeau, "Points of View," *Landscape Architecture* 76, no. 6 (1986): 72; Foresta, *America's National Parks and Their Keepers*, 68–73; Rothman, *The Greening of a Nation?* 58–63.

10. Whalen interview, March 27, 1993; Nadeau interview, October 6, 1998.

11. Nadeau, "Points of View," 72; Anne Hanley, "Golden Gate's Grass Roots," *Westways* 67, no. 3 (March 1975): 38–41.

12. *General Management Plan and Environmental Analysis, September 1980*, 23.

13. Ibid., 15–20; Godino, "Changing Tides at the Golden Gate," 34–38.

14. Martini, *Fortress Alcatraz*; Godino, "Changing Tides at the Golden Gate," 32–34; Hart, *San Francisco's Wilderness Next Door*, 107–9.

15. William Issel, "'Land Values, Human Values, and the Preservation of the City's Treasured Appearance': Environmentalism, Politics, and the San Francisco Freeway Revolt," *Pacific Historical Review* 68, no. 4 (November 1999): 61–77.

16. *General Management Plan and Environmental Analysis, September 1980*, 69–70.

17. Ibid., 72–84.

18. Ibid., 85–88.

19. Ibid., 88–91.

20. R. Patrick Christopher, James P. Delgado, and Martin T. Mayer, *Cultural Resources Management Plan, Golden Gate National Recreation Area* (San Francisco: Golden Gate National Recreation Area, 1982); Judd A. Howell, *Final Natural Resources Management Plan and Environmental Assessment* (San Francisco: Golden Gate National Recreation Area, 1987); for a time line that includes planning efforts through 1996, see the Chronology in this book.

21. Nadeau to Haller, January 23, 2002.

22. Herman Allcock, David Ames, Lynn Herring, Steve Leding, Ed Pilley, and Ron Treabess, "Alcatraz Island: Interim Management Plan, February 1973," HDC no. 409, File 116, GGNRA Archives; "Proposed Transportation Concession Prospectus, Alcatraz Island," and PFGGNRA memo, "Alcatraz—Ron Treabus [sic]," ca. June 15, 1973, both in Box 2, Golden Gate National Recreation Area, Sites: Alcatraz—Transportation, PFGGNRA I.

23. PFGGNRA memo, "Alcatraz—Ron Treabus [sic]."

24. *Assessment of Alternatives for the General Management Plan, May 1977: Golden Gate National Recreation Area, Point Reyes National Seashore* (San Francisco: Golden Gate National Recreation Area, 1977).

25. Allcock, Ames, Herring, Leding, Pilley, and Treabess, "Alcatraz Island: Interim Management Plan, February 1973," 6.

26. *Assessment of Alternatives, May 1977*; Rai Okamoto to City Planning Commission, November 17, 1977, Box 10, San Francisco Govt.—Dept. of City Planning, PFGGNRA I.

27. *Golden Gate National Recreation Area/Point Reyes National Seashore: Alcatraz Development Concept* (San Francisco: Golden Gate National Recreation Area, 1978);

National Park Service, Denver Service Center, and Royston, Hanamoto, Beck, and Abey, Engineers, "Structural Safety Hazard Study, Alcatraz Island, July 1, 1979," HDC no. 409, File 154, GGNRA Archives; *General Management Plan and Environmental Analysis, September 1980,* 37; Leslie Aun, "On the Rock: Park Service Staging Alcatraz Escape—From Extinction," *Federal Times,* February 1, 1988, 23–25, OCPA, Box 10, "News Clippings—February 1988," OCPA.

28. Judy Field, "The Rock: Visitors Have Freer Reign of Alcatraz Island Grounds," *Salinas Californian,* June 9, 1987, Box 9, "News Clippings—June 1987," OCPA; Aun, "On the Rock," 24.

29. James P. Delgado to File, "Mapping and Documenting Sea—Caves and Other Subterranean Features on Alcatraz Island," H30, Box 4, 1992 Cave Inventory, NRMR.

30. "Planning Spaces for People, Not Buildings," *National Observer,* June 23, 1969; Lawrence Halprin, *Alcatraz: The Future* (San Francisco: Golden Gate National Parks Association, 1988), 3.

31. Halprin, *Alcatraz.*

32. "Alcatraz Island Plan, First Draft, January 14, 1993," 4–7, Box 8, Alcatraz 1994, NRMR.

33. *Alcatraz Development Concept Plan and Environmental Assessment* (San Francisco: National Park Service, 1993); Aun, "On the Rock," 23; Sellars, *Preserving Nature in the National Parks,* 1–3.

34. *Alcatraz Development Concept Plan and Environmental Assessment,* 2–6.

35. Gregory Moore, interview with Hal Rothman, July 16, 1999; Rich Weideman, interview with Hal Rothman, July 17, 1999.

36. Weideman interview, July 17, 1999.

CHAPTER 5. ADMINISTERING GOLDEN GATE NATIONAL RECREATION AREA

1. Rothman, *The Greening of a Nation?* 58–63.

2. Jerry L. Schober, "Dog Policy, April 1976," Charles M. Sheldon to Superintendent, May 17, 1976, Douglas Weinkauf to William Whalen, June 27, 1976, Muriel T. French to Jerry Schober, April 16, 1975, and Richard M. Nason to GGNRA Superintendent, April 17, 1975, all in Box 1, Citizens' Advisory Commission, Committee on Pet Policy, PFGGNRA I.

3. Conrad L. Wirth, *Parks, Politics, and the People* (Norman: University of Oklahoma Press, 1980), 1–15.

4. Ray Murphy to Boyd Burtnett, September 21, 1976, and William Whalen to Matt Dillingham, September 29, 1976, both in Box 1, Citizens' Advisory Commission, Committee on Pet Policy, PFGGNRA I.

5. William J. Whalen to Matt Dillingham, September 29, 1976, and "GGNRA Dog Policy—Marin County," November 10, 1976, both in Box 1, Citizens' Advisory Commission, Committee on Pet Policy, PFGGNRA I.

6. Virgil S. Hollis to Silliam [sic] J. Whalen, September 7, 1976, Box 1, Citizens' Advisory Commission, Committee on Pet Policy, PFGGNRA I.

7. Ray Murphy to Boyd Burtnett, September 21, 1976, and Rolf Diamant, "Draft Dog Policy for San Francisco Unit, October 18, 1977," both in Box 1, Citizens' Advisory Commission, Committee on Pet Policy, PFGGNRA I.

8. Richard B. Hardin to Nancy L. Simpson, November 8, 1977, 1976, and Robert L. Chiappari to Jack Wheat, December 10, 1977, both in Box 1, Citizens' Advisory Commission, Committee on Pet Policy, PFGGNRA I.

9. John A. Godino, "Changing Tides at the Golden Gate: Management Policies

of the Golden Gate National Recreation Area and the Role of the National Park Service in Urban America" (Master's thesis, University of California, Santa Cruz, 1988), 37–42; "Pet Policy Hearing, June 14, 1978," Box 1, Citizens' Advisory Commission, Committee on Pet Policy, PFGGNRA I.

10. Golden Gate National Recreation Area Advisory Commission Minutes, May 23, 1978, 4, and Richard Hardin to Amy Meyer, September 14, 1978, both in Box 1, Citizens' Advisory Commission, Committee on Pet Policy, PFGGNRA I.

11. "Advisory Commission Proposed Rules for Pet Dogs in San Francisco, Lands of Golden Gate National Recreation Area," June 14, 1978, and "Citizens' Advisory Commission Minutes, 1978," September 27 and November 18, 1978, both in Box 1, Citizens' Advisory Commission, Committee on Pet Policy, PFGGNRA I.

12. Golden Gate National Recreation Area Advisory Commission Minutes, January 10, February 24, and May 12, 1979, all in Box 1, Citizens' Advisory Commission Minutes, 1979, PFGGNRA I.

13. Golden Gate National Recreation Area Advisory Commission Minutes, August 1, 1979, 6, Box 1, Citizens' Advisory Commission Minutes, 1979, PFGGNRA I; Florence Sarrett to Lynn Thompson, January 17, 1979, John Kipping to Golden Gate Citizens' Advisory Commission, May 9, 1979, and John L. Sansing to Frank Boerger, April 20, 1979, all in Box 1, Citizens' Advisory Commission, Committee on Pet Policy, PFGGNRA I.

14. *General Management Plan and Environmental Analysis, September 1980*, 37–49, 95–99.

15. Weinkauf to Whalen, June 27, 1976, Citizens' Advisory Commission, Committee on Pet Policy, PFGGNRA I, Box I.

16. Ivan Sharpe, "The City's Unofficial Nude Beach for Gays," *SFE*, June 16, 1981.

17. State of California Department of Parks and Recreation, *Mount Tamalpais— General Plan* (Sacramento: Resources Agency, 1979), in Box 12, GGNRA Archives, PFGGNRA II.

18. Jennifer Foote, "Hikers Not Deterred by Killings," *SFE*, May 3, 1981; John E. Douglas, *Journey into Darkness* (New York: Pocket Books, 1997), 101–2; Grover M. Godwin, *Hunting Serial Predators: A Multivariate Classification Approach to Profiling Violent Behavior* (Boca Raton, Fla.: CRC Press, 2000), 234–38.

19. Mike Mewhinney, "Planning Begins for 'Ring Around the Bay' Trail System," *Progress*, February 17, 1988.

20. "Ridge Trail Here at Last," *MIJ*, September 25, 1989, A8; Maura Thurman, "Bay Area Ridge Trail: 'This Is Only a Start,'" *MIJ*, September 25, 1989, A3.

21. Judd A. Howell, "Impact of Miwok Horse Concession on Trails in the Tennessee Valley," January 28, 1981, Golden Gate National Recreation Area Natural Resource Management, Department of Operations/Activities, 1980–1984, Box 1, Environmental Issues, 1980–1990, NRMR.

22. Gilbert Chan, "Rangers Battle Cyclists on Mount Tam Trails," *MIJ*, March 25, 1986, A3; Jill Danz, "Hey (Hey!) You (You!), Get Off of My Trail," *Outside Magazine*, August 1999, 26–35; Andrew G. Kirk, "Appropriating Technology: Alternative Technology and Environmental Politics," n.p., n.d.

23. Rothman, *The Greening of a Nation?* 58–63; Foresta, *America's National Parks and Their Keepers*, 68–73; Godino, "Changing Tides at the Golden Gate," 59–66.

24. Jacqueline Frost, "Wilderness Biking Ban Gets Airing," *MIJ*, February 4, 1985; Sharon Lewis Dickerson, "Bikers vs. Hikers on Wilderness Trails," *California Bicyclist*, April 1985; Harold Gilliam, "Wheels and the Wilderness," *SFC*, March 3, 1985; Gary Sprung, interview by Hal Rothman, February 19, 2000; Barbara Boxer to G. Ray

Arnett, September 21, 1984, Golden Gate National Recreation Area, Box 7, Trail Bike Letters, OCPA; 36 *Code of Federal Regulations* 4.2.C, 4.3; 16 *U.S.C.* 1133(c).

25. Harold Gilliam, "More on Wheels and Wilderness," *SFC,* April 14, 1985; Rhonda Parks, "Park Panel Reopens Bike Ban Decision," *PRL,* February 7, 1985.

26. Minutes, Natural Resources Meeting, February 18, 1988, "The Impact of Dogs, Horses, Bikes, and People on the Natural Resources of the Park," and Memorandum, Natural Resource Staff to General Superintendent, March 31, 1988, both in Box 3, Correspondence 1988, NRMR.

27. "Golden Gate National Recreation Area Marin Trail Use Designation Environmental Assessment, October 24, 1990," Marc Beyeler, "Trail Mix: Bikers Challenge Hikers on Narrow Mountain Paths," *California Coast and Ocean* (Fall 1991): 37–44, and "This Trail Closed to Bikes: Don't Let This Happen. Fight Back!" all in Box 3, Correspondence, 1991, PFGGNRA II; Sprung interview, February 18, 2000.

28. William Henry Malcolm to Brian O'Neill, November 19, 1990, and Bob Howell to Ed Wayburn and Amy Meyer, October 23, 1991, both in Box 5, Letters to Amy Meyer, 1991–1994, PFGGNRA II; Robert Howell to Senator Alan Cranston, October 3, 1991, Sarah Donnelly, November 17, 1990, and Dick Galland to Brian O'Neill, November 13, 1990, all in GGNRA Archives.

29. Jim Hasenauer, "IMBA Joins Lawsuit against National Park Service," and "They're Your Trails, Too—Get Involved," *IMBA Trail News,* January 1993.

30. Sprung interview, February 18, 2000; Ranger Activities Specialist to General Superintendent, November 20, 1990, "Trail Bike Use," Box 14, Mountain Bikes, PFGGNRA II; Hasenauer, "IMBA Joins Lawsuit against National Park Service."

31. Charlie Cunningham, Patrick Seidler, Steve Potts, and Mark Slate, "Civil Disobedience and the New Paradigm Trail," copy courtesy of Gary Sprung; Sprung interview, February 18, 2000.

32. Amy Meyer to Deborah and Sandy, "Bicyclist Lawsuit vs. the National Park Service, Declaration for the National Parks and Conservation Association, February 1, 1993," Box 5, Amy Meyer Correspondence, 1993–1994, PFGGNRA II; Maura Thurman, "Mount Tam Bicycle Patrols to Be Rangers' 'Eyes and Ears,'" *MIJ,* January 20, 1989; "Sierra Club Can Intervene in Bicyclists' GGNRA Lawsuit," *MIJ,* February 19, 1993; Edgar Wayburn and Amy Meyer to James Ridenour, October 10, 1991, Box 3, Correspondence 1991, PFGGNRA II.

33. Bartke to Haller, March 5, 2002.

34. Jan Silverman, "Fort Funston Treks Offer History, Wild Nature Scenes," *Oakland Tribune,* February 27, 1987; "Staff Report on Proposed Relocation of the Fort Point Coast Guard Station to East Fort Baker," January 15, 1987, Box 3, Correspondence, Early File, 1978–1986, PFGGNRA II.

35. Boyd Burtnett to Acting Unit Manager and Other Interested Parties, MINIWAREX-78, June 20, 1978, Box 2, L30, Military Operations, SOA II.

36. Ibid.; John H. Davis to General Superintendent, July 12, 1978, "Daily Operations, Golden Gate National Recreation Area," Box 2, L30, Military Operations, SOA II; Bartke to Haller, March 5, 2002.

37. Teresa Allen, "Fort Cronkhite Weapons Blasts Draw Concerns," *MIJ,* October 9, 1984; National Park Service Press Release, "Military Invasion Force to Strike Golden Gate National Recreation Area: Marin Headlands Closed Sunday Morning But Public Invited to Watch," October 30, 1979, Box 2, L30, "Military Operations," SOA II; Bartke to Haller, March 5, 2002.

38. Sellars, *Preserving Nature in the National Parks,* 65–66; Everhart, *The National Park Service,* 85–86.

39. Yvonne Rand interview, by Sara Conklin, July 23, 1993, GGNRA Oral History

Interview; Grover Sales, "The Man Who Gave Away the Green Gulch Ranch," *PS,*
April 26, 1985.

40. Sales, "The Man Who Gave Away the Green Gulch Ranch"; Rand interview,
July 7, 1993.

41. Barry Mackintosh, *The National Parks: Shaping the System* (Washington, D.C.:
Department of the Interior, 1991), 89; Foresta, *America's National Parks and Their Keepers,* 68–80; Rothman, *The Greening of a Nation?* 58–63.

CHAPTER 6. NATURAL RESOURCE MANAGEMENT IN A NATIONAL
RECREATION AREA

1. Sellars, *Preserving Nature in the National Parks,* 214–16; Foresta, *America's
National Parks and Their Keepers,* 133–36, 148–62; Ethan Carr, *Wilderness by Design:
Landscape Architecture and the National Park Service* (Lincoln: University of Nebraska
Press, 1998), 1–14.

2. Hal K. Rothman, ed., *"I'll Never Fight Fire with My Bare Hands Again": Recol-
lections of the First Foresters of the Inland Northwest* (Lawrence: University Press of
Kansas, 1994), 1–17.

3. *General Management Plan and Environmental Analysis, September 1980,* 1–11.

4. Judd A. Howell, *Natural Resource Management Plan and Environmental Assessment, Golden Gate National Recreation Area, California* (San Francisco: National Park
Service, 1982), 1.

5. Ibid., 2.

6. Ibid., 2–7.

7. Ibid., 2, 118–22; Stephen J. Pyne, *Fire in America: A Cultural History of Wildland and Rural Fire* (Princeton: Princeton University Press, 1982).

8. Sellars, *Preserving Nature in the National Parks,* 258–61; Rothman, *On Rims and
Ridges,* 277–81, and *The Greening of a Nation?* 53–64; Pet Policy Hearing, June 14, 1978,
Box 2, Pet Policy, PFGGNRA II; A. Starker Leopold et al., *Wildlife Management in the
National Parks* (Washington, D.C.: Advisory Board on Wildlife Management, 1963).

9. "Pigs Invade Coast," *Coastal Post,* January 21, 1985; Heidi Siegmund, "Feral
Pigs Menace Now Worries Feds," *PRL,* June 27, 1985; "Eat-Anything Wild Pigs Make
Marin Residents Bristle," *SJMN,* May 22, 1985.

10. Joan Reutingen, "Low-slung Feral Pigs Reach Shoreline Highway," and
"Wild Boars Loose in Marin County," May 1985, both in Box 8, Press Clippings,
OCPA; Brandon Spars, "Pigs All Too Plentiful on the Slopes of Mount Tam," *Marin
Messenger,* February 6, 1985.

11. Memorandum of Understanding between National Park Service and Marin
Municipal Water District, Audubon Canyon Ranch, Marin County Open Space District, California Department of Parks and Recreation, [and] Meadow Club, Box 2,
1985 Activities, NRMR; Joan Reutinger, "Great Big Pig Fence Erection," *Coastal Post,*
February 23, 1987.

12. "1985 Annual Report," SOA II; "Golden Gate NRA FY 1986 Annual Report
Highlights," 1986 Activities, Chief, Resource Management and Planning, to General
Superintendent, March 19, 1985, "1985 Activities," and Associate Regional Director,
Resource Management and Planning to Associate Regional Director Finance, April
15, 1987, all in Box 2, 1987 Activities, NRMR; Alison Willy, "Feral Hog Management
at GGNRA," Box 4, 1991 Correspondence, NRMR.

13. Dennis Wyss, "The Hunt Is On at Point Reyes," *MIJ,* January 26, 1992; Kevin
Knuhtsen, "Valentine's Day Massacre of Exotic Deer Planned," *PRL,* January 20,
1994, 1; Howell, *Natural Resource Management Plan.*

14. "Fish and Game Are Studying Point Reyes Exotic Deer," *PRL*, September 26, 1974; untitled folder, 59, Box 5, Natural Resources Management Plan, Notes, NRMR; Tom McCarthy, "Park Panel Proposes Eliminating Exotic Deer," *PRL*, November 24, 1993; Hunting at Point Reyes National Seashore, and John L. Sansing to Frank Boerger, ca. 1976, Box 16, Point Reyes National Seashore, Undertakings, Exotic Deer Reduction Program, PFGGNRA I.

15. "Fish and Game Are Studying Point Reyes Exotic Deer," *PRL*, September 26, 1974; Spencer Read, "Deer, Geese Hunt Proposal," *PRL*, October 1, 1981; Jay Goldman, "Seashore Hunting Proposal: Interior Department Directs Park Service to Consider Public Hunt," *PRL*, November 3, 1983; Henry W. Elliott III, Charles Van Riper III, and Lynn D. Whittig, "A Study to Assess Competition and Carrying Capacity of the Ungulates of Point Reyes National Seashore," Technical Report no. 10, March 1983, Box 16, Point Reyes National Seashore, Undertakings, PFGGNRA I.

16. Janine Warner, "Rangers Again Shooting Deer in Seashore: Some Carcasses Left to Rot," *PRL*, January 16, 1992, 1, 8; Wyss, "The Hunt Is On at Point Reyes"; S. Kibbe, "Rangers Massacre Deer," *PRL*, March 14, 1991.

17. Knuhtsen, "Valentine's Day Massacre of Exotic Deer Planned."

18. "Pre-Proposal, Predator Research, Golden Gate National Recreation Area," and Memorandum of Understanding by and between National Park Service, Golden Gate National Recreation Area, and California Department of Fish and Game Relating to the Study of Carnivores, both in Box 2, 1987 Activities, NRMR.

19. "GGNRA Site of Peregrine Falcon Reintroduction," National Park Service Press Release, May 29, 1983, Box 11, OCPA; Sylvia Lang, "Peregrine Falcons Set Free in Marin," *MIJ*, May 31, 1983; General Superintendent, Memorandum: Workshop to Prioritize Natural Resource Issues, February 8, 1990, Box 4, Correspondence 1990, NRMR.

20. Judd A. Howell to Henry G. Weston Jr., December 22, 1983, Box 1, 1983 Activities, NRMR; Natural Resource Specialist to Chief, Resource Management and Planning, November 29, 1984, Box 2, 1984 Activities, NRMR; Raptor Migration Observatory, Post-Season Briefing, "Raptor Migration Observatory, 3/5/86 Meeting Notes," Gregory Moore to Lawrence I. Kramer, March 20, 1986, San Francisco Foundation Monitor's Report, and Raptor Migration Observatory, "Summary of the 1986 Fall Migration," Box 2, 1986 Raptor Program, NRMR.

21. Raptor Migration Observation, Post-Season Briefing, and Buzz Hull to Judd Howell, November 24, 1986, both in Box 2, 1986 Raptor Program, NRMR.

22. Howell, *Natural Resource Management Plan*, 44–45; Natural Resource Management Specialist to General Superintendent, May 17, 1982, Box 1, Activities 1982, NRMR.

23. Achva Benzinberg Stein and Jacqueline Claire Moxley, "In Defense of the Nonnative: The Case of the Eucalyptus," *Landscape Journal* 42, 35–43; Erwin N. Thompson, *Defender of the Gate: The Presidio of San Francisco, A History from 1846 to 1995*, 2 vols. (San Francisco: National Park Service, Golden Gate National Recreation Area, 1997), 221–22, 228, 232–33; Alfred W. Crosby, *Ecological Imperialism: The Biological Expansion of Europe, 900–1900 A.D.* (New York: Cambridge University Press, 1986), 1–43.

24. Howell, *Natural Resources Management Plan*, 60–66.

25. Regional Plant Ecologist to Regional Director, September 30, 1985, Box 2, Correspondence 1985, NRMR.

26. Ibid.; Marin Unit Manager to General Superintendent, January 3, 1986, Box 2, 1986 Activities, NRMR.

27. Dale Champion, "A Plan to Chop Marin Eucalyptus," *SFC*, March 8, 1986; Press Release, "Citizens' Group Formed to Fight Clearcutting Proposal in Marin,"

November 12, 1986, Box 6, Natural Resources General, 1986, NRMR; Ed Miller, "Save the Eucalyptus," *MIJ*, August 1, 1987; Bruce Follansbee and Marylee Guinon, "Bad News Trees," *MIJ*, August 15, 1987; Anne West, "Why Trees Should Go," *MIJ*, October 20, 1987; "Dear Park Resident and Park Partners," September 23, 1988, Box 6, Eucalyptus Containment, 1988, NRMR.

28. Tom Cole, *A Short History of San Francisco* (San Francisco: Lexikos, 1981), 104–7; Gordon Thomas and Max Morgan Witts, *The San Francisco Earthquake* (New York: Stein and Day, 1971), 152–55, 188–94.

29. Sellers, *Preserving Nature in the National Parks*, 253–58; Pyne, *Fire in America*.

30. Judd M. Howell to Regional Director, Western Region, September 10, 1981, Judd M. Howell to Dick Hardin, Steve Olsen, Dick Danielson, Marvin Hershey, and Terry Swift, October 13, 1981, and Memorandum from Chief, Division of Resource Management and Planning, July 14, 1982, all in Box 1, 1981 Activities, NRMR.

31. *Fire Management Plan, Golden Gate National Recreation Area, February 19, 1985*, Box 5, NRMR; Chief, Resource Management, to General Superintendent, March 4, 1987, Box 2, Correspondence 1987, NRMR.

32. Tom Graham, "Control Burn Chars 250 Acres at Seashore," *PRL*, September 30, 1982.

33. John H. Davis to Outdoor Art Club, March 14, 1984, to Marin City Community Services District, March 12, 1984, to Marin View Community Association, March 14, 1984, to Tamalpais Valley Improvement Club, March 14, 1984, to Headlands Homeowners Association, March 14, 1984, to Marin Conservation League, March 14, 1984, to Muir Woods Park Improvement Club, March 14, 1984, all in Box 1, Correspondence 1984, NRMR.

34. Chief, Resource Management, to General Superintendent, October 18, 1984, Box 1, Correspondence 1984, NRMR.

35. *Fire Management Plan, Golden Gate National Recreation Area, February 19, 1985*, Box 5, NRMR.

36. Brian O'Neill to Curtis B. Mitchell, May 6, 1986, and Memorandum of Understanding, Prescribed Fire Management Boundaries between Golden Gate National Recreation Area and California State Parks and Recreation, May 6, 1986, both in Box 2, Correspondence 1986, NRMR; Memorandum of Understanding between Golden Gate National Recreation Area and California State Parks and Recreation, January 9, 1987, Box 2, Correspondence, 1987, NRMR.

37. Golden Gate National Recreation Area Annual Burn Program 1986, Box 2, Correspondence 1987, NRMR.

38. Chief, Resource Management, to General Superintendent, March 4, 1987, "Annual Burn Program 1987," and Brian O'Neill to Stan Rowen, March 10, 1987, all Box 2, Correspondence 1987, NRMR.

39. Sandy Ross to Brian O'Neill, December 4, 1987, and Brian O'Neill to Sandy Ross, December 16, 1987, both on Box 2, Correspondence 1987, NRMR; "Lots of Opposition to Controlled Burns," *SFC*, May 26, 1987.

40. Barry Taranto, "To Burn or Not to Burn, That Is the Question," *Mill Valley Record*, January 27, 1988; Mike Rowan, "Burning Mt. Tam for 'Safety's Sake,'" *Coastal Post*, February 1, 1988; Maura Thurman, "'Let Burn Fires Unlikely in Marin,' Experts Say," *MIJ*, September 18, 1988; Alex Neill, "Grand Jury Douses Plans to Use Controlled Burning on Mt. Tam," *MIJ*, October 12, 1991; Maura Thurman, "Park Plan Calls for Controlled Burns," *MIJ*, September 8, 1992.

41. Sellers, *Preserving Nature in the National Parks*, 150–55; Wright, *Wildlife Management in the National Parks*; Shankland, *Steve Mather of the National Parks*, 203; Rothman, *Preserving Different Pasts*, 52–73; Hart, *San Francisco's Wilderness Next Door*, 111–21.

42. Jerry L. Schober to Barry Vogel, July 27, 1976, Box 3, GGNRA Correspon-

dence, PFGGNRA I; Natural Resource Management Specialist to General Superintendent, June 29, 1981, Box 1, 1981 Activities, NRMR; "Golden Gate National Recreation Area Summary of Livestock Grazing for Calendar Year 1982," *Natural Resource
Management Plan and Environmental Assessment*, Golden Gate National Recreation
Area, California, 1984.

43. "Draft Range Management Guidelines, Golden Gate National Recreation
Area and Point Reyes National Seashore," 1987; "Range Management Guidelines,
Point Reyes National Seashore," April 1988.

44. Anne West, "Rangers Blamed for Gullies," *PRL*, November 25, 1987; Carl
Munger, "Diatribe Won't Help," *PRL*, December 3, 1987; William Barret, "Reply to
Letter," *PRL*, December 3, 1987.

45. Leon, "This Land Is Our Land," *Pacific Coastal Post*, January 11, 1988, Box 10,
February 1988, OCP; David V. Mitchell, "The Politics of Erosion," Box 5, Amy Meyer,
Letters to, 1981–1989, PFGGNRA II.

46. Brad Breithaupt, "Commission Urges End to Bolinas Lagoon Grazing Lease,"
MIJ, January 30, 1988; John Todd, "New Marin Range War: Borders vs. Cows," *SFE*,
February 8, 1988; "Knowing When to Stop and When to Start," *Coastal Post*, Febru-
ary 8, 1988.

47. Laura Impellizzeri, "Despite Angry Objection, Park Grazing Plan Supported," *PRL*, February 11, 1988; Maura Thurman, "Rangers, Ranchers in Accord,"
MIJ, February 12, 1988; "Protect Park Agriculture," Marin County *Independent*, February 20, 1988; Sarah Rohrs, "Park Advisory Commission Adopts Range Guidelines," Box 5, Amy Meyer, Letters to, 1991–1994, PFGGNRA II.

48. "A Move to Save State Coastline," *SFC*, March 31, 1967; "Bagley Proposes
Coastline Conservation Study Group," *MIJ*, March 30, 1967; California Coastal Zone
Conservation Commission, "California Coastal Plan, December 1975," Box 12, State
of California, PFGGNRA I.

49. California Coastal Zone Conservation Commission, "California Coastal Plan,
December 1975," Box 12, State of California, PFGGNRA I.

50. Rothman, *Saving the Planet*, 167; Daniel Yergin, *The Prize: The Epic Quest for
Oil, Money, and Power* (New York: Simon and Schuster, 1991), 744–48; James
Williams, *Energy and the Making of Modern California* (Akron: University of Akron
Press, 1998), 297–304; L. C. Soileau III to James G. Watt, February 11, 1981, Box 1,
Threats to the Park, NRMR.

51. Ed Smith, "Burton Denounces Watt for Oil-Drilling Proposal," *MIJ*, March
28, 1981.

52. Bob Norberg, "Sanctuaries' Drilling Ban May Be Reconsidered," Press Clippings, 1981, vol. 1, January–May, GOGA- 2376, Box 1, PCC; Jon Berry, "Anti-Drilling
Forces Win Offshore Oil Tilt," *PRL*, June 4, 1981; Rothman, *The Greening of a Nation?*
172–74.

53. Acting Regional Director to Director, February 18, 1981, Box 1, Threats to the
Park, NRMR; Rothman, *The Greening of a Nation?* 58–63, 172–74.

54. Paul Peterzell, "Drilling Warfare," *MIJ*, February 3, 1987; Paul Peterzell,
"Marin Coast Part of Oil Lease Plan," *MIJ*, February 5, 1987; Joan Reutinger, "Marin
Coast Target in New Oil Plan," *Coastal Post*, February 9, 1987; Rob Wells, "Hodel
Explains New Offshore Oil Plan," *PAC*, February 21, 1987; Timothy Polk, "No Hope
for Offshore Oil Compromise," *PAC*, February 27, 1987; Eric Brazil, "Cordell Bank
Ban Reported," *SFE*, May 2, 1989; "Drilling Ban off Point Reyes," *SFC*, May 3, 1989;
Dara Tom, "Bush Supports Monterey Bay Marine Sanctuary," *MIJ*, June 11, 1992.

55. John H. Davis to John Kriedler, March 8, 1983, Box 1, 1983 Activities, NRMR;
Burr to John, February 22, 1983, Box 2, Oil Spill Contingency Planning, NRMR.

56. To: District Managers, February 27, 1987, Box 1, Terri J. Tomas, 1982–88,

NRMR; To: Regional Director, Western Region, January 13, 1981, Box 5, GGNRA Undertakings, Resource Protection, PFGGNRA I; To: District Rangers, February 27, 1987, Box 1, 1987 Projects, NRMR.

57. Jon Stewart, "Fragile Paradise," *California Living Magazine,* December 16, 1984.

58. Sanctuary Coordinator to All Staff, November 6, 1984, Box 12, Oil Spill Contingency Planning, NRMR; Katherine Ellison, "Volunteers Un-Goo Birds off Golden Gate," *SJMN,* November 8, 1984; Mary Leydecker, "Slick Fouls Point Reyes," *MIJ,* November 9, 1984; Teresa Allen, "Slick Watch," *MIJ,* November 10, 1984; "Wash, Blow Dry for Oily Birds," *SFC,* November 12, 1984.

CHAPTER 7. CULTURAL RESOURCE MANAGEMENT

1. Rothman, *Saving the Planet.*

2. Martini, *Fort Point,* 41; Hart, *San Francisco's Wilderness Next Door,* 95–96; Minutes of the Executive Committee Meeting of the Board of Directors of the Fort Point Museum Association, January 28, 1971, G. M. Dean to Executive Committee, ca. January 1971, both in Box 3, A44, Minutes of the Board of Directors Meeting, Fort Point Museum Association, FPAR.

3. "Fort Mason Prison Plan Opposed," *SFC,* March 2, 1971; "Fort Mason Land Grab Proposed in Private Deal," *SFC,* October 22, 1971; "Strong Denial on Ft. Mason 'Grab,'" *SFC,* October 23, 1971; Donald Canter, "Deal for Ft. Mason 'Means Highrisers,'" *SFC,* October 19, 1971; "Galileo View on Fort Mason," *SFE,* April 8, 1972; Jim Wood, "Board to Get Galileo Campus Plan," *SFE,* April 19, 1972; Acting Director, Western Region to Director, National Park Service, June 12, 1972, Golden Gate National Recreation Area Briefing Book.

4. Golden Gate National Recreation Area Advisory Commission Minutes, October 5, 1974, 10, Box 1, GGNRA Citizens' Advisory Commission Minutes, 1974, PFGGNRA I; Phyllis and Harris Legg to John L. Foran, October 9, 1974, Box 1, GGNRA Land Acquisition Files, PFGGNRA I; Golden Gate National Recreation Area Advisory Commission Minutes, January 25, 1975, Box 1, GGNRA Citizens' Advisory Commission Minutes, 1975, PFGGNRA I; William Whalen to Amy Meyer, February 12, 1975, and Fort Mason Interim Use Subcommittee Report, March 11, 1975, both in Box 1, Citizens' Advisory Commission, Committee on Fort Mason, PFGGNRA I.

5. Memorandum to Fort Mason Sub-Committee, Golden Gate National Recreation Area Advisory Commission, Long-Term Cooperative Agreement with Fort Mason Foundation, March 16, 1981, Box 1, Citizens' Advisory Commission, Committee on Fort Mason, PFGGNRA I; Kay Keppler, "Fort Mason at 15," *North Beach Now,* March 1991.

6. Memorandum to Fort Mason Sub-Committee, Golden Gate National Recreation Area Advisory Commission, Long-Term Cooperative Agreement with Fort Mason Foundation, March 16, 1981, Box 1, Citizens' Advisory Commission, Committee on Fort Mason, PFGGNRA I; Keppler, "Fort Mason at 15"; "Fort Mason Committee, May 12, 1979," Box 1, Citizens' Advisory Commission, Committee on Fort Mason, PFGGNRA I; Sam Kaplan, "Fort Mason Pier: Creative Use of Military Surplus," *Philadelphia Inquirer,* July 12, 1981; Herbert A. Michelson, "Fort Mason an Eclectic 'Cultural' Park," *Santa Rosa Press Democrat,* May 21, 1987.

7. Bruce Bellingham, "GGNRA to Hold Hearings on Future of Blues Festival," *Marina Times,* October 1991; Michelson, "Fort Mason an Eclectic 'Cultural' Park"; "Golden Gate NRA, FY 1986 Annual Report Highlights," Box 3, Raptor Program 1987, NRMR.

8. Draft, Environmental Statement, Proposed Golden Gate National Recreation Area, California, February 18, 1972, Box 1, L-7619, Doyle Drive, 1973, CCF; William J. Whalen, interview by Sara Conklin, March 27, 1993, GGNRA Oral History Interview.

9. Delgado, *Alcatraz*, 40–41; Martini, *Fortress Alcatraz*, 140–41.

10. Golden Gate National Recreation Area Advisory Commission Minutes, November 19, 1977, "A Proposal to Develop an Indian Cultural Center on Alcatraz Island, California," 1974, Lucille Green, Louis R. Gomberg, and David Wolcott, "Proposal for a World Park on Alcatraz," November 19, 1977, and Forest Shaffer to Golden Gate National Recreation Area Citizens' Advisory Commission, November 19, 1977, all in Box 2, GGNRA Sites—Alcatraz, Proposals and Related Correspondence, PFGGNRA I; Rai Okamoto to City Planning Commission, November 17, 1977, Box 10, San Francisco Govt.—Dept. of City Planning, PFGGNRA I; Joyce Johnson, "The Grim Corridors of Alcatraz as a Tourist Attraction," and 1975, Box 1, PCC.

11. *General Management Plan and Environmental Analysis, September 1980*, 37.

12. Hart, *San Francisco's Wilderness Next Door*, 89–99, 104–5; Ariel Rubissow, *Cliff House and Lands End: San Francisco's Seaside Resort* (San Francisco: Golden Gate National Park Association, 1993), 34–35; Alan Cline, "A Hard Look: Recreation Area's Unsightly Sights," *SFE*, January 27, 1978.

13. Bartke to Haller, March 5, 2002.

14. Thomas interview, March 31, 1993; 1979 Annual Report of the General Superintendent, March 1980, 22–23, SOA II.

15. *General Management Plan and Environmental Analysis, September 1980*, 85–94; "The Secretary of the Interior's Standards and Guidelines for Federal Agency Historic Preservation Programs Pursuant to the National Historic Preservation Act," 16 *U.S.C.* 470, published in the *Federal Register*, April 24, 1998, 1.

16. *General Management Plan and Environmental Analysis, September 1980*, 20–21.

17. Charles B. Hosmer Jr., *Preservation Come of Age: From Williamsburg to the National Trust, 1926–1949* (Charlottesville: University of Virginia Press, 1982), 300–334; Rothman, *Preserving Different Pasts*, 186–220; Sellars, *Preserving Nature in the National Parks*, 136–38, 184; Foresta, *America's National Parks and Their Keepers*, 132–36.

18. Everhart, *The National Park Service*, 75–92; John C. Freemuth, *Islands under Siege: National Parks and the Politics of External Threats* (Lawrence: University Press of Kansas, 1991), 20–22.

19. Questionnaire, "Threat to Cultural Resources in the Parks," Golden Gate National Recreation Area, January 12, 1981, Box 16, N-42, Weather and Climate, General, CCF.

20. *Cultural Resource Management Plan, Golden Gate National Recreation Area, June 1982* (San Francisco: Golden Gate National Recreation Area, 1982), 2–5.

21. Ibid.; Anna Coxe Toogood, *A Civil History of Golden Gate National Recreation Area and Point Reyes National Seashore, California* (Denver: Denver Service Center, National Park Service, 1980); Erwin N. Thompson, *Historic Resource Study, Forts Baker, Barry, Cronkhite of Golden Gate National Recreation Area, California* (Denver: Denver Service Center, National Park Service, 1979), *Historic Resource Study: Seacoast Fortifications, San Francisco Harbor, Golden Gate National Recreation Area, California* (Denver: Denver Service Center, National Park Service, 1979), and *The Rock: A History of Alcatraz Island, 1847–1972, Historic Resource Study, Golden Gate National Recreation Area, California* (Denver: Denver Service Center, National Park Service, 1979).

22. *Cultural Resource Management Plan, June 1982*, 6–10.

23. Ibid., 10–15.

24. Ibid., 16–26.

25. Ibid., 27–54.

26. Stephen A. Haller, interview by Hal Rothman, May 10, 2000.

27. "Golden Gate National Recreation Area Annual Report, 1982," SOA II.

28. Ric Borjes, interview by Hal Rothman, June 2, 2000.

29. Minutes of the Meeting of the Golden Gate National Recreation Area Advisory Commission, October 10, 1991, Box 41, CAC Minutes, 5–17, OCPA.

30. "Standards and Guidelines for Federal Agency Historic Preservation Programs," *Federal Register,* April 24, 1998, 1–2.

31. Minutes of the Meeting of the Golden Gate National Recreation Area Advisory Commission, October 10, 1991, Box 41, CAC Minutes, 22–31, OCPA.

32. "Golden Gate National Recreation Area, 1979: Annual Report of the General Superintendent," "Golden Gate National Recreation Area Annual Report, 1981," "Golden Gate National Recreation Area Annual Report, 1982," and "Golden Gate National Recreation Area Annual Report, 1983," all in SOA II; Minutes of the Meeting of the Golden Gate National Recreation Area Advisory Commission, October 10, 1991, Box 41, CAC Minutes, 19, OCPA.

33. "Fort Point National Historic Site Annual Report, 1980," FPAR.

34. John A. Martini and Stephen A. Haller, *What We Have We Shall Defend: An Interim History and Preservation Plan for NIKE Site SF-88L, Fort Barry, California* (San Francisco: Golden Gate National Recreation Area, 1998), 81–83.

35. Bob Kirby, "Alcatraz Island, Annual Report, 1980," Golden Gate National Recreation Area A2621, GGNRA Archives.

36. Denver Service Center and Royston, Hanamoto, Beck, and Abey, "Structural Safety Hazard Study, Alcatraz Island, Golden Gate National Recreation Area, July 1, 1979," File 154, AD; "Golden Gate National Recreation Area Annual Report, 1982," 20; "Golden Gate National Recreation Area Annual Report, 1983," 57; "Golden Gate National Recreation Area Annual Report, 1990," Box 1, Annual Report 1990, OCPA.

37. James P. Delgado, "No Longer a Buoyant Ship: Unearthing the Storeship Niantic," *California History* 63, 4, and "What Becomes of the Old Ships? Dismantling the Gold Rush Fleet of San Francisco," *Pacific Historian* 5, 3; James P. Delgado and Robert L. Bennett, *Research Design for the Historical Archaeological Examination and Documentation of the Remains of the 1848 Sidewheel Steamship Tennessee at Tennessee Cove, Golden Gate National Recreation Area, Marin County, California* (San Francisco: Golden Gate National Recreation Area, 1978).

38. *PFGGNRA Greenbelt Gazette* 2, no. 1 (ca. October 1972), Box 6, File 115, KFC.

39. Rothman, *Preserving Different Pasts,* 172–75.

40. *Cultural Resource Management Plan, June 1982,* 18–20.

41. *General Management Plan and Environmental Analysis, September 1980.*

42. Minutes of the Meeting of the Golden Gate National Recreation Area Advisory Commission, July 30, 1992, Box 41, CAC Minutes., 16-20, OCPA.

43. Ibid., 22.

44. Ibid., 31.

45. Stephen A. Haller, *Post and Park: A Brief Illustrated History of the Presidio* (San Francisco: Golden Gate National Parks Association, 1997).

46. Jacobs, *A Rage for Justice,* 213, 367.

47. Gerald Adams, "Marshland Planned for Crissy Field," *SFE,* October 9, 1985; Amy Meyer to Judy Lemons, June 21, 1994, Box 5, Amy Meyer Correspondence, 1993–94, PFGGNRA II; John Hooper to Sala Burton, October 11, 1985, Box 12, Presidio Sierra Club Lawsuit—Correspondence, Individuals and Organizations, PFGGNRA II.

48. Brian O'Neill to Robert S. Rose, November 26, 1985, and Robert S. Rose to

Brian O'Neill, December 19, 1985, both in Box 12, Presidio Lawsuit Correspondence, PFGGNRA II.

49. John Fogarty, "Big Building Project at the Presidio Is Called Illegal," *SFC*, January 8, 1986; Dale Champion, "Park Service Backs Probe of Presidio Plans," *SFC*, January 9, 1986; Harold Gilliam, "Battle Cries Sound at Crissy Field," *SFCLE*, January 19, 1986; Amy Meyer to Judy Lemons, June 21, 1994, Box 5, Amy Meyer Correspondence, 1993–94. PFGGNRA II.

50. "Presidio Settlement Announced: Post Office to Be Demolished," July 16, 1986, Box 2, Post Office Settlement, PFGGNRA II; Amy Meyer to Judy Lemons, June 21, 1994, Box 5, Amy Meyer Correspondence, 1993–94, PFGGNRA II.

CHAPTER 8. INTERPRETING AN URBAN PARK

1. Barry Mackintosh, *Interpretation in the National Park Service: A Historical Perspective* (Washington, D.C.: National Park Service, 1986), 3–42; C. Frank Brockman, "Park Naturalists and the Evolution of National Park Service Interpretation through World War II," *Journal of Forest History* (January 1978): 19–29; Rothman, *Preserving Different Pasts*, 172–78.

2. Cooperating Association Coordinator to All Regional Chiefs of Interpretation and Visitor Services, May 27, 1977, and Site Manager, Fort Point to Cooperating Association Coordinator, Harper's Ferry, August 30, 1977, both in Box 14, K-1815, Interpretive Activities, Services and Facilities, FPAR.

3. Memorandum: Cooperating Association Future at GGNRA, Chief of Interpretation to General Superintendent, July 14, 1980, Box 1, A-42, Cooperative Associations, SOA II.

4. Ibid.; Memorandum: Development of a GGNRA Cooperating Association, December 11, 1980, Box 1, A-42, Cooperative Associations, SOA II.

5. Greg Moore, interview by Hal Rothman, July 16, 1999.

6. Moore interview, July 16, 1999; Judd Howell to Greg Moore, October 14, 1987, Box 2, 1987 Activities, NRMR.

7. Rothman, *Devil's Bargains*, 1–27; and *The Greening of a Nation?* 58–63, 172–79.

8. *General Management Plan and Environmental Analysis, September 1980*, 3–12.

9. Ibid., 29–35.

10. John Martini to Hal Rothman, June 16, 2000.

11. Martini to Rothman, June 16, 2000; Steve Haller, interview by Hal Rothman, June 15, 2000.

12. Martini to Rothman, June 16, 2000.

13. Ibid.

14. "Annual Report, Golden Gate National Recreation Area, 1977," 19, SOA II.

15. Ibid.; "Annual Report Highlights, Golden Gate National Recreation Area, FY 1986," Box 3, 1986, NRMR.

16. Martini to Rothman, June 16, 2000.

17. Ibid.

18. "1977 Annual Report," "1980 Annual Report," 22–27, both in SOA II.

19. "1981 Annual Report," 19–24, SOA II.

20. "1979 Annual Report of the General Superintendent, March 1980," 13–14, SOA II.

21. *General Management Plan; Interpretive Prospectus—Alcatraz* (1987); Steve Haller, telephone conversation with Hal Rothman, June 14, 2000.

22. "1983 Annual Report," 37, SOA II.

23. Doug Nadeau interview, October 6, 1998, Presidio Oral History; Lloyd Watson, "From the Ballpark to a National Park," *SFC*, March 21, 1986.

24. Moore interview, July 16, 1999; Nadeau interview, October 6, 1998.

25. Halprin, *Alcatraz*, 3.

26. Nadeau interview, 70; Halprin, *Alcatraz*, 8–14.

27. Rich Weideman, interview by Hal Rothman, July 17, 1999; Dwight Adams, "The Back Page," *Preservation* (1997): 128.

28. David Helvarg, *The War against the Greens: The "Wise Use" Movement, the New Right, and Anti-Environmental Violence* (San Francisco: Sierra Club Books, 1994), 148–54.

29. Deanne L. Adams to Roger Kennedy, March 3, 1997 (GOGA–Alcatraz, at NP-GOGA, 3/3/97, 4:08 P.M., from Park Service e-mail, copy provided to author.

30. Mary Kelly Black, March 14, 1997 (NP-WORI, 3/14/97, 4:49 P.M., and Frank Partridge, March 14, 1997 (NP-BICY, 3/14/97, 3:14 P.M., both from Park Service e-mail, copies provided to author; for Albright's views, see Donald Swain, *Wilderness Defender: Horace M. Albright and Conservation* (Chicago: University of Chicago Press, 1970), 206–56.

31. Rich Silverstein and Greg Moore, "Name-Branding the Parks" (public address at Presidio Stories: A Visitor Experience and Interpretation Symposium, San Francisco, April 14, 2000).

32. Silverstein and Moore, "Name-Branding the Parks"; Greg Moore, interview by Hal Rothman, July 15, 1999.

33. Silverstein and Moore, "Name-Branding the Parks"; "Help Grow Crissy Field: A Community Call to Action," *Renewing Crissy Field* 2 (Fall 1999): 1.

34. "Help Grow Crissy Field: A Community Call to Action," 1; "To Friends of Our National Parks," *Renewing Crissy Field* 1 (Summer 1999): 1.

35. John Martini, e-mail to Hal Rothman, June 25, 2000.

CHAPTER 9. THE PRESIDIO AND THE FUTURE

1. Oliver Stone, *Wall Street*, 35 mm, Twentieth Century Fox, Los Angeles, 1987.

2. Haller, *Post and Park*, 39–40; "The New Presidio," *SFC*, March 8, 1992.

3. Lisa Benton, *The Presidio: From Army Post to National Park* (Boston: Northeastern University Press, 1998), 86–87.

4. George B. Hartzog Jr., *Battling for the National Parks* (Mt. Kisco, N.Y.: Moyer Bell, 1988), 233–46; *National Parks for the Future: An Appraisal of the National Parks As They Begin Their Second Century in a Changing America* (Washington, D.C.: Conservation Foundation, 1972), 67–74, 197–236; Helvarg, *The War against the Greens*, 130–41; Foresta, *America's National Parks and Their Keepers*, 74–92; Rothman, *The Greening of a Nation?* 58–64.

5. James M. Ridenour, *The National Parks Compromised: Pork Barrel Politics and America's Treasures* (Merrillville, Ind.: ICS Books, 1994), 17, 80–81; for the impact of ANILCA, see Theodore Catton, *Inhabited Wilderness: Indians, Eskimos, and National Parks in Alaska* (Albuquerque: University of New Mexico Press, 1997).

6. Diana Scott, "Presidio for Sale," *Monitor*, December 28, 1999.

7. Huey D. Johnson, "The Presidio Trust: Blueprint for Privatization," *SFE*, December 2, 1996.

8. Amy Meyer to Steve Haller, February 11, 2002.

9. Jacobs, *A Rage for Justice*, 367; Robinson, "*You're in Your Mother's Arms*," 431–41.

10. Mary G. Murphy, "Fighting Over the Presidio," *Recorder*, October 27, 1993; Charles McCoy, "Astonishing Views and Many Opinions: Must Be the Presidio,"

Wall Street Journal, April 19, 1994; Bradley Inman, "Presidio Housing Battle," *SFE*, 1993; Benton, *The Presidio*, 88–90.

11. Brian O'Neill, interview by Sara Conklin, May 19, 1999, unedited transcript, 3, 5, Presidio Oral History Project.

12. O'Neill interview, May 19, 1999, 2.

13. Ibid., 9–11; Middleton interview, June 14, 2002.

14. Gerald D. Adams, "New Presidio Money Woes," *SFE*, April 10, 1991; John R. Moses, "Presidio's Uncertain Future," *SFI*, April 6, 1991; O'Neill interview, May 19, 1999; "NPS May Inherit Army's Problems at Presidio," *National Parks*, March/April 1991.

15. Doug Nadeau, interview by John Martini, October 6, 1998, Presidio Oral History Project, 62–64.

16. Middleton interview, June 14, 2002; Benton, *The Presidio*, 91; O'Neill interview, May 19, 1999, 14.

17. Benton, *The Presidio*, 92; O'Neill interview, May 19, 1999, 15–17.

18. Middleton interview, June 14, 2002; Amy Meyer to Steve Haller, February 20, 2002; John Reynolds, interview by Sara Conklin, unedited draft transcript, May 18, 1999, 3–5, Presidio Oral History Project; Benton, *The Presidio*, 92–93.

19. Don Neubacher, interview by Sara Conklin, April 27, 1999, unedited draft, 1–7, Presidio Oral History Project.

20. Duvel White, "GGNRA Asks Citizens to Envision Future of Presidio," *Star Presidian*, January 31, 1991; Benton, *The Presidio*, 93.

21. Jim Harvey to Presidio Council, November 6, 1991, Box 5, Presidio Council (Information mailed out by GGNRA), OCPA.

22. Neubacher interview, April 27, 1999, 10.

23. Harvey to Presidio Council, November 6, 1991; Neubacher interview, April 29, 1999, 11–12; Benton, *The Presidio*, 98–100.

24. Glenn Isaacson and Associates, "Summary of Baseline Financial Study," in Harvey to Presidio Council, November 6, 1991, GGNRA Archives; Keyser Marston and Associates, *Presidio Building, Leasing, and Financing Implementation Strategy: A Supplement to Final General Management Plan Amendment, Presidio of San Francisco, Golden Gate National Recreation Area, California, July 1994* (San Francisco: Golden Gate National Recreation Area, 1994).

25. Middleton interview, June 14, 2002; "Creating a Park for the 21st Century: From Military Post to National Park," *Final General Management Plan Amendment, Presidio of San Francisco* (Denver: Denver Service Center, National Park Service: 1994), 2–6; Neubacher interview, April 27, 1999, 11–13.

26. O'Neill interview, May 19, 1999.

27. Dick Brill, "Cradle of Aviation Fenced Down Middle," *SFP*, October 14, 1977; Benton, *The Presidio*, 106–10.

28. Gerald D. Adams, "Vast U.S. Plan for Presidio," *SFC*, October 14, 1993; Carl Nolte, "Big Worries about Plan for Presidio," *SFC*, October 15, 1993.

29. Gerald D. Adams, "6th Army Criticizes New Plan for Presidio," *SFE*, October 21, 1993.

30. Benton, *The Presidio*, 121; Nicholas Lemann, "The Kids in the Conference Room: How McKinsey and Company Became the Next Big Step," *New Yorker*, October 18 and 25, 1999, 209–16.

31. Robert Chandler, interview by Sara Conklin, May 14, 1999, 1–14, Presidio Oral History Project.

32. Ridenour, *The National Parks Compromised*, 210; Bartke to Haller, March 5, 2002; Meyer interview, February 25, 2002, 23.

33. Meyer interview, February 25, 2002; Eric Nystrom, "Mojave National Preserve: Draft Administrative History," June 10, 2002, 13–30, Mojave National Preserve, Barstow, California.

34. Meyer interview, February 25, 2002; Benton, *The Presidio*, 128–35.

35. Middleton interview, June 14, 2002; Bartke to Haller, February 5, 2002; Meyer interview, February 25, 2002, 24; Benton, *The Presidio*, 123–25.

36. Middleton interview, June 14, 2002; Martin Espinoza, "Presidio Inc.," *SFBG*, January 21, 1994, and "Presidio Plan Under Fire," *SFBG*, March 9, 1994; Benton, *The Presidio*, 125–27. Espinoza's credibility was often in question. Many believed he wrote what he wanted to, regardless of the facts, and Rich Bartke suggests that Espinoza's lack of credibility diminished his influence on park policy. In the end, Espinoza likely represents an extreme perspective, one that receives a hearing in the Bay Area because of the region's complicated politics. See Bartke to Haller, March 5, 2002.

37. Martin Espinoza, "The Presidio Power Grab," *SFBG*, January 12, 1994, and "The Shame of the Presidio," *SFBG*, March 30, 1994.

38. Amy Meyer to Steve Haller, February 20, 2002; Carl Nolte, "Congressman Tries to Block Presidio Plan," *SFC*, March 10, 1994, and "Congressional Foe of Presidio Knows His Pork," *SFC*, March 11, 1994; Gerald D. Adams, "Proposed Presidio Park Too Big, Says Lawmaker," *SFE*, March 10, 1994; "Help Save the Presidio," *MIJ*, March 17, 1994.

39. Brian O'Neill interview, May 19, 1999.

40. Rep. Nancy Pelosi and Rep. Barbara Boxer to Amy Meyer, September 19, 1989, Box 5, Government—U.S. House of Representatives, Nancy Pelosi, PFFGNRA II; John R. Moses, "Presidio's Future Uncertain," *SFI*, April 6, 1991; Ingfei Chen, "Army Says It Goofed, OKs Money for Presidio," *SFC*, February 12, 1992, and "Army Promises to Take Care of Presidio," *SFC*, November 14, 1992.

41. Seth Shulman, *The Threat at Home: Confronting the Toxic Legacy of the U.S. Military* (Boston: Beacon Press, 1992); Rothman, *Saving the Planet*, 196–99.

42. Benton, *The Presidio*, 115–16.

43. Middleton interview, June 14, 2002; Elliot Diringer, "EPA Fines Presidio for Mishandling Waste," *SFC*, May 10, 1994; Diana Scott, "Presidio for Sale," *Monitor*, December 28, 1999; Benton, *The Presidio*, 116–17; Meyer interview, February 25, 2002, 26.

44. Amy Meyer to Steve Haller, February 20, 2002; David McClure, "Closure Marks New Era for Presidio," *Star Presidian*, April 22, 1994; Robert D. Kaplan, *An Empire Wilderness: Travels into America's Future* (New York: Random House, 1998), 3–20.

45. "Army's New Role at the Presidio," *SFC*, October 21, 1993; Benton, *The Presidio*, 117; Bruce Bellingham and Maggie McCall, "The Presidio: Analysis and Report," *Marina Times*, May 1994.

46. Benton, *The Presidio*, 118; Bartke to Haller, March 5, 2002.

47. Pat Sullivan, "From Generals Admission to General Admission," *SFC*, May 7, 1994; Phillip Matier and Andrew Ross, "Army Wants to Stay the (Golf) Course," *SFC*, November 22, 1993.

48. Reynolds interview, May 18, 1999, 6, unedited transcript.

49. Benton, *The Presidio*, 118–19.

50. Gerald D. Adams, "San Franciscans Say Give Presidio to the Homeless," *SFE*, June 27, 1991; "An Urge to Act on Homelessness," *SFE*, June 28, 1991; Meyer to Haller, February 25, 2002.

51. Ingfei Chen, "Agnos Tells His Plans for Presidio," *SFC*, July 9, 1991; David

Crosson, "31 Leaders Visit Washington to Lobby for More Money for Homeless, Presidio," *SFE*, September 24, 1991; Erin McCormick, "Homeless Try Takeover of Presidio Apartments," *SFE*, May 3, 1994; Stephen Schwartz, "32 Held in Homeless Protest," *SFC*, May 3, 1994.

52. "Presidio Hospital Battle," *SFI*, December 14, 1993; "Retired and Disabled Vets Furious Over Letterman Closure, Ask Help," Marina *Times*, March 1992; Peter Tira, "Ongoing Battle to Save Letterman Medical Center," *SFI*, April 12, 1994; Benton, *The Presidio*, 237–38; Martin Espinoza, "The Presidio Power Grab," *SFBG*, January 12, 1994.

53. George Christopher, "The Presidio Should Be Made into a Campus for UCSF," *SFC*, March 12, 1992; "Paying for the Presidio," *SFE*, August 26, 1993; Martin Espinoza, "UC's Presidio Prescription," *SFBG*, March 30, 1994; Benton, *The Presidio*, 237–38; Bartke to Haller, March 5, 2002.

54. Marc Sandalow, "Babbitt 'Wearily Confident' about Future of Presidio," *SFC*, February 1, 1994; Peter Tira, "New Construction at Presidio," *SFI*, April 12, 1994; Carolyn Lochhead, "Push in House to Lease Parts of Presidio," *SFC*, May 11, 1994; Neil D. Eisenberg, "The Rape of the Presidio," *SFBG*, September 14, 1994, and "An Open Letter to the People of the Bay Area," *SFBG*, September 14, 1994; Martin Espinoza, "Death of a Park," *SFBG*, December 14, 1994; Meyer to Haller, February 25, 2002.

55. Michael Dorgan, "Swords to Plowshares: A Jewel of a Transition," *SJMN*, September 30, 1994; Gerald D. Adams, "New Era for Presidio," *SFE*, October 1, 1994; Carl Nolte, "Presidio Soldiers Furl Their Colors," *SFC*, October 1, 1994.

56. Nadeau interview, October 6, 1998, 66; Ric Borjes, e-mail to Steve Haller, July 7, 2000; Bartke to Haller, March 5, 2002; Donald J. Hellmann, "The Path of the Presidio Trust Legislation," *Golden Gate University Law Review* 28, no. 3 (Spring 1998): 319–98; Benton, *The Presidio*, 113–46; "The Presidio Sellout: A Chronology," *SFBG*, March 30, 1994; Scott, "Presidio for Sale."

57. O'Neill interview, May 19, 1999.

58. Middleton interview, June 14, 2002; Meyer to Haller, February 25, 2002; Mai-Liis Bartling to Steve Haller, September 21, 2000, copy in possession of the author.

59. Mai-Liis Bartling to Steve Haller, September 21, 2000, copy in possession of the author.

60. Middleton interview, June 14, 2002.

Bibliography

PRIMARY SOURCES

Government Documents

Babal, Marianne. *The Top of the Peninsula: A History of Sweeney Ridge and the San Francisco Watershed Lands, San Mateo County, California.* San Francisco: Golden Gate National Recreation Area, National Park Service, 1990.

Delgado, James P., and Robert L. Bennett. *Research Design for the Historical Archaeological Examination and Documentation of the Remains of the 1848 Sidewheel Steamship* Tennessee *at Tennessee Cove, Golden Gate National Recreation Area, Marin County, California.* San Francisco: Golden Gate National Recreation Area, 1978.

Delgado, James P., Robert L. Bennett, and Stephen A. Haller. *Submerged Cultural Resource Assessment: Golden Gate National Recreation Area, Gulf of the Farallones National Marine Sanctuary, and Point Reyes National Seashore.* Santa Fe: Southwest Cultural Resources Center, National Park Service, 1989.

Duffus, James. *Transfer of the Presidio from the Army to the National Park Service: Statement of James Duffus III, Director, Natural Resources Management Issues, Resources, Community, and Economic Development Division, before the Subcommittee on National Parks, Forests, and Public Lands, Committee on Natural Resources, House of Representatives.* Washington, D.C.: Government Printing Office, 1994.

General Accounting Office. *Transfer of the Presidio from the Army to the National Park Service: Report to Congressional Requesters.* Washington, D.C.: GAO, 1993.

Grassick, Mary K. *Fort Point: Fort Point National Historic Site, Presidio of San Francisco, California.* W. Va.: Harpers Ferry Center, Division of Historic Furnishings, National Park Service, 1994.

Keyser Marston and Associates. *Presidio Building Leasing and Financing Implementation Strategy: A Supplement to Final General Management Plan Amendment, Presidio of San Francisco, Golden Gate National Recreation Area, California, July 1994.* San Francisco: Golden Gate National Recreation Area, 1994.

Langellier, J. Phillip. *Historic Resource Study: El Presidio de San Francisco: A History under Spain and Mexico, 1776–1846.* Denver: Denver Service Center, National Park Service, 1992.

Livingston, Douglas. *A Good Life: Dairy Farming in the Olema Valley, A History of the Dairy and Beef Ranches of the Olema Valley and Lagunitas Canyon, Golden Gate National Recreation Area and Point Reyes National Seashore, Marin County, California.* San Francisco: National Park Service, 1995.

Mackintosh, Barry. *Interpretation in the National Park Service: A Historical Perspective.* Washington, D.C.: National Park Service, History Division, 1986.

———. *The National Historic Preservation Act and the National Park Service: A History.* Washington, D.C.: National Park Service, History Division, 1986.

———. *National Park Service Administrative History: A Guide.* Washington, D.C.: National Park Service, History Division, 1991.

————. *The National Parks: Shaping the System.* Washington, D.C.: National Park Service, Division of Publications, 1985.

————. *The United States Park Police: A History.* Washington, D.C.: National Park Service, 1989.

————. *Visitor Fees in the National Park System: A Legislative and Administrative History.* Washington, D.C.: National Park Service, History Division, 1983.

National Park Service. *Creating a Park for the 21st Century: From Military Post to National Park: Draft General Management Plan Amendment, Presidio of San Francisco, Golden Gate National Recreation Area, California.* Denver: Denver Service Center, National Park Service, 1993.

————. *Creating a Park for the 21st Century: From Military Post to National Park: Final General Management Plan Amendment, Presidio of San Francisco, Golden Gate National Recreation Area, California.* Denver: Denver Service Center, National Park Service, 1994.

————. *Draft General Management Plan Amendment, Environmental Impact Statement, Presidio of San Francisco, Golden Gate National Recreation Area, California.* Denver: Denver Service Center, National Park Service, 1993.

————. *Final General Management Plan Amendment, Environmental Impact Statement, Presidio of San Francisco, Golden Gate National Recreation Area, California.* Denver: Denver Service Center, National Park Service, 1994.

————. *Final General Management Plan Amendment, Presidio of San Francisco.* Denver: Denver Service Center, National Park Service, 1994.

————. *Muir Woods National Monument, California: Golden Gate National Recreation Area.* Washington, D.C.: National Park Service, 1987.

————. *Presidio Concepts Workbook: A Work-in-Progress Report for Public Review and Feedback.* San Francisco: Golden Gate National Recreation Area, National Park Service, 1991.

Robert Peccia and Associates. *Presidio Transportation Planning and Analysis Technical Report.* Washington, D.C.: National Park Service, 1993.

Thompson, Erwin N., and Sally Byrne Woodbridge. *Presidio of San Francisco, Golden Gate National Recreation Area, California.* Denver: Denver Service Center, National Park Service, 1992.

————. *Presidio of San Francisco: An Outline of Its Evolution as a U.S. Army Post, 1847–1990.* Denver: Denver Service Center, National Park Service, 1992.

United States. "Golden Gate National Recreation Area Addition Act of 1992. An Act to Authorize Inclusion of a Tract of Land in the Golden Gate National Recreation Area, California." Washington, D.C.: Government Printing Office, 1992.

————. "Omnibus Parks and Public Lands Management Act of 1996. An Act to Provide for the Administration of Certain Presidio Properties at Minimal Cost to the Federal Taxpayer, and for Other Purposes." Washington, D.C.: Government Printing Office, 1996.

U.S. House of Representatives, Committee on Natural Resources. *Golden Gate National Recreation Area/Presidio Management: Hearing before the Subcommittee on National Parks, Forests, and Public Lands.* 103d Cong., 2d sess. Washington, D.C.: Government Printing Office, 1993.

U.S. Senate, Committee on Energy and Natural Resources. *Authorizing Inclusion of a Tract of Land in the Golden Gate National Recreation Area, California: Report (to accompany S. 870).* Washington, D.C.: Government Printing Office, 1991.

————. *Management of the Presidio in San Francisco by the National Park Service: Hearings before the Subcommittee on Public Lands, National Parks, and Forests of the Committee on Energy and Natural Resources.* 103d Cong., 2d sess. Washington, D.C.: Government Printing Office, 1994.

U.S. Senate, Committee on Interior and Insular Affairs, Subcommittee on Parks and Recreation. *Golden Gate National Recreation Area and Farallon National Wildlife Refuge, California: Hearings before the Subcommittee on Parks and Recreation of the Committee on Interior and Insular Affairs, 93d Congress, 2d sess., on S. 2634, H.R. 10834, S.3187, S.2973, [and] H.R. 11013.* Washington, D.C.: Government Printing Office, 1975.

Newspapers

Daly City Record
Marin Independent-Journal
Pacifica Tribune
Pacific Sun
Palo Alto Times
Petaluma Argus-Courier
Point Reyes Light
San Francisco Bay Guardian
San Francisco Chronicle
San Francisco Chronicle and Examiner
San Francisco Examiner
San Francisco Independent
San Francisco Progress
San Jose Mercury News
Santa Cruz Sentinel

Manuscript and Archives Sources

All sources cited are held by the Park Archives and Records Center (PARC), Golden Gate National Recreation Area

Alcatraz Documents. Office of Resource Management and Planning. 1860–1988, GOGA-18340, HDC 409.
Central Correspondence Files, Golden Gate National Recreation Area, 1970–1996.
Fort Point National Historic Site Administrative Records, 1972–1990, GOGA-2275.
GGNRA Land Acquisition Papers, 1974–1978, GOGA-18339, HDC 479.
Katharine S. Frankforter Personal Papers and Records of Headlands, Inc., 1946–1975, GOGA-27066.
Natural Resources Management Division Records, 1980–1994.
Office of Communications and Public Affairs Records, 1974–1996.
People for a Golden Gate National Recreation Area Archives, 1972–1984, GOGA-2705.
People for a Golden Gate National Recreation Area Archives, 1985–1994, GOGA-2434.
Press Clippings Collection, 1966–1995, GOGA-2376.
Superintendent's Office, Golden Gate National Recreation Area, Archives, 1957–1977.
Superintendent's Office, Golden Gate National Recreation Area, Archives, 1977–1984, GOGA-2194.

HDC refers to Historic Documents Collection, the numbering system in use when manuscript and archives collections owned by Golden Gate National Recreation Area were maintained and housed by the San Francisco Maritime National Historical Park. The collections have recently been transferred and are now referred to by the Golden Gate National Recreation Area accession (GOGA) or catalog numbers. Archives staff can assist in locating these collections.

Oral Interviews

Borjes, Ric, interview by Hal Rothman, June 2, 2000.
Chandler, Robert, interview by Sara Conklin, May 14, 1999, Presidio Oral History Project.
Haller, Stephen A., interview by Hal Rothman, May 10, 2000.
Meyer, Amy, interview by Sara Conklin, Golden Gate National Recreation Area Archives, May 17, 1993.
Moore, Gregory, interview by Hal Rothman, July 16, 1999.
Murray, Ray, 1993, GGNRA Oral History Interview.
Nadeau, Doug, interview by John Martini, October 6, 1998, Presidio Oral History Project.
Neubacher, Don, interview by Sara Conklin, April 27, 1999, Presidio Oral History Project.
O'Neill, Brian, interview by Sara Conklin, May 19, 1999, Presidio Oral History Project.
O'Neill, Brian, interview by Hal Rothman, July 16, 2000.
Rand, Yvonne, interview by Sara Conklin, July 23, 1993, GGNRA Oral History Interview.
Reynolds, John, interview by Sara Conklin, May 18, 1999, Presidio Oral History Project.
Sprung, Gary, interview by Hal Rothman, February 19, 2000.
Thomas, Bill, interview by Sara Conklin, March 31, 1993, GGNRA Oral History Interview.
Weideman, Rich, interview by Hal Rothman, July 17, 1999.
Whalen, William interview by Sara Conklin, March 27, 1993, GGNRA Oral History Interview.

SECONDARY SOURCES

Articles

Adams, Dwight. "The Back Page." *Preservation* (1997).
"Army Won't Give Up All of a 4-Star Base." *New York Times,* August 12, 1994.
"Austerity Overcomes the Presidio: Sorrow and Joy Mix as Legendary Garrison Becomes a Park." *New York Times,* October 2, 1994.
Brockman, C. Frank. "Park Naturalists and the Evolution of National Park Service Interpretation through World War II." *Journal of Forest History* (January 1978): 19–29.
Calio, Suzanne. "Corrective Surgery for the Great Highway." *Landscape Architecture* (September 1978): 424–29.
Camia, Catalina. "House Passes Bill to Provide for Upkeep of Presidio Post." *Congressional Quarterly Weekly Report* 52, no. 33 (August 20, 1994): 2446.
"Clark Adds Sweeney Ridge to Golden Gate NRA." *National Parks* 58 (May–June 1984): 33.
Connor, John. "Bill for Revamping of Presidio Curbed by Panel in House." *Wall Street Journal,* August 5, 1994.
Craine, Kimber. "Golden Gate NRA: A Plan to Put Up a Parking Lot." *National Parks* 58 (November–December 1984): 34–35.
"Debate Surrounds Presidio's Future." *National Parks* 68, nos. 1–2 (January–February 1994): 10–11.
Delgado, James P. "No Longer a Buoyant Ship: Unearthing the Storeship Niantic." *California History* 63, no. 4.
———. "What Becomes of the Old Ships? Dismantling the Gold Rush Fleet of San Francisco." *Pacific Historian* 5, no. 3.

Del Rosso, Laura. "Newest National Park to Open in Urban Area." *Travel Weekly* 53, no. 70 (September 5, 1994): 14–15.

"Golden Gate Guardian Ends a Long Mission." *New York Times,* May 18, 1993.

"Golden Gate to Get Presidio Army Base." *National Parks* 63, nos. 7–8 (July–August 1989): 14.

Hellmann, Donald J. "The Path of the Presidio Trust Legislation." *Golden Gate University Law Review* 28, no. 3 (Spring 1998): 319–98.

"House Approves Creation of Entity over Presidio." *Wall Street Journal,* August 19, 1994.

Lemann, Nicholas. "The Kids in the Conference Room: How McKinsey and Company Became the Next Big Step." *New Yorker,* October 18 and 25, 1999.

McCoy, Charles. "Astonishing Views and Many Opinions: Must Be the Presidio." *Wall Street Journal,* April 19, 1994.

Nelson, Eric. "Presidio's Toxics Cloud Future As National Park." *San Francisco Business Times* 5, no. 3 (September 17, 1990): 1.

"NPS May Inherit Army's Problems at Presidio." *National Parks* 65, nos. 3–4 (March–April 1991): 12–13.

Ordano, Jo-Ann. "Changing of the Guard." *National Parks* 67, nos. 3–4 (March–April 1993): 30–37.

Paddock, Richard. "View from Presidio: Profits." *Los Angeles Times,* August 12, 1992.

"Presidio to Become National Park." *Planning* 59, no. 10 (October 1993): 35.

Rosenbaum, David. "Presidio Rehab Draws Fire." *ENR* 231, no. 19 (November 8, 1993): 24.

Rothman, Hal K. "'A Regular Ding-Dong Fight': Agency Culture and Evolution in the Park Service–Forest Service Dispute, 1916–1937," *Western Historical Quarterly* 26 no. 2 (May 1989): 141–60.

"Senate Panel Clears Bill on Presidio Trust Proposal." *Wall Street Journal,* September 23, 1994.

Stapleton, Katina. "House Panel Predicts Savings with Special Presidio Trust." *Congressional Quarterly Weekly Report* 52, no. 26 (July 2, 1994): 1788.

Tuttle, Liza. "At City's Edge: Urban Parks Provide Open Space and Recreation." *National Parks* 63, nos. 11–12 (1989): 37–40.

Books

Albright, Horace M., as told to Robert Cahn, *The Birth of the National Park Service: The Founding Years, 1913–1933.* Salt Lake City: Howe Brothers Press, 1986.

———, and Marian Albright Schenck. *Creating the National Park Service: The Missing Years.* Norman: University of Oklahoma Press, 1999.

Beers, David. *Blue Sky Dream: A Memoir of America's Fall from Grace.* New York: Doubleday, 1996.

Benton, Lisa. *The Presidio: From Army Post to National Park.* Boston: Northeastern University Press, 1998.

Brick, Philip D., and R. McGregor Cawley. *A Wolf in the Garden: The Land Rights Movement and the New Environmental Debate.* Lanham, Md.: Rowman and Littlefield, 1996.

Carr, Ethan. *Wilderness by Design: Landscape Architecture and the National Park Service.* Lincoln: University of Nebraska Press, 1998.

Catton, Theodore. *Inhabited Wilderness: Indians, Eskimos, and National Parks in Alaska.* Albuquerque: University of New Mexico Press, 1997.

Cohen, Michael P. *The History of the Sierra Club, 1892–1970.* San Francisco: Sierra Club Books, 1988.

Cox, Thomas R., Robert S. Maxwell, Phillip Drennon Thomas, and Joseph K. Malone. *This Well-Wooded Land: Americans and Their Forests from Colonial Times to the Present*. Lincoln: University of Nebraska Press, 1985.

Dasmann, Raymond F. *The Destruction of California*. New York: Macmillan, 1965.

DeLeon, Richard E. *Left Coast City: Progressive Politics in San Francisco, 1975–1991*. Lawrence: University Press of Kansas, 1992.

Delgado, James P. *Alcatraz: Island of Change*. San Francisco: Golden Gate National Parks Association, 1991.

Dilsaver, Lary M. Ed. *America's National Park System: The Critical Documents*. Lanham, Md.: Rowman and Littlefield, 1994.

Elkind, Sarah. *Bay Cities and Water Politics: The Battle for Resources in Boston and Oakland*. Lawrence: University Press of Kansas, 1998.

Elliot, George Henry. *The Presidio of San Francisco*. Washington[?]: 1874[?].

Everhart, William C. *The National Park Service*. Boulder, Colo.: Westview Press, 1985.

Foresta, Ronald A. *America's National Parks and Their Keepers*. Washington, D.C.: Resources for the Future, 1984.

Fox, Stephen R. *John Muir and His Legacy: The American Conservation Movement*. Boston: Little, Brown, 1981.

Freemuth, John C. *Islands under Siege: National Parks and the Politics of External Threats*. Lawrence: University Press of Kansas, 1991.

Gilbert, Henry. *Robin Hood*. New York: Blue Ribbon Books, 1912.

Gilliam, Harold, and Ann Gilliam. *Marin Headlands: Portals of Time*. San Francisco: Golden Gate National Park Association, 1993.

Goldman, Eric. *The Crucial Decade and After: America, 1945–1955*. New York: Knopf, 1966.

Halberstam, David. *Playing for Keeps: Michael Jordan and the World He Made*. New York: Random House, 1999.

Haller, Stephen A. *Post and Park: A Brief Illustrated History of the Presidio*. San Francisco: Golden Gate National Parks Association, 1997.

Halprin, Lawrence. *Alcatraz: The Future*. San Francisco: Golden Gate National Parks Association, 1988.

Hampton, Duane H. *How the U.S. Cavalry Saved Our National Parks*. Bloomington: Indiana University Press, 1971.

Harris, Ann G., and Esther Tuttle. *Geology of National Parks*. 3d ed. Dubuque, Iowa: Kendall/Hunt Publishing, 1983.

Harris, David V., and Kiver, Eugene P. *The Geologic Story of the National Parks and Monuments*. New York: Wiley, 1995.

Hart, John. *San Francisco's Wilderness Next Door*. San Rafael, Calif.: Presidio Press, 1979.

Hartman, Chester. *The Transformation of San Francisco*. Totowa, N.J.: Rowman and Allenheld, 1984.

Hartzog, George B. Jr. *Battling for the National Parks*. Mount Kisco, N.Y.: Moyer Bell, 1988.

Helvarg, David. *The War against the Greens: The "Wise Use" Movement, the New Right, and Anti-Environmental Violence*. San Francisco: Sierra Club Books, 1994.

Ise, John. *Our National Park Policy: A Critical History*. Baltimore: Johns Hopkins University Press, 1961.

Issel, William, and Robert W. Cherny. *San Francisco, 1865–1932: Politics, Power, and Urban Development*. Berkeley: University of California Press, 1986.

Jacobs, John. *A Rage for Justice: The Passion and Politics of Phillip Burton*. Berkeley: University of California Press, 1995.

Johnson, Marilynn S. *Oakland and the East Bay in World War II.* Berkeley: University of California Press, 1993.

Kaplan, Robert D. *An Empire Wilderness: Travels into America's Future.* New York: Random House, 1998.

Lears, T. J. Jackson. *No Place of Grace: Antimodernism and the Transformation of American Culture, 1880–1920.* New York: Pantheon, 1981.

Lewis, R. W. B. *The American Adam: Innocence, Tragedy, and Tradition in the Nineteenth Century.* Chicago: University of Chicago Press, 1968.

Liberatore, Karen. *The Complete Guide to the Golden Gate National Recreation Area.* San Francisco: Chronicle Books, 1982.

Lotchin, Roger. *Fortress California, 1910–1961: From Warfare to Welfare.* New York: Oxford University Press, 1992.

Markusen, Ann, Peter Hall, Scott Campbell, and Sabina Deitrick. *The Rise of the Gun-Belt: The Military Remapping of Industrial America.* New York: Oxford University Press, 1991.

Markusen, Ann, and Joel Yudken, *Dismantling the Cold War Economy.* New York: Basic Books, 1992.

Martini, John A. *Fort Point: Sentry at the Golden Gate.* San Francisco: Golden Gate National Parks Association, 1991.

———. *Fortress Alcatraz: Guardian of the Golden Gate.* Kailua, Hawaii: Pacific Monograph, 1990.

Morgan, Dan. *Rising in the West: A True Story of an "Okie" Family from the Great Depression through the Reagan Years.* New York: Knopf, 1992.

Nash, Roderick. *Wilderness and the American Mind.* 3d ed. New Haven: Yale University Press, 1982.

———. *World War II and the West: Reshaping the Economy.* Lincoln: University of Nebraska Press, 1990.

Olmsted, Nancy. *To Walk with a Quiet Mind: Hikes in the Woodlands, Parks, and Beaches of the San Francisco Bay Area.* San Francisco: Sierra Club Books, 1975.

Pyne, Stephen J. *How the Canyon Became Grand: A Short History.* New York: Viking, 1998.

Rawls, James J., and Walton Bean. *California: An Interpretive History.* New York: McGraw Hill, 1993.

Reisner, Marc. *Cadillac Desert: The American West and Its Disappearing Water.* New York: Viking, 1986.

Ridenour, James M. *The National Parks Compromised: Pork Barrel Politics and America's Treasures.* Merrillville, Ind.: ICS Books, 1994.

Robinson, Judith. *"You're in Your Mother's Arms": The Life and Legacy of Congressman Phil Burton.* San Francisco: Mary Judith Robinson, 1994.

Rothman, Hal. *America's National Monuments: The Politics of Preservation.* Lawrence: University Press of Kansas, 1994.

———. *Bandelier National Monument: An Administrative History.* Southwest Cultural Resources Center Professional Papers no. 14. Santa Fe: National Park Service, 1988.

———. *Conservation and Environmentalism in the American Century.* Chicago: Ivan R. Dee, 2000.

———. *Devil's Bargains: Tourism in the Twentieth-Century American West.* Lawrence: University Press of Kansas, 1998.

———. *The Greening of a Nation? Environmentalism in the U.S. since 1945.* New York: Harcourt Brace, 1998.

———. *Navajo National Monument: A Place and Its People.* Southwest Cultural Resources Series no. 41. Santa Fe: National Park Service, 1991.

————. *Preserving Different Pasts: The American National Monuments*. Urbana: University of Illinois Press, 1989.

————. *Saving the Planet: The American Response to the Environment in the Twentieth Century*. Chicago: Ivan R. Dee, 2000.

Rubissow, Ariel. *Cliff House and Lands End: San Francisco's Seaside Retreat*. San Francisco: Golden Gate National Park Association, 1993.

————. *Park Guide, Golden Gate National Recreation Area*. San Francisco: Golden Gate National Park Association, 1990.

Runte, Alfred. *National Parks: The American Experience*. 3d ed. Lincoln: University of Nebraska Press, 1997.

————. *Yosemite: The Embattled Wilderness*. Lincoln: University of Nebraska Press, 1990.

Schrepfer, Susan R. *The Fight to Save the Redwoods: A History of Environmental Reform, 1917–1978*. Madison: University of Wisconsin Press, 1983.

Scott, Mel. *The San Francisco Bay Area: A Metropolis in Perspective*. 2d ed. Berkeley: University of California Press, 1985.

Seabrook, John. *Nobrow: The Culture of Marketing the Marketing of Culture*. New York: Alfred A. Knopf, 2000.

Sellars, Richard West. *Preserving Nature in the National Parks: A History*. New Haven: Yale University Press, 1997.

Shankland, Robert. *Steve Mather of the National Parks*. New York: Alfred A. Knopf, 1953.

Shulman, Seth. *The Threat at Home: Confronting the Toxic Legacy of the U.S. Military*. Boston: Beacon Press, 1992.

Smith, Henry Nash. *Virgin Land: The American West As Myth and Symbol*. Cambridge: Harvard University Press, 1950.

Strasser, J. B., and Laurie Becklund. *Swoosh: The Unauthorized Story of Nike and the Men Who Played There*. New York: Harcourt Brace Jovanovich, 1991.

Swain, Donald. *Wilderness Defender: Horace M. Albright and Conservation*. Chicago: University of Chicago Press, 1970.

Udall, Stewart. *The Quiet Crisis*. New York: Holt, Rinehart and Winston, 1963.

Whitnah, Dorothy L. *Guide to the Golden Gate National Recreation Area*. Berkeley, Calif.: Wilderness Press, 1978.

Wirth, Conrad L. *Parks, Politics, and the People*. Norman: University of Oklahoma Press, 1980.

Index

Fort Point, 14, 15, 16, 27, 64, 103, 125, 126,
132, 133, 134, 135, 139, 141
Fort Point Museum Association, 16, 125, 135

General Services Administration (GSA), 20,
21, 22, 38, 126
Giacomini Ranch, 52, 55, 69
Giacomini, Gary, 51, 52, 82, 118, 119
Glacier, 108
Golden Gate and Gateway National
Recreation Areas, 78
Golden Gate Bridge, 8, 15, 33, 35, 67, 104,
121
Golden Gate National Parks Association
(GGNPA), 72, 73, 74, 94, 152–153,
157–158, 159–160, 163, 164, 168, 169,
170, 175, 179, 183, 185, 195, 200
Golden Gate National Recreation Area
(GGNRA), ix–xi, 27, 32, 46, 50, 52, 53,
58, 59, 61, 76, 86, 87, 171, 200–201;
acquisition strategy, 39; adaptive
reuse, 67, 139, 141, 148; avian species,
109–110; beaches, 82, 83; coastal
issues, 119–121; conceptual plan, 22;
cultural landscapes, 143–144; cultural
resources, 66, 101, 124–125, 131,
132–133, 134–135, 136, 137–140, 143,
44–145, 147–148; cultural resources
management plan, 133, 136; expansion
of, 41, 42, 44, 48, 50, 52, 53, 54, 55, 56;
exotic species management, 106; fire
management, 113–115; General
Management Plan (GMP), 60, 68, 76,
77, 82, 92, 102, 103, 117, 131, 133, 154,
157, 159, 167,168–169, 199; and
Generation X, 86, 87, 88; as Golden
Gate National Parks, 165; inholdings
of, 95; and interpretation, 149,
151–152, 154, 158, 159, 169; lands, 35;
management of, 62, 63, 81, 89, 97, 100,
102, 104; and the military, 93, 94; and
mountain bikes, 86, 88, 89, 90, 92;
natural resources management, 68, 99,
101, 107, 111, 122–123; Natural
Resources Management Plan (NRMP),
102, 103, 105, 106, 109–110, 113, 114;
pet management, 78, 82, 89; and pet
owners, 77, 82; planning of, 57, 75;
resource management, 84;
stakeholders in, 77; trails, 85;
transportation to, 64, 65; and zones,
63, 104, 131, 133, 136
Golden Gate National Recreation Area bill,
26, 27, 28, 30
Golden Gate Point Reyes General
Management Plan, 162
Green Gulch Ranch, 95, 96

Half-Moon Bay, 41
Halprin, Lawrence, 72, 73, 161
Hardini, Richard B., 80
Hartzog, George B, Jr., 59, 96, 97
Haslett Warehouse, 40, 41, 44, 133
Herbert, Edward, 36
Historic Preservation Act of 1966, 66, 67,
124, 125, 130, 138, 146
Hodel, Donald, 120
Holter, Anton G., 46, 47
Howell, Judd, 113, 116
Hughes, Betty, 42

International Mountain Bicycling
Association (IMBA), 90, 91

Jacobs, John, 46, 47, 69, 146
Jarvis, Howard, 49
Jarvis-Gann bill, 50
John Muir National Historic Site, 19, 57
Johnson, Lyndon B., ix, 49

Kent, William, 5–6, 7, 8, 14

Lagunitas Creek Loop, 46, 51, 55
Lands End, 63, 67, 83, 84, 103
Lane, Franklin, 3
Leopold Report of 1963, 101, 105, 112, 132,
143
Levine, Mel, 120
Limantour Estero, 63
Lincoln Park, 27, 84

Mailliard, William, 39–40, 126
Marin Conservation League, 51, 59,
Marin County, 13, 25, 33, 35, 36, 39, 40, 42,
46, 47, 48, 52, 54, 55, 59, 64, 65, 68,
78–81, 83, 88, 102, 104, 106, 112,
114–117, 119, 120, 134, 154
Marin County Board of Supervisors, 35, 37,
51
Marin Headlands State Park, 25, 27, 27, 36,
41, 63, 64, 65, 89, 93, 94, 103, 104, 108,
110, 135, 155, 159, 171
Marincello, 24, 27, 35, 46, 38, 46, 52
Maritime Museum, 156, 163
Martini, John, 156, 157, 168
Mather, Stephen T., 3, 34, 96, 173, 197, 201
Mesa Ranch, 47, 48
Meyer, Amy, 23, 42, 46, 47, 48, 59, 124,
126, 176, 187, 189, 196; and GGNRA
22–23, 29, 32; and PFGGNRA, 25, 33,
37, 69
Mill Valley, 112, 115
Miller, Clem, 12
Mission 66, 10, 19, 132, 150
Molinari, John L., 127